Finance and the Enterprise

FINANCE AND THE ENTERPRISE

edited by

Vera Zamagni

University of Cassino and
Johns Hopkins Center, Bologna, Italy

ACADEMIC PRESS

Harcourt Brace Jovanovich, Publishers

London   San Diego   New York   Boston
Sydney   Tokyo   Toronto

ACADEMIC PRESS LIMITED
24/28 Oval Road
London NW1 7DX

United States Edition published by
ACADEMIC PRESS INC.
San Diego, CA 92101

**A catalogue record for this book is available from the British
Library**

ISBN 0–12–775420–2

Typeset by Keyset Composition, Colchester, Essex
Printed in Great Britain by Hartnolls Ltd, Bodmin, Cornwall

Contents

List of contributors

Masahiko Aoki is a professor of Economics at the Universities of Stanford and Kyoto. His main contributions cover the theory of Japanese enterprise and the theory of organizational structures. His publications include *Information, Incentives and Bargaining in the Japanese Economy*, Cambridge University Press, Cambridge (1988), and he is editor-in-chief of the *Journal of the Japanese and International Economics*.

Giuseppe Conti is a researcher in Economic History at the University of Pisa. His fields of research are the history of credit and banking in nineteenth century Tuscany and the history of Italian shipbuilding between the two World Wars. He has published a book on the history of an Italian mortgage bank in the nineteenth century.

Giovanni Dosi is a professor of Applied Economics at the University of Rome "La Sapienza". His research interests focus on a dynamic theory of technical change. His publications include *Technical Change and Industrial Transformation*, Macmillan, London (1984), and he is the editor for Continental Europe of the *Journal of Industrial and Corporate Change*.

B. Greenwald is presently at Bell Communications Research.

Ken-ichi Imai is a senior fellow at the Institute for International Studies and Courtesy Professor at the Department of Economics at Stanford University, and also Director of Research at the Stanford Japan Center, Kyoto. Research interests include industrial organization, the economics of technological change, and the economics and management of the firm. He has served on both OECD and Japanese committees of experts on technology. Publications in English include several articles and essays in various collective books, and he is the editor of the *Journal of Evolutionary Economics, Entrepreneurship and Regional Development* and *Japan and the World Economy*.

William Kennedy is a member of the Department of Economic History at the London School of Economics. His main research

interest concerns the evolving relationships between financial system
and long-term growth in advanced economies; his most recent book i
Industrial Structure, Capital Markets and the Origins of Britis
Economic Decline, University Press, Cambridge (1987).

David C. Mowery is an associate professor of Business and Publi
Policy in the Walter A. Haas School of Business at the University o
California, Berkeley, researching the economics of technologica
innovation and the effects of public policy on innovation. He ha
testified before Congressional committees and served as an adviser fo
the OECD, various federal agencies and industrial firms. His variou
publications include *Technology and the Pursuit of Economic Growth*
University Press, Cambridge (1989) (with N. Rosenberg).

Giangiacomo Nardozzi is a professor of Economics at the Universit
of Milan. He has widely published in the fields of monetary theory
theory of growth, and lately comparative analysis of financial systems
His publications include *Tre sistemi creditizi: Banche ed economia i*
Francia, Germania e Italia, Il Mulino, Bologna (1983).

Joseph E. Stiglitz is a professor of Economics at Stanford University
Senior Fellow at the Hoover Institution and at the Institute for Polic
Reform and Research Associate at the NBER. He has made contribu
tions to the theory of market structures, the economics of the publi
sector, financial economics, macroeconomics, monetary economics an
the economics of development and growth, and was one of th
pioneers in the study of the economics of information. He is presentl
serving as consultant to Bell Communications Research, the Inter
American Development Bank, the State of Alaska, the Seneca Natio
of Indians and the World Bank, and is founding editor of the *Journa*
of Economic Perspectives.

Richard Tilly is a professor of Economic and Social History, an
Director of the Institut für Wirtschafts- und Sozialgeschichte at th
University of Münster. He has done extensive work on German
economic history of the nineteenth and twentieth centuries, wit
particular reference to the role and performance of financial institu
tions. Among his latest publications are *Vom Zollverein zum Indus*
triestaat. Die wirtschaftlich-soziale Entwicklung Deutschlands 183
bis 1914, Munich (1990). He is coeditor of the Journal *Geschichte un*
Gesellschaft.

Eugene White is a professor of Economics at Rutgers University, an
Research Associate of the National Bureau of Economic Research. Hi
publications include *The Regulation and Reform of the America*

Banking System, 1900–1929, Princeton University Press, Princeton 1983). His present research is on stock market crashes and problems of banking regulation.

Vera Zamagni is a professor of Economic History at the University of Cassino, and a visiting professor at the Bologna center of the Johns Hopkins University. She has done extensive work on Italian economic history, with special reference to state intervention, regional disquilibria and the evolution of standards of living. Among her publications are an economic history of Italy from 1861 to the present *Dalla periferia al centro: La seconda rinascita economica dell'Italia*, Il Mulino, Bologna (1990) an English edition of which is forthcoming from Oxford University Press).

ntroduction

is volume is the result of a collective effort by a group of economists
d economic historians to analyze the different systems of enterprise
ance that have developed over time in various countries that today
e industrially advanced. Common to all contributors is the view that
ere are differences which are substantial and persistent enough to
ll for more than a superficial explanation and, also, the persuasion
at such an explanation is more likely to be forthcoming out of a
ending of historical and theoretical approaches.

While all the chapters collected in this volume provide illustrative
aterial aimed at characterizing various components of the different
ancial systems, the chapters by Mowery and Conti are the most
mparative and systematic. Drawing mainly on these two works, but
ing hints springing from the other chapters as well, it is possible to
nclude not only that the existence of two alternative systems of
terprise finance is established beyond doubt, but that the under-
anding of the functioning mechanisms of the two systems has
ached a high degree of sophistication. Schematically, a comparative
ew can be set up as in Table 1.

The market-oriented system has developed, as is well known, in the
5 and UK, while the bank-oriented system has found its most
herent realization in Germany and Japan. In other countries,
ainly Belgium, France and Italy, an extreme version of the bank-
iented system has developed, in which the collusive relationships
tween the main bank and enterprises are exclusive, and the degree
concentration within industrial groups is very high. The financial
stitution at the center of such groups can no longer strictly be called
bank, but has been termed a holding, entrusted with the role of
oviding the industrial companies within the group with both the
eapest financial services and the controlling and coordinating
rvices, treating information in a much more secret way than banks
. It can be said that holdings provide the same services offered in a
nk-oriented system, but with more exclusivity and continuity than
nks. Holdings have therefore come to be seen as the institutional
swer to either a lack of banks ready to take long-term responsibili-

Table 1 Comparative view of systems of enterprise finance.

Main features of financial markets	bank-oriented	market-oriented
Predominant type of enterprise finance	External	Internal (self-finance)
Prevalent type of external funds	Bank credit (indirect finance) high debt/equity ratio	Equities, bonds (direct finance) low debt/equity ratio
Commercial banks and other enterprises' shareholdings in non-financial enterprises	Substantial	Limited
Formation in non-financial enterprises of cohesive and active controlling blocs with bank representatives	Frequent	Infrequent
Turnover of controlling blocs	Infrequent	More frequent
Role of main bank	Widespread	Not so common
Solution of crisis situations	Internal, supervised by main bank	External, through the market
Treatment of information	Confidentiality	Disclosure

ties, or a lack of good managers to make industrial enterprises viab
In the former case, groups of industrial enterprises have created the
own banks; in the latter case, "responsible" banks have ended
directly administering their associated industrial enterprises (see Ti
for a sketch of the Belgian case, and Mowery for an analysis of t
French case).

One aspect most of the chapters deal with in depth is the way
which information is processed by the different financial systen
Major concern is expressed by everybody at the implications
information asymmetries in the shaping of financial systems. Ke
nedy complains that in a system like the British one, where the sto
market is the means of allocating funds to new as well as establish
enterprises, the rules for disclosure of information have been for
long time particularly unsatisfactory, resulting in the starving of ne
branches of industry of funds, and alienation of investors fro
domestic industry at large. In the US case, investment banks we
created that performed the role of brokers, actively collecting a
circulating information with the public concerning investments
stocks. A number of legal and economic changes were introduced

:ilitate the working of the capital markets. And indeed US capital irkets have worked distinctly better than the British ones, but by means in a completely satisfactory way. As Greenwald and Stiglitz iclude in their chapter, "the process is best described as an olutionary one" (p. 33), with continuous pressure to introduce new vices that improve the working of markets arising as a result of 1arket failures." Imai, too, speaks of a sequential learning process, t, interestingly, the Japanese learning process he highlights is very 'ferent from the American evolutionary process sketched in the hite and Greenwald–Stiglitz chapters.

In the bank-oriented system the center of information is not the .arket, but the bank, collecting and circulating information through vast network of representatives sitting on the boards of directors of mpanies. Information concerns not only the relative safety of tending bank credit, but covers also the placement of new stock ith clients, who are often advised by banks (the same role performed ' US investment banks), as well as a variety of industrial and rategic information. But information, as Imai clearly explains, can so be created in this system as a result of exchanges of views among inkers and industrialists. Because of the tight organization of the stem, information often does not percolate into the market at large, hich is one reason for the relative underdevelopment of the stock :change as a collector of capital for industrial enterprises, that has :en noted in such systems.

If the assessment of the features of alternative systems of enter-'ise finance appears predominantly to be in terms of economic story, it is when we come to enquire about the causes as well as the iplications of the existence of alternative financial systems, and sort to economics, that we realize the significance of history. I think .e most convincing argument in this context is put forward in the 1apter by Greenwald and Stiglitz, when they state that in capital arkets price plays a secondary role, and the allocative mechanism is screening mechanism, in the provision of which "the role of stitutions is central". In capital markets, in fact, money is ex-1anged not against a good or a service that is surrended, but ;ainst *promise* of future return. The problem of making sure that the 'omise will be fulfilled is therefore crucial. Institutions have de-·loped precisely with the aim of connecting present promises with .ture returns.

But the architecture of institutions is more complicated than that of arkets, because the building blocks are much less standardized. It .n be argued that the market-oriented version of financial systems is kept institutions to a minimum and has mainly led to the

formation of institutions supportive of markets, while the ban
oriented financial system is much more lavish in the use of instit
tions – without, however, getting rid of markets, but using them
harmony with the configuration of the institutions. The argument
Imai's chapter is particularly appropriate in this connection. Im
argues that in Japan an interpenetration between the market and tl
organization principles has occurred, due to the existence of "failure
in the working of each principle in isolation. Indeed, in each econom
system we see such an interpenetration, but often one of the tv
principles serves as the guiding one, with the other in a subservie:
role.

In any case, institutions have an intrinsic historical dimension th
requires a historical analysis. Which original elements are to be he
responsible for such diverse institutional evolutions? The chapters l
Kennedy, White, Tilly and Imai focus on this question. Dealing wi'
"the first industrial nation," Kennedy has to go back in time a lor
way, to the English legislation of the first two decades of tl
eighteenth century, to identify the origin of the alleged "preferenc'
by English entrepreneurs for internally generated funds. The si
member limit on banking partnership, and the unlimited liability th;
were imposed by law as a result of excessive speculation, ma(
English banks more cautious in lending money and oriented the
towards highly liquid commercial credits, with the result of pushir
enterprises to rely more on internally generated funds, which is se(
in this view as a by-product of restrictive legislation, rather than ;
an exogenous "preference." To this it must be added that these banl
were note-issuing banks, something that strengthened their liquidi'
preference, while the Bank of England did not develop (probably as
consequence) a strong predisposition to act as a lender of last resoi
further contributing to the tendency of banks not to become involv(
in risky long-term financing, even when legislation was relaxed ar
changed. Kennedy concludes that "capital formation was therel
rendered more difficult, and the entire financial system made moi
unstable . . . by self-inflicted legal restrictions".

It is interesting to contrast Tilly's account of the origin of mix(
banking in Germany in the 1830s and 1840s, at the time
development of railroads and of the coal and iron industrial comple
To respond to the enlarged demand for long-term credit, joint stoc
banks were formed, without note-issuing rights, that soon becan
quite large and could rely on a state bank of issue with man
branches ready to perform the role of providing liquidity. These joir
stock banks were closely connected with a relatively small number '
large industrial customers, in a continuation of the pattern that ha

een typical of the private bankers which existed before the founda-
ion of the joint stock banks. Gerschenkron has interpreted the
iixing of long-term with short-term credit by German banks as an
istitutional innovation created by a country that wanted to catch up
vith Britain in the presence of a certain degree of backwardness in its
wn capital markets. Tilly is not completely happy with this explana-
ion, and though he does not discard it, he insists on the "political"
actors that have shaped the German financial system in enacting a
estrictive legislation concerning note issuing. We are back again with
egislation as the main origin of difference in the development of
nancial systems.

The US case as recounted in White's chapter is molded even more in
he logic of the impact of legislation. According to White, the role of
anks was reduced by the 1864 regulation of banking activity,
miting the size of loans that could be given to any one customer, and
reventing branch banking and buying of stocks by banks. Changes
n legislation that took place later, especially in the 1930s, did produce
ome redirection in American financial markets, without, however,
ltering their basic characterization. The chapters by Greenwald–
tiglitz and by Nardozzi confirm this dependence of American capital
narkets on regulation, underlining the complex feedback effects.

An excursion into the field of connecting in a systemic way financial
narkets with the rest of the economy has also been attempted in some
f the chapters of the volume. In the Aoki-Dosi chapter, finance has
een connected with three other crucial aspects of the organization of
nterprises, namely coordination of decisions, type of incentives
mployed, and innovative learning, with the aim of building arche-
ypes of different economic systems. In the words of the authors, the
esults are still at the stage of "a sort of 'Linnean' exercise of
lassification, in the perspective of an evolutionary theory" (p. 61).
Iowever, they show convincingly that the different shapes and
erformance of financial markets are connected to differences, some-
ime even more pronounced, in the other elements considered,
orming therefore more general and deep-rooted behavioral "coher-
nces" that encompass entire economies. The two polar archetypes
roduced in their work – the A (USA) and the J (Japan) models – do
ot share a single feature in any of the four fields investigated.

In the Mowery chapter, the interconnections between finance, size
nd degree of managerialization of enterprises, and the presence or
bsence of antitrust legislation are analyzed in a comparative
ramework; in the chapter by Nardozzi, too, the insistence on a
ystemic approach appears crucial to the arguments developed by the
uthor.

A final issue has been addressed in the chapters collected in thi volume. If it is established that financial systems differ, is it possibl to identify which is *best*, and whether historical developments mark progress towards optimality? The chapter by Nardozzi is entirel focused on this issue, but some remarks are advanced in othe chapters, too. According to Nardozzi, there is no compelling theoretic al basis for a clear-cut conclusion as to which can be considered th "optimal" financial structure. This is because such concepts a efficiency and stability, on the basis of which conclusions on optimalit should be drawn, are far from being unequivocal, and leave room for historically conditioned analysis that considers internal and externa coherence of alternative systems in different situations. For instanc there seems to be some sort of agreement in all the chapters that market-oriented system is allocatively more efficient in a stabl environment, while a bank-oriented system is more far-sighted an more conducive to the introduction of new technologies in a risk environment of radical change (see especially Aoki-Dosi).

The recent indicators that have shown some degree of convergenc between the two alternative financial systems, spurred by th increasing internationalization of finance (for empiric material on thi point, see especially the chapter by Conti) can be interpreted in a ne light if one accepts that there is no optimal model of finance. I bank-oriented systems have shown a renewed interest in the collec tion of funds through the stock exchange, and market-oriented system have increased their reliance on bank credit, this is in itself the bes proof of the fact that both systems of finance perform important task in an economy. However, all the contributors to this volume touchin upon this issue agree in pointing out that the observed convergence s far has been more a quantitative than a qualitative phenomenon leaving untouched the basic foundations of the two alternativ systems. Imai is the only writer who, at the end of his chapter, goes s far as to say that new challenges are in sight which might be s far-reaching as to be conducive to new institutional configurations o financial markets.

With the preceding brief review of the range of issues discussed, hope to have shown that the present volume, though perhaps no exhaustive, is in many ways provocative. It connects finance wit economic development through an analysis of the performance o corporations under different financial regimes, cast within an evolu tionary and institutional approach, with some effort at modeling. I offers a long-run comparative view that contrasts different paths o development up to the present, discussing the intriguing issues of th existence of an "optimum" path, and of convergence towards it. I

pans a large body of specialized literature. If the volume does not
ffer a full theoretical systematization of the relationships between
nance and economic growth, it can certainly claim to be a unique
ontribution towards new thinking.

Before closing, a word of thanks must be addressed to the Italian
ASSI Foundation, which in many ways has made possible the
ollaboration between economic historians and economists that char-
cterizes this volume.

Vera Zamagni,
University of Cassino

Theoretical foundations

CHAPTER 1

Information, Finance and Markets: The Architecture of Allocative Mechanisms[1]

B. GREENWALD AND JOSEPH E. STIGLITZ

Bankers and businessmen have long recognized the importance of finance, financial constraints, and financial institutions to the vitality and growth both of their enterprises and of the economy. Yet, while these financial factors may have played a central role in economic theories of the nineteenth and early twentieth centuries (see, e.g. Hawtrey, 1919), for almost a half century they have been subordinated to a secondary role by economic theorists. In seeking to explain business cycles, the most recent fad among American academic economists – real business cycles – attributes no role at all to financial institutions: while in the earlier new classical theories (and even much of Keynesian theory[2]) all financial analysis is subsumed under the control of the money supply.

In looking at macroeconomic theories of long-term growth, this narrowing of theoretical vision has been, if anything, even more extreme. Neoclassical growth theory ignored the role of financing institutions completely (e.g., Solow, 1956) and the few attempts to look at the role of financial markets (e.g., Foley and Sidrauski, 1970) focused narrowly on the effects of money supply decisions. In our view, while the former perspective is simply wrong, the latter approach not only represents a vast oversimplification, but it is a misleading one: the prescriptions which emerge, both with respect to micro- and macro-policy, are, at best partial, at worst, suspect. Thus, it is significant that in empirical economic analyses (e.g., in development economics and economic history) there is extensive debate on the role of financial institutions in stimulating growth which is almost invisible in the theoretical arena.

This chapter is divided into three sections. The first defines the economic problems with which the financial institutions are concerned. It argues that the central function of financial institutions is to overcome, or at least deal with, the information problems which, in their absence, would impede the agglomeration of capital and its transfer from those who have resources to those who can most effectively use the capital. The second section shows the variety of ways in which modern economies address these problems, identifying the strengths and weaknesses of the alternative mechanisms; it discusses briefly how these institutions have evolved, and identifies the legal and technological changes that were required for the development of these financial institutions. The third section explores the relationship between the financial constraints which arise out of the informational imperfections and the evolution of the firm. It serves to illustrate the impact of financial institutions on real resource allocation, and to suggest why neoclassical models which systematically ignored financial institutions and constraints may be seriously misleading.

The Role of Financial Institutions

There are two reasons for the development of financial institutions:[3] some enterprises require more capital than any single individual has at his disposal (the agglomeration function); and those who are in the best position to invest (to innovate, to monitor, etc.) are not necessarily those who have the resources (the transfer function[4]).[5]

To accomplish these functions, financial institutions must select among alternative uses of those funds (the selection function). They seek to encourage prudent behavior on the part of those to whom they have provided funds, to ensure that the funds are used in a way which will reap the providers of the fund the expected return, both by designing contractual (implicit and explicit) arrangements and by direct monitoring (the control function).[6]

It is important to realize, at this juncture, the basic differences between financial (capital) markets and other markets, in which goods are traded contemporaneously. In capital markets, money today is exchanged for a *promise* of returns in the future. The promise is always, in effect, a contingent promise: in the case of a bond, the promise takes the form, "I will pay a certain amount, provided that I can; and if I can't, certain other consequences follow . . .." In the case of equity, the promise takes the form, "I will pay a fraction of my profits. I will decide the fraction, and I will decide how profits are efined. Trust me! If I don't pay you a dividend, I will reinvest the ₁oney in the firm, and you will receive a return in the form of a ₁pital gain."

It is precisely this difference which explains why financial markets ₁re not, and cannot be, run as auction markets; why lenders, for ₁stance, do not simply lend to those who are willing to offer to pay ₁e highest interest rates. Those who promise to pay the highest ₁terest rates may not, in fact, be those for whom the expected return ₁ highest.[7]

Banks and other financial institutions are in the business of directly ₁locating resources, of making judgments about the best uses of ₁pital, or at least, about which users are most likely to pay the ₁omised returns. Prices (interest rates) play a role in the allocative ₁echanism – they define, for instance, the opportunity cost of the ₁nds; but the allocative mechanism is fundamentally a *screening* ₁echanism, in which prices play a secondary role. Thus, in contrast to ₁arkets for homogeneous commodities, in which the role of institu-₁ons (firms and market-makers) can reasonably be approximated by ₁e interaction of supply and demand, in studying financial markets ₁nd the allocation of funds, the role of institutions is central.

SIMPLE FORMAL MODEL

₁onsider a simple situation in which an agent (entrepreneur or ₁anager) offers participation in a project to investors. The amount to ₁e raised is V. Without these funds no project may be undertaken. ₁ssume that the project is completed after a fixed period and there is ₁ return, π, which is available for distribution to both investors and ₁he agent. This return depends on the amount of funds actually ₁ommitted to the project, k, which may be either greater or less than ₁', depending on whether the agent himself makes a positive or ₁egative investment, on the underlying attractiveness of the project, ₁, and on the actions taken by the agent, e, which include not only ₁ctive management of the project and effort expended, but also the ₁teps that the agent takes to appropriate the benefits of the project for ₁imself.[8] Formally:

$$\pi = h(k, e, \theta) \ , \ h_k > 0, h_e > 0, h_\theta > 0 \tag{1}$$

₁he return to investors, R, depends upon the way in which the total ₁eturn, π, is divided. For simplicity we will assume that a fraction, α, ₁s paid out to investors. Thus,

$$R = \alpha\pi = \alpha h (k, e, \theta) \tag{2}$$

In practice, π is neither observable nor known with certainty at the time funds are raised. Moreover, it may be only imperfectly observable by the time the project terminates. The level of investment, I may also not be observed *ex ante*, and may be observable only imperfectly and at high cost *ex post*. The same applies to the actions of the agent, e, and the attractiveness of the project. They will be difficult to observe, both before and after the fact. Finally, while may be specified *ex ante*, in many contracts (e.g., payment of corporate dividends) it is not.[9]

The central problems of financial management, in this context, are (1) how to determine an appropriate level of V (and the form in which V is raised) given the imperfect nature of information concerning all the determinants of R (these decisions affect both the beliefs of investors concerning what they might expect and the incentives of the agents), and (2) how to monitor and/or control (directly or indirectly completely, or more likely, partially) the variables θ, k and e, so that appropriate decisions in the interests of the investors are made.

Impediments to the development of financial markets

Given the importance ascribed to financial markets and institutions in modern economies, it is perhaps remarkable that they have developed so late. Though antecedents of modern capital markets have, of course, existed for a long time, the scale of modern institutions and the range of financial instruments which they offer are truly unprecedented.

Yet, upon further reflection, the natural impediments to the development of financial markets are stupendous, and we should, perhaps, be impressed that they work as well as they do.

Recent research has identified five central problems facing financial markets, which are related to the functions of financial intermediaries about which we spoke earlier. These problems arise, in varying form and in varying degrees, with essentially all financial instruments used to raise capital. In some cases, they may arise with such force as to make it virtually impossible to raise capital in the open market, or to use certain instruments (such as equity).

(a) The selection problem. The fundamental problem facing capital markets can be put starkly: there is an infinite supply of charlatans in the market, those who are willing to take others' money for their own uses. Moreover, like the students in our courses, all of whom believe at they are in the upper half of the class, even honest entrepreneurs re likely to have an inflated view of the likely returns to their rojects. And there is little reason to believe that the correlation etween individuals' beliefs in their returns and the actual returns re sufficiently high (even if we could solicit honest views concerning hat those expected returns are) to warrant allocating scarce funds 1 the basis of those expectations.

In terms of the model outlined above, the existence of an almost nfinitely elastic supply of charlatans means that at $V>0$ there is a ery large supply of projects at which $R \le 0$, either (i) because $k = 0$ nd/or (ii) levels of e are chosen which make π either zero or, if access credit is available in some form, less than zero,[10] or (iii) there was o real project opportunity, so that $\pi = 0$, given θ, for all values of k nd e, or (iv) because, after the fact, the unobservable true level of π, rhile positive, is reported to be zero by the agent. In any of these ases, there are a number of projects, N, which are indistinguishable om "valid" projects, for which the return $R^N \le 0$. If we denote the eturns of similar seeming legitimate projects as R^L and there are a xed number L of these, the average return to projects offered nvestors is:

$$\bar{R} = \left(\frac{N}{N+L}\right) R^N + \left(\frac{L}{N+L}\right) R^L \qquad (3)$$

nvestors will in the long run only make continuing investments if:

$$V(1+\rho) < \bar{R} \qquad (4)$$

/here ρ is an appropriate required expected rate of return encompassing both the time value of funds and returns for risk. Since $L.R^L$ fixed, determined by the available technologies and resources, for ny $V>0$, there is an N large enough and an R^N small enough so that $\bar{R} < (1+\rho)$ V. Thus, no financial markets consistently capable of aising positive funds will exist unless there are some limitations on N nd R^N.

We have perhaps put the matter too strongly in ascribing the election problem to the infinite supply of charlatans and dreamers. "he problem is actually more generic: it arises whenever there are symmetries of information between providers of capital and those eeking capital concerning the returns to projects. For instance, nsiders (the firm's managers and controlling shareholders) almost nevitably have more information concerning the firm's prospects than utsiders. They are most keen to sell the shares of their enterprise

when the market has overvalued them. When the market ha
undervalued them, they are obviously reluctant to sell their share
The market recognizes this, and there is considerable evidence tha
in the absence of other information to the contrary, the mark
interprets a firm's willingness to issue shares as a negative sign:
concerning its quality; that is, the price of shares falls dramaticall
upon (the announcement of) a share issue. Of course, firms are awa
of this, and this explains, in part, the relatively low reliance on ne
share issues. Indeed, in the absence of risk aversion, it can be show
that there would be no market for equities.[11] (But of course, in th
absence of risk aversion, the adverse risk-bearing effects which a
associated with the use of debt rather than equity finance would n
be present.)[12]

Finally, we should emphasize that the selection problem arises eve
when there is no asymmetry of information, and where borrowers ar
not intentionally cheating lenders. If there is a large supply
individuals who are overconfident of their abilities, investors have
problem of screening unproductive investments from truly productiv
investments. They cannot simply rely on the price system as
selection device.

While the selection problem arises in both credit and equit
markets, the scope that equity contracts provide for charlatans make
these contracts extremely attractive to them, and makes the selectio
problem central there.

(b) The enforcement problem. The equity contract is supposed t
pay equityholders a fraction of the firm's profits. But typically, th
contract leaves the fraction of the profits to be paid, as well as th
definition of profits, to the discretion of the firm's managers (board c
directors). The scope for diversion of funds for the use of managers o
of controlling shareholders appears to be great.

Indeed, even in the case of income bonds (where firms promise t
pay a certain amount to bondholders out of the firm's incom
provided that there is sufficient income), firms may manipulate th
definition of income in such a way as to evade paying amounts due, s
much so that currently income bonds are seldom used, in spite of thei
risk-sharing advantages to corporations.[13]

Formally, we have

$$R = \alpha\hat{\pi} \tag{5}$$

where $\hat{\pi}$ is the declared profit level. $\hat{\pi}$ may be substantially less tha
π.[14]

In this subsection, we have actually identified two separate enforcement problems: the difficulty of verifying the state of nature, or the variables upon which the payments to the supplier of funds are supposed to depend; and the difficulty of making the receiver of the funds comply with the terms of the contract. The latter problem is the one on which the literature on sovereign debt has focused, but the fact that there are large legal costs in enforcing a contract makes it apparent that this problem may be more pervasive. Indeed, the fact that in bankruptcy, owners of equity typically walk away with something, even though debt claimants do not have their claims fully satisfied, is evidence to the importance of these enforcement problems.

c) **The incentive problem.** Since firms' managers reap only a fraction of the returns from their managerial efforts, their incentives are attenuated (Ross (1973), Stiglitz (1974a), Jensen and Meckling (1976)). More generally, the interests of managers do not coincide with those of the shareholders. This has been made dramatically clear in recent takeover controversies.[15] These discrepancies affect a whole range of decisions.

d) **The management/public good problem.** Since, in principle, all shareholders receive the same amount per share, any efforts by a shareholder (or group of shareholders) to improve the quality of management (the return to their shares) rebounds to the benefit of all shareholders. (The same is true for any other class of claimants.) Therefore, management and efforts to improve management are public goods.[16] Thus, in corporations with widely held shares, the forces driving managers to serve shareholder interests may be particularly weak.

e) **The conflicting claims problem.** While the interests of all claimants within a class (shareholders, bondholders) coincide,[17] the interests of different classes of claimant frequently conflict. This too was seen most dramatically in several of the recent LBOs (leverage buy-outs) in the US, where the value of debtors' claims decreased dramatically as the value of equity claims increased.[18] While debt contracts show a cognizance of this possibility, with provisions which restrict the actions which the firm can undertake, the debt contract can seldom anticipate all the actions which the firm might undertake which might decrease the value of their claims. While future debt contracts are likely to provide some insurance against losses arising from LBOs, firms will, undoubtedly, devise new methods of transferring wealth from other claimants on the firm to themselves.

Difficulties facing equity issues:
an application of general principles

In terms of the model developed above, when equity issues are
undertaken as part of the continuing financing efforts of a long-lived
firm whose common stock is publicly traded, the population of
investors/shareholders changes continuously over time. Thus, there is
no longer a clearly identified investor population associated with a
particular investment project, whose interests the project's managers
can be required, at least in theory, to serve. This, in turn, calls into
question the definition of appropriate behavior of a project's mana
gers, since decisions which benefit shareholders at time, t, may
adversely affect the interests of shareholders at a later time, $t + 1$.[19,20]
The common answer to these difficulties both in law and economic
theory is to assume that in making decisions at time t, managers
serve the interest of current shareholders (i.e. those who hold stock at
time t).[21] For simplicity we will assume that there are only two
periods of interest. In the first, the managers of the firm make a set of
financing decisions, the market price of the firm's equity is determined
on an open market in response to those decisions (a reaction
anticipated by the firm's managers), funds are raised, and operating
plans are undertaken. In the second period, the results of the initial
operating and investment decisions are revealed and returns to
investors are determined accordingly. In addition, we will assume that
a fraction β of the initial shares is sold by shareholders after financing
decisions are announced in period one (and, therefore, a fraction $1 - \beta$
is retained through period two).[22] Formally, therefore, the proper
objective function for such a firm's managers is to maximize

$$\beta V_0 + (1 - \beta)\, \Gamma \alpha \hat{\pi} - c(k)\, \text{Prob}\,(\pi \leq R^*) \qquad (6)$$

where V_0 is the initial post-financing-decision market value of the
firm, Γ is the fraction of the firm held by its initial shareholders (this
is one if no new equity is sold), R^* now represents the promised level
of repayment on the firm's debts, $\hat{\pi}$ is declared profit, and c is the
penalty associated with bankruptcy; we now asssume that bankruptcy
penalties involving the reorganization of the firm increase with the
size of the firm. If an amount of new equity, E, is raised in the
financing period, then:

$$\Gamma = \left(\frac{V_0}{V_0 + E} \right) \qquad (7)$$

Assume further that a firm's managers have their own agenda to vhich they respond at least partially, reflected in their utility 'unction, which we represent as a function of θ, the nature of the project, k, and the resources devoted to the project, effort. For clarity, ve distinguish between e, the effort devoted to increasing π, and $\hat{e}$, the effort devoted to underreporting, which we model as simply a function of the discrepancy between π and $\hat{\pi}$, for any project. Thus, we represent the managers' utility function by $\hat{u}(e, \theta, k, \hat{e}(\pi - \hat{\pi}, \theta, k))$, where $\hat{u}$ embeds within it the managerial compensation schemes which define the financial rewards received by managers. It will be convenient in the following discussion if we simply represent the managers' utility in terms of the variables e, θ, k, and $\hat{\pi}$:

$$u(e, \theta, k, \hat{\pi}) \equiv \hat{u}(e, \theta, k, \hat{e}(\pi - \hat{\pi}, \theta, k)) \tag{8}$$

Then what actually is maximized reflects to some extent the managers' own utility:

$$\beta V_0 + (1 - \beta) \, \Gamma a \hat{\pi} - c(k) \, \text{Prob} \, (\pi \leqslant R^*) + \Psi u \tag{9}$$

and this is maximized, as before, subject to the constraint that

$$\hat{\pi} \leqslant \pi(e, k, \theta) \tag{10}$$

The weight the manager places on his own agenda (utility) is represented by Ψ. (The conventional principal agent literature assumes that Ψ is infinite, that is, the manager simply maximizes his own expected utility, given the incentive schemes in operation.)[23]

This model can be used to illustrate several of the impediments to equity markets to which we referred earlier:

a) The conflicting claims are reflected in difference in judgments concerning the weights to be associated with current market value versus future profitability, the parameter β above.[24]

b) As holding periods of shareholders become extremely short, β tends towards 1, and only the initial value, V_0, matters to managers. This, in turn, means that signals become overwhelmingly important relative to actual performance and, like financial markets without fraud sanctions (see the discussion below), equity markets will tend to collapse completely.[25]

c) The managerial incentive problem – the conflict between managers' incentives and that of the "firm" (whatever β is employed) – is reflected in the term

$$u(e, \theta, k, \hat{e}(\pi - \hat{\pi}, \theta, k))$$

which, we noted, is assumed to have imbedded in it the managerial incentive compensation scheme. It is generally not possible to find managerial compensation schemes (with risk-averse managers so that when they maximize their "utility," shareholder welfare (for any β) is maximized.

Coming to Terms with Capital Market Impediments: The Architecture of Allocative Mechanisms

In spite of these seeming impediments to the transfer and agglomera tion of capital, capital is transferred and agglomerated. This is one of the hallmarks of modern capitalism. We thus need to ask, how do modern economies overcome these impediments? What were the changes in the legal, economic, and social structure which facilitated the development of modern equities markets, and which enabled these markets to overcome the significant barriers to the effective func tioning of these markets?

Trust

Historically, in the absence of a well functioning legal system, there are two mechanisms which have worked to ensure the fulfillment of contracts: trust and reputation.

Trust played an important role in the early development of capital markets, in which financial transactions were often concentrated among members of a well-defined ethnic group or community. In such a context, social sanctions were a more effective instrument for the enforcement of contracts than economic sanctions.[26] (The fact that transactions occurred within a relatively small group also mitigated the information problem: the participants in the transactions likely had considerable information about each other.) It is, perhaps, ironic that the development of capitalist financial institutions depended, to a large extent, on non-capitalist ethics and control mechanisms, a point to which we shall return later.[27] But as economic development proceeded, the increasing scale of enterprise made it impossible to restrict raising and transferring funds within the members of a close knit community. Moreover, in some cases, social bonds within the community weakened, reducing the force of social sanctions as a discipline device.

ɔputation

ɔr reputation to be effective, there must be a continuing flow of ɔfits: otherwise there would be no incentive to maintain one's ɔputation. Reputations provide an effective barrier to entry, which ay allow the profits to be sustained. Again, we note an irony: the ability of capitalist financial institutions depends on limitations on ɪe degree of competition.[28] The flow of profits associated with banks, hich surely rank among the most important of the financial ɪtermediaries, arose, in most countries, from governmentally im->sed restrictions on entry, combined with the rights to print money ɾactional reserve banking). The profits generated by these govern-ent-granted monopolies depended, in part, on the assets which were ᴠailable in which reserves could be held. The fact that in England, ɔvernment debt provided a relatively safe investment opportunity ɪelding a positive return gave British banks the flow of profits, which ɔt only provided depositors with some direct insurance of the safety ˙their funds, but also provided banks with an incentive to maintain ɪeir reputation, an incentive which reduced the likelihood that the ɪnds would be invested in an excessively risky manner. In this view ɪen, the stability of the British government's national debt was ɔsely linked with the successful development of some of its financial ɪstitutions.

However, for reputation to be an effective incentive for those who ᴀise equity to pay a return to their investors, the firm must have ɪans to have future recourse to the equity market. But such future ᴣcourse to the equity market may have disadvantages as well: for it ᴀay imply dilution of the original owners' equity claims. Furth-ɾmore, each return to the equity market is a negative signal, with ɹverse effects on the firms' market value (see Gale and Stiglitz, ᴣ89). If it is not the desire for future access to the equity market hich provides the firm with an incentive to pay a return to equity ᴠners, what does? It is the legal strictures, which require that all ɪareholders (controlling and non-controlling) be treated the same, ɪd the limitations imposed by the legal system on the ability of ɔntrolling shareholders to divert funds to their own interests.[29]

ᴴhanges in legal structure

ɾust and reputation, while they may have sufficed for simpler capital ᴀarkets, by themselves were not sufficient for the development of

effective, widespread financial markets. For this, two innovations
the legal structure were required.

First, the principle of limited liability had to be recognized. Witho
limited liability, the costs that charlatans could impose on investo
would be unlimited, and investors would be unwilling to turn ov
funds to others about whom they had very limited information, even
those others included only a relatively small proportion of charlatan

Once limited liability constraints are imposed, so that $R^N \geq 0$, the
the average return to investors is bounded below by:

$$\bar{R} \geq \left(\frac{L \cdot R^L}{N + L} \right) \tag{1}$$

which may be small if N is very large relative to L, but whic
nevertheless provides the possibility of $V \geq 0$. Historically, of cours
limited liability has always been characteristic of debt contracts. Th
lender is not held responsible for the uses to which his money ha
been put. At worst, he loses his money. Hence, the early existence
borrowing and lending. However, in order to provide for the ris
spreading opportunities inherent in equity markets, explicit limite
liability laws for equity investors are essential. Unfortunately, limite
liability by itself would still, given an extensive supply of charlatan
create only limited opportunities for raising financial resources, sin
investors would pay only small levels of V for projects.

Second, a legal system which could effectively prosecute securiti
fraud[30] was required. Without such a system, the ability of fir
managers to divert resources is essentially unfettered, and again, th
costs of not knowing the honesty of the managers (or of n
monitoring borrowers' activities) would effectively deter most inves
ment. As it is, even with fraud statutes, the scope for manageri
diversion of funds for their own benefits (as recent episodes
managerial behavior in the face of takeover bids testifies) is n
insignificant.

Again, this condition can be expressed in terms of our simple mod
The actual levels of θ, e, k and, where π is unobservable, the declare
level of π, are determined by the objective function of a project
agent. Thus, in the polar case where he maximizes his own utility, h
behavior is defined by the problem[31]

$$\max_{e,\, k} u(e, k, \hat{\pi}, \theta) \tag{12}$$

where $\hat{\pi}$ is the declared level of profit and θ enters the agent's decisio
whether or not to bring a particular project to market. We hav

herto assumed essentially that u_e, u_k, and $u_{\hat\pi}$ are all less than zero
ence the tendency to strip the project's owners of any possible
.urn). However, once mechanisms for prosecuting fraud are in place,
e agent's objective function may now be specified in an entirely
ferent way. A contract may be written between investors and their
ent which merely specifies a promised return, R^*, on any given
oject. If "fraud" is interpreted as the payment of a penalty in the
ent of failure to deliver on such a promise, then the objective
action of the agent becomes:

$$\max_{e,\ k} u(e, k, \hat\pi, \theta) - \hat c \text{ Prob } (\alpha\hat\pi \leqslant R^*) \tag{12b}$$

ere $\hat c$ is the cost of "fraud," Prob $(\alpha\hat\pi \leqslant R^*)$ is the probability of
ing (found) guilty of fraud and, of course, this problem must now be
lved subject to the constraint that

$$\alpha\hat\pi = \hat R \leqslant \pi(e, k, \theta) \tag{13}$$

ice declared "dividends" must actually be paid. As $\hat c$, the penalty for
aud, becomes very large, agents will (a) always declare a value of
rofits" sufficient to provide the promised rate of return, where this
feasible; (b) take actions, e, and make investments, k, which ensure
at promised returns, R^*, can feasibly be paid and (c) avoid
idertaking projects where θ is such that condition (b) cannot be
lfilled with high probability.

Fraud penalties thus not only deal directly with the "enforcement"
oblem: they also have incentive effects. Furthermore, they may
hance the ability of good firms to signal that fact; when there is a
aud penalty, promises (R^*) convey information; better firms will, in
neral, promise more.[32] Moreover, fraud penalties deter charlatans
om entering the market. Thus, fraud penalties also enhance the
onomy's ability to solve the selection problem.

If effective fraud enforcement is interpreted to mean a level of c
fficiently high to ensure that promises are normally fulfilled, it will
ply that

$$\bar R \approx R^* \tag{14}$$

- the project universe as a whole and, with diversification, that

$$V = \bar R/(1 + \rho) \tag{15}$$

substantially positive. Historically, institutions such as debtors
isons have developed to serve precisely these fraud-policing func-
ns.
However, while such fraud control mechanisms may be essential to

the functioning of financial markets, they create a new set c
financing problems in solving old ones. Typically, the returns t
investment projects are uncertain, even to the agents who undertak
and manage them. Thus, as the cost of fraud, c, increases it not onl
deters fraudulent investors, but also deters legitimate projects. Th
chance of incurring fraud costs accidentally may either limit the scop
of projects, lead to serious underestimates of promised returns (an
hence, underfinancing), or deter the undertakings altogether. This i
especially likely if agents are risk averse. As a result, the vigorou
fraud control approach described above must be tempered either (a
by limiting penalties and/or (b) by developing approaches for excusin
fraudulent performance under circumstances beyond the agent'
control and/or (c) by providing financing without explicit retur
promises (i.e. equity finance). Yet these tempered measures, whicl
might be thought of as constituting an imperfect legal control system
reintroduce the original problems posed by the agent's privat
knowledge of e, π and k.

The modern corporation

The development of the large, modern corporation was, to a larg
extent, made possible by the improvements in financial markets, an
at the same time represented an intrinsic part of those improvements
We want to call attention to four aspects of these developments.

First, while the development of accounting practices and auditin
procedures made the *internal* control of the firm feasible, it als
enabled investors to monitor more effectively what was going o
within the firm. These accounting standards made it possible to defin
fraud more precisely and to detect it more easily. In the context of th
model, audit and punishment systems could be applied to reduc
deviations between $\hat{\pi}$ and π and deviations of e, k and θ from desirabl
levels.

Second, the large-scale firm could make use of systems of pee
monitoring to reduce the likelihood of fraud. In a small firm, th
owner/manager could doctor the books, with little scrutiny fron
anyone else. In a large-scale firm, with multiple checks, frau
(diversion of funds meant for the common interests of shareholders i
general to the interests of a few) required the complicity of a larg
number of individuals, making such diversion less likely.

At the same time, the modern corporation created an "interna
capital market." Funds could be transferred around the country
allocated to regions and used where returns were highest. Thi

ated a community to replace the ethnic communities, in which
mbers knew each other well, and while social sanctions might be
ited, economic sanctions (being fired, denied promotion within the
rarchy) could be quite effective.[33] (Indeed, in recent years, much
been written about the "culture of a corporation.") In most cases
hin the United States, the corporation developed a specialized
owledge associated with certain markets (products). As a result,
le capital was efficiently allocated within certain spheres, large
crepancies might arise between returns in different markets. But
informational and other problems discussed above provided an
oortant barrier to the flow of funds. (Chandler has rightly empha-
ed the importance of the lowering of transportation costs to the
elopment of national markets. The national markets in the US
e sufficiently large that diseconomies of scope set in when firms
empted to cross into new markets. The emergence of conglomerates
vides a possible exception – yet the failure of so many of the
glomerates suggests that these diseconomies were considerable,
weighing the obvious gains from arbitraging across markets.)
inally, corporations facilitate the functioning of the reputation
chanism. Firms create an asset called goodwill, based on their
utation, and it pays current owners to maintain that asset.[34] This,
turn, implies that investors may be more willing to provide
g-established corporations with funds. In effect, the firm's incentive
maintain its reputation reduces the investors' monitoring
ts.[35,36]

nture capital

dern corporations as mechanisms for allocating capital face two
blems. The first, which we have just discussed, is their specializa-
n within an industry. The second is specialization in certain
petencies relevant to the operation of large well-defined con-
uing enterprises with extensive but fragmented authority dele-
ed to individuals or groups of individuals. Both of these specializa-
ns may render corporations particularly unsuited to operate in
cent markets where success depends on familiarity with new
hnologies and demand behaviors on the one hand, and specific
racteristics (e.g., imagination, risk preference) on the other hand
ich are not prevalent in large modern corporations. Accordingly, a
proportionate amount of innovation arises in new and small
erprises. The problems we discussed earlier concerning the func-
ning of capital markets arise forcefully, and cannot be resolved

through the institution of the modern corporation. To fill this ga special institutions have grown up in the United States whi constitute the venture capital industry.[37]

The industry itself has many of the aspects of early financi market developments. Venture firms typically operate in a tight knit community, sharing projects among members of that communi and engaging, by design, in a continuing stream of projects. As result, reputation is critical to the effectiveness of the venture capit firms themselves, and strong cultural ties bind these firms togeth with investors. At the same time, the entrepreneurs who are fund by the venture capital firms are closely tied to and highly depende upon the venture capital firms. Consequently, venture capital firn tend to have detailed information on the operations of the projec they fund, and potentially strong sanctions in the event of misfe sance. The venture capital firms usually also have detailed specializ knowledge of the industries in which their entrepreneurs operate, that they are adept at evaluating relative entrepreneurial perforn ance. The similarities to early capitalist communities appear to l striking.[38]

Further impediments to efficient capital markets

We began this chapter with a list of problems which all financi markets face, and proceeded to show how certain changes in tl economic and legal environment had facilitated the development financial markets. We now want to raise some questions about ho some more recent developments may, in the near future, serve impede the functioning of capital markets.

First, we spoke earlier about the ability of corporations' manage to divert resources for their own purposes, and the role of the leg system in preventing fraud. Belatedly, managers have discovered th there is a wide range of *legal* ways by which funds can be diverted their purposes. In one recent takeover, the old managers walked c with $100 million. To make matters worse, in several states of tl USA, the legal system has reinforced the rights of managers, ar has made takeovers more difficult. Takeovers are one of tl mechanisms by which shareholders can ensure (or make it mol likely) that their assets are well managed, and that the mark reflects accurately the true value of those assets.

Second, the improvements in the secondary market for equiti have led to an increase in short-term trading of securities. Moreove an increasingly large fraction of funds on the market originate

•nsion funds, managed by fiduciary agents, many of whom are
dged by the short-run performance of their portfolio. In short, the
·oblems of which Keynes wrote more than a half-century ago, where
vestors focus on short-term returns rather than the long term, are
r more important today than they were when he was writing.

The consequences of this focus on the short term have been
scussed extensively elsewhere. Here, we note one additional effect:
e focus on the short term increases the signaling costs associated
ith issuing equities, and hence results in fewer firms issuing
uity.[39,40]

nance and the Evolution of the Firm

ne neoclassical theory of the economy pictures capital as a liquid: it
•ws smoothly throughout the economy, until the rates of return in
l sectors are the same. The picture we have drawn is markedly
fferent: the problems (largely informational in character) which we
ive described above create large barriers to the free flow of capital.
apital inside the firm is different from capital outside the firm. As a
·sult, there may be large differences in the observed rates of return
cross firms or sectors of the economy.

Why aren't the normal forces of arbitrage effective in overcoming
ese differences? Our analysis has provided an at least partial
iswer to this question: what we observe are *average* rates of return,
iy within a sector. Those outside the sector may be less able to select
iod projects within the sector, so their expected marginal returns
iay be much lower; and outside suppliers of funds may fear that (for
iy of the reasons delineated earlier) they may not be able to obtain
ie same rates of return on, say, new issues of equity.

But why don't existing firms borrow additional funds? First, firms
iay not be willing to borrow more, given the limited issue of equity,
r to do so would expose them to additional risk, which they cannot
vest. This is the fundamental difference between debt and equity:
hile debt entails a fixed obligation, equity does not; hence with debt,
iere is always a chance of bankruptcy. (See Greenwald and Stiglitz
988, 1990).)

Second, lenders may not be willing to lend: with asymmetric
formation, moral hazard, and enforcement problems, credit markets
ill, in general, be characterized by credit rationing. (See Stiglitz and
Veiss (1981, 1983, 1986, 1987).) Lenders are not concerned with the

marginal return to investment, only with the fraction of the t(
returns which they can appropriate. The total return in one se(
may be higher than in another, but the (expected) fraction which t]
can appropriate may be lower. Credit markets will not serve to equ
(expected) returns to investments.

Of course, industries with high returns will have an incentive
reinvest a large fraction of their high profits back into the enterpr
and this reinvestment will eventually drive down the rate of retu
Thus, there is a tendency for returns to capital to be equated *in*
long run, but the mechanism by which this occurs is quite differ
from that envisaged by the traditional neoclassical model. Moreove
and more importantly – new industries are constantly being crea1
Returns in these new industries may, accordingly, be significar
higher than in older, established industries, so that observed inequ
ties in rates of return may be persistent (though which industries
enjoying above-normal rates of return may be always changing).

Kalecki (1939), Kaldor (1956) and Robinson (1956) (and perh
Marx and Rosa Luxemburg) postulated models in which investm(
by firms was tied to their profits. In these models, the main sourc(
investment funds was firms' retained earnings.[41] For several deca(
these models have been criticized as *ad hoc* – whether they
realistic is quite another matter. The advances in the theory
financial markets described in this chapter have provided mi(
foundations for the kinds of constraints on financial markets wh
underlay these models. The assumptions concerning information {
contract enforcement are undoubtedly more reasonable than
assumptions of costless and perfect contract enforcement and per1
(or at least symmetric) information underlying the neoclassical mo(

We now show how these ideas can be used to develop simple mo(
of the evolution of firms. To begin with, we assume that ther(
equity and credit rationing: firms must rely on retained earnings
finance their investment. For simplicity, we assume that the outp
capital ratio is fixed at b, and the labor–capital ratio is fixed at l.
denotes the capital of the ith firm, and w the wage rate. Assume t]
the firm retains and invests a fraction s of its profits. Then:

$$dK_i/dt = sbK_i - swlK_i,$$

or

$$d\ln K_i/dt = m(w) = s(b - wl).$$

We thus obtain Gibrat's law: firms grow proportionately.

Assume the labor force grows at a fixed rate n, and that the rate

hange of real wages is a function of the unemployment rate (a real
hillips curve). Let aggregate capital be denoted by K:

$$K = \Sigma K_i. \tag{18}$$

ggregate employment is then:

$$L = lK. \tag{19}$$

he employment rate is then:

$$lK/N = e \tag{20}$$

here N is the aggregate labor supply. The real Phillips curve
ostulates that:

$$d\ln w/dt = g(e) = g(lk), \quad g' > 0 \tag{21}$$

here $k = K/N$.
n steady state:

$$g(e^*) = 0, \tag{22}$$

r

$$K^* = Ne^*/l \tag{23}$$

umming the firm capital accumulation equations over all firms:

$$dK/dt = d\Sigma K_i/dt = \Sigma K_i m(w) = m(w)\, \Sigma K_i = m(w)\, K, \tag{24}$$

r

$$d\ln k/dt = m(w) - n. \tag{25}$$

n long-run equilibrium, this implies that:

$$d\ln K/dt = m(w) = n, \tag{26}$$

r

$$w^* = m^{-1}(n) = sb - n/ls. \tag{27}$$

hus, in the long run wages adjust so that employment and capital
row at exactly the rate of the labor supply. It is easy to verify that
he dynamics described by the differential equations 21 and 25 give
ise to limit cycles.[42]

    The model we have just described is completely non-stochastic. If we
ostulate that there are some diseconomies of scale (if we think of the
umber of firms in the economy as fixed at N, firms that are much

larger than average are slightly less productive than smaller firm and that there is some randomness in the accumulation process, the

$$d\ln K_i/dt = M(w, K_i/K)\ \varepsilon_i, \text{ with } E\varepsilon = 1. \tag{2}$$

Define $v_i = K_i/K$, so, in long-run equilibrium with $d\ln K/dt = n$,[43]

$$d\ln v_i/dt = \hat{M}(w, v_i)\ \varepsilon_i - n. \tag{2}$$

The discrete time analogue to (29) is a stochastic process which, it c easily be verified, satisfies all of the Champernowne conditions. The exists a steady state distribution of (relative) firm sizes, in which t tail of the distribution satisfies (approximately) Pareto's law.[44]

Extension to firms which are equity but not credit constrained

The analysis can be extended in a straightforward manner to fir which are equity but not credit constrained. For simplicity, we use t Greenwald-Stiglitz (1988) model in which costs of bankruptcy give r to risk-averse behavior on the part of firms; and these costs bankruptcy are proportional to the scale of the firm. In that mod while firms can borrow as much as they wish at the actuarially f interest rate (which takes into account in an appropriate manner t probability of default), because increased borrowing gives rise to increased probability of default, firms choose to limit their borrowir They show that firms will have an equilibrium debt equity ratio, ϵ Thus, if their working capital or equity is denoted by E, their debt d^*E, and their total capital is $(l + d^*)\ E$. The change in the expect equity of the firm is then given by

$$dE_i/dt = b(1 + d^*)\ E - \rho d^*E - wl(1 + d^*)\ E_i = \mu(\rho, w)\ E_i. \tag{3}$$

where ρ is the safe rate of interest. It is clear that (30) is of exactly t same form as (17): our new model also gives rise to Gibrat's law. should also be clear that other specifications of firm risk-aversi (bankruptcy costs) and/or technologies can give rise to equatio describing the evolution of the firm of the form:

$$d\ln E_i/dt = \hat{\mu}(\rho, w, E_i). \tag{3}$$

To complete the model, we need to determine ρ. If we postulate th households have a savings function of the form:

$$S = s(\rho, w)\ Y, \tag{3}$$

1ere Y is household income, $wlK + \rho d^*E$, where   is aggegate
uity,

$$E = \Sigma E_i \tag{33}$$

1d K is the aggregate capital stock,

$$K = (l + d^*(\rho, w)) E \tag{34}$$

en in equilibrium, household savings must be equal to the increase
firm debt:

$$d^*(\rho, w)dE/dt = d^*(\rho, w) E\mu(\rho, w) = s(\rho, w)Y \tag{35}$$

ie steady state is determined by the pair of equations:

$$d^*(\rho, w) \mu (w, \rho) = s(wl(l+d^*) + \rho d^*) \tag{36}$$

1d

$$\mu(\rho, w) = n. \tag{37}$$

Substituting (37) into (36), we obtain:

$$d^* \{n - s\rho - swl\} = swl. \tag{38}$$

)rmally, we would expect $\mu_1 < 0$ (increasing the rate of interest
duces the rate of equity accumulation) and $\mu_2 < 0$ (increasing the
ige rate reduces the rate of equity accumulation). Similarly, $d_1 < 0$
icreasing the rate of interest that has to be paid on debt reduces the
timal debt equity ratio) and $d_2 < 0$ (increasing the wage rate, which
duces the profitability of output, makes production less attractive,
d hence reduces the desired amount of borrowing). Accordingly, so
1g as the savings rate does not decrease too rapidly as ρ increases (it
ems unlikely) as wages increase (which also seems unlikely), both
7) and (38) are positively sloped curves. It appears that there can be
ultiple steady states: a low wage, low interest rate equilibrium in
1ich firms have a high debt equity ratio; and a high wage, higher
terest rate equilibrium in which firms have a low debt equity ratio.
both equilibria, the steady state employment rate and per capita
tput are the same. The distribution of income and the economy's
1ancial structures differ across equilibria. In a more general version
this model, in which the capital output ratio may differ, then the
fferent equilibria will be associated with different levels of per capita
come.
It is easy to extend this model to incorporate stochastic elements, as
!ll as exogenously or endogenously determined changes in the rates
productivity growth, whether arising from learning by doing or
vestment in R and D (see Greenwald and Stiglitz (1990)). In the

latter case, differences in financial structure will be associated wit
different patterns of investment (differences in willingness to tak
risks): economic equilibria in which there is a low debt equity rat.
will be associated with higher rates of investment in R and D, an
accordingly higher rates of technological progress. The form:
development of these models would, however, take us beyond th
scope of this chapter.

The main points of this exploration would, moreover, be large!
unaltered by these final extensions. These main points are th:
modern theories of financial market imperfections (chiefly related t
informational problems) provide effective theoretical support f(
much of the existing less theoretical literature on the role an
importance of financial institutions, while also serving to rehabilita!
many of the early growth models and the conclusions concernin
economic development that arose out of the earlier informal liter:
ture.

Conclusions

There are a few simple messages underlying the analysis of th
chapter. Capital markets are different from other markets. They enta
exchanges of money today for a *promise* of a return in the futur
Ensuring that those promises can and will be fulfilled is a maj
concern of financial markets.

Difficulties in ensuring contract fulfillment presented a barrier t
the development of modern financial markets. (In the text, we note
five major impediments to the development of financial markets
Legal changes – the development of limited liability and enforceab!
fraud standards – combined with technological/economic advance
(e.g. in accountancy and auditing) facilitated, and in some cases wer
necessary for, the development of modern capital markets.

Still, there remains a tension: observed financial contracts ma
differ markedly from those that would arise in a world in which th
problems we alluded to earlier did not arise. For instance, th
functions of risk sharing would be well served by equity contracts; y
equity contracts suffer greatly from information asymmetry problem:
as well as enforcement difficulties, so that relatively little reliance i
placed on equity as a source of new finance.

These limitations on financial markets mean that financial market
function: markedly differently from the way envisaged in tradition:

oclassical theory. Rates of return across sectors may differ. The firm
xes on a role as an important financial institution. At the same
ie, these limitations, and the associated disparities in rates of
urn, give rise to two concomitant pressures. There is, first the
essure for financial innovations. Leveraged buy-outs and junk
nds represent two recent examples of these financial innovations in
e United States. At the same time, there will always be those who
ll seek to take advantage of existing and new contract forms for
eir own advantage, to define the boundaries of the fraud statutes,
d to exploit common perceptions of contract interpretations, and the
iitations of trust and reputation as contract enforcement mechan-
ns. Golden parachutes and a variety of other forms of managerial
trenchment in the United States are but two recent examples.[45]
The process is best described as an evolutionary one, in which the
ficiencies in the market give rise to new contract forms, which some
 those in the market gradually learn how to exploit, while the
arket gradually learns the deficiencies in those forms, giving rise, in
rn to still new arrangements. We suspect, for instance, that the true
ks associated with the junk bond, a financial form lying between
e standard bond and an equity, will only be fully recognized as the
onomy enters its next recession.[46,47] Since the behavior and func-
n of firms is closely linked with finance, with the contractual
rangements by which it raises funds, this evolution of financial
struments will be intertwined with the evolution of the firm. And
ice the behavior and evolution of the economy as a whole depend
 the behavior and evolution of the firms which comprise it,
derstanding the growth and development of modern industrial
cieties must begin by a study of the history and evolution of
ancial markets.

otes

inancial support from the National Science Foundation, the Olin Foundation, and
 Hoover Institution is gratefully acknowledged.
eynes must be given some of the blame for these developments: his aggregation of
g-term bonds and equities ignored the fundamental differences between these two
ns of capital, differences which play a central role in explaining business fluctua-
is.
f Keynes set the economics profession on the wrong road, Modigliani and Miller –
earing a quarter century after the publication of Keynes' *General Theory* – provided
 intellectual underpinnings for what was by then standard practice among
croeconomists. They provided a set of assumptions under which financial structure

truly made no difference. While for almost fifteen years following Modigliani and Mill
the profession sought to show that their result was more general than even they h
realized (see, e.g. Hirschleifer (1966), and Stiglitz (1969, 1972a)), it has been only in t
past fifteen years that we have gradually come to understand why the theorem is
little relevance. (See, e.g. Stiglitz (1988a) and the references cited there.)

The econometric work examining firm behavior, particularly with respect to inve
ment behavior, provides an important cautionary tale: while the earlier work of Ki
and Meyer (1959) had provided strong suggestions that, at least for many firm
financial factors were important in determining their investment behavior, the lat
work of Jorgenson and his co-authors (see, e.g. Hall and Jorgenson (1967)) employi
the so-called neoclassical theory of investment excluded these variables, simply becau
they (wrongly) believed that "economic theory" argued that they should have be
excluded. While "measurement without theory" may not be the best approach
understanding economic systems, and while it may be true that "data can never spe
for themselves," we should at least listen to the strong whispers of the data, and not
over-confident in our theories, particularly when they contradict common sense.

[3] There are other reasons, with which we shall be less concerned in this chapte
principal among these is risk diversification.

[4] In the natural life cycle of a firm, in the early stages the firm needs more capital tha
it generates, while in later stages it may generate more profits than it can profitab
invest.

[5] The adduced reasons for financial institutions are really reasons either for tl
existence of a capital market or for financial institutions. Below, we explain why cre
markets are not like auction markets, that is, why financial institutions are required

[6] Both the selection (or screening) function and the control function can be thought of
information problems: imperfect information is an impediment to the functioning
financial markets, and it is a principal objective of financial institutions to overcor
these informational impediments.

[7] This point has been emphasized by Stiglitz and Weiss (1981) and Stiglitz (1988b).

[8] From this perspective, greater efforts expended to divert funds from the firm to tl
manager represent smaller values of e.

[9] Moreover, α may itself be a function of other variables. The relationship between
and π will, of course, differ for different financial instruments.

[10] In this interpretation, π is profits after paying off debtors.

[11] These issues have been discussed at greater length by Greenwald, Stiglitz, and Wei
(1984) and Myers and Majluf (1984).

[12] There remain adverse incentive and selection effects. See, e.g. Stiglitz and Wei
(1981).

[13] Gale and Hellwig (1985) and the recent literature on sovereign debt (Eaton a
Gersovitz (1981), Eaton, Gersovitz, and Stiglitz (1986)) has emphasized the enforceme
problem.

A recent literature (under the rubric of "costly state verification") (Townsend (197￼
has developed, arguing that enforcement costs (or more precisely, the costs of tl
required verification) are less with debt than equity contracts. Providers of capital on
have to verify the state of nature if the borrower fails to make the promised paymet
As an explanation of the use of debt rather than equity, the theory has been criticiz
both on the grounds that the costs of verification do not appear to be that significat
(the other explanations accordingly seem more persuasive); more importantly, giv￼
that there *are* outstanding equities, for which, in the simple models at least, sta
verification is required, there are no marginal verification costs associated with issuin
additional equities.

As we noted above, the cost of verifying income/profits was an impediment to tl
early development of equity markets, and remains an impediment to the use of incom
bonds.

[14] This corresponds to point (iv) made in the discussion preceding equation.[(3)]

[15] Hannaway (1989) has emphasized the range of activities over which discrepancies
interests may arise. Information which may be of limited value to the firm may be

ısiderable value to the individual, in, for instance, signalling to others his competency
d command of the situation.
Shleifer and Vishny (1988) have, similarly, stressed managers' incentives for making
ımselves indispensable to the firm, thus increasing the rewards that they can extract
m the firm (managerial entrenchment).
This point has been emphasized by Alchian and Demsetz (1972), Grossman and Hart
ı80), and Stiglitz (1982, 1985).
Except, of course, to the extent that controlling shareholders can divert some of the
m's assets to their own interests.
The potential for this has long been recognized in the theoretical literature. See, for
tance, Stiglitz (1972a).
And in the absence of perfect information, later shareholders may not be able to
ıtect themselves by reducing their willingness to invest.
Only in special cases, such as where there is a complete set of state-contingent
urities, will there be no ambiguity about what the firm should do. See Stiglitz
ı72a, 1972b, 1974b) or Grossman and Stiglitz (1977, 1980).
It should be apparent, however, that only under severe restrictions will this policy, of
ıximizing the current market value, or expected utility of current owners, be
nstrained) Pareto efficient. See, e.g. Stiglitz (1972b).
The standard theoretical justification for such an assumption is that of an over-
ıping generations model, in which most wealth is held by older investors who sell it
for consumption of goods over time.
We suspect that that formulation exaggerates the extent to which employees in
ıeral follow self-interested policies. There appear to be many instances where
lividuals "do their job" – and do it well – not simply because their financial rewards
rease the better they perform. (This holds even if we take into account the increased
elihood of promotion for good behavior, and the increased likelihood of dismissal for
ır performance.) This is particularly true in managerial jobs where it may be little
ıre difficult to do a good job than a poor job, and individuals receive considerable
isfaction from doing a good job. The fact that their company is number one, or that
ıy have done better than their rivals, is satisfaction enough.
This only reflects conflicting claims among shareholders, not the conflicts between
ıreholders and bondholders.
The proof of this claim follows from a straightforward comparative statics analysis of
ı Greenwald-Stiglitz-Weiss (1984) model.
The recent literature on sovereign debt has made clear the limited effectiveness of
ınomic sanctions. See, for instance, Eaton, Gersovitz, and Stiglitz (1986).
Albert Hirschman has stressed a similar point in some of his recent writings.
The limitations on competition are endogenous, rather than exogenous, and in
ıilibrium, though existing firms earn positive profits, there are zero profits associated
:h entry. See, e.g. Stiglitz (1986).
Two other mechanisms are often suggested as imposing discipline on managers:
ıreholder voting and takeovers. There are good theoretical reasons for suspecting
ıt these mechanisms are of only limited efficacy, however (see Stiglitz (1982, 1985),
ıossman and Hart (1980)), and observation of firm behavior seems consistent with
ıs view.
As will be apparent from our discussion below, we are using the term fraud in a very
ıad sense.
Identical results obtain if he maximizes the more general objective function (equation

Certain technical conditions have to be satisfied for this to be the case.
The circumstances under which these are effective incentive devices are explored in
ıglitz and Weiss (1983).
See Eaton (1986).
Stiglitz and Weiss (1983) show that the intertemporal interlinking of loans (making
ı availability of funds at one date dependent on the firm's performance at an earlier
ıe) increases banks' expected returns.

[36] At the same time, it needs to be recognized that the information costs which give
modern corporation a role in allocating capital also give rise to considerable manager
discretion. While capital may be more efficiently allocated, some of the efficiency ga
are appropriated by the managers, with the providers of capital reaping only a part
the returns. While the mechanisms described in this chapter may limit the fraction
the returns which can be so appropriated, the total amount which managers can obt
in a large corporation may be enormous.

[37] The relatively small scale of most European markets in the period of the init
growth of most large corporations may account for the fact that European corporati
have tended to be less highly specialized than US corporations and, hence, ha
themselves substituted to a greater extent for the venture capital industry in t
United States.

[38] See Sahlman (1989) for a detailed description of the venture capital industry in t
United States.

[39] Greenwald, Stiglitz, and Weiss (1984) characterize the equilibrium size of the n
equities market for any given β. This result is obtained by examining how t
equilibrium changes as β changes.

[40] Summers and Summers (1989) and Stiglitz (1989) argue that an appropriat
designed turnover tax may be used to encourage longer-term holding of equities.

[41] In this view, then, Kaldor's formulation of the aggregate savings function m
provide a better description of the economy than Pasinetti's formulation (1962).

[42] The aggregate equations are of the form of the Volterra-Lotka equations; see Aker
and Stiglitz (1969). In the case where b is a function of the capital employment ra
(and hence of w), there is convergence to the steady state, but the path of converge
may entail oscillations.

[43] In effect, we are assuming that there are enough different firms that the law of la
numbers allows us to ignore, at the aggregate level, the variations in ε, and that
economies/diseconomies of scale are sufficiently weak that the slight fluctuations in t
distribution of K_i/K can also be ignored (i.e. we assume that $\Sigma M(w, K_i/K) K_i \varepsilon_i \approx m$
K).

[44] See Champernowne (1953) or Stiglitz (1969).

[45] The evolutionary nature of the market – and the fact that learning in t
environment appears, in one sense, quite rapid, and in another sense, quite limited –
illustrated by the S & L debacle in the United States. The S & Ls were quick to respo
to the new economic situation that they found themselves in in the 1980s, but th
seemed not to have learned from history the risks associated with having too larg
fraction of one's portfolio in correlated assets, nor did they grasp the possibility th
prices of real estate may fall dramatically. The S & L crisis has also made it clear th
the line between fraud and "moral hazard" may be a fine one. The crisis has for
changes in financial regulations, which in turn will give rise to adaptations of t
financial institutions.

Whether mortgage insurance and the development of national mortgage mark
represent permanent changes in financial structure, or the temporary (mal)adaptat
of markets to a situation in which, for several decades, real estate markets have h
relative stability – the problems of the Great Depression having receded into ancie
history – only time will tell.

[46] Though the junk bond itself may be partially a response to legal changes reduci
the economic costs of bankruptcy.

[47] See, for instance, Asquith and Mullins (forthcoming).

orporate Organization, Finance nd Innovation[1]

ASAHIKO AOKI AND GIOVANNI DOSI

troduction

his chapter deals with some theoretical issues concerning the lationship between financial institutions and business (non financal) corporations and its implications for innovation and other rporate behavior in contemporary economies. Let us introduce it ith three broad empirical historical phenomena which are relevant. rst, the forms of financing of production activities have changed ipressively in most of the industrialized countries over the developent process. Second, significant differences in financial institutions id in their relative importance among industrialized countries (and, ore so, in developing countries) have persisted. Third, a widespread aim, albeit not uncontroversial as an accepted "stylized fact," is that fferent financial set-ups have historically been an important conicive factor, or alternatively an important obstacle, to industrializain and growth.

In relation to the foregoing issues, the following major theoretical iestions emerge. What is the importance of financial institutions in ng-term growth? Do they significantly influence the rates and itterns of resource allocation? How do they influence the rates and rections of innovation? How do they influence the forms of corporate ganization? Did they evolve simply within a trend toward higher d increasingly common levels of efficiency? Can particular financial stitutions be related historically with particular patterns of corpote organization and behavior? The financial institutions simulneously play the roles of a provider of investment funds, a monitor corporate behavior and management, and a selection mechanism r would-be innovative endeavors. Hence, one is likely to find in the lationship between finance and industrial activity a powerful in-

fluence on the performance and paths of evolution of differe
economic systems.

We shall propose a few theoretical hypotheses on the basis of sor
of the above questions. The two authors have converged on broad
similar and complementary perceptions of those questions, via dif
rent routes. One of us (Aoki) has extensively studied the informati
and incentive properties of diverse institutional arrangements f
corporate firms. Specifically, the comparative organizational analy
of highly stylized "American" (A) and "Japanese" (J) firms h
clarified some reasonable conditions under which either of them mig
perform better than the other in efficiency terms, due to differe
informational and incentive characteristics. Quite concise theoretic
abstractions on the A and J firms as two polar archetypes, howev
suggest a need for the extension of the analysis to cover oth
empirical cases. In this comparative organizational perspective, sp
cific cultural traits and sociological variables, together with particul
sequences of historical events, would certainly be considered fund
mental to explaining why a particular set of organizational forms a
rules emerged: but once they emerged, no matter what the historic
reason, their workings may be analyzed in terms familiar to eco
omists, i.e., equilibrium properties arising out of their informatio
incentive, and financial control characteristics (Aoki, 1986, 198
1990b). The other author (Dosi) has focused on the features of t
processes of evolution, in particular on those features of technologic
and institutional innovation which are difficult to study in terms
their final equilibrium properties. On the bases of these differe
methodologies, however, we have come to a common appreciation, f
instance, of the importance of a theoretical analysis of the permane
tension that each economic system embodies, between incentives a
information flows which make it more or less efficient at performing
given set of tasks, versus its potential for discovering and developi
new things (products, processes, forms of organization); or that of t
differential influence of a variety of financial institutions upon t
innovative behavior of business organizations.

This chapter is organized as follows: in the next section we sh
review the general functions which corporate organizations, as well
markets, perform – to varying degrees and with varying success
irrespective of the particular institutional design. How do financ
institutions influence those various functions of the firm? Prelimina
to any answer to the question is, of course, a theoretical unde
standing of the internal structure and performance of the firm. In th
regard we suggest that the framework of standard agency theory
the firm prevents a unified account of diverse links between finan

and industry. The next section then attempts to develop what we believe to be a potentially richer theoretical framework, and examines the informational and incentive properties of different archetypes of organization and finance. The final section enlarges the proposed theoretical framework to account for innovation and environmental non stationarity.

Markets, Firms, and Finance: A Taxonomy of Functions and their Theoretical Interpretations

Whether economic activities occur through market exchanges or within organizations, they obviously involve a resource allocating function. Indeed, this property of economic interaction has been one of the central concerns of economic theory since its origin. However, as well as resource allocation, both markets and organizations perform other equally important functions. First, they involve a structure of information flows. Even the simplest exchange communicates information: after all, it is widely held that prices are a parsimonious device for communicating information in decentralized economic systems. This, however, applies under quite strict assumptions (e.g. market completeness and rational expectations). Moreover, the way information is distributed among agents affects their behavior: various sorts of asymmetric information models have highlighted the multiplicity of equilibria that can arise under different informational assumptions. In reality, things are even more complicated. Some information flows transit through the market. Many others do not; a lot of information flows occur within organizations. One can reasonably presume that the nature of such flows depends also on the structures of the organizations themselves, the "channels" they allow, the kinds of information they select. Also information flows are mediated between organizations by a variety of financial institutions. As a result, different financial systems are likely to generate different distributions of information across organizations.

Second, both markets and organizations involve incentive structures. Markets, in a Williamsonian terminology, involve "high power" incentives, in that they provide rather direct rewards and sanctions to economic behaviors. However, with asymmetric information and, more so, with environmental non stationarity, even market incentives are affected by information that the agents hold, their beliefs, their past experience, their problem-solving competences. A multiplicity of incentive structures is generated by the multiplicity of possible contractual arrangements. As illustrations, think of the different incentive structures associated with crop sharing versus land tenure (Stiglitz, 1974a), or in risk-sharing versus cost-plus contracts in R & D (Teece, 1988). Such a multiplicity of incentive structures is further expanded within organizations with different hierarchical ladders, promotion schemes, forms of reward, etc. Incentives for management at the apex of internal hierarchies may be varied depending on types of financial contracts provided by financial institutions.

Third, economic interaction involves forms of monitoring and control. Again, even if markets can be thought to provide more "high powered" forms of performance monitoring, this is not always so with asymmetric information: Akerlof's "market for lemons" is a good example (Akerlof, 1970). Within organizations, particular procedures of monitoring and control are associated with specific authority structures. Whether one believes (as most social scientists do) or not (as most economists do not) that power represents an autonomous dimension motivating behavior, it appears to hold that the variety of hierarchies in organizations implies differentiated criteria by which subordinates' behaviors are selected, performances are monitored, decisions are transmitted and implemented. Further, the variety of financial institutions exercises differentiated modes of financial control and monitoring on the behaviors and decisions of management at the apex of internal hierarchies.

Fourth, and finally, individuals and organizations learn, in the sense that they do not only refine their information about an unchanged external environment, but they also discover new products and production processes, new problems and new problem-solving rules. In a word, they innovate, and by doing so they also continuously change the environment in which they operate. Various financial institutions affect these evolutionary processes in differentiated ways by encouraging/discouraging different types of innovative activities on the part of individuals and organizations.

Let us emphasize that most of the economic theories of the firm have not dealt consistently with the entire set of functions as enumerated above and, less so, with the observed variety in their institutional arrangements of business organizations combining these functions.

The Marshallian tradition largely focuses on the allocative properties of the firm, whose very existence is justified mainly in terms of some asset indivisibilities and (bounded) economies of scale. Incentives and information issues are largely neglected.

The new contractual approach to the study of the firm, in which the firm is regarded as a nexus of principal-agency contracts involving investors, employees, and business partners, has made inroads since the early 1970s. What are the information and control relationships among these contracts? How are the incentives of agents aligned in the nexus? Agency theory regards the incentive content of contracts forming a nexus as essentially preconditioned by markets, in the sense that reservation utilities of contracting partners are exogenously given, and the pecuniary rewards for the supply of resources are *ex ante* specified in contracts, except for one class of contracting partners. This exception applies to residual claimants who receive the residual after all other contractual payments are made, that is, stockholders in the case of publicly held corporations. Because of their unique position, residual claimants are regarded as accountable as the principal designer of the nexus of contracts for the purpose of efficiency. However, details of management and operating decisions need not be specified in contracts, and the drawing of actual contracts with other agents may be delegated to management, if management is effectively placed under market-oriented financial control. This can be done in the following hierarchical order.

First, top management may be controlled directly through the board of directors providing proper incentive contracts for managers and monitoring management decisions on behalf of residual claimants. But who monitors the monitor? There is the market for corporate control (i.e., the selection of the board) and, if the incumbent board fails to meet stockholders' interests, takeover discipline may be imposed on it. Thus corporate management decisions of the firm, such as on investment, employment, corporate finance and the like, are assumed to be effectively controlled in the direction of maximizing the present value of residuals. Management control over operating activities, in turn, may be hierarchically decomposed by means of hierarchical layers of incentive contracts. At a higher level, management acts as a surrogate for residual claimants (the principal) *vis-à-vis* management at a lower level, as well as outside agents such as suppliers and distributors. At the bottom level of the hierarchy, operating employees control only their own effort level, within the framework of incentive contracts provided by management.

The assumed information structure within the hierarchical nexus is roughly as follows: in designing incentive contracts, the principal is supposed to know *ex ante* the probability distribution of relevant events affecting the outcome of the agent's action, whereas only the agent is able to have access *ex post* to the eventual realization of events. The prior knowledge of the principal may be thought as deriving from formal learning exogenous to the nexus, as well as from

the principal's own higher order decisions that shape the actio
environment of the lower level. Because of this information asym
metry, any incentive-compatible contract has to accrue informatio
rents to the agent who has on-site information regarding its actio
environment. But within this inevitable "agency loss," the principa
may be able to control the agent's action in its own interests b
properly designing incentive schemes consistent with market con
straints. Thus, according to principal–agency theorists, the firm i
nothing but a "legal fiction which serves as a focus for processes i
which conflicting objectives of individuals are brought into equilibriun
within a contractual framework" (Jensen and Meckling, 1976). Ac
tions of agents are induced by incentive contracts consistent witl
market competition, and the control-monitoring function of the firm i
only tacit.

Interestingly, Coase (1988), regarded as the pioneer of the con
tractual approach, recently criticized such a state of contractua
theory. He held that because of contractual theorists' preoccupatio
with the incentive provision function of the firm, another importan
aspect of the firm, i.e., "organizational coordination" – which saves o
costs of market transactions – has largely been left unexplored. Coas
maintains that this gap is undesirable, and unsatisfactory for under
standing "the institutional structure of production in the system as a
whole." In the nexus-of-contracts approach, hierarchical ordering o
information distribution and flow within the firm seems to be take
for granted: on the contrary, we argue later that modern firms need t
be analyzed within a richer informational variety.

From the evolutionary perspective, the neglect of explicit treatmen
of the specificities of control/authority mechanisms associated witl
organizational hierarchies is equally unsatisfactory. Even if on
accepts that any one particular organizational structure has emerge
as the result of some original contractual process, one must at leas
admit that, thereafter, this same structure has some inertia: it i
largely event-independent, and resilient to recontracting on th
grounds of subsequent information acquired by the contracting
parties. Indeed, with generalized asymmetric information and
transaction costs, Williamson's model has shown that discretionary
behavior within the context of hierarchies may outperform markets
precisely because of their irreversibility features. Relatively sticky
organizational rules moderate the risk of opportunistic behavior by
introducing some combination of incentives and administrative control, with limited recontracting possibilities.

Finally, we want to emphasize the almost complete neglect in most
contemporary industrial organization theories of the specificities of

ompetences and skills that each firm embodies and that obviously
ffect performances. It is true that some competence-related issues
ave been addressed in "human capital" models and in "incentives-to-
earn" models. However, a fundamental dimension is still missing,
amely those relatively tacit and changing organizational capabilities
which cannot be imputed to individual workers, but, rather, are the
ollective outcome of particular interactive procedures within the firm.
As one of us has discussed at greater length elsewhere (Dosi, Teece
and Winter (1991)), this lack of attention to specific firm competences
mpedes any satisfactory analysis of the innovative capabilities of
lifferent firms. Somewhat complementarily, as the other author has
hown, it also obscures one of the main sources of differential
erformance between firms and countries (Aoki, 1986, 1990b).

Our endeavor, in the following, is to proceed some modest steps
oward a deeper theoretical understanding of the nature of the firm,
vhich can account for the coexistence of the functions discussed above
n a unified framework and recognize an observable variety of their
ombination. In doing so, we specifically emphasize the following
oints:

a) Different patterns of business organization and different modes
   of interaction with other agents imply diverse combinations
   amongst those functions, and thus different performances. There
   might be some different organizational designs which are roughly
   equivalent in terms of performance. However, others may be
   shown to present specific or general "inferior"/"superior" characteristics.

b) An intrinsic tension may appear amongst the above organizational functions: in particular between those combinations which
   are conducive to relatively high performances on the grounds of
   current technologies and markets, and those other combinations
   which are more conducive to learning and innovation, possibly at
   the expense of current performances.

c) The modes of financing and the link between business firms and
   various financial actors influence the ways firms combine their
   various functions, and also their long-term innovative success.

Coordination, Incentives, and Financial Control

There are alternative ways to represent different institutional com-
inations of the functions performed by the firm, depending on

particular methodological inclinations. Even the authors of this work have pursued the inquiry with rather different approaches. One of us has interpreted the general properties of the firm in terms of outcomes of bargaining games. That is, the distribution of quasi-rents arising out of firm-specific coordination are subject to explicit/implicit bargaining among constituent members of the firm. Therefore institutional interdependence between, for example, employees, corporate management, other firms, and financial institutions, needs to be explicitly specified. Some institutional arrangements may be able to approximate the rational outcome as described by the cooperative game theory under certain environmental conditions, but others may not (Aoki, 1986).

The other author has been inclined to a much more "institutionalist" representation of business organizations, with more emphasis on "routinization" and on the role of extraeconomic, highly inertial, variables as guides to economic behavior (Dosi, 1984, 1988a; Dosi and Orsenigo, 1988). Organizations are viewed, following Nelson and Winter (1982), as involving also some sort of "truce" between conflicting interests: hence, the precarious status of any incentive-compatibility that is possibly achieved, and also a big allowance for "disequilibrium" behavior.

However, for the purposes of this chapter, the two views are not inconsistent and somewhat complement each other, in that together they highlight the economic properties of specific institutional arrangements as well as the "rationality" of different micro-behaviors under different organizational set-ups. For our purposes here it does not matter whether one believes that some contractual agreements between rational individuals are the ultimate "philosophical" foundation of organizations, or alternatively that various institutions "philosophically" exist prior to the individual perception of self-seeking goals, and shape their "economic rationality." What is crucial is that different behaviors may be informationally feasible and incentive-compatible under different forms of economic organization. Hence, no matter what the general theoretical preference, one may take any comparative exercise on the equilibrium performance of different organizational regimes, at least as a "thought experiment" on the economic viability of particular institutional developments.

With these premises, let us proceed to a simple comparative analysis by presenting archetype models of a combination of internal coordination, incentives, and financial control (and innovation in the next section), and compare them with the alternative principal/agent model discussed in the previous section. This analysis is inspired by the comparative analysis of stylized archetypes of the "American" and

ιe "Japanese" firm discussed by one of the authors (Aoki, 1986, 1988,
990b). However, the following presentation may suggest a broader
pplicability of the analysis than to those two extreme archetypes.

oordination: hierarchies versus knowledge-sharing

irst, we compare two archetype modes of internal coordination of
ctivities pursuing given strategic business decisions on investment,
ιles targets, etc. (We will consider modes of financial and other possible
ɔntrols over strategic business decision later.) Suppose that predeter-
ιined strategic decisions need to be implemented as a joint effort by
ιultiple subunits of an organization (say, a chain of shops), technologi-
ιlly mutually interrelated. The costs of each shop performing a certain
ιsk depend upon uncertain events. In order to achieve the overall
rganizational goal most efficiently, however, it is not necessarily good
ɔr each shop to select the cost-minimizing method of doing its own task
ι a decentralized way, for this might overburden other shops.
'he choice of operating methods by individual shops must be
oordinated.

One archetype mode of coordination, which we call the hierarchical
ιode and shall refer to as the *H-mode*, is implicit in the agency model
f the firm, and its essence may be reiterated simply as follows.
ιanagement has knowledge concerning the prior probability distribu-
ons of events affecting the cost conditions of shops, and chooses the
ιsks for all shops that will jointly minimize the total expected cost of
chieving the strategic goal. Each shop is required to perform the task
hosen by management. As events evolve, the chosen set of tasks may
ot achieve *ex post* the minimization of total cost. But since there has
een already an effort to minimize such discrepancy, operating task
hould proceed as planned and *ex post* information available at shops
ɜ to be communicated to (or be monitored by) management for the
evision of its subjective probability distributions of events, which may
e utilized only for the improvement of next-round centralized
lanning.

An alternative archetype mode is more participatory. Suppose that
ιe centralized planning by management only sets a preliminary
ramework for actual operations of each shop. Suppose that, as time
oes by, each shop utilizes its own observation on-site for the revision
f its prior probability distribution of events (in a Bayesian manner)
nd communicates this information horizontally with other shops
possibly with the help of centralized communication facilities) for the
ιurpose of fine-tuning the coordination of tasks. This coordination

mode based on information sharing, referred to as the *S-mode*, car
improve on cost performance per time because of better utilization of
on-site information. Such gains cannot be without cost, however. The
participation of each shop in learning (the revision of prior distribu
tions) and communications involves costs in terms of effort expendi
ture, and the diversion of attention to non-routine kinds of operations
including possible bargaining among shops over operational coordina
tion.

Thus, the contrast of two archetype modes involves a tension almost
universally present in any organization, i.e. the tension between
economies of specialization (specialization in specific operational tasks
as well as the separation of planning and operational tasks), versus
gains from learning and knowledge-sharing. The comparative analysis of informational efficiency of the two modes has been recently tried
by various authors (Aoki, 1986, 1990b; Cremer, 1990; Itoh, 1987)
According to those studies, the H-mode outperforms the S-mode when
operational environments for shops are relatively stable or drastically
changing. In both cases, decentralized learning may not add so much
information value (saving of costs), and the sacrifice of economies of
specialization may not be worthwhile. In the intermediate case where
environments are continually changing (but in relatively recognizable
ways), the S-mode may outperform the H-mode, provided that the
learning capability of each shop and the communicability among
shops are high enough. In this case, gains from decentralized learning
and knowledge-sharing may be greater than losses from the sacrifice
of economies of specialization.

In actual organizations, elements of both H-mode and S-mode may
be combined in varying degrees and in complex ways. However, the
results of a comparative analysis based on simple archetype models is
not entirely devoid of empirical implications. For example, the
American automobile and steel industries, which dominated world
markets up to the end of the 1960s with a relatively small set of
homogeneous products, predominantly exhibited aspects of the H-
mode, whereas the Italian textile and garment industry, as well as the
Japanese automobile and steel industries, attuned to small-to-medium
batch production of a large variety of products, predominantly exhibit
aspects of the S-mode. We shall postpone discussion of the implications for innovation to the next section.

Incentives: markets versus promotional hierarchies.

As discussed in the previous section, the essence of the incentive
structure captured by the agency model of the nexus of contracts is its

market orientation, in spite of its preoccupation with incentive design. It is assumed that there is only one type of residual claimant, and the agency theory explores various types of incentive schemes precisely to extract the maximum residual, while guaranteeing the exogenously determined expected utility levels for agents. The market-oriented incentive mode, referred to as the *M-mode*, may be thought as being well aligned with the H-mode of coordination, because the information efficiency of the latter depends upon specialized skills of operation and planning. Specialized skills which can be acquired through formal training and are universally applicable may be supplied through well-defined job markets. If an agent can acquire a firm-specific information-processing capacity (skill) through internal training, the principal may have to accrue information rent to the agent in designing an incentive-compatible contract. However, the principal can offer long-term contracts to newcomers such that the amount equivalent to the discounted present value of the information rent is extracted as a training cost in the training period (Riordan, 1990), since the new agent does not have any bargaining power to prevent the principal from doing so before the acquisition of firm-specific skills themselves.

Conversely, as soon as elements of the S-mode of coordination set in, the exclusive reliance on the archetypical M-mode of incentive structure becomes problematic. Since the S-mode involves inter-shop communication of learned results by shops (or employees) to coordinate their operations, the information-value net of training and communication costs created by the S-mode is of a collective nature, and not decomposable into individual contributions. In other words, the skills of participants in the S-mode can be accumulated and are useful only within the context of the S-mode and may be appropriately characterized as "network-specific" (as distinguished from "firm-specific," Mailath and Postlewaite, 1990). Accordingly, market-transferable, individual contracts cannot be written *ex ante* for individuals.

An archetype model of incentive structure combined with the archetype S-mode coordination may be constructed in two steps: the collective level and then the individual level. First, and collectively, the net information value created by the S-mode may be subject to internal distribution between the participants of the S-mode (the employees of the firm) as a whole, on one hand, and the "firm," on the other. Since the net information value can be generated by the active involvement of all employees in learning on-site, and by communications among themselves, they are likely to have credible collective bargaining power for a share in the value by the threat of withdrawal

of cooperation (Aoki, 1990a). Conversely, if the information value is
be snatched away by the competitors of the firm unless the evolvi
information is utilized effectively on-site as well as between shops, it
incentive-compatible for both the employees and the firm immediate
to agree on the sharing of information value to be created a⟩
cooperatively to engage in the S-mode of coordination (Binmo⟩
Rubinstein and Wolinsky, 1986).

An interesting question is why the employees cannot appropria
the whole value of the network by themselves. Why cannot th⟨
purchase the network (the S-mode) collectively and replicate
guaranteeing themselves the whole value? Mailath and Postlewa⟩
(1990) pose this question and argue that, if there are intangib
benefits which individual employees receive from the "firm" a⟩
which are not verifiable by each other, a share of the inform⟩
tion-value created by the network is likely to go to the firm, as t⟩
size of the network becomes larger. There are many possibilities f⟨
the emergence of such intangible benefits. The firm's provision of t⟩
incentive-monitoring mechanism for individual performance with
the S-mode may in fact realize such a possibility. That is, t⟩
guarantee of a share in information value to the employees as a who⟨
does not automatically induce the level and kind of efforts ⟩
individual shops and employees appropriate for the efficient operatic
of the S-mode. Individuals may try to free-ride, whereas individu
shops may develop and assert their own group-centric goal (a larg⟨
share in information value) wastefully, taking up time and resource
The collective sharing of information-value needs to be supplement⟨
by a proper mechanism for monitoring individual performance.

In order to achieve individual efforts appropriate for the S-mo⟨
which are incentive-compatible, the incentive-monitoring mechanis⟩
needs to have the following properties. First, since the S-mode reli⟨
upon decentralized information-processing (and problem-solvin⟨
based on knowledge sharing, participating employees need to ⟩
encouraged to develop information processing capacities appropria⟩
for a specific network built in the firm (learning). Second, shops a⟩
individuals need to be encouraged to cooperate and to restrain t⟩
assertion of subgroup-centric interests. As Koike has emphasized in
series of works (1984, 1988) in the Japanese context, the nurturing ⟨
network-specific skills in general, and the capacity for problem-solvin
on-site in particular, may require a wider-range understanding of t⟩
working of the network. Skills versed only in a specific compone⟩
task of the organization may not contribute to the information⟨
efficiency of the S-mode as under the H-mode. Such wider-rang
understanding may be nurtured by experiencing various interrelate

tasks, through the rotation of jobs. The rotation of employees between shops may also facilitate knowledge-sharing among shops, and restrain the development of an egocentric coherent subgroup.

One possible way to encourage wide-range learning and cooperative efforts may be to create promotional hierarchies of ranks (there may be multiple hierarchies for various job categories, such as clerical employees, blue-collar employees, engineers, etc.) and administer them from the organizational perspective. Suppose that new employees not trained for network-specific skills are placed at the bottom rank of an appropriate hierarchy and that they are promoted to higher ranks over time according to their learning achievements evaluated in relatively wide dimensions as well as their cooperative contributions (e.g. in teaching junior employees, communications ability, teamwork, etc.). A particular level of compensation and other benefits is associated with each rank, but not with a specific task. Imagine that employees are rotated over various jobs through administrative assignments by the management. Employees of the same rank may be assigned to different tasks, while employees assigned to the same tasks may be of different rank because of differences in general learning achievements. There are elements of seniority in ranking, because learning takes time. But employees of the same job tenure may well be ranked differently according to their learning achievements. One who fails to progress in rank hierarchy, because of failure in learning and/or poor cooperativeness may be ousted from the rank hierarchy and have to seek another job elsewhere. Since this might represent a negative signal concerning the person's qualities, he might be unable to obtain another position of equivalent rank, and a substantial loss in income may be inflicted upon him. Thus the organizational "administration" of rank hierarchies and job assignments might function as an effective incentive-monitoring mechanism to induce learning and cooperation useful for the S-mode (MacLeod and Malcomson (1986)). Let us denote this mechanism as the *R-mode*.

It may be appropriate to comment here on the so-called "internal labor market," as this is often confused with the R-mode incentive structure. It is certainly true that both share a feature, in that employees are made mobile among jobs within the firm. But the internal labor market is characterized by "job ladders," i.e. the progression over mutually related but well-defined job categories, not by mere ranks of pay and status. Also, the mobility of employees over job ladders is realized by the matching of the posting of vacant jobs by the employer with the applications of employees. Only if there is an excess of demand for jobs by equally qualified employees is selection to

be made on the basis of seniority. On the other hand, only when th
supply of jobs exceeds the internal supply, the market is made ope
externally. In the R-mode, on the contrary, task assignments as we
as rank assignments are administered by the personnel department o
the firm. For these reasons, the internal labor market may b
classified as a variant of the M-mode, rather than of the R-mode.

There tends to be a rigidity in the level of employment under th
R-mode, as it is designed to promote internal learning over tim
Within this rigid framework, however, employees' skills may b
flexibly utilized because of the relative ease of rotation and transfer o
employees through administrative job assignment. On the other hanc
the M-mode incentive system can be relatively flexible in th
adjustment of employment, as it can absorb and release worker
through labor markets as needs arise. Conversely, the interna
reallocation of employees is rigidly limited, as job categories ar
defined in external labor markets. We will discuss below som
implications of the rigidity–flexibility dilemma in terms of innovativ
activities of the firm under each mode.

As in the case of the coordination mechanism, real-world firms ten
to combine elements of both archetype modes of incentive structur
Generally speaking, however, in Western economies the incentiv
systems tend to be relatively more characteristic of the M-mod
whereas in Japan the R-mode tends to dominate.

Modes of finance and corporate control: markets versus banks

It has been argued by several authors that, historically, one ca
distinguish between two basic modes of finance-industry links, ofte
classified as the market-oriented system and as the bank (credit
oriented system (Rybczynsky, 1985; Berglof, 1990; Dosi, 1990). In th
market-oriented system, historically approximated by Britain and th
USA, ownership titles are traded relatively freely on stock market
and variations in the stock values are taken to represent the mai
impersonal disciplining mechanism on corporate behavior. Growth i
financed mainly through retained profits and, to a lesser extent, b
bonds and new equity issues. In the bank-oriented system, historicall
observed in Continental Europe and in Japan, banks and othe
financial organizations have played a more direct role in industri
growth. They have holdings of company shares, and their holdings ar
relatively stable and concentrated; the ratio of bank credit to tot
assets of the nonfinancial corporate sector is relatively high, and
"voice" mechanism of control – in Hirschman's terminology – is ofte

xercised to influence the strategic decisions of management. Recent-
, as the internally accumulated financial resources of nonfinancial
mpanies have grown, the importance of bank credits in financing
rowth, as well as the frequency and strength of the banks' "voice,"
ave tended to decline, but stable stockholding on the part of banks
ill insulates corporate firms in the bank-oriented system from hostile
keovers through the market for corporate control.

Let us discuss the finance–firm links in terms of financial control
ver strategic decisions of the firm by distinguishing four archetype
odes – the M-mode, as envisioned in the agency theory discussed in
ie foregoing section, an RB-mode, a WB-mode and an SB-mode,
hich are introduced below.

The now classic treatment by Modigliani and Miller of finance
ieory distinguishes debt financing and equity financing only in terms
f return characteristics (i.e., fixed returns with a probability of
efault, versus residual claim). As is well known, they argued that in
ie absence of taxes, and with perfectly competitive markets, the
ioice between these two methods of finance does not matter, from
ie viewpoint of stockholders. Implicit in this claim is the assumption
iat the inside manager who enters into debt contracts (possibly in
ie form of a bond) is the agent of stockholders. But are bank credits
ssentially the same as bond issues from the viewpoint of corporate
ontrol? The Modigliani-Miller theory assumes that there is a clear-
it point of bankruptcy, at which stockholders' control and liquidation
re separated. But it is often observed that bankruptcy does not
ecessarily lead to liquidation, but rather to reorganization attempts
y specialists (often the bank as creditor cum stockholder). How can
e analyze the implications of this phenomenon?

Recently Aghion and Bolton (1988) have suggested an interesting
icomplete contract model of finance, trying to answer these and
ther questions. They argue that the essence of debt contracts does
ot lie in their return characteristics, as commonly believed, but in
ie *ex ante* arrangements regarding the distribution of control. As
ing as good profitability continues, the outside investor (the bank)
oes not intervene, and the inside manager keeps managing; other-
ise the outside investor (bank) takes over management and reorga-
izes or liquidates. Within the specific context of their model, they
howed that such a contract can achieve *ex ante* Pareto optimality
hen the inside manager has a strong preference for carrying on
usiness as usual (rather than "liquidating" in a bad profit state or
innovating" in a good profit state). An external investor with control
ights may be excessively "innovative" in good profit states (as in the
ase of a takeover raider), while inside management may try to

survive wastefully on other people's money in bad profit states. Indeed, Aghion and Bolton's model of debt contracts captures some important elements of financial control in a "mature" bank-oriented system in which, in the normal state of affairs, the bank's voice within the corporate governance structure is not loud, and inside managers' discretionary power is strong, while in crisis situations the bank's power becomes visible and plays an essential role in the reorganization or liquidation of failing companies. In such a bank-oriented system, the takeover of failing companies can occur, but takeover is usually exercised by banks, rather than occurring via the market for corporate control, as in market-oriented systems. Thus the financial control mode, in which there is an *ex ante* agreement between management and the bank about the transfer of control contingent upon profit states as described by Aghion and Bolton, may be distinguished from *relational banking*, which we often observe in developing countries. In the latter setting, banks are often owned and controlled by industrialists, and are used as instruments for raising funds for their firms. Moreover, risk diversification is limited in such circumstances. We refer to this relational banking system as the *RB-mode*, which, for our purposes, also includes all those cases where a bank formally owns one or a few firms, but is completely "tied-in" with them: the future of the bank goes together with the fortune of the companies with which it is linked. On the other hand, in the developed banking system *à la* Aghion and Bolton, not only control rights shift between banks and industrial firms, depending upon the latter's wealth position, but also banks normally diversify their lending among many industrial firms. We refer to this system as the *WB-mode* (the weak bank control mode). Finally, we refer to those banking systems in which strong financial control by banks is exercised over industrial firms regardless of the latter's wealth position as the *SB-mode* (the strong bank control mode).

Types of modal combination

Empirically, one can easily observe varying combinations among the dichotomic organizational characteristics discussed so far. Some of these combinations may turn out to be plausibly "inferior" to others in efficiency terms, but they can historically persist, due precisely to that same institutional inertia which makes the continuity of "superior" combinations easier. Among "superior" ones, however, there may not be simple ranking. One combination may be superior in certain technological, market and cultural conditions, but not in others. It is

ite likely, therefore, that any observed structure of a corporate
>nomy will be quite complex, barring simple stylizations. However,
us list a few representative archetypical combinations below, at the
k of oversimplification, in an attempt to provide a sort of com-
rative taxonomy.

H-M-M. This is the combination of the hierarchical internal
>rdination with the market-oriented incentive structure and mar-
t-based financial control. This archetype is the one which more
>sely corresponds to the model of the firm as a nexus of agency
ntracts discussed in the previous sections, and may be referred to as
e A-model of the firm hereafter. One may say that this model
>resents a sort of "neoclassical image" of Anglo-American firms.

H-M-RB. The H-mode internal coordination and the M-mode
centives are combined with "relational" banking. One is likely to
serve something similar to this combination in several developing
untries (authoritarian coordination, segmented and localized labor
arkets, and oligarchic industrial control), which tend to hinder
rticipating behavior on the part of the labour force and to make
m-specific development of skills more difficult, while fostering
llusive rent-seeking strategies by firms.

H-R-SB. This is the combination of hierarchies in both coordina-
>n and incentives (rank hierarchies) with strong bank control. If
nks degenerate into a single monolithic national system, this model
ay come somewhat to resemble the socialist firm (the S-model)
der central planning. Note that, for corporate organizations to be
ective (in terms of whatever organizational goals) while at the same
ne utilizing individual initiatives, they may need to combine
ntralization (the H-mode or the R-mode) and decentralization (the
mode or the M-mode) in coordination and incentives. If the coordina-
>n mechanism and incentive structures are both centralized, as in
is model, organizations may be stifled by bureaucratic burdens and
k of individual initiative. Moreover, in the single monolithic
nking system, the allocation of financial resources is apt to be
ided by political expediency, and financially failing firms are often
lvaged by refinancing, leading to an excessive survival rate for
efficient firms, a phenomenon known as the "soft-budgeting prob-
n" (Kornai, 1980).

S-R-WB. The S-mode mechanism of internal coordination and the
mode incentive structure are combined with the WB mode of
ancial control. This combination is related to the archetypical
panese model (the J-model) as developed by one of the present

authors (Aoki, 1988, 1990b), but it need not be limited to it. We hav
already mentioned that the S-R combination is effective for th
development of network-specific skills geared towards continuall
changing market and technological environments. But what about it
combination with the WB-mode? Is it accidental or not? Whos
interests does the "inside" manager represent in the J-model? W
argue, first, that the combination is essential and second, that th
"inside" manager represents the dual interests of financial investor
and employees embodying network-specific skills.

Let us begin with the first proposition. You will recall that in th
S-mode coordination, within the framework of strategic decisions
problem-solving is delegated to the lower level of functional hierarchy
while relatively free communication among constituent units at th
lower level is practiced. However, in order to guarantee that th
constituent units at the lower level do not engage in collusive behavio
aimed at rent-seeking, sacrificing the organizational strategic goals
the actions of lower units must be properly monitored. This monitor
ing requires more than just checking whether they perform hierarchi
cally decomposed directives. It needs to be assessed whether econ
omically meaningful information is created and efficiently utilized o
a shared basis at the lower level. In turn, on the side of monitoring
this requires the knowledge of how the internal information networl
operates. Such knowledge may be most effectively nurtured by th
experience of active participation in the network. Under the M-mod
of financial control, however, top management is likely to be selecte
from the "external" market of managers, separated from the interna
network of information. Thus, from the information-monitoring poin
of view, the WB-mode of financial control, which assures the control o
the internal management on the conditions of internal informationa
efficiency, is more likely to be consistent with the S-mode of interna
coordination.

Second, note that for rank hierarchies to work as an effectiv
incentive mechanism, it is desirable that ranks extend "indefinitely'
upward. If progression in rank hierarchy is known to cease at a
certain rank, shirking may occur at that point (e.g. in the form of th
lack of effort sometimes observed among middle management in th
S-firm). Of course, the indefinite extension of rank hierarchy in a
literal sense is not feasible. Suppose, nonetheless, that internal rank
hierarchy could extend up to the top management. What about th
incentives of top management then? We have suggested that unde
the WB-mode of financial control the degree of discretionary power o
top management is positively correlated with the level of profit. To
managers of J-model firms are thus likely to be engaged in competi

n over profit ranking, subsequent to the successful completion of
ternal competition over promotion. Competition over ranking is thus
ade open-ended through the combination of the R-mode of incentive
ructure with the WB-mode of financial control.

Let us now turn to the second proposition. We have already argued
at some sharing of the net value of information is more likely in the
R combination. But strategic management decisions – such as on
vestment, diversification, and employment levels – obviously exert
a impact on the lifetime earnings of employees by affecting their
sitions in rank hierarchies in the short run as well as in the long
n. Therefore it is rational for them to negotiate with management
garding possible trade-offs between the current pay level, the level
their own effort, and, generally, management policy decisions. Such
gotiation may be in the interests of investors as well. The
egotiation" between the financial investor and employees need not
direct and explicit, but may be mediated by management. In fact,
e can prove the following interesting result: if, on the one hand,
ployees are committed to the level of effort expenditure at which
tal information value (albeit not their share therein) net of the total
sutility from work is maximized, and, if, on the other hand,
anagement strikes some balance in its decisions between the
terests of financial investors (as represented by the bank) and
ployees – with distributive shares as weights – then, from the
ewpoint of both financial investors and employees, Pareto efficient
d incentive-compatible outcomes are likely to emerge (as it approxi-
ates the generalized Nash bargaining solution cum subgame perfect
uilibrium; cf. Aoki, 1986, 1988).

Note that in the WB-mode, the bank cum stockholding does not
ace pressure on management for continual share price maximiza-
on, yet is committed to the supply of financial resources as far as the
elivery of satisfactory yields, defined in the debt contracts, is secured.
n the other hand, internally promoted management may be more
fective in identifying employees' interests and their bargaining
wer in striking some balance of interests between them and the
areholders.

orms of Corporate Organization, Finance and Innovation

far, we have suggested that different institutional combinations
tween modes of coordination, incentives, and financial control may
ell lead to different forms of behavior and economic performance of

firms. This is even more so if one allows for the innovative activities o business firms. Already, in the previous section, we have considered the potential for learning under different organizational set-ups However, we purposely limited the representation of "learning" t those activities involving information-processing, somewhat akin t Bayesian procedures of estimating random variables with stationar means and finite variance. What happens if there is some largel; unknown dynamic in these variables, or if agents may "create" new events by their own actions? After all, as argued elsewhere (Dos 1990), these are precisely the consequences of innovative activities More formally, these activities imply the discovery and/or the adjust ment to events which *ex ante* are "unique" (and thus hardly allov Bayesian learning) and are not enumerable.

In dynamic terms, firms are required to develop skills allowin; them to explore an ever-expanding opportunity domain (Dosi an Orsenigo, 1988; Nelson and Winter, 1982; Amendola and Gaffard 1988). In turn, these skills may be highly specific to particula technological tasks and particular networks within firms. They ma; well seem redundant and uneconomical on the grounds of given technological and market conditions, yet still be crucial to th long-term viability of a firm. Here, a possible tension emerge between short-term performance optimization regarding existing pro ducts and known technologies, on the one hand, and learning abou radically new opportunities, on the other. Contemporary firms alway face some aspects of this dilemma and try to deal with it in ways tha can hardly be managed, *ex ante*, with optimizing criteria. Rather firms will develop various forms of innovative *loci* and procedure without being able to precisely attribute pay-offs to individua activities and projects. Firms in a few industrial sectors undertak part of their research activities in specialized units (typically R & I laboratories). Others do not. Even those which happen to undertak formal R & D-based research, also rely on more "informal" activitie of innovation diffused throughout the firm, including the shopfloor (fo sectoral evidence and taxonomies, see Pavitt, 1984; Levin *et al.*, 1987 Dosi, 1988a).

This represents a general informational and competence dilemma the ability to develop innovations with some bearing on the genera organization and strategies of the firm differs, and indeed is likely t be separate from the ability to conduct and perform "business a usual." In turn, the latter ability may imply a potential absence o innovative capabilities by many members of the organization, neglec of potentially useful information and, ultimately, loss of opportunities s is where the analysis of the coordination, incentive, and finance perties of firms links with the evolutionary analyses of non sta- ary environments. For example, it is straightforward that in the hetypical A-model of the firm – with its high degree of functional rarchy and specialization, decisions concerning the directions of ovative search, the introduction of new products and techniques, or n the modification of existing ones must be placed quite high in the ategic management. In such an institutional set-up, efficiency via cialization has precisely the corollary of positively avoiding nges in individual behaviors which are not planned *ex ante* in the ign of the organization. In the case of the J-firm, more decentral- d information-processing and knowledge-sharing among related ctional units appears to be more conducive to local innovative ustments on the basis of in-house knowledge (e.g. on shop-wide duction procedures, on particular product characteristics, etc.). wever, it does not seem to provide any strong endogenous incen- s to approach R & D activities which may require a new firm-wide anizational set-ups, new researchers and scientists acquired from ernal markets, etc. In all cases, the very nature of organizations ich make the latter, to different degrees, informationally viable and entive-compatible (hence, efficient) under conditions of limited (or atively predictable) innovative opportunities, limits the incentive to eriment with radically new ideas. It is hard to imagine an anization with positive incentives for all its members stopping m doing what they are "supposed" to do and fiddling around with ir brilliant ideas on how to reorganize the firm, its production mix, .! All this is for good efficiency reasons, but these same reasons y well also represent an evolutionary limitation, in that they trict the incentive to innovate.

This limitation is strengthened by the very nature of the innovative cess. As several works have shown (Freeman, 1982; Rosenberg, 74 and 1982; Dosi, 1988; Aoki and Rosenberg, 1989), innovation not generally be represented as a linear process, stemming from genous scientific discovery and ending with economic exploitation. ther, it most often involves complicated forms of feedback among ional technological opportunities, perceived market opportunities, d organizational responses. That is, there is a good part of ovative opportunities which are endogenous to corporate dynamics. ferent organizational frameworks imply diverse links with custom- , suppliers, competitors; diverse degrees of reliance on endogenous lls versus exogenous (especially scientific) sources; and diverse rees of exploitation of new technological paradigms via the

formation of new firms. In addition, the allocative criteria associat
with bank- or market-oriented finance are plausibly important, t(
We want to touch only on the last factor here.

Any system must rely for its evolutionary potential on its capabi
ties of innovative exploration. As argued elsewhere (Dosi, 1990), t
distribution of innovative trials may well be biased toward "mistake:
and thus any system which selectively operates too quickly agair
below-average performing companies may actually discourage innov
tion. On the other hand, less "selectiveness" means more inefficie
slacks and lower average performances. It is a fundamental evol
tionary dilemma. Relatively big and diversified firms somewh
mitigate this dilemma internally, through their rules for fund alloc
tion across divisions and across products. Bank-oriented systems, in
few cases (e.g., Japan, Germany and Sweden), appear to allow mo
internal experimentation by established companies, as the banks te:
to have more detailed and differential knowledge about those firr
and do not have to draw too heavily on their current and/or avera:
performances. Market-oriented systems, on the other hand, tend
value existing firms largely on the grounds of common knowledg
inevitably drawing on current performance. However, they seem mo
frequently to give opportunities to new innovative firms to explo
new technological trajectories. Relatedly, these systems have gene
ated new financial organizations, such as venture capital firms, whic
interestingly, embody some "special" management knowledge ai
play an active ("voice") role toward customer firms, similar to th
observed in many bank-oriented systems.

More generally, the institutions governing the allocation of financi
resources to business firms influence the criteria and speed
selection among agents displaying different economic performance
the variety of directions in the exploration of yet unexploited technol
gical opportunities; and the rate at which innovative capabilities a
accumulated within firms. There is no easy way to map the
"evolutionary" properties into the comparative taxonomy develop
earlier in the previous section. Indeed, this is a major field of researc
namely: how effectively do those different archetypical models hand
the dilemma between informational coordination and incentive-co:
patibility, on the one hand, and innovative exploration, on the othe
Building on the foregoing analysis, one can advance some tentati
conjectures.

First, as argued at greater length in Dosi (1990), bank-bas
financial systems are likely to be more conducive to "far-sighte
corporate strategies of incremental accumulation of innovative co:
petences, even when they involve relatively uncertain returns and

relatively far-away future. A weaker selection force on the financial 1e puts less pressure on the management for short-term profitabil-
ア. This, together with rank-based incentives and relatively low anagement mobility, makes corporate commitment to long-term mpetence accumulation incentive-compatible for the members of the m.

Second, there might be some "critical threshold" in the richness of novative opportunities which any one environment provides that akes the A-model evolutionarily viable. That is, only when the obabilities (not necessarily known to the agents) are high enough at new discoveries can be economically exploited, market-based 1ancial systems are able to foster innovative research via venture- cking and market selection of new innovative firms. This is possibly so the reason why the A-model has not historically been particularly ccessful in technologically less-developed countries. In fact, an -incentive mode requires a pre-existing abundant availability of :ills, a developed market for them, and, equally important, an location of financial resources to technological activities which – on e grounds of sheer common knowledge – present, especially, in ggard countries, an extremely high probability of failure. Converse- , WB-modes of financing appear to be more conducive to the cumulation and "targeting" of initially scarce innovative skills, rtly sheltered from short-term profitability evaluations on the ounds of market "common knowledge."

Third, environments which are permanently characterized by unex- oited opportunities and unexpected innovations somewhat distort e notion of incentive-compatibility as discussed earlier. Under chnological stationarity or quasi-predictable change, incentive-com- tible behavior within firms, or for that matter by firms *vis-à-vis* 1ancial investors, can be measured against some widely shared rdstick of efficiency. However, in an innovative world, evolutionary ability must involve some incentive to "break the rules," both within ms and by the firm as whole. In so far as each corporate ganization, no matter how "innovative," can innovate only to a nited degree without dramatically losing its efficiency, some finan- al institution must back "deviant" exploratory behavior. Notionally, th market-based and bank-based financial systems could do this ually well. Empirical evidence so far apparently suggests that the -model (in the American, but not in the British case) has adapted ther flexibly to that function. However, some analysts interpret the me phenomenon in an opposite way: Keith Pavitt, for example, ggests that widespread innovative exploration via the birth of new ms is in fact a by-product of the failure of the A-model to foster innovative behavior within incumbent firms (a related argument is Pavitt, 1991).

Conclusions

Building on the analysis of different functions performed by corpora organizations – in terms of information coordination, incentiv performance control and innovative learning – we have suggested sort of comparative institutional taxonomy (see Fig. 2.1). Each arch type of firm, in order to be economically viable, defines its inform tion-efficiency and incentive-compatibility in relation to both internal organizational mechanisms and its relationship with exter institutions such as those governing the labour market and finar (e.g. with stockholders, banks, etc.). Hence one can theoretica describe various notional combinations between internal governar structures and industry-finance links. In that context we have tried present four basic "models" or archetypes, ranging from one cha acterized by market-based incentives, hierarchical information flow and market-based finance, on the one hand, to an opposite type

	S Information sharing / H Hierarchical	M Market-oriented incentives	R Rank hierarchies	Financial regime	Institutional archetype
C O O R D I N A T I O N	S Information sharing			M (Market based)	A-model (The "anglo-american" model)
	H Hierarchical	X			
	S			RB (Relational banking)	D-model ("Developing countries" model)
	H	X			
	S		X	WB (Weak bank-based)	J-model (The Japanese archetype)
	H				
	S			SB (Strong bank-based)	S-model (The centrally planned economy)
	H		X		

Figure 2.1   A comparative taxonomy.

odel based on generalized hierarchical relations, on the other. Then, e explicitly added the requirement of innovative learning in each rm, and of financial allocations to innovative research. Permanent nnovative opportunities, we have argued, may well introduce a ermanent dilemma between the revealed efficiency of each institu- onal set-up and its evolutionary viability, as manifested by its ability successfully generate innovations.

In a continuously changing world, internal governance structures of rms and industry–finance links must be assessed on their dual, and ossibly conflicting, roles of determining efficient performances – on he grounds of given technologies and innovative exploration. Our axonomic exercise of basic archetypes of such corporate structures nd finance modes certainly falls short of any explicit analysis of their ifferent evolutionary properties, and lacks a thorough historical nvestigation highlighting particular empirical examples closer to ach theoretical model. Indeed, the foregoing discussion should be onsidered as a theoretical introduction to a comparative analysis of he differentiated patterns of change of corporate and financial nstitutions: in a biological analogy, a sort of "Linnean" exercise of lassification, in the perspective of an evolutionary theory of their rigins and change.

Note

M. Aoki's research was supported by the Japanese Ministry of Education and by he grant of the Research Institute of System Analysis, NTT Data, to the Japanese conomy Program at the Center for Economic Policy Research, Stanford. Giovanni Dosi's esearch was supported by the Designated Research Center of the ESRC at SPRU, niversity of Sussex, and by the Italian Ministry of Education ("Progetti 40%").

Historical taxonomies

inancial History in the Age of
ndustrialization:
. Selective Survey

CHARD TILLY

eparation of this chapter pursued the doubtlessly immodest goal of
nbining a comparative historical sketch of financial institutions
th the use of modern financial theory, to the end of producing
idelines for future research. In practice it attempts to link analyses
financial behavior with economic history. It discusses a number of
ordinates connecting recent contributions to financial economics, on
e one hand, with the history of financial institutions, on the other.
 concern lies with the age of industrialization, that is, with the
ghteenth, nineteenth, and twentieth centuries; apologies are thus
e to those readers having a less parochial view of financial history.
If I read the record correctly, the most fundamental point raised in
e recent literature of financial economics concerns informational
iciency, i.e., the extent to which economic actors enjoy equal access
 information concerning returns and risks of investment opportuni-
s in their relevant economies. Most of the chapter is therefore
ected to the way financial institutions handle the "information
oblem." "Financial institutions" are broadly defined, taken here to
er to rules governing financial decision making (North, 1986;
chter, 1988). The concrete subject matter of the chapter is, however,
rrowly circumscribed. It first takes up the question of capital
arket efficiency and discusses some pertinent recent historical work.
e chapter then turns to a treatment of the history of enterprise
ance, paying special attention to the concept known as the "Mod-
iani-Miller Theorem." The last part of the paper widens the
rspective by offering an "ideal-typical" sketch of the development of
ancial institutions in a small set of important industrializing
untries, covering the period from the eighteenth to the twentieth
nturies, and stressing the dichotomy between markets and

organizations (or hierarchies). A few summary and speculati observations form the conclusion.

Quantification: An Apology to Raymond Goldsmith

I was tempted to introduce my topic quantitatively, by drawing on t work of Raymond Goldsmith (Goldsmith, 1969 and 1985). That wo represents, after all, a major attempt to link financial structure a economic development using the comparative-historical approach. studies, to my knowledge, are more comprehensive than Goldsmith which covers nearly 300 years and some 20 countries. Nevertheless resisted the temptation, and for two reasons. First, many of t national and temporal differences in financial structure identified Goldsmith's work result from definitional variance across countri and time. The numbers do not speak for themselves, at least n without a great deal of elaboration or translation which would ha been inappropriate for the purpose at hand. Second, the basic da and ratios built therefrom do not, with some exceptions, correspond a well-articulated theory of financial behavior or development.[1] The are some interesting correlations, but no clear connection with caus explanations. In short, the Goldsmith data do not help much in t initial search for connections between financial behavior and histori al change, though, as we shall see, those data are useful for a numb of specific comparative purposes.

The Relevance of Efficient Capital Markets

Less systematic and comprehensive, but far more to the point concern here, is some recent historical work on the performance financial markets (Eagly and Smith, 1976; Edelstein, 1982; Mirowsl 1981 and 1987; Neal, 1987; Snowden, 1987; Tilly, 1989b). This work largely quantitative and econometric in nature, and closely tied current financial theorizing, in particular to the capital asset pricir model (CAPM) and the related efficient markets hypothesis (EMH). call attention to this work not because it shows that econom historians can handle sophisticated financial theory, but because raises – at least implicitly – the question of whether and ho

ll-organized financial markets could have contributed significantly
industrial development.
I begin with a discussion of work on the eighteenth century. Eagly
d Smith and, most recently, Neal, have shown that early in that
ntury, sophisticated financial practices in London and Amsterdam
nerated "efficient market" results associated with international
pital movements and international financial integration. Mirowski
rroborates the findings of these authors with respect to the
phistication and "maturity" of financial institutions and practices –
a finding of widespread information on prices, of continuously
oted prices, the presence of numerous professional arbitrageurs,
ear rules to guarantee the transfer of securities, etc. – but chal-
nges the suggestion that this was in any substantial sense a
econdition of British industrialization. The challenge is based on
antity effects. For not only was the market for shares a small one,
 begin with, but it declined from the early part of the century
wards, becoming thinner and ever more sporadic. At the same time,
a number and size of joint-stock businesses were growing; but they
re not making use of the London financial market. The question is:
ny not? The preferred answer would seem to be that capital-seeking
terprises (except for some canal companies) found other sources of
nds – such as relatives, wealthy neighbors and, increasingly after
50, banks – both more accessible and cheaper. If there was an
terregional flow of funds from savers to investors in the period of the
dustrial Revolution, then it was via the country bankers in surplus
d deficit regions, whose payments through correspondents in the
ndon money market, according to Pressnell, executed the transfer.
ressnell, 1956; Cottrell, 1980.)
Nevertheless, the view that the London capital market had an
portant role to play in early British industrialization has not died
sily. If not through shares, then through government debt; and if
t positively, then negatively. For in the latter third of the eight-
nth century, the organized British capital market – the London
ock exchange – came under the dominance of government debt. One
 the traditional explanations of Britain's Industrial Revolution, we
ay recall, was the significant fall in the rate of interest in the
ghteenth century, a fall related to the improved status of govern-
ent finances and of government debt. In the course of the eighteenth
ntury, a supraregional market for such debt was fashioned. It has
en argued, indeed, that this debt was quite widely held (Dickson,
 67). Its increase in the 1770s, and especially after the 1790s, could
us have had considerable weight; and in fact it has been alleged to
ve attracted savings which would otherwise have financed invest-

ment in industry or the industrial infrastructure, i.e. governme
borrowing during the period 1790–1815 is said to have "crowded o
private investment (Williamson, 1984). However, this argument a
assumes well-functioning market linkages, which must be question
One investigation of the matter, for instance, has focused on inter
rates and found no relevant shift which could have motivated t
crowding-out effect posited (Hein and Mirowski, 1987). And as Mok
has written:

> Dealing with the supply of savings on an aggregate level, however, is
> even more misleading than an aggregate analysis of labor markets. Such
> an analysis assumes the existence of "a" capital market which allocated
> funds to competing users, presumably on the basis of an expected rate of
> return and riskiness. There were capital markets in Britain during the
> Industrial Revolution, and it is important not to neglect them. Certain
> developments, especially the growth of transport networks, would have
> been slowed down considerably and possibly aborted, had it not been for
> capital markets. In the early stages of the Industrial Revolution,
> however, they played a secondary role in the process and certainly were
> far removed from the naive well-functioning market which allocates
> resources efficiently in neo-classical growth models.
>
> (Mokyr, 1985: p. 35)

Strictly speaking, the crowding-out argument does not imply a capi
market which passes EMH tests, but the point should be well take
nevertheless.

Although the discussion may seem to have moved quite a distan
away from historical applications of the CAPM or EMH, I think th
the movement was relevant, for the "prior" of quantity effects
financial markets on the real economy is an important issue. Beari
that in mind, we stay with the history of "The First Industr
Nation," Britain, and move ahead several decades, picking up Mich
Edelstein's important study of the British capital market in the "A
of Imperialism." Drawing on previous work, Edelstein argues that
typical financial needs of domestic business enterprise over much
the nineteenth century, local banking connections and the provinc
stock exchanges sufficed, even in the 1860s, when the switch to t
joint-stock form of business became more prevalent. That is, up to t
1870s, or perhaps even the 1880s, the failure of domestic busine
firms to utilize the London stock exchange is no sign of "mark
failure." From then on, large-scale domestic industrial enterpri
gained access to the London capital market, but here it increasing
competed for funds with foreign governments and enterprises. F
latively speaking, indeed, domestic capital-seekers fell behind forei
ones, whose share by one estimate rose toward the end of the period
over 50 per cent.[2] Edelstein's study of realized returns on portfo

ivestment in this market, however, utilizes the CAPM to show that
reign investment "paid." Edelstein did not formally test the efficien-
 of this market (with autoregressive techniques), but his results
rongly suggest that bias was of minor importance and that foreign
ivestment was a rational market result.
Criticism of Edelstein's work there has been, to be sure, but in fact
has not generally focused on his use of the CAPM. Instead it has
een directed toward limitations of the data set utilized. Though large
omprehending 566 securities for the 1870–1913 period), it repre-
nts only "first-class" and "second-class" investments, and excludes
ie securities of new and untried or unranked enterprises (and
overnment institutions) which entered the London market only
riefly or not at all. Thus as W.P. Kennedy has written:

> It is therefore entirely consistent with Edlestein's results that although
> within the sample group no evidence of bias towards foreign issues
> appears, the capital markets were in fact deeply biased away from
> favouring most home industrial projects, particularly those in risky areas
> of new technology. Furthermore, some of Edlestein's findings confirm the
> existence of bias even within his special sample . . . . [E]ven for his
> restricted sample, Edelstein finds that trading in Australian, Indian and
> home long-term negotiable debt instruments remained partially isolated
> (segmented) from their dealings in their US counterparts . . . .

Kennedy suggests a systematic undervaluation of most domestic
idustrial securities to have been present, and asserts that

> Edelstein's conclusion appears to be only partially valid. The UK capital
> market surely improved but at best by reducing segmentation within the
> classes of established securities, leaving the segmentation between these
> securities and the newer, less familiar, often riskier, issues of domestic
> firms unchanged or even increased. This segmentation . . . ensured that
> only inadequate market channels, or even none at all, existed to
> arbitrage the differences between the yields created by the application of
> new technologies abroad and those earned by the same technologies in
> Britain.
>
> (Kennedy, 1987: pp. 146–7)

Some responses to the criticism are possible. Edelstein suggests, for
xample,

> that first- and second-class returns are fairly good estimators for the full
> spectrum's movements . . . . An important reason for this finding is the
> interaction of all parts of the spectrum. In the nineteenth century, many
> wealth holders owned assets in both the best and worst parts of the
> national portfolio. It is plausible to assume that they allocated their
> funds according to their relative profitabilities and risk, and, hence,
> provided a strong equilibrating force. Perhaps a stronger equilibrating
> force was the presence of publicly traded companies in nearly all UK
> industrial sectors by the end of the nineteenth century.
>
> (Edelstein, 1982: pp. 115–16)

Thus the criticial question turns on a "prior": the definition of th
relevant capital market and the quality and volume of securitie
traded in it.

Since the German and American capital markets have bee
explicitly and favorably compared with the British, studies of th
former covering roughly the same period are of some interest. Th
Germany study follows the Edelstein methodology and concludes, a
did that author, that foreign portfolio investment "paid" (Tilly, 1989a
On the one hand, foreign securities promised – and yielded –
significantly higher rate of return and higher risks than did compa1
able domestic ones. On the other hand, those returns and risks wer
lower than investments in domestic equities. This may well hav
represented satisfaction of preferences of those investors desiring jus
that combination of risks and returns which foreign securitie
embodied. Interestingly, the data reveal a bias in the German capita
market against foreign securities. When a correction is made for th
distinction between debt and equity, a higher rate of return is seen 1
have been "required" to induce investors to hold foreign securitie
than to hold domestic ones. The excess returns measure, however, 1
not statistically significant. One notes, finally, a double long-ru
tendency for the yields and risks of foreign securities to decline; an
the accompanying convergence of yields and risks among differe1
security groups (see Fig. 3.1). This supports the notion that expecte
returns can explain German foreign portfolio investment pretty wel
and also that their realization was not achieved at the expense «
forgone domestic investments to the degree contemporaries believed

In contrast to the British case, the German capital market wa
much more strongly oriented toward domestic users of capital in th
period. New issues of securities suggest a significant increase in th
domestic share of the market between the 1880s and the First Worl
War: up from 35–40 per cent to between 65 and 70 per cent. Indeed,
has been suggested that such a shift might throw doubt on the ver
application of the CAPM to this case.[3] But what has attracted mo1
attention is another related point: the fact – particularly noticeabl
after the 1890s – that in Germany the strong flow of funds to domest
industrial enterprise was largely equity, and that it was associate
with high rates of investment and industrial growth, whereas i
Britain the most readily observed association was between vast flow
of funds abroad and fixed-interest debt instruments, on the one han«
and virtual domestic industrial stagnation, on the other. This contras
had to do, many have suggested, with the development in Germany «
the large, mixed banks combining commercial and investment bank
ing activities, and the absence of such an institutional link betwee

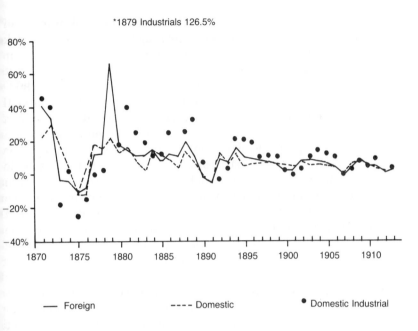

*1879 Industrials 126.5%

— Foreign   ---- Domestic   ● Domestic Industrial

Figure 3.1   Mean realized returns on traded securities in Germany (in 1913 prices, weighted by amounts outstanding in 1900).

money and capital markets in Britain. What I find particularly striking here – and puzzling – is that the minor differences in capital asset pricing results recorded by no means reflect the deep institutional contrast between the two capital markets which accompanied them.

The American capital market study by Snowden focuses exclusively on the equity traded on the New York stock exchange. He asks the important question: "Did the stock market allocate funds efficiently among the competing investment alternatives that arose in the corporate sector during the process of industrialization?" (Snowden, 1987: p. 328). Various tests of the EMH are conducted to investigate this issue, utilizing one aggregate and three sectoral indices. The basic finding of this study is that statistically significant departures from the ideal of an efficient market can be identified, the most striking of these being concentrated in the years before 1914, and especially in the subperiod 1900–14. Snowden's interpretation emphasizes two institutional factors: (a) for the pre-1914 period the cyclical instabili and dependence of stock exchange returns on price and money mark(instability, related to the absence of a central bank;[4] (b) the rap growth of domestic industrial securities traded and of investe involvement in the New York stock exchange from around 1900 1 1914, in the face of the continued absence of any regulation of th security issuing business. This second factor created, *ipso fact* informational segmentation, since most of the new investors, i contrast to the previous dominant groups, were non-professiona (Snowden, 1987: pp. 349–51; Carosso, 1970). Even in this perio however, departures from "rational stock prices" were probably n "substantial" in an economic sense, for given contemporary financi data and computational capacity, the statistical departures from EM norms represented only modest "market failures." The pre-New De New York stock exchange thus emerges from this as a relativel efficient institution. Contrary contemporary criticism of the stoc exchange is seen as exaggerated. However, what falls by the waysid in the analysis, once again, is the initial concern with that capit market's allocation of funds to finance American industrializatior This role is presumed, not examined. The connection between capit market efficiency and industrial growth remains open.

The Importance of Enterprise Financial Structure

This section of the chapter examines the receiving end of th intermediation process: the demand by non-financial enterprises fo finance. It is concerned with the identification of informationa asymmetries and institutional responses thereto. In this connectior the idea described as the "Modigliani–Miller Theorem" deserve: discussion, for it is relevant to financial history. And yet I believe it i: fair to say that business and economic historians have failed, on th whole, to take up the challenge to their work inherent in th Modigliani-Miller view. It is probably no coincidence that Jonathar Baskin, a financial economist, rather than an economic historian should make the first historical attempt to deal explicitly with thi: theory (Baskin, 1988). In fact, there is considerable tension betweer the theory, which taught the irrelevance of sources of enterpris finance and in particular of the relative shares of new equity, debt anc retained earnings for enterprise performance, and the historica record, replete as it is with stories of enterprise success and failure closely related to differences and shifts in financial structure. Baskin correctly identifies asymmetric information among investors and between investors and users of capital as the basic problem. In the process, he discusses two concepts in the recent literature which might help resolve the "tension" mentioned: "signaling effects" and "agency problems," two sides of the separation of enterprise ownership and control.[5] In the following I take up Baskin's suggestion by looking at another slice of the historical record.

As a first approximation one may characterize industrialization in the nineteenth century as a process of discontinuous technological change which generated scale economies and waves of demand for capital far exceeding the resources of individual investors. This necessitated the development of institutions capable of mobilizing outside savings, and gave rise to the separation of enterprise ownership from control, most clearly with generalized use of the business corporation with limited liability. We note here in passing that, according to the Modigliani–Miller theorem, limited liability did not reduce the total risk of any business enterprise, but merely redistributed it from owners to creditors – a point we will come back to. Nevertheless, the corporation was basically a capital-mobilizing device which could transcend individual accumulations of wealth and, as such, is interpretable as an institutional response to relative capital scarcity, if not an ideal one.[6]

Technological change, then, underlay the rising capital demands of the nineteenth century. However, in most of the industrializing countries the prior emergence of a large government debt proved to be a conditioning factor of critical importance. In these countries something like a "financial revolution" took place which lent stability to government finances and which made its debt a relatively secure financial investment. This had happened earlier in Holland and Great Britain, but by the nineteenth century swept other countries in Europe and America as well.[7] In the first half of the nineteenth century, indeed, financial markets in which securities were publicly traded were virtually synonymous with the market for government debt.

This historical phase shaped subsequent experience. When the railroads – which were largely organized as corporations with limited liability and which became the principal successors to governments as users of financial capital in the nineteenth century – came upon the scene in the 1830s, they could be seen as civic improvements having public or governmental attributes. Close ties with government existed from the start, involving the delegation of eminent domain rights, land grants, stipulations for carrying government troops and mail, frequently government guarantees of interest on bonds, and even provision for eventual purchase of the property by the government. More importantly, however, the financial instruments they issued closely resembled government debt – down to the practice of providing for semi-annual coupon payments to bondholders. For these, like government debt, mainly took the form of fixed-interest securities, as bonds or as preferred stock. It may be suggested that their similarities to government securities eased the acceptance of railroad securities by investors. Railway equity was much less widely traded. In Great Britain, the US and Germany, local investors expecting indirect gains from railroads took up most of the common stock, the aim being less financial returns than control of the enterprise. Efforts were made to suggest that private share subscription represented a private subsidy of the public interest. Where the railroads' organizers felt it essential to sell common stock to a wider public, they offered a fixed-interest payment to shareholders for the duration of the construction period. This thus came close to being a temporary form of preferred stock and, once again, reflected recognition of the inferior information possessed by "outside" subscribers. Common stock offered without such security would have been viewed with suspicion by most, as evidence that insider sellers no longer saw advantage in holding it, i.e. as objects of adverse selection. Creditors apparently required further reassurances. Interesting, in this connection, are a number of devices which anticipated the Modigliani–Miller view on creditor risks *vis-à-vis* limited liability companies, e.g. the rule in many British companies holding debt issue to the value of the unpaid portion of share capital, or the American railroad practice of issuing convertible bonds (which offered an equity option). Issuing debt secured by liens against the real property of the enterprise was yet another device strengthening creditors and the market for enterprise debt (Baskin, 1988).

One is hardly surprised to read of the much greater difficulties which railroads – and later industrial corporations – encountered in fashioning an anonymous market for their common stock, for valuation of the latter required more information than did fixed-interest debt. The late-nineteenth century prominence of that halfway house, preferred stock, has already been mentioned. Its use reflected the information-for-valuation problem (though enterprise control was also a factor). Three aspects of the difficulties are worth noting at this point. First, the use of par value of common stock as a norm, a practice which encouraged analogy with debt instruments (and which went so far as to provoke a tax-law interpretation of stock dividends as income) (Baskin, 1988: p. 226). Second, the attempt by corporate enterprises to regularize their dividend payments and, indeed, to tilize financial accounting practices to justify stable dividends. Third, he association between excessively high dividend pay-outs by corpoate managements and their wish to "make a market" for their ommon stock. These last two observations reflect the central importnce of cash flows as signals to potential investors. All three points, iowever, are examples of the importance of signaling in the presence f asymmetric information on returns and risks.

Perhaps in part owing to such practices, a market for corporate ndustrial securities began to emerge which encompassed debt and quity, and whose scope has since then continued to widen. Contemiorary concern with the difference between debt and equity appears o have reflected a serious informational problem. This applies articularly to the financial structure of enterprise. The Modigliani-Miller view that valuation of corporate enterprise – assuming perfect nformation – did not depend on financial structure overturned the ilder view, which Baskin has termed the "pecking order" hypothesis. t states that firms finance and desire to finance investment expansion out of first, retained earnings, then debt issue, and lastly equity ncreases. The reason for this preference hierarchy lies in the eluctance of managers to signal, by means of equity increases, an inwillingness to increase debt obligations (this, in turn, being related o investors' assumptions about incentives to a solid managerial ierformance being greater in the presence of debt than with more quity, and, hence, reflection of an agency problem). Thus "the irediction of the theory is that debt ratios depend on the amount of ast retained earnings relative to the quantity of investment" (Baskin, 1988: p. 213). The Modigliani-Miller interpretation saw corporate nterprises caught in a trade-off between the risk of bankruptcy limiting their debt) and tax advantages of increased debt loads. In nost industrial countries up to 1914, however, tax laws gave little ncentive for high debt levels. And what we find in the financial iistory of corporate industry in such countries as Great Britain, the JS, France or Germany in this period, in any case, is the overvhelming predominance of self-finance through retained earnings. If ine includes railroad companies in the analysis, the importance of lebt increases, particularly for the US, but the generalization neverheless stands, all the more strongly, indeed, as one follows the mpirical record through the twentieth century (Creamer, Dobrovolsy and Borenstein, 1960; Davis, 1967; Caron, 1975; Levy-Leboyer, 1978; Cottrell, 1980; Tilly, 1986; also Baskin, 1988).

In general, looking more closely at this record, one tends to find a iositive correlation between faster enterprise growth and the use of iutside finance, particularly of equity increases – both over cross-sections of enterprise and over time. It is likely that this had to do with the varying desire of insider-owners to maintain control – a motive little discussed in the Modigliani-Miller theory. Slow growers took on little new equity. There are some interesting international differences, however. In the US, rapid enterprise growth proved possible without loss of control, as managements widened the scope for preferred stock or non-voting common stock. (A sharp growth surge and merger by the Pennsylvania Railroad in 1871 is alleged to have had a signal effect in this regard.) In Great Britain, there was some echo of this development in enterprise growth at the end of the nineteenth century, and preferred stock and debenture issues remained the main vehicle of outside finance. In Germany, however, rapid enterprise growth (without railroads) reflected rapid growth in equity, at least until the twentieth century. Moreover, there was an interesting trade-off in the German experience between the state of the capital market and the form of finance: as the stock market boomed and stock prices rose, industrial enterprises expanded by issuing new equity; in slacker times with relatively low rates of interest, they issued long-term debt. The reason for the former practice has been seen in the strong influence wielded by banks within industrial enterprises. They could break down owner-manager resistance to equity issues because control need not be affected thereby and because, given banks' prominence in the German capital market, equity issues did not represent negative signaling. The latter (temporal) pattern suggests that neither equity nor debt issue need have represented negative signaling *per se*: it all depended on the context.

Financial Institutions and Market Imperfections

Broadly speaking, financial institutions have developed in response to informational needs and the gains of specialization related thereto. In part this reflects "market failures," e.g. where scale economies, barriers to resource mobility or asymmetric information render coordination via the competitive market mechanism unfeasible. According to Gerschenkron's celebrated typology of industrialization, late industrializing countries faced significantly larger capital demands relative to savings than had the pioneer country, Great Britain, and they found the latter's relatively atomized and decentralized credit and capital markets inadequate. They innovated, in a sense, organizational substitutes for those markets, e.g., on the ntinent the "universal banks," or in more extreme cases (such as arist Russia), state institutions (Gerschenkron, 1962). In general, is development was marked by the emergence of larger decision its, or as some scholars have pointed out, by hierarchies increasing-substituting for markets (Daems, 1975).

The simplifying Gerschenkronian typology deserves some elabora-n. It would no doubt be misleading, for example, to suggest that itish industrialization involved no significant change in financial termediation. After all, it was quite an innovation for the Scots to velop an efficient supraregional system of branch banking in the ghteenth century. Great Britain, we should not forget, was the untry that created the first nationwide banking system, the three-red system embracing the Bank of England, the London money arket and the country banks, and that country which then trans-rmed the latter into a nationwide system of joint-stock deposit inking (Cameron, 1967). It is fascinating to see how those basic stitutions, the country banks, evolved, to tell the story, for instance, how eighteenth-century attorneys-at-law with investment-seeking ients – the "money scriveners" – met at the quarterly assizes to nclude their financial business, and of how they came to recognize e gains of specialization as bankers, and became such (Pressnell, 56). This was the country which innovated general incorporation ws and which encouraged widespread use of the corporation and nited liability for business purposes. And this was the country, ially, whose stock exchange in London became a central part of the orld's most important capital market in the nineteenth century Iichie, 1986). Nevertheless, the characterization of pre-1914 Britain an economy which executed its financial business very largely rough relatively small firms operating in competitive markets, i.e. rough the market, can stand.

The contrast between British and Continental banking institutions well known. The small, new country of Belgium pioneered the velopment of holding companies, initially in the form of investment nks. This it did by expanding the Dutch creation of 1822, the ciété Générale pour favoriser l'Industrie Nationale des Pays-Bas, om 1830 on into the dynamic Société Générale de Belgique. This stitution, along with a similarly constructed rival, the Banque de elgique, may be seen as a response to imperfections in the then isting Belgian capital market, imperfections related to the capital-tensive character of Belgian growth sectors at this time (coal-ining, iron and steel, and transportation) and the reluctance of elgian wealthholders to invest in those industries directly. Initially, terestingly, these institutions were truly "mixed banks," combining note issue with investment banking activities. Difficulties experience in the crises of 1838 and 1848, however, forced them to abandon th note-issuing business. In the 1830s and 1840s, moreover, the Belgia "mixed banks" had already launched a new institution, the inves ment trust or holding company (1835: Société de Commerce d Bruxelles; and Société Nationale pour Entreprise Industrie et Con merce) (Cameron, 1967: p. 135), to stimulate, as it were, indire public investment in Belgian industrial companies. By the 1860s an 1870s, the Belgian mixed banks, despite these creations, had then selves become very largely holding companies, with well over half the Société Générale's entire portfolio consisting of industrial secu ities (Cameron, 1967: p. 147; also Daems, 1975: pp. 38–9). Thu Belgium's place in the typology of financial development is clearl associated with the institution of the holding company, even if the fu legal separation of commercial banking from investment bankin operations did not occur until 1935, a result of the banking crisis the 1930s (Daems, 1975: pp. 38–9).

Universal or mixed banking attained its purest form in nineteent century Germany. As with Belgian investment banks, German mixe banks were a response to capital market imperfections, and began t grow in the 1830s and 1840s in association with the development the railroads and the heavy industrial complex spawned by railroa building, i.e., in response to the growth of relatively capital-intensiv sectors. The limits of their own resources (and difficulties experience in shaping collective cooperative organizations) encouraged privat banking firms to organize joint-stock banks with limited liability. B the 1850s a number of these institutions were in place, and the gradually became independent of the private bankers who ha founded them. Indeed, by the 1870s they began competing the latte out of existence (Pohl, 1982). Nevertheless, they followed the sam "mixed banking" program. For political reasons, German goverr ments did not grant note-issuing rights to such banks, those right being virtually monopolized by government-controlled institution whose development may thus be deemed complementary to that of th mixed banks. In Germany, a formal organized capital market cer tered around the principal stock exchanges in Berlin and Frankfur on-Main did emerge in the nineteenth century, but its importance a an alternative to the mixed banks was much more limited than i Great Britain.

I pass over the French case, permitting myself only two brie references. One is to that celebrated institution, the Société Général de Crédit Mobilier (founded in 1852), which no doubt contributed great deal to the spread of mixed banking in Europe, since it cause

val bankers to adopt some of its methods. It was perhaps significant
at the Crédit Mobilier's greatest successes were realized abroad and
ere associated with French capital exports, for this was to become
pical of French financial institutions (Cameron, 1961; Levy-Leboyer,
978). That motivates my second observation, namely that in France,
ixed banking did not become the norm. The system which emerged
as rather a mixture of British deposit banking and Belgian invest-
ent banking; and the importance of the formally organized capital
arket – underscored perhaps by the French savers' well-known
reference for fixed-interest securities (especially the *Rentes*) – was
oser to the British than the German case. This may have been to do
ith differences in the distribution of wealth and income in the
untries mentioned (Born, 1977; Daems, 1975).

The case of the US, finally, though not part of the Gerschenkronian
pology, is worth considering. The comparative characteristic which
ands out most is the very large-sized enterprises which had emerged
y the end of the nineteenth century. This was in part, no doubt, a
esult of the capital market's growth in the period which was
ssociated first with railroad growth, and then, from the 1890s on,
ith industrial enterprises, including the oft-discussed "merger move-
ent" which produced many of the giant enterprises referred to. Scale
conomies in finance played an important role in bringing about this
esult, associated also with the mobilization of large sums of capital
rom abroad (mainly Britain) (Davis, 1967; also Michie, 1986). A
elated factor was regulation of the American banking system, for one
f the (probably unanticipated) products of that regulation was the
xtreme concentration of bank funds in New York, the country's main
nancial market, where most of the large-scale enterprises were thus
reated and financed (Sylla, 1972). However, another characteristic of
the American case" deserves mention. That is that the triumph of
ierarchy over market exemplified by giant enterprise also reflected
echnological change in response to relatively expensive skilled labor,
nd not just availability of capital. It is striking, after all, that in
ontrast to the Belgian and German cases, the giant American
nterprises were much less concentrated in branches of industry
vhich were capital-intensive (Daems, 1975; Chandler, 1977).

There have been some attempts to quantify the original Gerschenk-
onian insights, e.g., by relating country estimates of bank-owned
ssets to those of total assets, but measurement problems have
recluded clear results (Good, 1973; Sylla, 1979). One interesting and
ossibly relevant measure undertaken by Ray Goldsmith relates the
ssue of securities – government debt plus corporate stocks and bonds
– to estimates of total national assets and of total assets held by

financial institutions, country by country (Goldsmith, 1985: Appen(
A). The results – reproduced in Table 3.1 – are suggestive, I thir
First of all, one notes the special position taken by Germany. T'
differences *via-à-vis* Great Britain correspond to conventional asse.
ments of the latter's financial structure: in Great Britain "securiti;
tion" of financial relationships – private holdings of securities dist
buted via security markets – had developed much further than
Germany, where financial intermediation, and particularly the use
bank credit, took the place of formal financial markets. One shou
acknowledge, certainly, that government ownership of railways
Germany (since 1879) and the much wider use of the corpora
enterprise form in Britain also contributed to the contrast cite
However, one must also point out that consideration of forei;
portfolio investment would enlarge the degree of "securitization"
asset holdings in Britain relative to Germany. This last point
relevant to a second observation on the ratios given in Table 3.1: th
the degree of "securitization" in the US would be considerably reduc.
were we to deduct from securities issued those held abroad (ar
especially in Britain). Nevertheless, securitization had gone mu.
further in the US than in Germany. It was highly concentrated
shares, which were not widely held abroad. This reflects, even mo.

Table 3.1   Securities and asset structure, five countries, 1850–1913.

Securities as % of total assets

	1850		1875		1913	
	Govt	*Other*	*Govt*	*Other*	*Govt*	*Other*
Great Britain	13	6	7	8	5	18
Belgium	5	7	4	9	7	10
France	4	2	8	8	8	11
Germany	2	1	2	3	4	4
USA	3	8	5	13	2	12

Securities as % of assets of financial institutions

	1850	1875	1913
Great Britain	322	161	207
Belgium	527	232	167
France	525	268	139
Germany	109	80	62
USA	162	258	258

Source: Goldsmith, 1985: Appendix A.

han the British data, the very wide use made of the corporation as a usiness form (Davis and Gallmann, 1978). Third, French "securitizaion" was quite striking, especially if we could allow for French foreign nvestment, and conforms to standard pictures of French investors nd their preference for *Rentes* and other fixed-interest securities. In o country was the share of fixed-interest securities higher than in 'rance. Finally, Belgium's position is striking with regard to the high roportion of shares it issued (in 1875 an estimated 7 per cent and in 913 8 per cent of total assets). This could well reflect the pyramiding f ownership associated with the Belgian economy's important holding ompanies.

To draw upon Gerschenkron's typology does not imply endorsement f all of its claims. It has "relative backwardness" explaining instituional innovation. In slight contrast I would like to call attention to an lternative explanation of cross-country variation in financial instituions: political constraints and priorities.[8] In so doing I draw on the inancial and banking histories of Germany, Great Britain and the JS. I begin with Germany.

The development of mixed banking (in its "ideal-typical" form) nvolved a relatively small number of large banks combining shorterm credit and money market activities with long-term capital narket finance, maintaining at the same time close connections with a relatively small number of large, industrial customers. This pattern irst emerged in the relations between private banking firms and the apital-intensive railroads. That supports Gerschenkron. The relevant political factor, however, concerns the nature of bankers' short-term iabilities. Neither private bankers nor the joint-stock banks they ounded – with a few minor exceptions – obtained note-issuing rights, vhich remained a virtual government monopoly. The reason for this goes back to the fiscal needs of the German states and to negotiations eading to the German customs union, the *Zollverein*, in 1833. To cut a long story short, monetary integration involving the then-predominant coinage was a necessary part of revenue apportionment among he member states, and eventually called for regulation of paper noney and, hence, of banknote issue (associated with seignorage ights) as well. For fiscal and political reasons, the sovereigns in these ndividual German states clung to these rights. However, in the 1850s and 1860s the Prussian bank of issue expanded to become *de facto* the German bank of issue.

The significance of this development lies in the fact that banks of ssue must hold relatively liquid portfolios, in order to be able to redeem their notes in cash when they are presented for payment. That dictates an emphasis upon short-term credit, secured, if possible, by liquid assets. Thus, neither banks of issue nor their logical – ar chronological – extension, deposit banks, would be fruitful grounds f the growth of a large business in the underwriting of capital issue and for the concentration on the needs of a relatively small number large industrial companies. The German private bankers and the corporate successors worked increasingly with the current accou funds on deposit with them, but these were liabilities the repayme of which was more predictable and controllable than were th liabilities of banks of issue and deposits. This was in part because th customers represented a selected circle with well-monitored paymen needs. The historical result was a division of labor which left most pure payments and short-term trade credit business of the economy the government bank of issue and most of the industrial credit an also the security issue business to the private bankers and the protégés, the corporate "mixed banks." In addition, the latter foun themselves increasingly able to turn to the former for paymen services, cash, and for short-term discount credits when the nee arose. By establishing a dense network of branch offices covering mos of Germany, the Prussian Bank contributed to a significant reductio in transaction costs of trade and finance, illustrated, for exampl through the setting of one rate of interest and fixed exchange rates fc bill payments anywhere in Prussia as early as 1848. Thus, to som extent, even before the 1870s, the mixed banks could build thei growing business upon the security that the bank of issue could an would supply it with liquidity, if necessary (Tilly, 1989a: p. 193).

These arrangements continued after 1875 with the founding of th *Reichsbank*, which took over the assets and network of the Prussia Bank, building it – with the development of giro facilities an hundreds of branch offices – into one of the most efficient payment systems in the world. In subsequent years, the powerful support tha mixed banks gave German industry and trade rested in part on th payments network and liquidity guarantee it provided.

In Britain the predominant country banks were banks of issue, an the joint-stock banks which eventually replaced them were deposi banks. In both cases, these relatively liquid liabilities dictated mainte nance of portfolios with liquid assets. They provided no encourage ment to development of investment banking activities of the Germa type. This was tradition. However, the other side of the Anglo German contrast concerns the role of the Bank of England, th government's bank. It remained until the First World War a private profit-making enterprise over which the government had no officia controls. It had special status, but its operations largely reflecte profit-maximizing aims. Thus commercial banks, discount houses, an

e rest of the money market, could not reckon as a matter of course
ith the Bank of England as a liquidity guarantor, for its assistance
ould not depend on the need, but on its own position. In con-
quence, they had to maintain highly liquid positions themselves. As
ggested earlier, this ruled out movement into more adventurous
elds such as the investment banking German joint-stock banks
gaged in.

In the US, banking regulation was very early a dual phenomenon
volving fiscal interests of both federal and state governments.
itially, regulation affected banks of issue, from the Civil War (and
ational Banking Act of 1864) on, increasingly deposit banks as well.
ual regulation had a number of corollaries, the most important of
hich were the ban on branch banking and the absence of a central
ank which could serve as a lender of last resort. Whatever unantici-
ated advantages might have stemmed from pyramiding of deposits in
ew York banks (mentioned earlier), the US system was extremely
risis-prone; and pressures for the establishment of a central bank
ith lender of last resort functions grew. However, for various
asons, not even the founding of the Federal Reserve System (FRS)
1 1913 put an end to dual regulation and the instability which
ccompanied it. This experience had two important implications.

First, it reveals a strong negative correlation between the political
ower of small-town and rural bankers, on the one hand, and support
r branch banking and central banking controls such as those of the
RS on the other (White, 1983). The political economy of this
rrangement lies in the fact that whereas the private costs of bans on
ranch banking were borne by a small number of bankers, the social
osts were widely diffused, while the potential private costs of
ranching (to local bankers) were direct and readily perceived. There
as thus an asymmetry in the distribution of incentives to political
ction, similar to that which affected advocates of free trade and tariff
rotection in the nineteenth century.

Second, up to the First World War the dual system of regulation
as marked by the absence of a central bank which could provide
nder of last resort functions as well as routine refinancing facilities.
hus, one pillar of the European money markets and the banks that
perated in them was missing in the US, and therefore a broad money
arket dealing in bills of exchange and bankers' acceptances failed to
evelop there. Coupled to other restrictions on commercial bank
perations, this fact helps explain why investment banking functions
emained largely separated from commercial banking ones in the US
efore 1914, and why the most adventurous, most prominent, and
ost successful American financial institutions in this period were

private bankers engaged in investment activities, and not joint-stock banks, which in Europe by 1900 had all but totally eclipsed their private banker rivals (Born, 1977: p. 176).

A key question to raise in cross-country comparisons of financial institutions concerns the degree of competition. Casual and not-so casual evidence suggests that highly competitive financial markets predominated in Great Britain, e.g. in the London money market and London capital market. In spite of concentration among the joint stock banks at the end of the nineteenth century, the credit market appears to have remained highly competitive. How efficient these arrangements were in an overall sense would seem to depend on the importance of segmentation among asset types and of informational asymmetries (particularly as between capital seekers and capital suppliers). It is certain that British capital market institutions did not take a long-run view of domestic security issues *ex ante*, tending to see each transaction as a killing to be exploited to the utmost. That close connections between banks and industry did not develop was part of this same syndrome (Cottrell, 1980; Tilly, 1989a). Why institutions which might have taken a long-run view and developed close industrial ties did not emerge is not clear. Daunting barriers to entry are not readily apparent.

The Continental story is quite different, of course. The creation and early successes of the investment and mixed banks represented new competition for existing financial institutions (such as the Rothschilds and altered the terms on which industrial enterprises could raise capital. Where several such institutions came into being almost simultaneously, for instance as in Belgium in the 1830s, or in France and Germany in the 1850s, the displacement effects could be amplified, and the entire process of investment made quite unstable. This is the kind of process which Schumpeter (in his *Theory of Economic Development*) had in mind.

However, there were longer-run issues at stake. As indicated mixed banks entered into close relations with the industrial enterprises they financed. These relations included the development of control mechanisms by which the banks could monitor and influence the behavior of industrial enterprise. This was a multifaceted nexus First, banks obviously wished to protect their investments (especially of firm-specific information). Second, banks could increase their profits by pursuing industry-control policies, e.g. inducing market-sharing output and pricing decisions among competitive firms under their control. Many examples of such attempts are documented, especially in nineteenth-century Germany, e.g., the steel rail cartel forced on West German producers by creditor banks in 1876; or the completion the steel works cartel under bank pressure in 1904. To take an ~ious American example, J.P. Morgan's consolidation of US rail- ids in the 1890s fits the relationship quite well (Carosso, 1987). ird, in the long run, the returns to control depended on bankers 1 holding companies being able to enlist the support of investors o bought either the industrial securities intermediated, or the ires of the banks or holding companies themselves. After all, ikers themselves faced a liquidity constraint and a need to "turn ~r" their own portfolios. The willingness of investors to take :urities from those intermediaries, one may presume, resulted from • existence of costs to individuals of acquiring information on ~ersification possibilities. "Control" may have reduced the return on :urities below what a perfect market would have produced, but the ins to diversification for small investors could nevertheless have ~n positive, given transaction costs of individual diversification. In s connection it is interesting to note that the shares of the German ~at banks were in strong demand in the pre-1914 period. They nained at such a premium, despite large capital increases, that the :t of raising new capital fell considerably for the banks in the 70–1914 period (see Fig. 3.2). At the same time, large banks were ~ored disproportionately, a factor which fueled ongoing concentra- n after the 1880s.[9]

The historical-empirical evidence on financial control of industry is indant, though not without controversy. That investment and xed banks of the Belgian, French or German type consciously and ively pursued the goal of controlling the railroads and industrial terprises they financed is documented in hundreds of individual isodes (Cameron, 1961; Levy-Leboyer, 1964; Tilly, 1966; März, 58; Landes, 1969; Kocka, 1978; Pohl, 1982). To those may be added zens of chapters from American railroad finance and, in addition, ~ries on the "money trust" as related by, among others, the ll-known Pujo Committee of 1913 (Redlich, 1951; Carosso, 1970; inting, 1971; Martin, 1976). Industry control by means of presentation in the key decision-making organs of the companies icerned has been studied extensively; somewhat less so, the related estion of ownership and control of voting shares. This is not the ice for a comprehensive survey, but two points of detail may be of erest, one related to Belgian and German evidence and one to the rman case only. First, representation in German top management itrol organs has involved both bankers in industry, and vice versa. wever, the bulk of evidence suggests that bankers held more portant positions in industry than industrialists did in banks; and is is true today (Jeidels, 1905; Riesser, 1910; Kocka, 1978; Pappi,

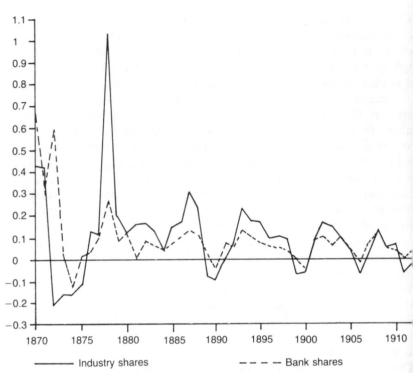

Figure 3.2 Mean realized return on German industry and bank share 1870–1913.

Kappelhoff and Melbeck, 1987). The observation is of interest, since revisionist school of thought has long existed which downplays th power of the bankers, with the help of the "mutual power" argumen For Belgium during the postwar period, the best evidence shov holding company directors occupying strategic positions in th country's corporate sector, rather than being controlled by directors enterprises in other branches (Daems and Van der Wee, 1974 Second, since the nineteenth century, German bankers have had ea: access to the voting rights of shares held on deposit with the (*Depotstimmrecht*). This meant that bankers rarely had to devote significant proportion of their own resources to mobilizing the desire number of votes in important shareholders' metings. Certainly, th trust of their customers was not unrelated to the banks' pa performance as intermediaries of desirable securities, and this itse required large equity capitals. In recent decades this practice has bee restricted, but still exists.

The issues just discussed fall under the heading "finance capita m," an old-fashioned concept which somehow lives on (Hilferding, 910; Davis, 1967; Daems, 1975). That concept's validity depends on he degree of competition in the financial and industrial sectors of the conomy, and implies that greater concentration and market power cated initially in the former, and thus controlled development of the atter. I think there have been phases in the history of most of the ow-industrialized economies in which that relationship has held. ritain may be the exception which proves the rule. The rule certainly pplied to Belgium during most of the nineteenth century; indeed, ccording to one careful student of the question, it fits the Belgian se right up to the 1960s (Daems, 1975). It may be appropriate for ermany from the 1850s to perhaps the 1890s, though much depends a the branches of industry one looks to (Kocka, 1978). For France he fit is very weak, except for perhaps a few foreign investment rojects; the financial independence of nineteenth-century French dustry is proverbial, and the capital-intensive industries which were ssociated with industrial dependence in other countries were less rongly developed in France (Caron, 1975; Levy-Leboyer, 1978). ven in the US there was a phase – from the 1890s to the First World ʹar – which was arguably a case study in "finance capitalism," volving, once again, the capital-intensive railroads and heavy dustry. What about Italy from the 1890s to the 1920s? The case has en made (Gerschenkron, 1962; Cohen, 1977; Toniolo, 1984).

"Finance capitalism" was limited by the growth in size of the dustrial enterprise itself, the use of retained earnings, and an aproved credit status to establish contact with investors directly or shop around for alternative institutional sources of financing. This as related to a broadening of the capital market and the develop-ent of competition in the financial sector, which improved the terms a which industrial enterprise could raise capital. In some countries et another factor, the role of government, altered the lines of aancial dependence and the financial structure in general. This came especially apparent after the First World War, particularly in urope, where government institutions became involved in financing dustrial reconstruction on a fairly broad scale, and where govern-ent resources in general grew relative to those of the banking ctor. In the main industrial countries, however, the big movement this direction came in the 1930s. This was not everywhere a rmanent change in direction, but I would hesitate to suggest that nance capital" is on the way back. As mentioned above, the concept elf is an antiquated one. It does have one virtue, however. It minds us that questions of power and control are an important part the story of the development of modern financial institutions.

Summary and Conclusions

This chapter has discussed three important issues in the history of modern financial institutions. The first concerns the development and performance of organized capital markets. Its provisional conclusion would seem to be that price formation in pre-1914 capital markets (stock exchanges) reflected fairly efficient arrangements, but that such efficiency was no indicator of the contribution of formal capital markets to industrial finance and economic development. Efficient capital asset pricing in such markets is neither a necessary nor sufficient condition of growth-provoking financial intermediation. What is needed are operational models which link the latter to both informational flows and capital asset pricing. An obvious point perhaps, but an important one, I believe.

A second issue concerned the financial structure of enterprise and was connected with the Modigliani-Miller proposition (on the irrelevance of financial structure). The historical evidence suggested that capital-seeking enterprises and investors used adjustments in financial instruments and financial structure as a response to informational asymmetries. Various forms of enterprise control by financial institutions can be seen as means of overcoming those asymmetries. The Modigliani-Miller hypothesis, it may be suggested, could be a useful tool in subsequent work on the history of enterprise finance.

The third issue of financial history taken up in this chapter is tantamount to an attempted overview of financial development, with special regard to Gerschenkron's well-known views on banking institutions. In addition to "relative backwardness" (which in this context is about the same thing as relative capital scarcity), I suggest that political factors deserve consideration as determinants of how financial institutions develop. This is felt to avoid the suggestion of an inevitably efficient challenge-response syndrome which Gerschenkron's backwardness typology seems to have emphasized. However, the efficiency of institutions remains an important issue whatever the historical results. One may see relative backwardness as a force generating informational problems and, in response, institutional innovations in which large-scale organizations or hierarchies replace relatively atomistic competitive units, and in which allocation by hierarchy replaces allocation through formal markets. The question then becomes one of assessing the costs as well as the benefits of such large scale organizations. In this chapter it is argued that some of the inefficiencies associated with large-scale organizations, and in particular with bank control of industry, were limited by (a) certain returns

ontrol in the form of lower costs of risk diversification, and (b)
inuing competition within the financial sector itself. Admittedly,
e may have been additional costs of large-scale organizations –
as neglect of small-scale credit needs – not discussed in the
pter but which deserve attention. From this chapter and from the
ature it surveys, four final points can be made:

t, there is a positive connection between the growth-inducing
ts of financial institutions and the degree of competition the latter
associated with. The relationship should be seen in Schumpeterian
as, that is, as allowing for high profits to innovators which cannot
ompeted away immediately.

cond, the hypothesis that factor endowments, comparative cost
antages and the resultant structure of an economy were an
ortant determinant of the demand for capital and, hence, for the
ncial institutions which developed in it, should continue to be
n seriously, even if one must acknowledge that structure and
parative advantage could themselves be affected by financial
lopment.

ird, it makes sense to see economic control of enterprise – in
icular by financial institutions – as a response to informational
rences among investors and itself an investment which yields a
ive return. In the period observed here, however, equity own-
ip was too concentrated for a "market for control" via takeover
and mergers to develop. There were close connections between
ger activity and enterprise disappearances, on the one hand, and
k market prices, on the other, but the connection may reflect
ng more than the structural shaping of enterprise decision-
ing.

urth, financial crises deserve careful attention, not only as
ators of system weakness but also as a factor conditioning
tutional development, e.g., the opening up of new paths of
lopment, or the closing off of possible alternatives to "the road
n." To take some British examples, there is the Overend &
ney crisis of 1866, which appears to have sealed the fate of
nturous investment banking in Great Britain, the City of
gow Bank failure in 1878, which put an end to unlimited liability
ritish joint-stock banking and may have paved the way for
entration there; and there is the Baring crisis of 1890, which,
ng other things, exposed the weakness of the Bank of England's
ion and may have altered the business operating procedures of
Bank of England and the joint-stock banks. The list of examples
d be easily extended, as books on the subject by Charles

Kindleberger and others indicate. Crises have obviously been part a parcel of the emergence of modern financial institutions.

Notes

[1] For better or worse, there is no "Quantity Theory of Finance" to which Goldsmi data could be oriented. For the abundance of linkages between monetary the monetary history and monetary statistics, see the recent survey by Bordo (1987).

[2] Two points: A not unimportant part of Edelstein's argument is that swings in Brita foreign investment over the period were significantly influenced by swings in dome investment, particularly that of the "population-sensitive" kind. The implication is t weak representation of domestic industry in the British capital market reflecte relatively weak demand for capital, rather than imperfections of the market. Revi of previous estimates of British foreign investment in this period is in process caution in the use of figures such as those cited here is urged. It seems, for exam that there was more British direct investment abroad than hitherto believed (e.g. in form of "free-standing companies"), and probably less portfolio investment. (See these points, Platt, 1986; Wilkins, 1989; Cottrell, 1990.) Moreover, some of the "Brit portfolio investments (foreign securities issued in London) were taken up by Lon representatives of foreign banks or foreign investors.

[3] With significant shifts in portfolio shares, the mean-variance approach breaks d unless all components of the portfolio are highly and positively correlated. In this c however, diversification effects will be small.

[4] It is well known that American monetary instability before 1914 had much to do v seasonal swings in payments, and that crises generally reflected the coincidenc strong cyclical and seasonal movements. On this see Goodhart (1969) and Miron (19

[5] By "signaling effects," I mean the use by investors and creditors of behavio capital-seeking enterprise as indicators of the latter's financial status (its profitab and riskiness) for which direct information is unavailable. "Agency problems" refe the absence of incentives ensuring that enterprise managers (agents) perform as we the owners (principals) wish or expect them to. A discussion of signaling and o aspects of informational asymmetries in relation to the Modigliani-Miller theor given in Stiglitz (1988a). A section of the fall 1988 issue of *The Journal of Econo Perspectives* is devoted to the Modigliani-Miller hypothesis.

[6] One notes also that corporative enterprises in the nineteenth century freque raised deep agency problems, involving corruption, embezzlement, and so on. Not a these were the result of limited liability, however, but of size.

[7] Two further observations: (a) "financial revolutions" were not necessarily perma and could be undone; and (b) "financial revolutions" were in a sense frequently imp upon borrowing countries by the bankers and investors of the capital-expor countries and represented the imposition of Western European standards of credit thiness.

[8] I claim no originality in this, for Sylla (1972) made a similar argument in regar the US case.

[9] Statistical investigation of the connection between bank size and the risk-corre realized return on bank shares shows it to be negative (in a number of tests invol variation in sample size and composition); examination of the connection between k mergers and the price of bank shares (1870–1913) reveals it to be significantly posi See Pohl (1982) and Tilly (1986).

inance and Corporate Evolution
Five Industrial Economies,
)00–1950[1]

VID C. MOWERY

roduction

recent years, historical research on the evolution of corporate anization in the industrial economies has expanded dramatically, rred in large part by the pathbreaking work of Chandler and by ghtened interest in the development of an institution of central ortance to the economic growth of these nations. How has the lution of corporate structure been affected by the structure of the ncial systems within these economies? National financial systems e exerted an important influence on the development of the lern corporation, but appear to have done so largely through litating, rather than being solely responsible for, organizational ovation. The level of involvement by financial institutions in orate management and evolution varies across the economies ussed in this chapter and across industries within these econ- es. As such, the financial system was an important influence on the "selection environment" within which firms developed (see Dosi *et* 1990), but this environment reflected the operation of other ors as well.

he relationship between the evolution of industrial and financial ctures is an interactive one that displays many of the hallmarks of ath-dependent process (Dosi, 1988); the array of economic and nological opportunities available to one firm or to one economy y contrast with those faced by another firm or economy.[2] For this son and others, cross-sectional comparisons of financial and indust- organization may be somewhat unreliable. Differences in the lution of corporate organization in the United States, Great ain, France, Germany and Japan during the past century are

indisputable. The linkage between the financial environment and
evolution of the corporation is unclear, however, as is the influenc
the path of corporate evolution on corporation and national econo
performance. Moreover, intranational differences in corporate eve
tion across industries appear to be as significant as differences acr
nations. The industry-specific influences of technology and mar
demand were important determinants of corporate evolution throu
out this period.

The chapter begins with a brief overview of the arguments
Gerschenkron (1962) and Chandler (1977, 1990), whose resea
presents important perspectives on the role of the financial system
industrialization and corporate development. I then survey the his
ical evolution of the financial systems and leading corporations of
US and Great Britain, focusing particularly on the implications
cross-national differences for the development of industrial researc'
critical element in the international competitive fortunes of th
economies. This comparison is followed by briefer surveys of finan
and corporate development in the German, French, and Japar
economies. Broadening the comparative analysis to include evide
from these economies calls into question the generality of the linka
between financial and corporate evolution that appear to stand
starkly in the US–British comparison. The conclusion considers s
of the conceptual issues raised in this historical comparison.

Gerschenkron's Historical Analysis of Financial Evolution

Gerschenkron's discussion of relative backwardness rejected Rost
argument (1960) that all industrializing economies must pass thro
a similar sequence of phases. Gerschenkron based an alterna
description of the process of industrialization on his analysis
nineteenth-century Europe. For Gerschenkron, the spread
industrialization within Europe meant that the "relatively backw;
economies in Europe often followed a path that differed from tha
early industrializers. In most cases, these followers employed
technologies created in the leading economies, but did so in diffe
institutional surroundings. The institutional and other correlate
industrial development differed considerably across economies,
the extent of relative backwardness and timing of industrializa
were crucial determinants of these correlates. Anticipating n
recent scholarly work that stresses the path-dependent natur

echnological change, Gerschenkron argued that the process of ndustrialization depended heavily on the initial conditions.

Gerschenkron's key argument for the concerns of this paper deals vith financial innovation in the relatively backward economies of 'rance and Germany during the nineteenth century:

> The industrialization of England had proceeded without any substantial utilization of banking for long-term investment purposes. The more gradual character of the industrialization process and the more considerable accumulation of capital, first from earnings in trade and modernized agriculture and later from industry itself, obviated the pressure for developing any special institutional devices for provision of long-term capital to industry. By contrast, in a relatively backward country capital is scarce and diffused, the distrust of industrial activities is considerable, and finally, there is greater pressure for bigness because of the scope of the industrialization movement, the larger average size of plant, and the concentration of industrialization processes on branches of relatively high ratios of capital to output.
>
> (1962: p. 14)

n France, according to Gerschenkron, institutional innovation in inance included the foundation of the Credit Mobilier and the evelopment of industrial banking. In Germany, the great industrial anks were the institutional response to the underdeveloped state of omestic capital markets and limited supplies of domestic capital.

Gerschenkron's analysis focused on the industrialization of the arious national economies within a region long characterized by xtensive intraregional flows of people, ideas, culture, and (increasing-y, during the nineteenth century) capital. The political and economic npulses for industrialization in relatively backward economies and he availability of technology presumably were facilitated by these onditions. Nevertheless, other scholars (Rosovsky, 1961; Sylla, 1972; 'amamura, 1972) have discussed the relevance of Gerschenkron's nalysis to the industrial development of two other far more distant relatively backward" economies during the nineteenth century, apan and the United States, focusing on the growth of *zaibatsu* anks within Japan and the role of investment banks and industrial ecurities markets in the US.

Gerschenkron has been criticized (Cameron, 1972) for his explana-on for the lack of bank involvement in the finance of early British dustrialization, and some evidence for France, Germany, Japan, and 1e United States (keeping in mind that Gerschenkron's original rmulation did not cover these last two economies) does not support ll elements of his hypothesis. Nevertheless, Gerschenkron's discus-on provides a useful organizing framework for discussing the role of nancial institutions in industrialization. Moreover, the hypothesis

that the responses of national financial systems to the demands c
industrialization depended on the initial structure of these system
closely parallels one part of Chandler's analysis of the growth c
corporate organization. For Chandler, the development of corporat
structure compensated for weaknesses in national systems of distribu
tion and marketing of consumer goods in a fashion that wa
analogous to financial innovation in Gerschenkron's analysis. Th
evolution of both financial and industrial structures depended fund&
mentally on the initial state of development of these systems in all c
the economies examined below. Obviously, the interaction betwee
the evolving financial and corporate organizational structures als
affected the development of each.

Chandler's Analysis of Corporate Evolution in the United States

Chandler (1977, 1990) and others have identified a number •
attributes that characterize the modern corporation. Among the mo&
important elements are (a) the control by the manufacturing firm •
multiple functions in addition to that of production, including marke
ing, distribution, and R & D; (b) increased size; (c) a reduction i
family control and management and the replacement of owne
managers with professional managers; and (d) greater produ
diversification. These elements are common to modern firms in mo
industrial economies, but the timing of their appearance, the
importance in different industries, and the speed with which the
spread within different national economies, seem to differ.

Chandler's argument was developed in greatest detail for th
United States, and a brief recapitulation will illuminate the points
contrast between US and foreign corporate evolution. During th
latter half of the nineteenth century, Chandler suggested, technologi
al innovation in communication and transportation (the telegraph ar
railroad) considerably increased the "span of control" of a single firr
binding together the US national market and facilitating coordinatic
within a single organization of a more extensive range of activitie
Simultaneously, innovations in production technologies in food proce
sing, metallurgy, petroleum, and chemicals increased the capiti
requirements of firms in these industries. Innovations in productic
technology significantly increased the minimum efficient scale
production in these manufacturing industries, expanding the share

ιe national market that a single plant could serve. These technolo-
cal innovations also confronted entrepreneurs with unprecedented
²quirements for coordination of both upstream and downstream
:tivities with those of production, and created opportunities to exploit
:onomies of scale and scope.[3]

Chandler distinguishes among three groups of manufacturing
dustries. The first group, including furniture, leather, shoes, and
xtiles, was not significantly affected by process innovation during
ιis period. Within these industries, firms either retained their old
·oduction technologies and corporate structure, or (as in the cordage
dustry) mergers attempting to exploit economies of scale or of scope
iled. A second group included firms in consumer foodstuffs (e.g.,
wift, Armour, Pillsbury, Anheuser-Busch, Pabst), and light machin-
·y (McCormick Reaper, Singer Sewing Machines). A lack of well-
²veloped channels for distribution and (in some cases) retail sale of
ιeir products meant that these firms integrated forward into
stribution through such innovations as the ownership of refrigerated
ειght cars, warehouses for the distribution of sides of beef, or
·oduct service and sales outlets for complex light machinery. The
odest capital requirements of production and distribution operations
these industries, however, as well as the large cash flow thrown off
ν successful operations, meant that these firms did not require
.ternal finance for their strategies of vertical integration (initially
rward and subsequently, as in the case of McCormick Reaper,
ιckward). Among other things, this ability to finance reorganization
om cash flow meant that financial institutions did not become
volved in oversight of management or corporate organization, and
νners remained in control of many of these firms well into the
rentieth century.[4]

The second group of manufacturing firms includes the more
·pital-intensive sectors of petroleum, nonferrous metals, chemicals,
bber, and heavy electrical machinery. The revolution in the tech-
ιlogies of production and distribution significantly increased the
·pital requirements faced by these firms and (by raising fixed costs)
·ay have created greater incentives for horizontal agreements to
ntrol prices and output, often under the sponsorship of trade
sociations (see Galambos, 1966; Lamoreaux, 1985). Here, the
ιique public policy environment of the United States exerted a very
·portant influence on corporate evolution. The passage and in-
²asingly stringent judicial interpretation of the Sherman Antitrust
:t severely reduced the number and effectiveness of such interfirm
reements. A number of scholars have suggested that the merger

wave of the 1892–1904 period, particularly the surge in mergers afte
1897, was in part a response to this new juridical environmen
Finding that the legality of informal or formal price-fixing an
market-sharing agreements was under attack, firms resorted t
mergers, creating firms that substituted intrafirm for interfir
methods to control prices and markets.[5]

In contrast to the other groups of firms, the increased capit
requirements and the need for financial advice and assistance i
mergers led these firms to rely heavily on external sources of financ
The primary sources were the New York securities market which w
rapidly expanding its listings of industrial securities during this peri
(Navin and Sears, 1955), access to which required the services
investment houses whose foundation and growth often had bee
based on railroad finance in earlier decades.[6] Outside financie
facilitated many large mergers and imposed new organizational ar
management structures on the firms that they created. The size of tl
firms resulting from these mergers, the mergers' financial requir
ments, and their oversight by major financial houses also hasten
the replacement of owners by managers. Significantly, the sectors i
which new internal organizational structures were developed throug
merger were those in which organized industrial research ar
technical progress would expand rapidly during subsequent decades

Following the foundation of large, multifunction firms, stror
pressure for diversification and internal reorganization grew ar
influenced the evolution of corporate structure during and after tl
1920s. As the expansion into additional functions (e.g., marketing,
& D) created greater incentives for diversification (in some cases,
pointed out by Penrose, 1959, in order to fully utilize firm-specif
capabilities), the internal management structure of the firm becan
increasingly inadequate. The result was the development of tl
so-called "M-form" firm, which separated strategic from operatir
responsibilities and created an internal capital market for the alloc
tion of funds to investment in different product lines. During tl
postwar period in the US, conglomerate firms developed intern
management structures that emulated the M-form, albeit for lines
business with little if any operating relationship with one another.[7]

In addition to changes in the capital intensity and minimu
efficient scale of production technologies in many US manufacturir
industries, three factors influenced the timing and spread of the
new corporate structures. They are central to a comparative applic
tion of Chandler's analysis to the development of corporate organiz
tion in other industrial economies during 1900–50.[8] The first a
arguably the most important factor affecting corporate evolution w

. development of the domestic market for consumer goods, which *.*wned many of the pioneering US corporations. Where a mass *.*rket for branded, packaged products (e.g., cigarettes, photographic *.*1, etc.) was lacking, large, internally financed firms to serve this *.*rket were slower to develop, and often did not do so through the *.*nbined management of production and distribution. Integration of *.*duction and distribution required that this mass consumer market *.* a domestic market, as Chandler and Daems (1974) argued in *.*nparing US and European corporate development:

.. when there was enough of the mass market Europe started to *.*evelop continuous process techniques to produce a few low-priced *.*ackaged products. Unilever, Nestlé, Royal Dutch Shell had similarities *.* American counterparts. The basic difference was that they had to *.*narket in many countries rather than in a single market. This resulted *.*1 a much more diversified and decentralized multi-nation organization .. until World War II producers in European nations and Japan had to *.*ely much more heavily on foreign markets than did Americans. In all *.*raditional industries and many new ones European manufacturers *.*eached their markets through middlemen, exporters and importers. *.*hese middlemen, rather than manufacturers, became responsible for *.*narketing the product and for coordinating the flow from manufacturer *.* consumer.

(p. 23)

. second and closely related factor was the level of sophistication of *.*nestic channels of distribution and marketing and raw materials *.*ply. Where these were well developed, particularly for consumer *.*ducts, the combined management within a single firm of produc-*.* and distribution was less essential. These first two factors were *.*st important for firms serving the consumer market.

*.*he final factor affecting the development of corporate structure in *.*ndler's schema is the state of development of the national *.*ncial system. The development of modern firms in heavy manufac-*.*ng was heavily influenced by the availability of external sources of *.*nce, and especially, by the intervention of financial institutions in *.*porate management. External finance of corporate development *.* contributed in the US to the growth in size of the modern firm *.* to the replacement of owner control by that of managers. *.*ancial factors nevertheless appear to be of subsidiary importance – *.* causes of change in corporate structure were primarily technolo-*.*l and demand-driven. The characteristics of economic and corpo-*.* development during this period in the US also meant that the *.*ncial system affected the development of corporate structure for *.* one of the three groups of US manufacturing firms discussed *.*ier. The national financial system was by no means the sole

determinant of the overall structure of US industry or of t
corporations participating in a broad range of sectors. Equa
important were the character of consumer demand and technologi
change.

Moreover, as White notes, the structure of financial oversight
corporate development was heavily affected by public policy. T
prominent role of investment banks, rather than commercial ba
lending, in the 1897–1902 merger wave resulted in large part fr
federal and state restrictions on commercial bank ownership of stoc
and limitations on the size of their loans to any single corpor;
borrower.[9] During 1901–12, for example, more than 77 per cent of t
external funds raised by US nonfinancial corporations were deriv
from the sale of securities, a share that declined only slightly duri
1923–9, to 74.1 per cent. The Glass-Steagall Act of 1933 furtl
reduced the role of commercial banks in long-term industrial finan
Despite their prominent role in financing the foundation of many
the largest US manufacturing firms in the late nineteenth and ea
twentieth centuries, Chandler (1990) argues that the direct invol
ment of investment bankers in the management and oversight
these firms declined after their establishment.[10]

The state of development of the US national financial mar|
nevertheless may have influenced US corporate development ir
manner similar to the influence of the relatively backward distri|
tion system for consumer products in the late nineteenth century
economy. Had the market for industrial securities been fully
veloped and easily accessible to firms without the intervention of W
Street investment banks, these banks would have exerted far |
influence on the subsequent development of the firms raising fui
through the equity markets. Although stock ownership would h;
become dispersed through successive equity issues, the replacemen|
owners by managers, as well as the internal rationalization
corporate structure, might well have been slower and less complete,
was the case in Great Britain.[11]

Relative backwardness thus affected US corporate evolution in
least two ways – the integration of distribution and production ;
the involvement of financial institutions in corporate managem
and strategy. The British experience (see below) also suggests t|
even a highly efficient industrial securities market may fail to prov
investors with the information needed to evaluate relatively ri;
investments, making it difficult for new firms to tap the equ
markets. This argument raises still another, "Schumpeterian" dim
sion of relative backwardness, the possibility that financial or cor
rate organization in a developing economy is more dynamic;

icient than that in the developed economies, where dynamic
iciency may be sacrificed for static allocative efficiency.[12]

eat Britain

Britain, the transformation and reorganization of major firms
urred later than in the United States, and was less complete in
portant respects. Hannah (1980) characterized the British corpo-
e landscape in 1919 as follows:

n 1919, the characteristics associated with the modern corporate
economy were rare in Britain. Large corporations were less common in
lmost all industries than in the United States; in some sectors, such as
lectrical machinery and steel, there were also many fewer than in
ermany . . .. The loose holding company and the family firm remained
much more common structures, despite the development of modern
managerial enterprises among some of the largest firms in certain
ectors.

(pp. 59–60)[13]

s slower development of modern corporate structures reflected a
nber of influences, including but not restricted to the financial
tem. Mass markets for consumer packaged products may have
eloped more slowly within Great Britain, although the rise of giant
ns within the food and allied industries (Lipton, Lever, and others)
ected the emergence of a mass, urban consumer market. Even
hin this sector, however, a well-developed British system for
nestic distribution and marketing through independent firms
int that the integration of mass production with large-scale
ribution did not occur as rapidly as it did in the United States.[14]
the extent that the integration of these activities drove the
elopment of the diversified, multifunction firm in the United
tes, the absence of integration may have retarded similar develop-
its in Great Britain.

aradoxically, the development of modern corporate organization
also hampered by the sophistication of the British financial
em, which combined an extensive market for securities (before
4, primarily domestic and foreign railroad and government secur-
s) with minimal bank involvement in industrial finance. Long-term
k lending historically had played a minor role in British industrial
nce; the data in Table 4.1 suggest that before 1950, financial
itutions in Great Britain accounted for a smaller share of national

financial assets than in any of the four other economies discussed
this chapter. Corporate equities also played a less significant role
the finance of British industry than in the United States,
observation consistent with the data in Table 4.2.

According to Kennedy (1987), the modest role of equity finan
reflected the inability of potential purchasers of equity to obt:
reliable information on the quality of equities, especially those issu
by new firms. Investment banks, such as J.P. Morgan & Co., wh
had been crucial in underwriting new issues and establishing (alb
imperfectly) the quality of industrial and railroad securities dur
this period in US financial markets, largely were absent from Brit
industrial securities markets. As a result, British firms in 1
technologically progressive, capital-intensive industries of au
mobiles, electrical machinery, and chemicals, all of which were lead
in establishing new forms of corporate organization in the Uni
States, encountered serious difficulties in raising funds through 1

Table 4.1 Financial intermediation ratios, 1895–1950[a].

	1895	1913	1929	1939	195(
France	–	17.0	27.3	–	27.2
Germany	26.2	30.1	36.7	40.4	33.1
Great Britain	15.4	17.3	18.4	21.0	30.5
Japan	30.6	33.4	41.2	39.1	31.7
United States	20.0	21.3	16.4	28.8	29.1

Source: Goldsmith (1985): p. 136
  [a]"Financial intermediation ratio" is defined as the ratio of the assets of financial institutions t
domestic and foreign financial assets.

Table 4.2 Share of domestic corporate stock in Financial Assets, 1895–19

	1895	1913	1929	1939	195(
France	–	10.4	6.1	–	14.4
Germany	5.7	9.0	13.2	8.5	11.5
Great Britain	24.3	21.2	22.1	24.1	19.2
Japan	15.0	12.1	12.5	20.2	11.1
United States	22.2	27.5	34.6	20.3	14.9

Source: Goldsmith (1985): p. 153.

British equity markets. In Great Britain, the lack of involvement of financial institutions with the highly efficient market for industrial securities meant that the market for industrial securities acquired the features of a market for "lemons" (Akerlof, 1970) – credible evidence of the quality of investments was not available, and investors in securities avoided those of firms in the "new industries."

In addition to impeding the development of British firms in these sectors, the limited involvement by British banks in corporate management and the modest role of equity finance meant that British firms, even those in relatively capital-intensive sectors such as steel, remained controlled by their owners for a much longer period than was true in the United States:

> ... such a large proportion (58 per cent) of the 82 largest British industrial companies ... were characterized in 1935 by a dominant ownership interest, and so few (9 per cent) by no discernible dominance of ownership (33 per cent were marginal cases), that [P. Sargent] Florence believed that any proclamation of the managerial revolution in the Britain of the mid-thirties was quite unjustified. Instead, in the largest companies there appear to have been very many cases where control was exercised by virtue of partial ownership.
> (Payne, 1978: pp. 212–13)[15]

The delayed development of modern corporate organization that resulted from the limited involvement by financial institutions was reflected not only in the persistence of management control by founding families of many British manufacturing firms well into the 1940s, but also in the absence within British manufacturing of an extensive middle-management hierarchy. As Chandler has observed, it was the growth of middle management, in response to the increasing size and range of functions performed by the American manufacturing firm, that increased the demand for professional management education and aided the shift in control of the large firm from owners to managers.

The slower development of modern corporate organization in Great Britain was reflected in the structure of the late nineteenth century merger waves in the US and Great Britain. The British merger wave in the late nineteenth and early twentieth centuries was smaller than that of the US, which spawned many of the firms that developed new organizational structures and professional management. Fewer firms and assets were absorbed than in the United States.[16] The British merger wave also involved a narrower range of industries, primarily brewing (reflecting the development of tied houses in response to licensing restrictions) and textiles. Both British and American manufacturing experienced another wave of mergers after the First World

War. In the United States this merger wave had a less dramatic
impact on firm and market structure than its predecessor.[17] The
British merger wave of the 1920s, in contrast, resulted in the
formation of such major modern firms as ICI and Unilever. The giant
centralized firm thus did not develop in Great Britain until well after
the first American merger wave.[18] Even where large mergers among
British firms took place, they often produced an awkward collection of
poorly coordinated, fiercely independent subsidiaries, rather than a
streamlined or efficient structure.[19] The opposition of directors to the
extinction of their firms or the closing of their factories often meant
that inefficient and excess capacity survived mergers.

The large merger wave in US manufacturing was followed by a
shakeout period, but by 1919 turnover among firms had dropped
sharply and market structure among the largest firms was to remain
fairly stable for the next 60 years (Edwards, 1975; Kaplan, 1964). In
British industry there was no comparable transition from instability
to stability in market structure after the First World War. The
survival rate of large British firms appears to have been substantially
lower than that of the largest American firms in the early years of
this century; an increase in the survival rate of British firms
comparable to that of the early twentieth century in the US appeared
in Great Britain only in the 1940s.[20] Although survival may not imply
efficiency, this evidence suggests that the transition to modern
corporate organization in British industry occurred later than in the
United States.

Although important, however, the financial system was not the only
factor contributing to the slow development of modern corporate
organization within Great Britain. A weak antitrust policy slowed the
emergence of large firms through mergers. British firms interested in
reaping the benefits of industrywide coordination of price or output
were able to choose from alternatives ranging from trade association
to complete merger; legal sanctions against such interfirm cooperation
were only modest.[21] Trade associations were a primary vehicle for
such arrangements, which spread throughout the manufacturing
sector. These agreements were encouraged by the government during
the 1920s and 1930s in industrial rationalization programs.

It may be claiming too much to argue that the mild antitrust
climate failed to encourage mergers, or the rationalization of such
mergers in British industry as did occur, but this environment
reduced firms' incentives to pursue technological change and other
means of competition, especially after the demise of free trade.
Informal or formal interfirm cooperation allowed the survival of firms
that were smaller and less efficient. Nevertheless, Great Britain was

t the only industrial economy with a weak antitrust policy during
s period. A weak antitrust policy and the spread of domestic and
ernational cartels in Germany, for example, were associated with
e growth of capital- and research-intensive firms. It is the interac-
n among a number of factors, including antitrust policy, education,
d finance, that underlay the slow development of modern corporate
ganization in Great Britain (Mowery, 1984).

dustrial research in the US and Great Britain

n important aspect of corporate behavior that was influenced by the
fferent structures of British and American corporations was indust-
al research. In addition to smaller size and continued family control,
e contrasting structure of British and US manufacturing firms
ntributed to the slower development of industrial research within
ritish industry. Although industrial research is only one dimension
the development of the modern firm, it is an extremely important
e, contributing to the development of new products and processes
ith substantial public returns. Moreover, industrial research within
e firm contributed to diversification and corporate survival among
e US firms that were early investors in this activity.

Throughout the period 1900–50, British firms invested less in
ndustrial research than did American enterprises. Freeman's analy-
s (1962) of data on expenditures from the 1950s and Sanderson's
nalysis (1972) of employment data from the 1930s both conclude that
esearch intensity in British firms averaged about one-third that of
American manufacturing firms. Although this comparison does not
ontrol for transnational differences in the size distribution of firms,
he largest British firms appear to have been even further behind
heir American counterparts in research activity than were smaller
British manufacturers.[23]

The organization of British industrial research, which contrasted
with that of the United States during this period, may also. have
undermined its effectiveness. The persistence of extramural research
within Great Britain, in addition to the lower levels of overall
industrial investment in research, appears to have impaired the
innovative performance of British firms. The different histories of
corporate development in these two economies produced different R
& D systems, with direct consequences for innovative and competitive performance.

In the United States, the interaction between evolving firm struc-

ture and in-house research was of great importance to the develo
ment of the modern industrial firm. In Britain, this interaction w
largely absent. The modest importance of intrafirm industrial m
search reflected the lack of dramatic change in the structure of t
British firm. When compared to the development of US corpora
organization, the more gradual pace of change in British industry ca
be attributed in part to the peculiarities of the British nation
financial system. The financial system, however, was only one
several key factors in the divergent paths of development followed I
US and British corporate structure.

Other Industrial Economies: France, Germany, and Japan

Introduction

Research on the development of the financial system and intern
corporate organization is less abundant for other industrial economie
In particular, we lack comprehensive measures of corporate structur
or even of the structure of the financial system for this period tha
would support a more detailed or rigorous comparison. Nevertheless
some clear contrasts among these nations are apparent from
comparison based on secondary sources. The smaller size of mas
markets for consumer goods of the sort that supported the growth c
large firms in the US and Great Britain meant that the reorganiza
tion of the corporation in France, Germany, and Japan took plac
mainly in the relatively capital-intensive manufacturing industrie
that depended on external financing. Much of the contrast among th
manufacturing sectors of the US, Great Britain, France, Germany
and Japan thus reflected differences in the profile of consume
demand; only within the capital-intensive capital goods industrie
does one observe the interaction between financial and corporate
evolution that proved significant in the United States.

Industrial securities markets appear to have played a very modes
role in the finance of domestic corporations through much of the
1900–50 period in Germany, France, and Japan, in contrast to thei
significant role in the US and Great Britain (see Table 4.2). Differ
ences among the financial systems within these three economies
therefore mainly concern differences in national banking systems and
the contrasting relationships between banks and industrial firms
Despite the "relative backwardness" of all three nations relative to

Great Britain, and Gerschenkron's citation of two of the three in his original article, this comparative discussion provides only mixed support for the Gerschenkron thesis, for the period 1900–50 (admittedly, a period that lies somewhat outside of that discussed in Gerschenkron's work).

France

A combination of slow growth in domestic markets for both consumer and industrial commodities and the lack of a close relationship between industry and the national banking system meant that modern corporate organization developed slowly in the French economy during the twentieth century. Domestic markets for consumer goods did not support the rapid growth of firms serving them within France before 1950, reflecting slow population growth, severe losses in the First World War, and possibly, a somewhat more skewed distribution of income than either the United States or Great Britain. Even outside of this sector, however, firms remained smaller, owner control was significant, and intrafirm diversification was modest until after the Second World War. Despite Gerschenkron's mention of the French banking system as an important force for modernization and industrialization in the second half of the nineteenth century, financial institutions exerted little "modernizing" influence on French industrial firms in the twentieth century.

Because of the lack of close relationships with commercial or investment banks, as well as the small size of French markets for industrial securities, French firms during the late nineteenth and early twentieth centuries appear to have relied primarily on internal resources for investment. Caron (1979) cites Malinvaud's estimate (published in 1973) that French industrial firms self-financed as much as 80 per cent of investment during 1910–13. Since other scholars (Levy-Leboyer, 1978) suggest that industrial demand for external finance grew rapidly during this period, the Malinvaud-Caron estimate may understate somewhat French firms' reliance on internal sources for investment funds. Although the Credit Mobilier and other large French banks had mobilized considerable sums of capital for French domestic railroad investments and for loans to foreign governments and enterprises during the nineteenth century, French industry did not rely extensively on this source of funds. "Relative backwardness" in France apparently was associated with innovation in financial intermediaries, but not with innovation in industrial finance. Despite the fact that industrial securities accounted for a substantial portion of the shares listed on the Paris Stock Exchange during the 1890–1911 period (as much as 66–67 per cent), the overall size of the market for industrial securities was so small (according to Caron (1979), securities accounted for only 6 per cent of net industrial product in 1913) that self-financing remained the dominant policy. Corporate equities accounted for a far smaller share of national financial assets in France than in Great Britain or the United States through most of the 1900–50 period (Table 4.2), while financial institutions were less prominent than in Japan or Germany (Table 4.1).

Demands by external financial sources, such as the investment banks of the US or the industrial banks of Germany, for renovation of internal corporate organization and management thus were absent during much of the pre-First World War period in France. Moreover, reliance by French firms on internal sources of capital did little if anything to loosen control of these firms by owners. In the aftermath of the First World War, which brought with it severe inflation, Levy-Leboyer (1980) suggests that French firms, seeking substantial additional resources for investment, developed holding companies to accumulate capital.[24] Corporate capital requirements drove innovation in the financial system after the First World War, rather than the reverse:

> ... the creation of chains of holding and subholding companies was a continuous process; they had been set up on the initiative of industry and were to answer its needs in a period of abnormally rapid industrial development. Thus the classical relationship between business and financial intermediaries, in which the latter are described as controlling the former, had been reversed; industry had taken the lead in building financial structures to make up for the impoverishment of the country and the deficiencies in the banking system.
>
> (1980: p. 146)

The relationship between corporate and financial development during this period in France thus appears to reverse that observed in the US; industrial firms were responsible for institutional innovation in the financial sector, rather than vice versa.[25] French holding companies remained under the control of the owning families, and provided a substitute for the intrafirm diversification taking place at this time in German, US, and (to a far smaller extent) British firms.[26] The holding company structure emerged from industrial requirements for capital, and enabled owners to retain control of large segments of French industry. Intrafirm control of diversified production and other activities was pursued through the holding company, but this control and involvement rarely extended beyond purely financial relaonships. During the 1920s and 1930s cartel agreements among the ubsidiaries of various holding companies further reduced pressures or restructuring and innovation.

Some of the consequences of these developments for French corporate structure are summarized by Levy-Leboyer:

> Previous studies have established that earlier in this century industrial integration was lacking in France, so firm size, measured by total assets, was smaller than in other industrial economies. In the 1920s, for example, Alsthom (the leading electrical-equipment manufacturer) and Saint-Gobain (the glassmaker and chemical producer), the two largest French corporations in terms of share capital issued, were only 5 to 7 percent as large as Imperial Chemical Industries or the German giant I.G. Farben. Similarly, industrial firms were slow to use their experience, whether technical or commercial, to diversify into new products or processes . . ..
>
> Large French firms were slow not only in adopting a strategy of diversification but also in taking up the new organizational forms . . . the use of this new structure [the M-form] was not expanded in the interwar years and in many cases was even discontinued. In 1950 . . . far more of the largest firms were organized as loose-knit groups in which one firm had large shareholdings, or *participations*, to use the French term, in the others. For managerial purposes, they did not offer an efficiency comparable to that of the multidivisional organization; their predominance indicates a continuing preference, voluntary or not, for indirect rather than direct control over operations.
>
> (1980, pp. 118–19).

The slower development of modern corporate organization in France may have hampered the competitive performance of French industry during this period. The collapse of the Citroën industrial empire in the early 1930s, for example, reflected the lack of coordination between production and market demand that General Motors had overcome through the development of a staff charged with coordinating production and projected market demand (see Chandler and Salsbury, 1971).[27]

Germany

German firms are widely cited as pioneers in the development of technology- and capital-intensive heavy industry, aided by funding and close supervision from large industrial banks. Large firms in the sectors singled out by Chandler as critical to the development of the modern corporate structure through external sources of finance – electrical machinery, chemicals, and primary metals – grew rapidly in the German economy after 1870. By the early 1900s, according to Kocka (1980),

> While only 23 percent of all manufacturing and crafts workers were in operating units with more than 50 employees in 1882, their proportion had risen to 42 percent by 1907. Mining, engineering (including electrical engineering), chemicals, and textiles led this trend toward concentration. In each of these industrial areas, more than two-thirds of all employees worked in plants with more than 50 employees. The least concentrated areas were the manufacture of clothing, food, and wood and leather products.
>
> (p. 79)

With the significant exception of packaged consumer products in foodstuffs and other sectors, the leading sectors in corporate restructuring and technological innovation in the German and US economies during this period were broadly similar.[28] In addition to large size, German firms appear to have adopted strategies of diversification, based in part on in-house industrial research, by the early twentieth century.[29] Indeed, Beer (1958) and others have suggested that German firms in the chemicals industry were leaders in the development of industrial research within the firm.

A small number of large banks grew to dominate the German financial system after 1870; the significant role of financial institutions in the German economy throughout the 1900–50 period is revealed in Table 4.1. They provided long-term loans to corporate customers, and organized the issue of shares in industrial enterprises.[30] The German banks combined commercial and investment banking to a greater extent than did the financial architects of corporate mergers and growth in the United States during this period (and hence were known as "mixed" banks).[31] Senior executives from German banks were well represented on the supervisory boards of German firms before and after 1914:

> Before 1914, bank directors made up the largest single group among the supervisory board members of German joint-stock companies and occupied 20 percent of all positions. In 1913–1914, the Deutsche Bank had representatives on 186 other companies' boards. A few leading bank directors had accumulated up to forty-four seats each on supervisory boards before World War I, and by 1930 some held as many as a hundred. Not surprisingly, the supervisory board was the most important channel through which the large banks exercised direct and continuous influence over industrial firms.
>
> (Kocka, 1980: p. 91)

As in the United States, the performance and contribution of the German credit banks to corporate development were heavily affected by regulatory and other government policies. According to Tilly

)86), the Prussian state bank provided extensive short-term com-
rcial credit, enabling the large banks to focus on long-term lending,
which less liquidity was required in reserves. The state-owned
ussian Bank also provided the mixed banks with ready access to
dit when they encountered sudden demands for liquidity. Both of
ese characteristics of the policy environment supported the credit
nks' focus on relatively long-term corporate lending to large
lustrial enterprises. The data in Table 4.2 also suggest that by
mparison with Great Britain or the United States, corporate
uities were far less significant in German industrial finance.

The German financial system thus appears to have exerted a
werful influence on corporate development and on national econ-
ic performance. Tilly's comparison (1986) of the efficiency of the
ctoral distribution of British and German banks' lending concludes
at German bank lending yielded a more efficient yield-variance
adeoff, based on available opportunities, than did British banks'
tivities during 1880–1913. There are four qualifications to this
rtrait. First, as was noted earlier, the lack of a strong mass market
r consumer goods meant that an important sector for the develop-
ent of the US corporation did not expand rapidly within Germany
ring this period.

The dramatic growth in the role of the German industrial banks
)pears to have followed, rather than to have led, the formation of a
imber of large German enterprises.[32] Tilly (1974) argues that many
erman industrial firms initially did not rely on the banks for equity
debt finance:

... there was a clear tendency for industrial enterprises to resort more to
external financing as the 1870–1913 period went on ... there seems to
have been a fairly close negative relationship between the size of
industrial enterprise and dependence upon external finance. The larger
the enterprise, apparently, the less fear its management had of losing
control through indebtedness.

(p. 162)[33]

Third, the early development by German firms of organized indust-
al research predates the period of major intervention in corporate
ganization and management by German industrial banks. As Beer
d others have noted, a number of German firms had begun
gnificant industrial research programs, either entirely in house or
ised on close collaboration with universities, by the 1870s, well
fore the attainment by the industrial banks of substantial power
d influence over corporate development. Indeed, Beer (1958) cites
e passage of the first comprehensive German patent law in 1876,
ther than developments in finance or corporate structure, as a

central factor in the origins and growth of German industr
research. Nevertheless, major expansion and institutionalization
industrial research occurred only in the 1880s and 1890s.[34] The ma
role of industrial banks in the finance of German enterprise also d(
not appear to have uniformly replaced owner control with manager
control – families such as Siemens, Krupp, Stinnes, Thyssen a
others retained significant control over the operation of their fir
well into the twentieth century, and holding companies similar
those in France facilitated such control.[35] Finally, Tilly (1986) su
gests that new, relatively small enterprises were not well served
the German mixed banks. To the extent that these firms were mo
innovative (an assumption, rather than an empirical stylized fact), t
concentration of German banks on lending to large firms may ha
impeded economic performance,[36] although this impediment almc
certainly was less significant in Germany than in France, Japan,
Great Britain.

Japan

The Japanese case combines elements of the German and Fren
histories. Industrial banks, engaged in long-term lending to industri
enterprises, were combined with family-controlled holding compani
(the *zaibatsu*) and diversification through the holding compan
rather than through the firm, as was the case in French indust
during the post-First World War period. As in Germany, financi
intermediaries played a more important role than in Great Britain
the United States (Table 4.1). Corporate equity was somewhat mo
important in the Japanese national balance sheet than in the Frencl
but equity finance was far less prominent in Japanese industry tha
in Great Britain or the United States. Although the pace of Japanes
industrial development was extraordinarily rapid and quickly pr
duced major industrial firms, little is known about the development (
the internal organizational structure of these firms, nor are the
accounts in English of the role (if any) of industrial research withi
pre-1950 Japan.

Japanese industrialization and the *zaibatsu* both had their origin
in government sponsorship after the "opening" of Japan in the 1860
The core of many *zaibatsu* activities during the late nineteent
century was the operation by favored families of factories establishe
by the Japanese government as demonstration projects, or the sale
goods to the government by these enterprises at premium price
During the last decades of the nineteenth century, many *zaibats*

ınded or absorbed private banks, supplementing the system of
tional banks established by the government in the 1870s. Despite
ɛ rapid emergence of banks under the control of major industrial
milies, an institutional innovation that appears quite consistent
th Gerschenkron's argument, considerable disagreement remains
ɛr the contribution made by *zaibatsu* banks to the early develop-
ent of manufacturing firms. Yamamura (1978) argues that during
ɛ initial phase of Japanese industrialization, lasting from the 1860s
the 1880s, organized banks played little if any role in financing
rporate development.[37] The limited role of external finance also may
ɪve reflected the fact that industrial development during this period
cused largely on textiles, an industry with modest capital require-
ents.

The period from the 1880s to the First World War saw the
organization of the growing *zaibatsu* on a holding company basis
ɪd the expansion of lending activities by the *zaibatsu* banks.
lthough loans and purchases of equity shares in affiliated industrial
rms by the *zaibatsu* banks expanded during this period, Yamamura
ɪisagreeing with Patrick, 1968), argues that

> . . . contrary to the long-maintained proposition that the banks, especial-
> ly the large ones, were a dominant factor in providing industrial capital,
> a close examination of the data seems to reveal that the importance of
> large banks as owners of individual shares and as individual financiers
> during this period has been significantly overstated.
>
> (1978: p. 240)

ɪnly during the 1920s and 1930s, when with strong government
ɪncouragement the *zaibatsu* and other enterprises embarked on
ɪrge-scale investments in capital-intensive sectors such as steel,
lectrical machinery, chemicals and ordnance, according to Yama-
ɪura, did the *zaibatsu* banks become major lenders of long-term funds
ɔ Japanese firms, especially to firms not affiliated with *zaibatsu*.[38]
'he *zaibatsu* of this period closely resembled the French holding
ɔmpanies, combining extensive cross-corporate equity holdings with
ɔntinued owner control. In contrast to the French case, however, in
apan this structure was associated with rapid growth and structural
hange.

The development of Japanese corporate and financial institutions
ɔntradict several of Gerschenkron's arguments (keeping in mind that
ɪerschenkron did not originally apply his schema to Japan). The
ɪapanese financial system does not appear to have been a major
ɪnfluence on the early phases of corporate development and
ɪndustrialization. The initial stages of Japanese industrialization were
ɪentered on the growth of labor-, rather than highly capital-intensive

sectors (contradicting another of Gerschenkron's arguments). '1 firms engaged in manufacturing at this time do not appear to h; relied heavily on external sources for their capital.

Three other aspects of Japanese corporate evolution deserve b; mention. As in France and Germany, the absence of a mass mar. for "modern" consumer products largely prevented the developmen; large, multifunction firms in consumer goods that combined prod; tion and distribution. This reflected conditions of demand as well the highly developed domestic distribution system.[39] The developm of advanced industrial and financial firms also did not result in 1 loss of significant control by the founding owner families – fam control of the *zaibatsu* remained strong until 1945. Finally, and ag; in some contrast with the situation in other industrial economies this time, Japanese manufacturing retained a dualistic struct; within even its relatively capital-intensive sectors:

> If all establishments of less than 100 operatives are considered together we find that plants of this size contributed 45 to 50% of the gross output of Japanese manufacturing in 1934. Of the total amount of gainful employment in industry, they accounted for not less than 65% and probably more. This is a conservative estimate which allows for a large amount of part-time employment in small-scale industry. It may be contrasted with the corresponding figure for the United States. Here only 29% of all manufacturing wage earners were employed in plants of 100 workers or less in 1935.
>
> (Lockwood, 1968: p. 205)[40]

In Japan, as in other industrial economies, the national financi system can explain some but by no means all aspects of the corpora and industrial structure that developed during the first half of th century.

Conclusion: Some Conceptual Issues

In the introductory section of this chapter, two broad issues wei singled out for discussion: (a) the relationship between intern; corporate organization and corporate performance; and (b) the rel; tionship between a national financial system and the structure of th firms affected by it. This historical survey yields a clear answer 1 neither of these issues. In this section, I discuss the evidence an suggest some reasons for the uncertain verdicts.

Linkages between corporate structure and firm performance appe; to be very clear in the comparison of British and US corporat structure and industrial research. Nevertheless, it is dangerous even in this comparison to single out corporate structure as central to the exclusion of others – other factors, including public policies in antitrust, financial regulation, and education, were of great importance.

This issue becomes even cloudier when one considers the limited historical evidence from Japan, Germany, and France. Holding-company structures (the prewar *zaibatsu* and postwar *keiretsu*) that in Japan are associated with rapid economic growth and industrial development are cited in analyses of French economic development as impediments. Moreover, contemporary paeans to the virtues of "network" and "post-modern" corporate organization that emphasize the value of equity participations and various forms of joint ventures and alliances in domestic and international markets also seem to recommend a form of holding company structure, rather than a vertically integrated corporation or the conglomerate structure, as the preferred form.

Uncertainty concerning the relationship between internal firm structure and performance reflects the lack of a solid theoretical basis to favor impersonal capital markets over more complex, "hybrid" relationships for resource allocation. Chandler suggests that intrafirm mechanisms proved to be more efficient than market institutions as allocative mechanisms for long-term investment and the strategic development of the firm, and as structures for the coordination of complex transactions. In this view, the efficiency advantages of modern corporate organization (advantages that have rarely been empirically documented in detail) had both static and dynamic dimensions. It is equally possible, however, that static and dynamic efficiency clashed in truly Schumpeterian terms in the development of the modern, multifunction firm. For example, the restructuring of corporate organization in the US was accompanied by significant reductions in interfirm competition and increases in market power, which made little if any contribution to static allocative efficiency.

In his most recent work (1990), Chandler raises trenchant criticisms of the performance of US managers in the 1960s and 1970s, the architects of highly diversified conglomerate firms. However valid these criticisms, they do not explain how the "selection environment" that promoted the development of putatively efficient, multifunction firms changed. Why did the quality of management decision-making decline? The discussion of the advantages of intrafirm mechanisms for the allocation of capital in Chandler or in other studies of multidivisional and conglomerate firms,[41] rarely specify limits to the superiority of intrafirm control. Yet such limits clearly exist.[42] The

disappointing performance of many conglomerate mergers of th
1960s and 1970s (see Ravenscraft and Scherer, 1987), for example
has increased interest in dismantling these putatively omniscien
decision-making units.[43]

Managerial sentiment on the relative merits of intrafirm and
market-based mechanisms for allocation appears to have shifted
heavily in favor of the latter, with little clear assessment by scholars
or practitioners of the specific factors influencing the merits of visible
or invisible hands. The revival of faith in the power of external capita
markets to optimally allocate funds across sectors and across time ir
mature industries and firms is coupled with growing concern over the
impact of the efficient US capital market on the growth of high
technology firms.[44] The venture capital market and other institutions
previously hailed by some scholars for spawning innovative firms and
new industries now are criticized by others for their myopia and
insufficient support for technology development over the long run.

Ceteris paribus, beyond some number of units or level of
"cospecialization" or "technological relatedness," intrafirm allocation
decisions may be inferior to those of the market. Nevertheless, in the
British economy of the early twentieth century, the size and degree of
diversification of many firms apparently were below thresholds that
were necessary for more dynamic growth and development. German
and American firms in some industries, however, were of sufficient
size to exploit these strengths. Where does the threshold lie? The lack
of answers to this question reflects the paucity of theoretical or
empirical analysis of the boundaries or internal structure of the firm,
as well as the likelihood that this threshold varies across industries
and over time.

As this summary of the debate suggests, the study of the internal
structure of the firm and the relationship of this structure to the
firm's behavior and performance remains in its infancy. There are
surprisingly few strong empirical results. Empirical analysis of one
important dimension of firm behavior, product-line R & D investment data, suggests that measures of firm structure explain little if
any cross-sectional variance (Cohen and Mowery, 1989). Industry-
specific fixed effects remain as important as firm-specific fixed effects
in explaining R & D investment behavior, and both sets of "naive"
measures outperform measures of corporate structure. This empirical
indeterminacy also has undercut recent efforts to detect some relationship between corporate takeover activity in the United States and
corporate R & D investment – so far, there is disagreement on
whether these effects are positive or negative (see Hall, 1988; Gorte,
1989); Lichtenberg and Siegel, 1989).

Turning to the second issue, the relationship between national
financial systems and corporate evolution, it is useful to distinguish
between the influence of the financial system on the establishment of
new firms and industries and the influence of the system on the
day-to-day governance of corporate enterprises. Tilly (1986) argues
that financial institutions can contribute to the mobilization of capital
or the finance of investment in new, and therefore relatively risky,
technologies in two ways: (a) financial institutions can improve
information available to investors about asset quality; and (b) financial institutions may be able to diversify and hedge against risk more
efficiently than individuals and accommodate the needs of risk-loving
entrepreneurs and the preferences of risk-averse investors.
Gerschenkron's discussion implicitly allows for these functions of the
financial system, but his analysis emphasizes the sheer size of the
capital requirements of late industrialization in explaining the important role of financial intermediaries. For Chandler, the financial
system plays a strictly secondary role in the development of corporate
structure, relative to those of technological change or national market
structure. Chandler does acknowledge an important role for financial
institutions in the development of the governance of the modern
corporation. The early involvement of financial institutions and
external finance in the organization and foundation of the firm,
according to Chandler, hastened the replacement of owner-managers
by professional managers and diversified and diffused corporate
control. The organizational structure that resulted from these changes
in turn transformed many aspects of the innovation process in
capitalist economies through its expanding investment in industrial
research and development. Still another role for national financial
systems, broadly defined, is hypothesized in the discussion by Dosi *et
al.* (1991) of financial factors in the "selection environment" of firms.
This influence on corporate development, however, may be as much a
result of industry-specific factors (free cash flow), as it is national in
origins and scope.

The historical evidence concerning the influence of financial institutions on corporate structure is as indeterminate as that on corporate
structure and performance. Comparison of Great Britain, the United
States, and Germany seems to suggest a strong causal relationship
between the financial system and corporate organization. The cases of
Japan and France, however, where industrial firms exerted a fairly
significant influence on the development of financial institutions, are
less supportive of this argument. Moreover, as was noted above, the
historical analyses of the relationship between the financial system
and corporate evolution consider only a fairly narrow range of

manufacturing industries. If one is concerned with the determinants of international differences in overall industrial structure, other variables, such as the structure of consumer demand and the state of development of domestic distribution and marketing systems, must be brought into the picture. There are few theoretical reasons to expect a nation's financial system to be an exogenous influence on corporate structure. Both institutional structures are jointly determined outcomes of a complex set of environmental influences, in which industry-specific conditions will figure prominently.

Discussion of the financial system's influence on corporate development also poses the Schumpeterian tradeoff quite clearly. Consistent with the spirit of Gerschenkron's analysis, a number of scholars have suggested that short-term allocative efficiency in the financial markets of early industrializers impaired the long-run dynamic efficiency of these institutions. British banks did not lend long-term funds to industry and did not engage in the underwriting of securities issues on the London market. Although the short-term allocative efficiency of the British financial system in the early twentieth century appears to have been high (regional interest differentials were smaller than those of the United States or Germany),[45] the system was far less effective in mobilizing capital for riskier investments with a more distant payoff.[46]

The inability of British industrial securities markets to convey sufficient information about the quality of their securities meant that domestic firms in such industries as automobiles, chemicals, or electrical machinery were not able to rely on the securities markets in the early twentieth century. In the "late industrializers," however (a group including Germany, Japan, and the United States), institutions developed that were able to provide the credible information on the quality of securities that was needed for capital to be mobilized through this channel for investment in emergent industries.[47] In Germany and Japan, close involvement of bankers with industrial borrowers lowered the risks and agency costs associated with long-term lending. As in the evaluation of corporate organization, however, we lack measures of efficiency or of agency costs that would lend specificity and concreteness to this analysis.

Despite the critical tone of this discussion, the concept of "relative backwardness," which underpins both Gerschenkron and Chandler, assuredly remains an important concept for comparative .historical analysis. One can distinguish at least three analyses of the effects of backwardness. For Gerschenkron, relative backwardness affected institutional development in latecomer economies converging on "industrialization," a state that presumably was identical for both

1eers and latecomers. In positing a common endpoint, schenkron shared some of the assumptions of the hypothesis that industrializing societies go through an identical sequence of stages.

)ther recent analysis of the role of backwardness in postwar nomic growth (Abramovitz, 1986) devotes little attention to institu-1al innovation, but examines the influence of backwardness on the ·e with which latecomers "catch up" with leaders, as well as the dual exhaustion of the potential for rapid growth within the ·comer group. Both of these analyses appear to assume that the 1tier that latecomers are approaching and that pioneers are upying remains relatively fixed.

'omparison of these five industrial economies during 1900–50, as 1 as the experience of Japan during the later postwar period, 'gests yet another role for relative backwardness. Institutional ovation, especially when combined with changes in a (loosely ined) technological opportunity set, can fundamentally alter the jectory of development of the latecomers. That is, backwardness y not simply enable latecomers to catch up quickly with the neers, but may facilitate their overtaking the pioneers, through rning from the leaders, institutional innovation, the exploitation of v technologies, and investment in more rapidly growing sectors. e experiences of the US and Germany, compared with that of Great tain, during the pre-1950 period[48] seem to resemble such a process, 1 this broad framework describes some elements of Japan's rapid ·rtaking of the United States during the post-1945 period (see senberg and Steinmueller, 1988; Mowery and Rosenberg, 1989).

)espite the extensive attention devoted to the topic, empirical and ·oretical analysis of the contributions of economic backwardness to ·nomic growth, as well as the analysis of the process of "catchup," nains fruitful. Separating the contribution of backwardness from ·se of other sources of growth, however, will remain a very difficult alytic and empirical challenge. Moreover, the analysis of the eraction between the environment and the structure of the institu-ns that play central roles in economic change requires additional ·oretical and empirical work on the economics of institutional velopment.

·tes

·eparation of this chapter was supported by the Alfred P. Sloan and Sasakawa Peace indations, and by the Technology and Economic Growth program of the Center for ·nomic Policy Research at Stanford University.

[2] David (1975) and Arthur (1988) discuss path-dependent models of technolog change; Dosi (1988c) has a useful survey of this broad body of work. This chap argues that a portion of the observed path-dependence of a given economy's devel ment may reflect its institutional structure, as well as the vicissitudes of technolog change.

[3] " ... the new mass producers became modern enterprises only when they integra forward by creating their own extensive organizations for sales and distributi (Chandler, 1980a: p. 23).

[4] " ... because these enterprises successfully combined the advantages of h throughput and high stock turn, they were self-financed. The cash flow generated fr the high-volume output and sales provided ample funds for both working and fi: capital, so these pioneering firms rarely went to capital markets for funds. Wl supplementary funds were needed, they obtained them through short-term loans fi local commercial banks. As a result, the ownership of these firms remained in the hai of the founder, a few close associates, and their families" (Chandler, 1978: p. 1(Chandler's historical argument is broadly consistent with the analysis of the "select environment" that influences firm development in Dosi et al. (1990): "The availability free cash flows is perhaps the key regulator of selection. If a firm or business generating sufficient cash flow to sustain itself and take care of reinvestment needs a opportunities, it will typically be able to survive. If it does not, then it will ne additional debt or equity financing. To obtain funding of either kind exposes the firm capital market discipline that might not otherwise intervene" (p. 16).

[5] See Stigler (1968). The Supreme Court ruled in the *Trans Missouri Association* ca in 1898 and the *Addyston Pipe* case in 1899 that the Sherman Act outlawed agreements among firms on prices or market sharing. Data in Thorelli (1954) a Lamoreaux (1985) indicate a sharp increase in merger activity between the 1895–8 a 1899–1902 periods. Although the Sherman Act may have motivated many horizon mergers during this period, Chandler argues that the ultimate success or failure of t mergers depended on the underlying technological and other determinants of t competitiveness of the resulting firms: "Although the Sherman Anti-trust Act had be passed in 1890, it clearly had little impact on the outcome of the nation's first gro merger movement. Technology and marketing, not legal constraints, were the criti factors in determining the size of firms and the structure of industries" (1978: p. 11)

[6] "The merged enterprise, for example, was unable to rely on current cash flow finance its activity . . .. Moreover, the merger itself often required outside fun particularly if some of the firms joining a consolidation insisted on cash as well securities in exchange for their stock. So the mergers of the 1890s led industr enterprises for the very first time to rely on Wall Street and other capital markets funds. By the First World War industrial securities had become almost as acceptable investment portfolios as those of railroads and governments.

"One result of such financing was that investment bankers began to sit on the boa of the new industrial corporations. Of more importance, the stock ownership – alrea dispersed through the process of merger – became even more widely scattered . . .. these merged enterprises ownership became separated from management from alm the very beginning" (Chandler, 1978, p. 112).

[7] "The separation of operational decisions from the strategic capital decisions w realized in the early decades of the twentieth century. This organizational change w only the beginning of the complete professionalization of capital management; whi has found its extreme application in the conglomerate movement in the 1960s. Wh was then the effect on the economic and financial efficiency of investment strategy? It a fascinating question which only can be tentatively answered with Oliver Williamso challenging hypothesis. The multidivisional and conglomerate firms have provid management with an efficient tool to plan and carry out investment. This organiz tional form is, in fact, a mini capital market. Cash flows and retained earnings are r earmarked anymore but can flow to the division with the best economic outlook for t future. This is an important innovation within the capitalistic system. The declini marginal productivity of capital caused by the continuous ploughback of earnings in t

e activity, is circumvented in the divisional and conglomerate structure, where
eral opportunities compete for retained earnings" (Chandler and Daems, 1974: pp.
2). The recent performance of highly diversified firms has led a number of
ctitioners and some scholars (including Chandler, 1990) to suggest that there exist
ortant limits to the effectiveness of the intrafirm capital market; see below for
itional discussion.

handler's most recent work (1990) provides a comparative analysis of the evolution
orporate structure in the US, Germany, and Great Britain.

he modern vertically integrated industrial concern could not obtain the necessary
ding from the banking sector. Federal and state regulation inhibited the ability of
ks to first grow in size with industry and continue provision of short-term loans and
ondly to fund long-term investment by buying stocks. Consequently, investment
ks helped corporations issue bonds and stocks that were sold primarily to the public
other financial intermediaries" (White: p. 166 this volume).

. . . as the knowledge and experience of the full-time managers on the board
reased and as the new enterprise succeeded in financing its current operations and
g-term growth primarily from retained earnings, the influence of the financiers
ned. Only in the industries having the largest capital requirements (the
ctrical-equipment industry is a notable example) did the leading enterprises retain
with the bankers who had provided funds in their earlier years, so that
resentatives of the banks continued to sit as outside directors on their boards"
andler, 1990: pp. 81–2).

Although Orsenigo (1989) and others argue that its "market-oriented" financial
tem, in which equity finance, rather than bank lending, is prominent, was a very
ortant factor in the emergence of new, relatively small firms as important agents in
commercialization of biotechnology and microelectronics in the postwar US
nomy. The "startup firm" appears to have been far less significant in the pre-1940
economy, however, despite the fact that equity finance loomed large in this period.
contrast between the two periods suggests that other factors, such as public R &
nvestment, new forms of financial intermediation (venture capital), and antitrust
cy (Mowery and Rosenberg, 1990) were of greater importance in the postwar
minence of the US startup firm than a static comparison across postwar industrial
nomies would suggest.

A similar argument is made by Dosi et al. (1988), who argue that ". . . markets
not deliver information about or discount the possibility of future states of the world
ose occurrences are themselves externalities resulting from the present decisions of
aviorally unrelated agents. Under such circumstances there may be trade-offs
ween Ricardian [static] and Schumpeterian efficiency" (p. 23).

Comparing the industrial composition of the 200 largest firms in the US and British
nomies in 1919 and 1930, Hannah found fewer British firms within this class
gaged in the manufacture of nonelectrical machinery, far more British firms among
top 200 located in the food and allied products sector, and a larger number of British
ns located in textiles. Interestingly, the primary metals, electrical machinery, and
micals industries were equally well represented in the British and US lists of the
largest firms (Hannah, 1980). The contrasts between a classification of the largest
tish firms in 1905 and the largest US enterprises in 1909, however, are greater,
ording to Kocka (1980): "In 1905, most of the largest British firms produced
sumer goods, especially textiles and food, while firms in the so-called new industries
hemicals, electrical and other machinery and transportation equipment – were not
so well represented" (p. 99).

The economies of speed gained across the Atlantic by the visible hand of the
nager were often readily available in Britain through the 'invisible hand' of the
rket. Markets work well where the costs of information and transactions are low,
these are likely to be lowest in the kind of compact, industrialized urban region in
ich most British industries were located . . . markets could offer advantages that
weighed the rival benefits of internal organization – primarily economies of scale
efficient scheduling of flows – at least in the short run. When tested by competition

in the British context, the invisible hand was often apparently superior to the visit hand of the managerial firm" (Hannah, 1980: pp. 63–4).

[15] Hannah (1980) corroborates this conclusion, noting that "The separation of ow ership and control, for instance, had not progressed far enough to displace founding family directors from company boards; 110 of the 200 largest firms in 1919, or ! percent, had family board members, as did 140, or 70 percent, in 1930, and 119, or 59 percent, in 1948" (p. 53). Hannah attributed continued family dominance to ". . . tl highly developed but diverse [British] capital market. No real equivalent existed Great Britain, at least before the 1930s, of the investment bankers of the United Stat or the industrial banks of Germany, which controlled new capital for transportation a industrial enterprises" (p. 55).

[16] See Hannah (1974b): p. 10.

[17] See Salter and Weinhold (1980): p. 4.

[18] ". . . the large industrial enterprises in Britain at the end of the First World W; were either integrated, centrally administered entrepreneurial companies or feder tions of family (or entrepreneurial) enterprises which were legally but not administr tively combined within a holding company. As a result there were very few lar central offices manned by professional managers and served by extensive staffs. At tl top, owners managed and managers owned . . . the organisational framework did n exist in the UK, as it did in the US, in which to develop the new techniques of mode management" (Chandler: 1976, p. 40).

[19] See Payne (1967); Hannah (1974a) and Chandler (1980b).

[20] See Hannah (1976c): pp. 117, 167.

[21] Hannah (1980) states that "in important respects – particularly in coordinating sal policies and securing monopolistic control over prices – cartels were an alternative merger that was open to European entrepreneurs but closed to their counterparts in tl United States. Firms that preferred to maintain a single-unit structure in Britain we therefore free to do so while, at the same time, reducing competition by joining a cart in the 1930s and during World War II, in fact, these arrangements were active encouraged by the government. United States industrialists like Gerald [sic] Swope, tl dynamic president of the American General Electric Company, accustomed to tl antitrust tradition, were advised by bankers in Britain that they need not create larg centralized corporations through mergers for their European operations; mark competition could be regulated through agreement with other firms, and there was th no need to acquire them" (p. 67). Macrosty (1907) and Lucas (1937), among other provide detailed accounts of price and output agreements among firms in a wide ran; of industries.

[22] Reader (1979) notes that "it was settled policy in ICI (Imperial Chemical Industrie to avoid competition with customers or suppliers which meant, in effect, avoidir competition with virtually every manufacturing company of any importance in tl United Kingdom. For many years, accordingly, ICI kept clear of the range of chemic products associated with industrial alcohol, which were supplied by the Distiller Company Ltd. and which were of considerable importance in the fields of organ activity opening up in the late 1920s and early 1930s. Similarly, in order to avoid givir offence to Courtaulds, important customers for caustic soda, ICI, unlike Du Pont, ke well clear of rayon and cellophane" (p. 174). Chandler (1990) also argues for th important role of British antitrust policy.

[23] In 1933, 116 of the firms in a sample of 160 US firms listed among the 200 large manufacturing firms had R & D laboratories; in 1936 only 20 of the 200 large; British firms had such facilities. The contrast for the postwar period is similar] dramatic – 164 of the 200 largest US manufacturing firms in 1948 had researc laboratories, and 40 of the top 200 British firms had in-house R & D facilities as 1946. The data on US firms are taken from the National Research Council surveys industrial research and the tabulations of the 200 largest firms compiled by Profess Alfred Chandler. The British R & D and firm data are drawn from Chandler's u published tabulations and Andrade (1946).

[24] ". . . financing from sources that had supplied funds in the past was now less readi

able . . . inflation during and after the war wiped out past savings and prevented funds from being accumulated in the capital market and in the banking system Given the imbalance between the need for and the availability of funds, industrial s had to devise practical solutions for their credit requirements" (Levy-Leboyer, : p. 143). Kindleberger's survey contains a similar assessment of the late 1920s: *facto* stabilization of the franc in 1926, however, touched off a five-year recovery •d, but one in which a heavy reflow of capital enlarged the money supply, rendered Bank of France liquid, and with substantial profits left the banks concerned with •rnment bonds and foreign exchange but with little activity in lending to industry" dleberger, 1987: p. 23).

•e development of Japanese corporate and financial institutions during this period below) also displays some interesting similarities with the French case.

aint-Gobain therefore tended to act as a holding company with 45 percent of its s revenues derived from its own industrial activities, 25 percent from its idiaries, and 30 percent from purely financial operations. Nor was this a unique many companies' accounts show the same shift in resources from their own ities to those of subsidiaries" (Levy-Leboyer, 1980: p. 147).

gnificantly, by this date André Citroën had already forced off his board of directors representatives of the banks and steel companies that he had appointed, under sure, in 1927 (see Levy-Leboyer, 1980).

imilarities between the development of the modern corporation in Germany and its ation in the United States are striking . . . the distribution of the largest ufacturing firms among industrial groups was similar in Germany in 1907 and the ed States in 1909. In both cases, the large firms clustered in capital-intensive, nologically advanced industries, especially those producing iron, steel, and other ds, on the one hand, and machinery, instruments, and transportation equipment on •ther" (Kocka, 1980: p. 99). As was noted earlier, these patterns contrasted with the •strial composition of the largest British firms at this time.

n 1907 only five of the 100 largest firms remained undiversified; twenty years er there had been 14 such firms among the 100 largest" (Kocka, 1980: p. 80).

•cording to Tilly (1974), "Between 1895 and 1908, German joint-stock companies unted for 43, and industrial companies for 31 percent of all new issues in the Berlin : exchange, while in England at about the same time joint-stock shares accounted ome 22 per cent of total new stock exchange flotations" (p. 162). Kocka (1978) es that "it was the establishment of the joint-stock company which offered the •s the means of influencing industrial enterprises. The issue of shares and bonds normally done with the help of the banks; it was the joint-stock companies which gave a certain clarity to the published accounts of an industrial enterprise and thus itated the financial engagement of outside investors. But above all, the joint-stock oany brought to the industrial concern an internal structure which allowed the •s (which also were organized in this form) to exercise a direct influence on its rs" (p. 566).

lly (p. 80, this volume) cites data from Goldsmith (1985) in noting the significantly ller share of nongovernment securities in the German national financial asset folio, by comparison with France, Belgium and the US, and suggests that this lower of "securitization" of finance in Germany reflected the lending activities of the nan credit banks.

lly (1982) has noted that the prominent role of the credit banks in German orate development was not associated with merger activity on a scale comparable to in the US or even Great Britain during the late nineteenth century. In his view, ively liberal state incorporation laws in the US facilitated such merger activity, an rvation that once again underlines the difficulties of establishing a tight cause-and-t linkage between financial systems and corporate evolution.

lly's observation appears to conflict with Kocka's argument (1980) that reliance by nan firms on external financing declined in importance through the early twentieth ury.

eyer-Thurow (1982) argues that industrial research in the chemicals industry had effects on barriers to entry and corporate stability that were similar to the effects t industrial research appears to have had in the United States at a later date: "One of indirect effects of industrial research was to make it harder for a new firm to enter field. No new dyestuffs firms were successfully founded between the mid-1880s ₴ 1914; the corporations already dominating the dyestuff business in the early 188 before industrial research made headway, were still in the top rank in 1914" (p. 38)

[35] See Riesser (1911). Kindleberger (1987) argues that "...Thyssen and Stin pursued policies of friendly relations with a number of banks, without wedd themselves to any one, and the chemicals industry made large profits for years whicl plowed back so that banks had little influence with those companies" (p. 9).

[36] "New and medium-sized enterprises, of the kind with which one might associ innovation, could not expect to obtain ready access to such secondary markets and th depended on ready credit. To the extent that innovation, risk, and newness (and size enterprise are linked, and insofar as new issues on the Berlin capital market indic the nature of the credit banks' business, the latter was not primarily risk ₴ innovation-oriented" (1986, p. 148).

[37] "The bankers, still groping for the fundamentals of sound modern banking practi in the new industrial age, were not yet ready to participate in industrial financing. examination of bank records and recent empirical studies conducted by Japan scholars make it clear that most bank funds tended to flow to agriculture ₴ commerce" (p. 239).

[38] "During the third period, the inter-war years, we find that the ownership and cont of Japanese industrial firms underwent significant changes. Most notable among th is the rapid rise of the financial control of, and increased ownership of, industrial fir by the *zaibatsu* banks. Concentration of product and capital markets continued a rapid pace, and mutual shareholding and interlocking directorships continued increase. It also was during this period that nearly a dozen holding companies, b large and small, appeared.

"The First World War, which made Japan a fully fledged industrial power, profoun changed banking practices. The larger banks, which were beginning to be cal *zaibatsu* banks, began to advance significant sums in long-term loans to industrial fir in such capital-using industries as the heavy, chemical, and utility industries. M importantly, these new recipients of long-term bank loans were not, as earlier, a sn number of firms which had close *zaibatsu* connections, either having been establisl partly by *zaibatsu* capital (such as the Oji Paper Company) or being one of the *zaiba* industrial ventures developed from plants bought by the *zaibatsu* interests from Meiji government at the beginning of the 1880s. One could say that the *zaibatsu* ba became, during the 1920s, investment banks of the German type" (Yamamura, 1978 244).

[39] "During the two and a half centuries when Tokugawa Japan was closed foreigners, the Japanese people created and refined unique tastes for their consumpt goods and also developed a highly complicated market organization, composed of tra of middlemen between producers and consumers. Furthermore people in modern Jap continued to live, eat and wear [*sic*] in traditional modes. Their houses, foods ₴ clothes were still supplied by traditional carpenters, peasants, fishermen and handlo weavers. This ingrained taste and established market organization turned in mode Japan to be the greatest barrier for the development of mass-production ₴ mass-marketing in consumer goods industries, and were also primarily responsible the fact that in Japan the pioneering firms in consumer goods industries could ₪ develop along the American line of vertical integration of successive product processes and of manufacturing, marketing and purchasing" (Nakagawa, 1974: p. 20)

[40] According to Lockwood, this pattern was not greatly altered by the forced-dr industrialization for wartime of the 1930s and 1940s: "In Japan, as elsewhere, ₪ exigencies of war conferred advantages on the large enterprise. Significantly, howev small- and medium-size factories tended on the whole to maintain their relative posit through the thirties, clustering as subsidiary establishments around the great ar plants" (p. 203).

'The capital market in an environment of U-form firms was earlier regarded as a less
n efficacious surveillance and correction mechanism for three reasons: its external
ation to the firm places it at a serious information disadvantage; it is restricted to
**marginal adjustments; it experiences nontrivial displacement costs. The general
ce of the M-form organization has superior properties in each of these respects. First,
s an internal rather than external control mechanism with the constitutional
hority and expertise to make detailed evaluations of the performance of each of its
rating parts. Second, it can make fine-tuning as well as discrete adjustments. This
mits it both to intervene early in a selective, preventative way (a capability which
capital market lacks altogether), as well as to perform *ex post* corrective
ustments, in response to evidence of performance failure, with a surgical precision
t the capital market lacks (the scalpel versus the ax is an appropriate analogy).
ally, the costs of intervention by the general office are relatively low. Altogether,
refore, a profit-oriented general office in an M-form enterprise might be expected to
ure superior performance to that which the unassisted capital market can enforce.
e M-form organization might thus be viewed as capitalism's creative response to the
dent limits which the capital market experiences in its relations to the firm . . ."
illiamson, 1975: pp. 158–9). Compare this assessment with Rumelt's recent skeptic-
concerning internal capital markets: "Given mobility, the [middle] manager must
per his view of how a project's future influences his reputation or income with the
sibility that he will no longer be in the organization. The net effect is that mobile
nagers will discount future cash flows more heavily than would be indicated by their
sonal discount rates on wealth or their employer's cost of capital. Given the fact that
management must choose among the projects that are actually proposed, the
poration as a whole will appear more myopic than are its members" (Rumelt, 1988:
153–4).

osi *et al.* (1990) propose that technological "competences" and interrelatedness are
criteria for defining the limits of corporate "coherence," but these criteria are
icult to define or measure *ex ante.*

'However important it may have been in practice, the internal capital market
ory of merger motives is subject to some serious limitations. If the units acquired to
orb excess cash are managed poorly, the hoped-for capital gains will not materialize.
o, internal capital markets are often highly politicized, and it is not clear that they
ceed better than 'arms length' markets in generating the information and incentives
ded to allocate funds into their most profitable uses" (Ravenscraft and Scherer,
37: p. 214). A recent journalistic account of corporate restructuring echoes this
olarly assessment: "Only 20 years ago senior managers spent their time building
glomerates through acquisition . . . . Companies became trapped in the worst of all
rlds. Some 7 out of 10 acquisitions turned out poorly. Management often failed to run
liverse group of companies well. [Union] Carbide's [Robert D.] Kennedy [CEO]
misses the whole concept: 'All that stuff about balancing the cash generators and the
h users sounds great on paper. But it never worked. When corporate management
s into the business of allocating resources between businesses crying out for cash, it
kes mistakes.' The investment community, he says, is 'a better sorter-outer'"
siness Week, 11.7.88: p. 142).

ee Ferguson (1983, 1988); Reich and Mankin (1986); Borrus (1988); White House
ence Council (1988); Florida and Kenney (1988); *Business Week*, 6.26.89.

". . . throughout the nineteenth century significant regional differences in interest
es on short-term commercial paper and mortgages, let alone on more risky assets,
sted in the US. Although a national short-term commercial paper market had begun
appear by 1900, differentials on mortgages narrowed more slowly. The economic
velopment of the southern part of the US, favoured by climate and resources, was
bably greatly retarded by capital market imperfections. Similar differentials
eared in Germany. Because the Great Banks 'did not care for that class of business'
resented by local deposit banking and the extension of commercial credit to small
ders, historians have argued that serious misallocation of resources occurred in
perial Germany. In contrast, these marked regional and, to some extent, sectoral

differences in interest rates on mortgages and short-term commercial credit appe have been largely eradicated in Britain no later than the 1860s" (Kennedy, 1976 157–8).

[46] "To understand the role of finance in industrial development, we must disting between financial *intermediation* via capital markets and financial *integratio* accommodate long-run planning by capitalist firms. From the market-oriented per: tive of neoclassical economic theory, the higher the degree of financial liquidity closer we are to social optimality. When we bring long-run investment planning int picture, however, we must ask to what extent the operation of the capital mark compatible with the needs of industry" (Best and Humphries, 1986: p. 223).

[47] "A classic problem of the second best appears to have operated in Britain before 1 A part, but only a part, of her set of capital markets operated better than anyone e Had Americans or Germans had the facilities to obtain such high yields with such risks as did Englishmen, perhaps they too would have taken fewer of the risks w their own capital markets forced upon them. But the Americans and Germans did have the facilities and they did bear, collectively, the risks associated with 1 nineteenth century technical change. As a consequence their growth rates 1 substantially higher than Britain's as their level of per capital wealth surpasse rapidly approached that of Britain" (Kennedy, 1976: p. 174)

[48] David's work on biased technical change in the nineteenth-century US econ (1975: Chapter 1) illustrates one important difference between the US and G Britain in their trajectories of development that was driven by the interactio differences in labor and natural resource endowments with technological evolution

CHAPTER 5

Historical Patterns of Finance in Great Britain: A Long-Run View

WILLIAM P. KENNEDY[1]

Introduction

This chapter seeks to present an historical overview of the evolving nature of enterprise finance in Britain. This subject is timely, for although enterprise finance has long attracted much attention in British economic history, its importance is even greater than is often appreciated. Long, inconclusive debates over the adequacy of British entrepreneurs (Aldcroft, 1964; Wiener, 1981); over the adequacy of British education and managerial recruitment (Barnett, 1986; Pollard, 1989); and over the adequacy of Britain's patterns of industrial organization (Elbaum and Lazonick, 1986) – to cite only a few – have gravely suffered because participants have failed to recognize in each of these instances the pivotal role played, for better or for worse, by the adequacy of the financial system.

Today it is commonplace in Britain to expect that incompetent managers (or managers even suspected of incompetency) will face hostile takeover bids for the companies they blight. Quarrelsome octogenarians are no longer left in the unbroken peace they enjoyed as late as the 1930s to preside over ruin (Tolliday, 1986: pp. 86–8). The crucial questions do not now concern whether takeover bids will occur, but when, and with what effect. The issue is decided in financial markets. Poorly trained and unqualified managers pursuing inappropriate R & D policies are now similarly exposed to external discipline through the financial system, while those pursuing superior R & D policies are rewarded. Again, the extent to which this desirable outcome occurs is routinely seen as reflecting the adequacy of the financial system. Industries characterized by too many small firms, each operating inefficiently, are likely to be swept by merger waves fuelled by share dealing and frenzied financial activity, while industries dominated by large, inefficient firms are likely to be subject to "restructuring" in one guise or another. The pace at which merge and restructuring occur, and the adequacy of the organization structures that result, are again properly seen as tests of the financ system, as are the terms on which new initiatives can secure suppo

Indeed, the importance of the financial system derives from its ve pervasiveness. The way in which productive assets are priced affec virtually every important decision – capital and labor allocation consumption and investment plans, the choice of production tec nique, the distribution of economic power. The numbers generated financial markets constitute the signals that necessarily guide mark economies. This pervasiveness means that the adequacy with whi the financial system functions determines in large measure over; economic performance. Unfortunately historians, to the detriment their discourse, have only slowly come to comprehend this, ofte focusing instead on secondary phenomena while the more influent; causal mechanisms centered on the financial system are neglecte This is not to claim that the operations of the financial syste determine everything by themselves. Educational traditions an government policies, to note only the most obvious additional facto; are essential elements of the environment in which financial syster operate and which influence financial operations as well as bei; influenced by them. Nevertheless, to the extent financial syster reflect the underlying fundamentals of the economies that suppo them – mirroring individual preferences (including preferences f leisure and intensity of work) and available technology – education traditions and government policies are exposed to strong, frequent decisive, pressures.

It is not sheer ignorance or willfulness alone, however, that h caused historians only slowly to recognize the centrality of financi systems. The intellectual tools needed to assess in detail the adequa and importance of such systems have emerged in operational for only within the last 25 years. In the absence of these tools historic research (and much practical work) lacked focus, being guided mo by erratic intuition than by (somewhat less fallible) systema; thought. Moreover, the first phase of the development of these too produced a persuasive, comforting message: competitive capital ma kets were efficient, as economists understand that term. This fir development phase, which might be illustrated by the work of Euge; Fama (1970, 1976), was persuasive because it took little effort to se as the model predicted, that no simple, obvious unexploited (leg; arbitrage opportunities existed in competitive financial markets. T message was comforting because little more was necessary for t;

icient regulation of financial systems than to ensure the mainte-
nce of competition.

Subsequently, however, the development of the study of financial
stems, building on the undeniable achievements of the first phase,
s become skeptical and increasingly pessimistic about the "effici-
cy" delivered by ostensibly competitive capital markets. For example,
pers by Schiller (1981) and Roll (1984) found evidence of price
latility, even in financial markets with many well-informed traders,
at was difficult if not impossible to explain on grounds other than
ndamental (but unspecified) market weaknesses. In a massive
oss-section study, William C. Brainard *et al.* (1980) found, contrary
the expectations engendered by belief in an efficient financial
stem, a large, unexplained drop in the stock market valuation of the
esent value of after-tax cash flows of American companies in the
riod 1972–4 (calculated with either a constant real discount rate or
inflation-adjusted bond rate). David J. Ravenscroft and F.M.
herer (1987) have found persistent, widespread stock market
nfusion over the value of American mergers, with the share price of
quiring firms on average first rising then falling relative to the
arket as a whole, leaving the net impact of mergers either neutral
negative. Steven M. Fazzari *et al.* (1988) have found evidence for
e period 1970–84 that small, rapidly growing American firms faced
disturbingly large differential in the cost of internal and external
nds, despite the undeniable coverage and sophistication of the US
ancial system. Colin Mayer and his collaborators (1987) have found
arked, persistent differences in corporate funding patterns among
e large OECD countries over the last two decades, with the most
tensibly competitive financial systems – those of the US and the UK
being found to service the least impressively performing economies.
flood of theoretical explanations, stressing matters such as transac-
ns costs, tax distortions, agency costs, real bankruptcy costs and
ymmetrically distributed information, have been advanced to
count for the anomalies and perceived defects of the so-called
icient markets hypothesis.[2]

This recent ferment in theoretical and applied research on capital
arkets offers opportunities for historians to view the performance of
tional financial systems in new and advantageous perspective,
inging under closer scrutiny in their narratives aspects previously
glected or misunderstood. They now have access to a variety of
odels in which to frame their enquiries, leavened with a myriad of
estions directed to institutional arrangements and operational
actices. Moreover, historical perspective, especially when honed by

international comparisons of varying national experiences, affords
rich variety of circumstances with which to probe the explanator
power of alternative models of financial behavior. History matters, fc
models which are persuasive only for a limited experience are les
likely to offer useful insight into the future than are those that ca
persuasively account for a wide variety.

To contribute to such an international comparison, this chapte
presents a narrative account of the evolution of Britain's financia
system, with three central themes: (a) the changing relationships •
nonfinancial enterprises and financial intermediaries; (b) the genera
availability of the information needed for rational, efficient inves
ment decisions; (c) the means available to limit agency costs. To mak
this task manageable within an essay, most historical detail and th
texture of the inevitable complexity of events must be suppresse
What remains is necessarily a highly stylized account, but one whic
attempts to capture the essence of Britain's experience and to brin
forward for closer examination the most salient features.

The Bubble Act and its Legacy: British Capital Markets to 1826

Although most of the attention of this chapter will be devoted to th
last one hundred and fifty years, to understand more recent develo}
ments it is necessary to begin the story much earlier, in the la*
seventeenth century, before the onset of the classical Industri;
Revolution, but at a time when the pace of economic activity wa
clearly accelerating. Between 1660 and 1720 there occurred a
amazing efflorescence of early British capitalism. W.R. Scott ha
estimated that there were 150 joint-stock companies in existence i
1695 and that in the year of frenzy that led to the Bubble Act of 172(
an additional 190 distinct company promotions can be identifie
(Scott, 1912 vol. 1: p. 327; vol. 2: pp. 445–58; quoted in Mirowsk
1981: p. 565). Although the companies formed in the 60 years befor
1720 spanned an extraordinary array of activities – including mun
cipal water supply, the distillation of salt from sea water, mining
glass making and foreign trade – many of the largest, judging fror
contemporary trading activity and coverage in the rudimentar
financial press of the day, were banks and insurance companie
(Mirowski, 1981: pp. 560–6), suggesting that opportunities in this are
were perceived to be particularly promising.

'he degree of promise might be inferred from the experience of the ɪk of England. The Bank was first granted a Charter of Incorpora-ɪ by Parliament in 1694, in return for a loan of £1.2m., £500,000 of ɪch was in the form of the Bank's own notes, all bearing interest at er cent. From its creation, worried by the continual emergence of p-pocketed competitors in the banking business, the Bank of ɡland sought a monopoly of joint-stock banking in England and, in ɪrn for further support of public credit in 1697, secured Parlia-ɪt's acquiescence. However, this failed to eliminate competition, ɪch emerged most notably from the Sword Blade Company, formed ɡinally to make hollow sword blades but after 1702 coming to deal ɪitles to sequestered land, and by this circuitous route gradually ɪbracing banking as well. Matters came to a head in 1708 when the ɪk's Charter was once again up for renewal and Parliament was ɪe pressed than usual by the demands of war finance. This time the ɪk of England had greater success and, to howls of criticism, ɪured a more tightly drawn monopoly, restricting banking com-ɪitors to partnerships with no more than six members, each facing ɪimited liability for the partnership's debts. This position was ɪther strengthened in 1720 with the passage of the famous Bubble , which made the creation of a large stock of freely transferable ɪres a criminal offence. The six-member limitation, combined with ɪimited liability and an effective prohibition on openly transferable ɪres, ensured that banking partnerships would be created and ɪolved only with difficulty. These restrictions formed the basis for ɪk and company formation for more than a century, until 1826.

'ogether, the restrictions had two broad consequences. First, they ɪrkedly slowed the development of English banking. The number ɪ size of banks and other intermediaries seeking charters in the ɪ seventeenth and early eighteenth centuries reveals the perceived ɪand that existed then for banking services. This demand was ɪmately met by a cautious Bank of England, determined to take full ɪantage of its favored position, and by a host of much smaller firms ɪpelled by law either to limit their activities to a smaller scale than ɪy would have otherwise chosen, or to undertake greater risks. The ɪk of England concerned itself chiefly with the highly profitable ɪvision of financial services to the state throughout the eighteenth ɪtury. Its limited private business consisted of maintaining in ɪdon deposits for wealthy individuals and discounting bills of ɪhange for selected London merchants, activities which earned it derisive title of "the Bank of London." This was a highly lucrative ɪiness which many customers and potential competitors wished was ɪe widely shared. While the costs to England of the Bank's favored

position in government finance may be safely assumed to have be
large, much greater costs arose from the arbitrary restriction on bar
size imposed by the six-member limit to banking partnerships. The
restrictions ensured that individual banks would remain small a
that opportunities for widespread diversification of bank loans a
discounts would be sharply limited. They also acted to limit t
commercial intelligence that could be gathered by any one ban
maintained for over a century, the restrictions served to embed with
English economic life segmentation and circumscription of inform
tion much more deeply than the slow and expensive transport a
communications of the age warranted. The immediate costs of the
restrictions may be approximated by comparing the development
banking in England and Scotland during the eighteenth century.

The six-member partnership rule did not extend to Scotlar
Scottish law set no restrictions on the number of partners; that w
left to private negotiation, with the result that some banks in the la
eighteenth century counted their partners in the hundreds. Ad
tionally, partnership shares were relatively easily transferred
negotiation, although unlimited liability remained. Consequent
Scottish banking partnerships were larger and better funded th
their English counterparts. They maintained a network of branch
and serviced their customer base more thoroughly, as reflected in t
higher level of banking assets per capita found in Scotland, despi
average incomes there being lower than in England. They provid
more innovative services, offering customers interest-bearing depos
and extending credit through the cash account. Perhaps most signi
cantly, their wider capital base and intelligence network produc
better diversification and greater stability, sparing Scotland the f
trauma of the banking panics that periodically swept England, despi
the greater exposure of most Scottish banking partnerships
industrial and commercial risks.[3]

Secondly, the Bubble Act interrupted for more than a century t
development of an ability by non-financial firms to raise mon
directly from the public. Dispute exists regarding the costs imposed I
this interruption. Philip Cottrell (1980: p. 10) has argued that t
costs were small, an "inconvenience," not a major obstacle, noting th
even after the Bubble Act was finally repealed in 1825, partnershi
remained the favored form of business organization for a further ha
century. In contrast, Dubois (1938: p. 11) wrote that "the Bubble A
was a latent menace in every board room and lawyers' chambe
when problems of business organisation were deliberated" (quoted
Lammert, 1989a: p. 13). Certainly the Bubble Act postponed for mo

in a century widescale experimentation with the corporate form of
ganization. Although Parliament and the Crown awarded corporate
arters from time to time throughout the eighteenth century, these
re expensive, and obtained by few firms. Thus the development of
e legal and practical framework needed to support a viable joint-
ck form of organization was greatly stunted. Certainly, the specula-
e excesses and agency costs revealed by the mania of 1719–20
ant that joint-stock companies would have been formed more
wly and cautiously in any event, whether a Bubble Act had been
creed in 1720 or not (Pollard, 1965). Moreover, developments during
e eighteenth century in the law and practice of partnership made it
more flexible, accountable and predictable form of organization,
lucing the need for joint-stock enterprise. Prohibition, however,
imately exacted a high toll. Flexible as it eventually became, the
rtnership could not serve efficiently as an organizational vehicle for
ge-scale capital formation. Some form of joint-stock organization
s ultimately necessary, but prohibition stifled the continuous
perimentation, the learning-by-doing, required to discover how a
stem of joint-stock enterprises should best be operated. Reliance for
ull century on unlimited liability partnerships not only delayed the
vitable learning process (which to this day is still going on, perhaps
an increasing pace), but also further contributed to an avoidable
d undesirable segmentation of information, creating islands of
ormation only tenuously linked to one another. Such isolation made
difficult if not impossible to eliminate yield differentials and,
ause of the obstacles created for the information-intensive activity
diversification, made capital formation and commercial activity
en riskier than they intrinsically were.

The consequences of the Bank of England monopoly of joint-stock
nking and the Bubble Act interacted with and reinforced each
er. By handicapping the ability of enterprises to raise external
ance directly, the Bubble Act served to make them more dependent
internally generated funds and on bank support. Yet, perversely,
e six-member limit on banking partnerships reduced the banking
tem's ability to respond to this heightened demand, leaving an
fficient, artificial dependence on internal finance. Capital formation
s thereby rendered more difficult and the entire financial system
de more unstable – within an environment intrinsically unstable
e to endemic warfare of varying intensity and vulnerable to climatic
ocks – by self-inflicted legal restrictions. Sustained for over a
itury, this process established deep within the embryonic English
ancial system a profound orientation toward short-term commercial

finance, since the intentionally small size and limited resources
English banks ensured that long-term bank lending carried with
inordinate risks. This short-term orientation of the English bank
system, eminently rational within the institutional constraints of
period, was reinforced through a process of natural selection. Ba
failures in the eighteenth and early nineteenth centuries tended
strike most frequently ventures which sought to combine bank
with a limited range of industrial or manufacturing activities. T
soundest banks, those which eventually grew to dominate the Engl
system of country banking, depended upon a wide range of cc
mercial interests and avoided the inevitable concentrated hazards
the production and distribution of a single commodity (Pressn
1956: p. 53). In this way, the natural bond between banks and
most credit-hungry, capital-intensive ventures was kept weak a
tenuous in England. Similarly, non-banking enterprises, prohibited
the Bubble Act from publicly issuing or trading transferable shar
although not restricted in the numbers of permitted partners, w
kept smaller and more unstable than was necessary. The combinat
of small, unstable banks lending to small, unstable firms inevita
limited information flows and created an environment even m
crisis-prone than the difficult circumstances of the time dictated.

Of course, as is universally known, these obstacles and difficul
did not in the end prevent Britain from experiencing the world's f
Industrial Revolution. At a cost, the obstacles and difficulties could
and were, surmounted. The technology of the time did not requ
many large concentrations of illiquid physical capital, and most of
time the traditional means of private negotiation sufficed well enou
to support growth that, while unduly hazardous, was neverthel
highly vigorous by international standards. In the few instances wl
private negotiations and private partnerships were inadequate
direct application to Parliament for public incorporation with limi
liability could be made, as was done with the canal and turnp
companies that sprang up in the last half of the eighteenth centu
and with the large overseas trading companies. This pre-indust
method of pooling large concentrations of wealth – a method obviou
capable of supporting considerable economic development, all
expensively – survived far into the nineteenth century. It was
means by which even the railroads, the most capital-intensive proje
of the nineteenth century, were largely financed. But as we shall
later, this process of development launched the British finan
system upon a path that was to create substantial problems for
future as well as having made early industrialization unnecessa
painful.

he Rise of the Joint-Stock Company: British Capital Markets, 826–78

he avoidable financial instability inflicted upon England by the x-member limit on banking partnerships finally became intolerable `ter the financial panic of 1825–6, perhaps (on the basis of highly ìperfect national income data for this early period) the most severe ' the nineteenth century. Earlier in 1825, non-financial companies ìd been freed from the restrictions of the Bubble Act on joint-stock `ading. Next, long standing criticisms of restrictions on English ìnks, fueled by appreciation of the virtues of Scottish banking ;lapham, 1926: p. 273), were finally acted upon and within a year ìnks (outside a 65-mile radius from London) also had the right to `ganize themselves into joint-stock companies with freely transfer-ìle shares and the right to sue and be sued in the name of their ìblic officers. Unlimited liability remained. The new freedom that ìnks now had to expand their businesses, however, was tempered by ìe Bank of England's opening of branches in the provinces (Clapham, ì26: p. 275). Given that banking partnerships and businessmen in ìneral were in 1826 and 1827 busy ascertaining their solvency in the ìake of the panic, and that the newly authorized joint-stock banks ìerated with unlimited liability, in the face of new competition from ìe Bank of England, now at last taking an active interest in `ovincial banking affairs, the new organizational form was adopted ìickly, 32 joint stock banks having been formed by 1833 (Clapham, ì26: p. 279; Cottrell, 1980: p. 16, cites 33 banks). In 1833, ìndon-based banking partnerships finally succeeded in their agita-ìn for joint-stock status, although they were prohibited from note ìue. After 1833, joint-stock banking companies with unlimited ìbility quickly became the predominant form of bank organization ìroughout Britain, although many private banking partnerships ìmained.

The new organizational form quickly acted to break down barriers ìtween banks and non-financial enterprises. Banking partners had `ten had considerable non-banking business interests – indeed, not frequently the cash generated by non-bank interests had led ìsinessmen to open banks. The new organizational form allowed and ìcouraged this tendency to develop much further. Moreover, the new ìructure allowed banks to become more readily highly capitalized, as ìe recurrent waves of bank stock flotation makes clear (Clapham, ì26: p. 278; Holmes and Green, 1986: pp. 1–22). With closer ties to ìcal industry, and the bigger risks that increasingly capital-intensive

technology was creating – the 1830s saw the first of the railwa
manias that marked the beginning of a richer, more technologica
advanced age, even as England was consolidating the gains of earli
advances – joint-stock banks, despite capitalization greater than th
of their country bank predecessors, quickly faced a choice of curtaili
their activities, or achieving a broader, more diversified and th
more stable geographical and business base, or running an increas
risk of failing in a crisis (Holmes and Green, 1986: pp. 33–5).

Banking activity was at the forefront of Britain's buoyant econom
performance in the later 1830s and 1840s, as railway construction g
well under way, exerting its influence both directly and throu
complex linkages to the rest of the economy. With banking expansi
inevitably came failures, no doubt often due to the unfortuna
realization of intrinsic risks, increasingly embodied in the sha
swings of economy-wide business cycles, although stern Victoria
readily attributed them to weak or dishonest management. In d
course, with the Joint Stock Banking Act of 1844, Parliament ma
bank promotion more difficult, stipulating issuance of a charter fro
an increasingly stringent Board of Trade, and a minimum capital
£100,000, divided into shares of at least £100 each (an amount equ
at that time to a year's wages of a semi-skilled worker) (Cottre
1980: p. 34). At the same time, the Bank Charter Act of 18
curtailed the note issue of existing banks and prohibited ne
creations from ever having the right to issue bank notes. These Ac
checked the rate of expansion of the banking system but by no mea
stopped it, although only 12 new banks were created between 18
and 1862, when a consolidated Companies Act once again establish
a more permissive regime. Most of the expansion in the peri
1844–62 came from the continued growth of joint stock banks found
earlier.

As banks (and insurance companies) developed in the new circums
ances, important changes were gathering pace in the laws governi
non-financial companies, which were to have a profound impact on tl
relationship between banks and business. The essence of the
changes was that companies were offered a means of bypassing ban
and raising money directly from the public. From the repeal of tl
Bubble Act to the mid-1850s, company formation had gradual
become easier. Unlimited liability remained, but the corporate right
sue and be sued in the name of company officers – an important leg
right which directly reduced the cost of doing business – became mo
common. However, it was expensive to obtain this right, and tl
application for a corporate charter was vulnerable to interference

ther interested parties (Cottrell, 1980: pp. 40–4). At the same time,
n increasing number of companies were availing themselves of the
pportunity to obtain limited liability by seeking incorporation in
rance or the United States. While there were considerable misgiv-
igs within the British business community about the wisdom of
outinely granting limited liability to all who sought it, benefits were
lso discerned, not least by those such as the Christian Socialists who
aw in limited liability a means of more tightly linking the interests of
mployers and men by means of some form of profit sharing (Saville,
955). Such a linkage could never come about if workers were to be
xposed to unlimited liability for their employer's debts while having
t best only a minority stake in the business. Thus a number of
nfluences came together to cause an abrupt and radical liberalization
n the procedures for the formation of companies with limited liability.
ns had happened in 1846 with the repeal of the Corn Laws and in
849 with the repeal of the Navigation Acts, with the changes to
ompany law the English government relinquished, on lesser grounds
erhaps, but no less decisively, close control over another activity in
vhich previously it had been deeply involved, namely the determina-
ion of what bodies should have the right of incorporation and with
vhat degree of personal liability.

Thus, after the consolidating Companies Act of 1862, which in-
luded banks and insurance companies within its provisions,
ncorporation with limited liability was made easily and cheaply
vailable virtually for the asking, thereby making it possible for
nterprises of all types, banks and nonbanks alike, to raise capital
hrough stock exchanges on which equity claims to capital could be
eadily traded. This was a natural way to extend the negotiations
vhich had traditionally been the means by which long-term capital
ad been raised, and indeed re-established practices that had
lourished in the 60 years before 1720, the year of the Bubble Act. The
atural course of this development is revealed by the manner in which
he new access to limited liability was taken up. For most of the
quarter century after 1862, limited liability was used primarily to
nake less risky the kind of capital formation that was the essence of
he partnership mode of organization. Equity participation was still
ngaged in largely by those who had some kind of personal knowledge
f a business, albeit as time went by this personal connection
;radually grew less evident than was the case before 1862. Neverthe-
ess, it was not until the domestic boom of the 1890s that the personal
inks among investors were broken on a substantial scale, and direct
ersonal knowledge of investment projects was widely replaced by

information gathered through the mechanism of the stock exchange consisting mainly of brokers and an increasingly influential financi press.

The slow increase of recourse by both companies and investors the stock exchanges for raising capital may be attributed to two ma factors: a strong residual mistrust of limited liability dating back least to the early eighteenth century – the Bubble Act, after all, w an accurate reflection of a widely held, if intemperate, contempora view – and the incredible paucity of information the new limite companies were required to provide to their shareholders, a lack information which was repeatedly to vindicate the mistrust. Th Companies Act of 1844 had stipulated a minimum level of subscribe capital and disclosure provisions that included half-yearly returns shareholders and externally audited balance sheets, both of whic were to be filed with the newly created Registrar of Joint Stoc Companies and made available for public inspection. But by 1862, th only disclosure required was an annual return of shareholders. The can be little wonder, then, that some sort of personal knowledge wa considered essential before rationally embarking upon an investmen The consequence of this was that despite a new-found ability to appe directly to the investing public, banks remained for most companie an indispensable source of external funds, hard bargaining amor small and selected groups of well-informed participants general yielding more mutually satisfactory outcomes than wider appeals to more ignorant audience often uncomfortably aware of its ignoranc And as the scale of operations needed for profitable operations i many different lines of activity steadily increased – as occurred i industries as diverse as brewing, steel fabrication, sewing, cotton, an flour milling – resort to such external funding was increasingl necessary.

For their part banks also expanded in order to meet this deman increasing their capital base and striving for improved diversificatio in terms both of the geographical coverage and the industrial scope their lending. However, the demands of commercial and industri finance, particularly long-term finance, grew too fast for the Britis banking system to support safely without a further fundamenta reorganization. The rash of mid-Victorian bank failures, reaching crescendo with the failure of the City of Glasgow Bank in 187 vividly illustrated the dangers of local banks lending heavily to loc businesses trying to expand rapidly.

Two main routes were available to the British banking system i the quest for a more reliable means of consciously shouldering greate long-term risks. The first route depended upon the banks organizin hemselves to withstand safely the risks inherent in long-term, often lliquid, investment; the second upon an altered relationship to the nstitution gradually emerging as Britain's central bank, the Bank of England. The first route, internal reorganization of the banking system, had two dimensions. The first dimension, long familiar to banks, was continued diversification in terms both of the geographical area serviced by deposits and loans and of the business activities generating the demand for them. The second dimension was a deepening of the capital base of the banking system in order to permit banks to take an explicit equity stake in the businesses of selected clients. The first dimension was fully realized and resulted in a vast process of merger which greatly contracted the number of deposit banks in the clearing system, while leaving the surviving banks widely diversified across both the nation and the economy. The second dimension was partially realized in that bank amalgamation was accompanied by a slow increase in capitalization relative both to the assets and liabilities of the banking system. The gradual increase in capitalization, however, was used to support extensive diversification (that is, traditional short-term, self-liquidating bank advances and loans to a broader client base) rather than more intensive equity involvement with non-bank enterprises.

Two related factors serve to explain why banks did not move toward closer equity involvement with non-bank enterprises. First, such involvement was discouraged by the long traditions of behavior which comprised the canons of sound British banking practice. For decades the greatest danger faced by the small banks that had made up the British banking system was to become too enmeshed in their clients' businesses – in short, to fail to distinguish between a bill and a mortgage. The wave of mid-Victorian bank failures served to reaffirm in changing circumstances the traditional wisdom. Naturally, many of the joint stock banks established after 1826, such as the Birmingham and Midland Bank (later, and still today, the Midland Bank) had close, generally profitable links with local business (Holmes and Green, 1986: pp. 30–1, 62, 79–82). These informally developed links, often growing out of bank directors' outside business interests, constituted a potential basis for more formal, consciously planned equity-type participation. But in the crisis atmosphere following the City of Glasgow debacle, which coincided with a prolonged downward phase of the business cycle, even strong, profitable banks like the Birmingham and Midland Bank did not have the resources to do more than attempt to limit the damage inflicted by close ties to businesses experiencing at least temporary difficulty. What resources these banks had were devoted to extensive diversification of short-term

commitments, combined with a systematic attempt to reduce longer
term commitments to existing (and surviving) clients, a reduction
brought about by gradually but persistently reducing the existing
accommodation as loans and advances fell due (Holmes and Green
1986: pp. 63, 67, 79–82).

The second, related factor why closer equity involvement between
banks and enterprises did not emerge in the 1870s and 1880s was
that closer involvement directly conflicted with the process of exten
sive diversification, the most obvious solution to the difficulties of the
time. Extensive diversification was only in part accomplished b
existing banks seeking to diversify their deposit bases and loan
portfolios directly through their own efforts. Much more importantly
extensive diversification was accomplished indirectly by agreed mer
gers between banks. But a merger was unlikely to occur as long a
one of the potential partners had suspect advances among its assets
or even relations with clients that might prove time-consuming and
complicated for the enlarged bank to handle. Thus British bank
looking for merger partners in order to achieve rapid extensive
diversification were best served with "clean" balance sheets, unen
cumbered by too close ties to clients. This motive, too, served to help
sever the close ties to local industries that had developed since 1826.

In this environment it was improbable that the British banking
system would be able to reorganize itself rationally to shoulder more
equity risks on its own. The only outside source of help even remotely
available was the Bank of England. This route to change would have
involved the Bank of England accepting more explicitly its role o
lender of last resort and being willing to extend accommodation, no
doubt at a suitably (and necessarily) stiff price, on all first-class paper
offered to it for discount, much as the contemporary *Reichsbank* did
(McGouldrick, 1984: pp. 334–45). As it was, the Bank of England
reserved the right to determine as events unfolded the quality o
paper eligible for discount. While this allowed the Bank to exercise
remarkable control over the huge London money market while itsel
possessing only a small (and shrinking) reserve in relation to its task
it shifted the bulk of the burden of adjustment on to the banking
system at large, forcing individual banks to carry larger reserves o
higher quality in order to avoid insolvency in the event of a crisis
during which the Bank of England dramatically raised its discount
requirements. As was shown in the quarter century before 1914
particularly during the Baring Crisis of 1890–1, the Bank of England
was becoming increasing adept, within its limited resources, at
controlling the money supply and preserving the integrity of the
British financial system without generating great shocks for the

nderlying real economy. The problem was that its own resources ere not sufficient, nor, at a further remove, was the government's ommitment to the Bank sufficient, to permit a stance more suppor- ve of long-term capital formation.

The banking and economic crises of the late 1870s marked the end f an important era in the evolution of the British financial system. A elatively brief period of strengthening links between banks and onfinancial enterprises drew to a close. The banking system set out istead upon an alternative path in which the cheap, efficient and rofitable provision of short-term finance was paramount, with close quity-like links to nonfinancial firms seen as a positive obstacle to nis ideal. This chosen path of development was to provide many dvantages: British companies (and many others) almost anywhere in ne country could borrow short-term more cheaply from British ommercial banks than foreign firms could borrow from foreign ources anywhere in the world; the British financial system, shorn of liquid long-term commitments and buttressed by the great wealth of ong-sustained economic growth, possessed an enviable solidity and tability. But these advantages were purchased at great cost. Above ll, information about long-term risks became more tightly circum- cribed within firms themselves. This information was not diffused hrough the banking system, as occurred in important continental uropean economies or, albeit to a lesser extent, in the US, where ntermediaries continued to take, for better or worse, an important ong-term interest in nonfinancial firms. Nor was the information iffused directly among the investing public at large by means of a eliable system of public disclosure of corporate affairs, complete with n informed, impartial financial press and with mechanisms for wners to respond to information in order to regulate efficiently the ianagers of their enterprises. The late Victorian financial system as whole could not effectively supplement the personal contacts that ad earlier guided long-term investment. Banks were too removed om active long-term risk taking and, as we shall see, stock xchanges were too vulnerable to manipulation, fraud and ignorance engender real confidence, their mechanisms and procedures too nformed to be effective. Yet the British economy had grown so large nd complex that individual personal contacts ceased to be adequate r sustained, well-diversified investment.

The consequence of this lack of information about long-term ivestment opportunities was that no one, no individual or institution, ossessed the knowledge necessary to make efficient, rational invest- ient decisions across the entire spectrum of opportunities generated y the economy, adequately weighing all alternatives for risk and return. Because efficient diversification could thus not take place, risk-adjusted yield differentials could not be equalized, leaving resources suboptimally allocated. By itself, this "capital blindness" was not a new phenomenon. What was new, however, was the economic and technological environment in which it occurred. Britain had long depended upon international trade to sustain its wealth. Relatively high population densities and limited natural resources ensured this dependence. Britain's technological lead, allied to long-established commercial connections around the world, secured for her a favored position in the international economy. Continued British prosperity, however, depended upon maintaining a technological lead at a time of increasing capital intensity. This became particularly important as manufacturing techniques pioneered in Britain were successfully adopted in poorer countries. If other nations, also competing for international markets and resources, were to acquire technological advantages over Britain through superior investment allocations, Britain's relative prosperity would be undermined. Within this context of heightened international competition and the increased capital intensity of accelerating technological change, the financial system took on a new importance.

The Rise of the Stock Exchange: 1878–1914

The withdrawal of banks (and other financial intermediaries, see Kennedy (1987: pp. 120–34) for further discussion) from willing involvement in long-term capital formation after 1878 once again left the burden of this task to individuals supported, if at all, only by the mechanism of company law, fortified, as we have seen, by the easy availability of limited liability after 1862. Private British groups, usually acting without extensive institutional facilities for collecting information and for diversifying widely and efficiently, achieved the great bulk of the not inconsiderable capital formation and structural change which occurred during the late Victorian and Edwardian eras. Perhaps the most important way in which systematic, organized change was brought about in Britain after 1870 was through the diversifying behavior of established, viable firms with proven technical capabilities and trade connections. These firms accomplished change by using their cash flows from profits and depreciation either to alter the character of their activities by creating new product lines or to enlarge themselves by expanding existing profitable operations,

ey also used their established credit to issue bonds or to secure –
rhaps by mortgaging tangible assets – medium-term, fixed-interest
ins from a variety of sources (including banks). In any event,
iether change occurred within firms or through the creation of new
ms, it was accomplished by tapping relatively small, highly seg-
ented pools of savings. When personal or internal resources were
sufficient and short-term bank accommodation was too limited and
ky, British firms and entrepreneurs seeking additional resources
re forced to turn to the other main route to expansion made
ailable by the liberalized company law, the stock exchanges, which
peal of the Bubble Act, coinciding with the railway booms, caused to
increasingly animated.

In principle, the stock exchanges offered a means of overcoming the
rvasive segmentation spawned by networks of highly localized
siness contacts. Provincial exchanges, which had been established
ring the railroad booms of the 1830s and 1840s, were essentially an
tension of the close circle of local associates, since those who traded
ere were generally well aware through personal knowledge of the
rcumstances of the quoted firms (Thomas, 1973: pp. 137–9). Provin-
il exchanges were an important means of providing liquidity for
vestors in local businesses, but gross new issues on them, both fixed-
terest debt and equity, equaled an amount no more than 5–10 per
nt of the annual amount of gross domestic capital formation in the
ars immediately preceding the war (Lavington, 1921: p. 208). The
ntribution of provincial exchanges to the reduction of segmentation
is thus sharply limited. The London capital market dwarfed those of
e provinces and was correspondingly more important as a source of
w funds. Gross new domestic issues in London equaled an amount
uivalent to 23–8 per cent of annual gross domestic capital formation
1911–13 (Lavington, 1921: pp. 200–6). However, the main functions
the London capital market were concerned with government issues,
reign loans, and railroads or other public or semipublic utility
curities, both foreign and domestic, rather than with domestic
dustrial finance.

There are good historical reasons why this was so. Although the
ndon market was an amazing mechanism of great capacity and
xibility, it operated in a legal environment only just beginning to
apple with information problems that were to become familiar in
id-twentieth century capital markets. The lax disclosure require-
ents stipulated by the consolidated Companies Act of 1862 invited
ncealment and manipulation. The legal requirements governing
anagerial behavior and the disclosure of company affairs were so
inimally drawn as to place the company's directors in virtually

unchallengeable and generally unmonitored possession of the com pany's assets. In late Victorian Britain, the extent of the ignorance shareholders and creditors without direct access to a company internal accounts may be estimated by the fact that not until 190 were companies once again required, as they had been from 1844 1856, to submit accounts for an annual audit. Not until 1907 wer companies compelled to file publicly an audited balance sheet. Sin the relevant 1907 Act failed to specify that the published balan sheet be current, some public companies seeking secrecy chose to f the same balance sheet year after year (Edwards, 1981: pp. 3–4).

In the light of the inherent informational weaknesses in Britis capital market operations, it is not surprising that the mone ventured through them went very largely to the purchase of "knowr securities. There were a number of ways in which securities becam "known." They might be the oldest securities traded on the exchang government debt stock. The price of these could certainly vary, bu the instrument itself was well understood and obeyed known laws behavior. In the first quarter of the nineteenth century, as Britai came to enjoy a gradually increasing external payments surplus, th securities of foreign governments began to appear in London in larg quantities. Their numbers grew rapidly, and at first they tended to b indiscriminately equated with domestic government stocks, but th was quickly changed. Painful experience in the 1820s taught investo to distinguish among issues more carefully. Sovereign borrowers cam to be judged on their reputations and a good record became a increasingly valuable asset, assuring the holder an attentive receptio in the market and keeping down interest costs if an issue were agree upon. The same evolution occurred in the marketing of home railroa securities, which had by the late 1880s become thoroughly respectabl as the memories of the excesses of the 1830s and 1840s faded und the impact of a long succession of dividend and coupon paymen reliably made. The unmistakable sign of complete acceptance wa extended to selected home railroad debentures in 1889 when the were accorded trustee status (Morgan and Thomas, 1962: p. 110). Th next group of securities gradually to win favor in London were foreig railroads, with colonial issues most preferred, followed by the issues proven North and South American lines. Domestic nonrail compani began to appear in the later 1860s; most of these issues represente established coal, iron, steel and heavy engineering firms takin advantage of the new provisions for limited liability to ease th burden of their relatively large fixed costs. These issues too wer occasionally attended by unscrupulous promotions, but the pruden Victorians who made up most of the investing public seldom straye

r any time from familiar securities. Finally, there was throughout
ιe nineteenth century an accumulation of other foreign securities,
rimarily those of land, finance and investment companies, mining
ιd other raw material extraction concerns, and a few industrial and
ιmmercial enterprises. In each case, a learning experience took place
ş investors strove to discriminate among issues of varying intrinsic
ιality. What is striking in the great rise of the London stock
κchange is not that spectacular frauds occurred, but that they were
˙ such small magnitude compared with the volume of securities
ιrchased. The Victorians circumvented remarkably well the dangers
hich tenuous control information imposed upon them, although at a
ιgh cost of lost opportunities, by buying selectively and cautiously.
  With the established Victorian financial intermediaries removed
om an active, direct role as either managers or risk-sharing agents
ι private industrial capital formation, careful selectivity – usually
·ring on the side of caution, although occasionally prone to an
ηbridled wave of short-lived optimism – emerged as the most reliable
ιfeguard available to the individual investor not possessing inside
ιowledge of a company's affairs. As the first wave of conversions of
rivate partnerships took place in the late 1860s and 1870s, inter-
ιediaries appeared who helped uninformed, or only partially in-
ιrmed, investors discriminate among issues. These intermediaries,
ften local accountants or solicitors who were familiar with the
artnerships they were proposing to convert to limited companies and
ιcing an interested but skeptical market, generally drew up careful,
ιutious assessments of the businesses for the consideration of
ιtsiders and insiders alike. Moreover, these early company promo-
ırs commonly insisted that the amount of "new" money raised be
ιmited to 25–30 per cent of the value of the issue, the remainder
eing the (conservatively) assessed value of the vendor's or issuing
roup's assets (Jeffreys, 1938: pp. 298–9). The early promoters, such
ş David Chadwick, perhaps the most successful of this early group,
enerally stayed with the companies they had launched in some
rofessional capacity – for example, Chadwick, an accountant, served
ş auditor – thus providing vital reassurance to those whom they had
ιcouraged to invest.
  The early company promoters succeeded in establishing limited
ιmpanies as legitimate and often attractive investment vehicles. In
ιe late 1870s, for example, Chadwick's failure rate was only one
ιmpany in ten promoted, a ratio that compared well with the failure
ιte of private partnerships. However, this impressive record was not
ι be sustained, for it had depended upon favorable temporary factors.
irst, the early promotions were primarily local affairs in which even

many outsiders had enough knowledge through routine busine
contact and general awareness to gauge the plausibility of t
putative companies prospectuses'. Such discernment rarely surviv
the transfer of the locus of promotion from its native region to t
London stock exchange. Thus while London promotions could reach
far wider market – the provinces generally being more aware
London prices than those of their neighbors – the audience w
generally less well informed, a fact which encouraged repeated cyc
of exploitation and revulsion of investors. Second, and perhaps m
importantly, once the bulk of eligible established businesses had be
converted from partnerships to limited companies, the task of co
pany promotion became more demanding and complex as go
candidates for flotation became harder to find. It was one matter
manifestly not without its own problems – to assess the value of
established enterprise; it was another matter, even less tractable,
estimate objectively the future earnings of a less-seasoned ventu
and to ensure, somehow, that the new venture actually got under w
in some rough accordance with its published prospectus.

Unfortunately for Britain's future development, the inherent wea
nesses in the Victorian system of company promotion were to
revealed most fully in the launching (or relaunching) of key indu
tries, particularly those of crucial importance to late nineteen
century economic growth – electricity, chemicals (particularly orga
chemicals) and motor vehicles. These and closely allied industri
were crucial because of their extraordinarily fast rates of growt
sufficient in fact to have an important impact on overall aggrega
growth rates (Kennedy, 1987: pp. 22–77), and because of their roles
providers of productivity-enhancing inputs to the rest of the econom
Overall economic performance in the late nineteenth century was
large measure determined by these industries, and in each ca
disastrous company promotions severely handicapped their subs
quent development in Britain.

The first to pass through this baleful cycle of overblown optimis
inevitable financial collapse and prolonged investor revulsion was t
electrical industry. British inventors and entrepreneurs played a
important part in the early development of the industry, whi
attracted inventive minds around the world. The eventual achiev
ment of a practical incandescent lamp, accomplished essentia
simultaneously in the US and Britain in 1878, dramatically signal
the beginning of commercial promise in the electrical industry.
trickle of promotions became a flood in 1882. Although Pollar
estimate (1989: p. 48) of £23m. raised for the industry in Britain
the years 1880–2 appears too high, the true figure was nevertheless

arge one. The electrical mania ended late in 1882, as reality punctured fantasy. Subsequent recriminations revealed false prospectuses (particularly concerning patent rights), gross manipulation of share prices (often involving frenetic short selling by stockbrokers), the plundering of company assets by managers, and a whole host of practices that were dishonest in spirit if not (yet) in law. Although many writers (Clapham, 1938: pp. 130–2; Pollard, 1989: pp. 47–8, 51–2) have asserted that the Electric Lighting Act of 1882, granting municipalities the power of compulsory purchase after 21 years, was responsible for the collapse of the boom, this claim is hard to sustain. A little experimentation with the present discounted value of hypothetical dividend streams, even using a discount rate as low as 3 per cent, the approximate nominal yield on consols, reveals that only a fantastic projection of dividends could fully account for the 90 per cent drop in the share prices of the early British electrical companies as a result of the 1882 Act. Using generous dividend projections, especially for later years, a low discount rate, and a low final purchase price it is possible to account for perhaps 25 per cent of the actual drop in share prices by rationally changed expectations. Using a dividend projection rate 50 per cent greater than that recorded for all British industry in the period, a discount rate of 3.5 per cent, and a compulsory purchase price equal to the initial capital costs, an estimate far less generous than that actually received by virtually all companies that were eventually purchased by municipalities, allows one to attribute less than 50 per cent of the 1882 share price collapse to the 1882 Act. If one goes further and uses as terminal purchase prices the prices actually paid by municipalities and employs a discount rate equal to average total return on stock exchange investments, the Act can be shown to have influenced fundamental share values very little (based on the value of discounted dividends), because municipalities in fact paid generously to take over private companies. The conclusion is inescapable that the slow development of the British electrical industry in its first decade of existence was caused primarily by its disastrous launch on an unregulated, uninformed, unintermediated stock exchange, and not by factors such as ill-advised legislation.

The legacy of the disastrous launch was that successful British firms had to grow with painful slowness, relying upon internal funds or traditional private negotiations. For example, the General Electric Company (which is today by far Britain's largest electrical equipment manufacturer), although formed in 1889 and by 1914 Britain's largest British-owned electrical manufacturing company, did not go public until 1900 and then only to provide liquidity for insiders, not to raise new money. The company's shares were so infrequently traded that it

did not have a regularly published share quotation before 191
Consequently the British industry showed no ability to maintai
investment and construction over the business cycle. Although Britis
companies managed to benefit from the later stages of the buoyar
phases of the cycle, they tended to lose market share to foreig
manufacturers and to imports during the depressed phases of th
cycle, and were always badly prepared for the initial stages of th
upswing. The feeble state of British manufacturers prevented the
from becoming involved in the financing of electricity-generatir
companies and hence contributed to the links between manufacture
and utilities being notoriously weak in Britain, where harmonizatio
of standards proved much more difficult to accomplish than in oth
advanced countries where links, particularly financial links, betwee
manufacturers and utilities were closer. With the fortunate exceptio
of the northeast of England, the same problems hindered th
realization in Britain of economies of scale in generation, causin
British electricity supply prices to be excessively high, a factor whic
also contributed to the slow growth of demand for electricity. Th
perpetually straitened financial condition of firms in the Britis
electrical industry discouraged systematic research and developmer
and contributed to the strange phenomenon of an industry heavil
reliant on scientific knowledge recruiting few scientifically traine
men. Lack of demand for a scientifically and technically traine
workforce meant the provision of this training, especially in highe
education, was stunted, a development which severely hindere
future growth. Britain was not to begin to make good the handicap
the poor start in this vital industry until the interwar period.

The automobile industry's experience was similar. The first Britis
motor company, the British Motor Syndicate, was floated in 1895 fc
£150,000, later raised to £1,000,000, by Harry Lawson (Lewchul
1985: pp. 7–8). As in the initial electrical industry flotations, most
this money went to buy or to license obsolete patents. Ultimatel
Lawson succeeded only in launching struggling firms that barel
managed to stay in business, while the industry in France wa
establishing itself as the most productive in Europe, a position it wa
to retain until the First World War. Thus, despite the motor vehicl
industry being well suited to Britain's industrial traditions, unlik
electrical engineering, and despite the relatively high incomes whic
made the British vehicle market potentially the largest in Europ
after a spectacularly unsuccessful financial launch the industr
developed comparatively slowly. Finally, beginning in 1904, wit
many successful foreign examples before them and the extent of th
home market sharply outlined by burgeoning imports, new money di

ɔw into the industry. However, the stock exchange persisted in vishing money most generously on the biggest lemons in an ⸱dustry now showing signs of becoming extremely profitable (Saul, ⸱62: pp. 32, 40). Moreover, the bursts of money available to the ⸱dustry were erratic. In 1907, overseas troubles, this time in the US, ⸱ce again suddenly disrupted Britain's financial markets, forcing ꞏveral firms into liquidation. Consequently, during a feverish world-ide boom in car sales, the domestic British industry could raise ꜩternal money only with great difficulty (Kennedy, 1987: pp. 139– ⸱)). Little was obtained from the stock exchange in 1908, and nothing ꞏ all in 1909–10. During this time imports poured in, and by 1911, as ꞏe stock exchange showed signs of recovering its nerve, Henry Ford ꞏd settled in to dominate the lower end of the market with the ⸱odel-Ts gushing from his new Trafford Park plant.

As the experience of the motor vehicle industry revealed, by the ꞏrn of the twentieth century Britain's stock markets could, at least ꞏtermittently, mobilize sufficient money to sustain a rapidly growing ⸱dustry. The launch of the motor industry, while hardly successful, as less disastrous than that of the electrical industry, where ꞏitain's lag was more pronounced. But stock exchange support was ꞏratic and expensive, to the industry's detriment. First, heavy ꞏpendence on the stock market for external funds made the British ⸱dustry, by international standards, unusually vulnerable to exces-vely volatile financial markets, choking off funds when firms in her countries could continue to get finance from more stable ꞏurces. It was ironic that the Panic of 1907, which originated in the ꞏS, disrupted British vehicle industry finance much more severely ⸱an its American counterpart. Second, dependence on external ⸱ance, in conditions of acknowledged inadequate corporate financial ⸱sclosure, attached a particularly high importance to dividend pay-ents by firms. A firm could maintain its ability to raise fresh money ꞏly by continually signaling through large dividend payments the ꞏh yields it could earn (Lewchuk, 1985: pp. 16–18). This require-ent aggravated the problems caused by dependence on external ⸱nding, because when markets were disturbed firms could raise no ꞏsh money yet had to maintain high dividend payments in order to ꞏfeguard access to the market in calmer future times. Thus, in times ꞏ stress, when investment was most vulnerable, British vehicle firms ꞏre markedly less able than foreign ones to preserve continuity and ꞏomentum in their development plans, both because they were more ꞏpendent on less reliable external funding and because they could ꞏtain less of internally generated funds. No doubt recourse to ꞏternal funds allowed the British industry to grow more rapidly than

it could otherwise have done, but at the cost of always being les
financially secure, an insecurity which kept investment horizons shor
and cautious.

The experience of the chemical industry differed from that of moto
vehicles and electricity in detail, but not in effective outcome. In thi
case, the attention of the stock exchange was lavished on th
formation of United Alkali in 1891, a great dinosaur of a compan
that was briefly, before its inherent obsolescence became evident, th
largest chemical company in the world. This squandering of money o
a giant lemon was in marked contrast to the vast indifferenc
accorded dynamic firms such as Nobel Explosives and Brunner, Mond
both of which were financed, with difficulty, in the traditional manne
of private negotiation. The outcome of this pattern of developmen
was to yield a chemical industry composed of moribund giants steadil
losing market share to a small group of dynamic firms that ha
managed, against the odds, to become established. This combinatio
produced for Britain a particularly undynamic industry which grev
much less rapidly than the cartel-ridden industries in other advance
countries.

The peculiar inability to launch new firms successfully, particularl
in new industries, had a serious, cumulative effect upon Britisl
economic performance in the decades before 1914. First, it resulted i
industries with the greatest growth potential and brightest futur
being underrepresented in the domestic economy, with less promisin
industries being correspondingly overrepresented. This constraine
growth directly. Growth was also constrained indirectly. An industria
structure overweighted toward "mature" industries made foreig
investment unnaturally attractive. Through foreign investment it wa
possible to obtain higher yields in such familiar activities as govern
ment, railroad, and public utility finance than could be obtained fron
those activities at home. To the extent that domestic British industria
investment was rendered difficult and unattractive by weaknesses i
capital markets, relatively familiar and safe foreign investment wa
made even more attractive. Moreover, Britain's long financial experi
ence overseas resulted in the ready availability in London of a wid
array of well-known foreign financial instruments, an availabilit
which served only to highlight the problems in forging profitabl
domestic financial links between investors and industrialists seekin
long-term external funding.

These influences can be seen in the portfolio behavior of wealth
Victorians, who had the best access to investment opportunitie
(Kennedy and Britton, 1985: pp. 62–74). Portfolio choice among thi
group tended to follow distinct patterns. Active businessmen investe

avily in a small set of activities, often including their own family
ns, which they knew well from personal experience. These men
ded not to be highly diversified, and thus their undertakings were
erently risky; if things went badly, there was little hope of raising
litional finance except on the most onerous terms. On the other
nd, rentiers and professional men who did not have close business
tacts tended to avoid domestic industry altogether and instead
centrated their holdings in a variety of "safe" foreign and domestic
ivities. Thus British entrepreneurs operated in a highly risky (but
en rewarding) environment, while other great British wealth-
ders had very little exposure to domestic industry. Informational
aknesses embedded deep within the financial system prevented
ective risk sharing among these groups, exposing the one to greater
ks and depriving the other of useful opportunities. This pattern of
tfolio behavior in turn generated a structure of prices for risky
ets that undervalued domestic entrepreneurial efforts. It is here,
her than in vague cultural predispositions, that historians should
k an explanation for so-called entrepreneurial failings in the
torian economy. Moreover, once foreign investment became an
ablished feature of the Victorian economy, it created a structure of
nand that disproportionately stimulated demand for Britain's
ditional staple exports, further hindering the expansion of newer
lustries. This aspect of the Victorian economy struck with particu-
force the managers of foreign firms manufacturing new products,
ecially capital goods, in Britain. They saw clearly that Britain's
raordinarily heavy foreign investment deprived them of the orders
it made their colleagues' operations back home so much more
fitable (Kennedy, 1987: pp. 148–63).

This process, fundamentally driven by Victorian capital markets
h their attendant weaknesses, resulted in a serious failure of
tain to establish new, technologically based industries before 1914,
spite the occasional careless commitment of large amounts of money
these industries through the stock exchange. The slow development
these industries in Britain, industries primarily producing capital
ds, directly contributed to the slow productivity growth experi-
ed throughout the British economy at this time. Slowing growth,
urring after a long period of buoyantly rising real incomes,
urally exacerbated labour relations by removing the lubricant of
expanding real product available for sharing among cooperating
ups. Ominously for the longer term, failure to shift the structure of
economy on to a more modern, forward-looking basis badly
ndicapped, if it did not destroy outright, Britain's ability to
intain relatively high per capita incomes. Instead, output remained

concentrated in long-established industries. Thus even before t‍
outbreak of war in 1914, the British economy was facing ‍
increasingly difficult adjustment. The war made adjustment mu‍
more difficult.

Hesitant Steps Towards a Difficult Adjustment: 1914–39

The First World War created great economic problems for Britain. ‍
the outbreak of the War, perhaps as much as one-third of Britai‍
capital stock lay overseas. Of this vast accumulation, perhaps 10–‍
per cent was irretrievably lost in the turmoil of war and revoluti‍
and its aftermath. More immediately pressing, Britain's great n‍
stock of short-term financial claims on the rest of the world w‍
replaced by a massive overhang of war-related short-term clair‍
against Britain, a reversal which seriously complicated moneta‍
policy. Servicing the short-term debt held overseas and restorir‍
depleted capital stocks both at home and overseas was complicated ‍
the fact that the prewar process of foreign accumulation not only l‍
the domestic capital stock smaller than it otherwise would have bee‍
but it also diminished the ability of the economy to regenerate itse‍
Decades of heavy foreign investment sustained either by exports ‍
traditional staples or by the reinvestment of the earnings of overse‍
assets had left a shrunken domestic capital goods sector, much ‍
which was oriented towards well-established activities, rather th‍
towards the newer ones, such as electrical engineering or the ma‍
production of consumer goods, upon which future prosperity d‍
pended. Additionally, traditional export markets had been succes‍
fully penetrated by other producers and many of these were perma‍
ently lost. To the extent the interlopers had important c‍
advantages – either through lower wages (such as those enjoyed ‍
Indian textile producers), or through superior technology (such as th‍
enjoyed by American producers newly exporting to Latin Americ‍
or, worst of all, through some combination of lower wages a‍
superior (or at least comparable) technology (such as that enjoyed ‍
the Japanese in a range of activities spanning textile manufacture ‍
shipbuilding) – the loss of traditional export markets was inevitab‍
The war, however, had accelerated the process and made Britai‍
adjustment correspondingly more painful.

The financial system was not well placed to respond effectively ‍
the new, harsher environment. The financial channels dug befo‍

14, particularly those leading overseas, continued to exert a
werful attraction. Despite discouragement from the Bank of Eng-
nd, anxious to defend the pound at its prewar gold parity, foreign
vestment on a substantial scale soon reappeared, fueled perhaps by
widespread suspicion that the pound was overvalued and that
reign assets were therefore artificially cheap, to be snapped up while
e opportunity lasted. Domestic capital formation proceeded slowly,
rtly because of net disinvestment in depressed staples plagued by
ercapacity and partly because of restrained expansion in newer
tivities hampered by lack of reasonable access to external finance.
Much against their will, the great clearing banks came to be much
ore closely involved with industry than had been typical before the
ar. The banks had lent heavily to industry during the war. Almost
l of this was for traditional short-term accommodation which, in the
ceptional circumstances of wartime production pressures and infla-
n, was readily rolled over. The wartime involvement was further
mented by bank support for expansion undertaken in the incredibly
timistic days of the short-lived postwar boom of 1919–20. When the
evitable contraction began in the second half of 1920, what had been
ewed by the banks as short-term (if generous) lending came
creasingly to be seen as undesirable long-term commitments to be
uidated as soon as prudently possible. The essential features of
ese commitments were that they were unanticipated and that they
ere perversely motivated. The banks did not enter into this long-
rm involvement with their industrial clients actively seeking an
uity stake in attractive ventures. Instead they were sucked into
se involvement with the most vulnerable of their clients, while
ofitably expanding enterprises financed themselves by the tradi-
nal means of internal sources, private negotiation, short-term bank
ans, or new issues on the stock exchanges. Once again, inadvertent-
, the resources of the commercial banking system were directed
vay from the most dynamic and potentially most profitable sectors of
e economy, and into a variety of dead-ends.
The perverse orientation of the commercial banking system was
irrored in the orientation of the Bank of England. Because the
mmercial banks were so heavily exposed to floundering industrial
ntures, the Bank of England became increasingly concerned for the
ability of the entire financial system. Its solution was to seek
rough a series of organizations, first the Securities Management
rust, formed in 1929, and then the Bankers' Industrial Development
mpany, formed in 1930, the "rationalization" of important indus-
ies, such as steel and cotton, that employed many workers, that
ved large sums to the banking system, and that suffered from

overcapacity and low (or nonexistent) profitability. The Bank *
England achieved little with its initiatives (Tolliday, 1986). First, th
Bank had very limited resources to commit to domestic rationaliza
tion. Second, the Bank, like the banking system as a whole, foun
itself enmeshed with clients in a long-term relationship which it ha
neither wished nor anticipated. Thus, the Bank, again like th
banking system as a whole, possessed neither the experience nor th
expertise to bring about fruitful rationalization in the industries *
which it had a large-scale stake. Such limited opportunities as di
exist for restructuring declining industries were largely lost throug
awkwardly conducted negotiations.

The absence of an active contribution by the banking system t
industrial renewal in the interwar period should not obscure les
dramatic, but vitally important contributions. Most obviously, Britai
was spared the trauma that paralyzed the US when the financia
system collapsed there between 1929 and 1933, a collapse so total tha
the US did not regain 1929 levels of income and output until 194
and then only under the stimulus of war. The weaknesses of th
British financial system did not include paralysis, and inherer
conservatism paid handsome rewards in the extraordinary events *
the early 1930s. Moreover, the resilience of the banking syste
permitted traditional methods of finance to work reasonably well in
hostile environment. The sharp fall in interest rates in the early 193(
encouraged housebuilding, which in turn stimulated a wide range *
industries from construction materials to electrification to road buil
ing. Improving levels of business activity generated the cash flow
most firms needed to sustain investment. Cheap money also mad
recourse to external funding, either through short-term bank loans *
through the stock exchanges, easier. Moreover, economic collapse *
virtually all those overseas areas where Britain had invested s
heavily over the preceding century meant that, for the first time sinc
the end of the Napoleonic Wars, Britain made no net investmer
abroad in the decade of the 1930s. Indeed, Britain was the recipient *
funds being repatriated or seeking a safer haven in an unprecedentec
ly hostile world.

On balance, the interwar period found the British financial syste
in a process of transition. Banks were drawn into a closer an
longer-term relationship with industrial clients, albeit in a pervers
and negative manner. The Bank of England came to recognize a
obligation for the adequacy of domestic industrial finance and slowl
and painfully began to develop a capacity to discharge this duty. Mo
private enterprises outside the troubled sectors of cotton, steel, co
and shipbuilding financed themselves much as they always had

ugh retained earnings, short-term bank loans, and private
otiations. Because of the utter economic collapse overseas, how-
r, British domestic industrial finance in the 1930s at least
efited from the undivided attention of merchant bankers, broker-
houses and the rest of the City of London, while pursuing
ansion in trying circumstances. Adjustments, while far from
pleted, were at least under way.

9 to the Present: the Road to Recovery?

Second World War was even more destructive of Britain's
nomy than the First had been. The domestic capital stock was run
n in order to sustain maximum mobilization for the war effort. An
ady shrunken stock of overseas assets was further drastically
uced. Massive foreign debts were incurred to finance critical
time imports. Export markets, already ravaged by the trade
apse of the 1930s, appeared more remote and uncertain than ever.
vever, unlike the decade after 1918, Britain was able to adjust to
postwar conditions in circumstances of unprecedented interna-
al expansion, although from a very low base.

owever, Britain was unable to benefit fully from the unexpectedly
yant conditions, due to serious policy errors arising from state
mpts to direct economic activity. Although these errors were
espread, they can be most easily illustrated by the steel industry.
troubled steel industry had attracted official interest in the
rwar period, and as a vital raw material of war, it had continued
be of urgent concern after 1939. As an essential construction
terial, its importance did not decline with the advent of peace. The
l industry, however, found itself in a policy straitjacket which
vely retarded its postwar expansion. Rigid price controls under-
ued steel, with the result of greatly stimulating demand, while
ving steel firms with too little retained earnings to increase
acity significantly. Government-subsidized investment, insensitive
market demands, blind to costs and erratic in availability, was
gularly inept, yet low levels of profitability prevented the industry
m attracting external finance.

n part because of the perceived failures of state direction of the
nomy, the machinery of massive intervention began to be disman-
l in the early 1950s; and with only short-lived interruptions this
cess has continued until the present (although one may wonder

whether the recent policy of privatization of loosely regulated ind
tries with marked degrees of market power will not create its o
crop of errors). Consequently, the bulk of British capital format
continues to be allocated by processes and institutions that h
strong historical roots. Perhaps most importantly, the long traditior
enterprise self-finance remains deeply entrenched. British enterpris
perhaps to a greater extent than those of any other developed nati
depend upon internal resources for expansion.[4]

Important changes nevertheless have taken place in the Brit
financial system which make it very different from what it was
1939. The Companies Act of 1948 was a true watershed, fin
requiring a degree of financial disclosure that permitted comp
outsiders to obtain an unprecedentedly clear picture of comp
assets and earnings, placing managers for the first time un
informed public scrutiny. This and subsequent laws passed with
same objective have vastly enhanced the capabilities of Britai
public capital markets to direct financial resources in a knowledgea
and responsible manner.

Three aspects of this development are particularly important. Fi
financial innovations have extended the scope of public capi
markets. These innovations have many forms, such as interest rate
currency swaps, traded options, enlarged futures markets, and
extended range of instruments that may be converted into equity
specified circumstances. Of this large and growing array of inno
tions, perhaps the most important is the emergence of the misnan
"junk bond," which promises to open up for a critical range of clie
access to areas of the long-term capital markets previously reserv
only for mature "blue-chip" firms. If this promise is fully realized
ability of markets to direct resources to their most productive uses
be greatly improved, and the often-observed gap between inter
rates of return on capital and the external cost of funds will
reduced.[5]

Another aspect of the process whereby firms seek to deal m
directly with ultimate lenders than by borrowing from banks is
increasing recourse made by highly creditworthy firms to their abi
to sell short-term commercial paper to lenders directly through op
credit markets.

A second development has been the emergence of an unlist
securities market (USM), with a supporting network of special
market makers and brokers. This development gives stock exchan
access to smaller, newer firms than previously, while still maintaini
some degree of market scrutiny; a multi-tiered stock market gi
recognition to the special needs of firms in different phases

`elopment. A third development, following directly from the re-
ns embodied in the 1948 Companies Act (and elaborated subse-
`ntly), allows increasing use of stock exchange trading to effect
`tile takeover bids with the intention of making more effective use
`orporate assets, thereby opening up a channel of market control
ependent both of the banks and the bankruptcy courts. This marks
important change from the past, when the only course open to
gruntled shareholders was passively to sell their holdings.

`hese developments in the use of Britain's public capital markets
`e been accompanied by changes in the behavior of Britain's large
`aring banks. These banks are gradually cultivating closer, longer-
m ties with client firms and are using their huge, diversified asset
`e to shoulder real equity risks. Through venture capital, merchant
`king, or stockbroking subsidiaries, Britain's banks are now
empting to play a more aggressive, systematic role in British
porate finance. However, as the experience of the National West-
`ster Bank with the Blue Arrow flotation of October 1987 has
`wn, this new development in banking can be hazardous and costly,
`l is by no means an easy road to enhanced profitability. Neverthe-
s this aspect of banking development seems likely to continue to
`w in importance.

`he combined developments in banking behavior and public capital
`rkets can be seen as an important new stage in Britain's financial
`velopment. With only limited and partial exceptions, most notably
` period from 1826 to 1878 and the very recent past, when banks
`e sought out profitable long-term links with industry rather than
`ving such links determined by adverse selection, Britain's financial
`tem, to borrow Colin Mayer's useful distinction (1987), has been
`rket- rather than bank-driven. The changes since 1950 have
`erally served to make market processes more informed and more
`ctive. These changes have been accompanied by efforts on the part
banks and other financial intermediaries to be more closely and
`re profitably involved in private sector finance. Such involvement,
`wever, is clearly taking place within an environment decisively
`ped by market forces and trading opportunities. Britain's financial
`tem is likely in the foreseeable future to become even more firmly
`rket-driven than it has been in the past. In this sense, Britain's
`ancial traditions, while definitely evolving, remain intact.

`dvocates of competition in financial services maintain that recent
`velopments in public capital markets, combined with closer equity
`ks between banks and client firms, will result in a greater volume
skilled investment, free from the anti-competitive tendencies
`ged to have inhibited bank-dominated financial systems in the

past. Banks will play a crucial role, but their ability to sh
themselves from competitive pressures at the expense of the econ
as a whole will be reduced, both by the increased range of alterna
means of enterprise finance and by an increasingly articu
antimonopoly policy. In this competitive environment banks wil
compelled in future to use more fully for less reward, particularl
support of small innovative firms, their resources, their accumul
market intelligence, and their opportunities for systematic diversif
tion. If this requires a systematic expansion of the capital base of
banking system, it would represent a desirable reallocation of
sources and would also suggest that the system's capital base
been too small previously. Although this line of development does
hold out the promise of radically improving Britain's econo
performance in the short run, the longer-term prospects appear t
brighter. Long standing weaknesses are being corrected and
capabilities are being added, to an important degree by for
financial institutions taking an active part in the finance of Bri
domestic enterprises.

It is necessary, however, in closing, to note an alternative v
(expressed most recently by Colin Mayer (1987)) which holds t
beneficial competition in financial markets may not be realized wit
Britain's tradition of financial evolution. In this view, recent deve
ments in the operations of public financial markets, far from facili
ing the skilled, long-term risky investment upon which gro
ultimately depends, only increase the scope for short-term opportu
tic behavior. Banks, for example, will be less likely to aid firm
crisis if they have a significantly reduced ability to profit from th
firms' recoveries, should they occur, because the firms, once recove
can turn to the open capital markets for funds more cheaply t
those offered by the rescuing banks (unless, of course, banks ext
rescue aid in the form of equity participation). Similarly, the man
ment of a firm exposed to hostile takeover bidding will be m
reluctant to undertake a long-term investment program if it incre
the likelihood of an unwanted takeover bid before the program
reach fruition, triggered perhaps by the kind of delay common to
ambitious, complex effort. Moreover, while the threat of a hos
takeover bid undoubtedly serves to discipline managers, the discip
may not be an efficient one. Corporate raiders generally expect h
premiums before undertaking a bid, for they risk substantial st
and shoulder heavy expenses, while all shareholders stand to ben
from a takeover, or indeed, even from an attempted but unsucces
takeover bid. Thus "free riders" will create a gap, possibly a large
between the intrinsic value of a firm and its market value w

hares are widely dispersed; a gap which can be difficult to close under resent arrangements (Grossman and Hart, 1980). If this view, with s emphasis on inherent market weaknesses, arising most fundamentally from limited information, is correct, competitive marketased financial systems will inevitably be myopic, forever bound by ndesirably short horizons which no amount of institutional tinkering an correct. In this case, fundamental improvement in Britain's conomic performance cannot be achieved within the bounds permited by the evolution of Britain's traditional financial system, but must wait the adoption of an entirely new tradition.

Notes

In writing this chapter I have greatly benefited from the suggestions, comments and criticisms of Charles Goodhart and Leslie Pressnell. Any remaining errors are my responsibility alone.
For examples of the theoretical lines of argument, see papers by Hart (1975), rossman and Hart (1980), Stiglitz and Weiss (1981), and Bernanke (1983).
Factors other than differences in banking organization and practice have been dvanced to account for the more rapid growth of Scottish than English per capita ncomes during the eighteenth century. There is nearly consensus among historians nat Scotland's greater provision of education fostered highly advantageous human apital formation, but educational provision was only remotely linked to banking. It has lso been argued that agriculture, an activity relatively (but not completely) neglected y banking, played a vital role in Scottish development, as did the ready availability of atural resources in the form of iron and coal (Campbell, 1985: pp. 1, 106). evertheless, Scottish banks were too closely involved with too many key industries nd growing firms for an important link between banking and economic development to e denied. The case for a link existing has been well argued by Warren Lammert 989b).
Smaller American firms also appear to be undeniably dependent on internal esources. See Fazzari *et al.* (1988) for an interesting cross-section attempt to measure ne difficulties US firms face in raising external funds, and a discussion of the aacroeconomic costs of these difficulties.
It might be noted in passing that the advent of "junk bonds" constitutes a triumph of cademic financial theory, since the willingness of fund managers to hold relatively w-grade bonds depends crucially upon newly operational strategies for creating fficiently diversified portfolios. While it has long been known in principle that portfolio ability can be achieved without requiring that each individual portfolio component as low expected variance, the operational means of achieving stability in practice with wer-grade assets has only recently been devised. Although critics forcefully argue that ore experience is needed to obtain information of sufficient quality to assess ccurately the risks embodied in the new instruments and to make reliable calculations f optimal portfolio balance, the principle of the utility of "junk bonds" is almost niversally conceded.

CHAPTER 6

The Effects of Bank Regulation on the Financing of American Business, 1860–1960

EUGENE N. WHITE

In the last decade the rapid changes in corporate finance have becom a focus of public concern. Hostile takeovers and leveraged buyou dramatically replaced some firms' equity with debt. Overall, durii the 1980s, corporations bought back more than one-sixth of the outstanding stock, making American business more leveraged than any time since the Second World War.[1] Many economists ar policy-makers fear that higher corporate leverage will precipita more business failures in the next recession, creating the potential f a general liquidity or solvency crisis.[2] Federal tax policy is most oft held accountable for these developments, and the relatively low level of leverage earlier in the century, when income taxes we nonexistent or less distortionary, is held to be the norm. Howeve early twentieth century corporate finance was far from a free mark outcome, and the distinctive emphasis on equity finance was primari the consequence of the regulation of financial intermediaries.

This chapter assesses the contributions of institutions, regulatic and taxation to the development of modern industrial finance fro the mid-nineteenth century to the mid-twentieth century. In th survey, the early twentieth century emphasis on equity finance argued to be primarily the result of the regulations placed c commercial banks. Although commercial banks had been the preem nent source of funds for business in the first three-quarters of th nineteenth century, they were displaced by the securities marke when regulations limited the size and type of their investments. Whi government intervention did not impede the establishment of moder industry, it did have profound consequences for corporate control. Th sale of equities to the general public meant that managers were n osely tied to their bankers and were instead directly subject to the essures of the securities markets.

New regulations and higher taxes altered the character of Amer-an corporate finance during the New Deal and Second World War, viving the use of debt and restoring, to a limited degree, the role of anks. Since 1960, rapid financial innovation has transformed the ancing of business, but these changes largely represent an accelera-on of earlier postwar trends.[3] Most policy recommendations have cused on altering the tax structure to reduce the incentives for using bt; however, a more general reform should consider the regulations at have limited the participation of financial institutions in the ancing and governance of modern American enterprise.

nance and Enterprise in America, 1850–1913

efore 1840, American industrial goods were produced in small orkshops with a few employees; the only important exception to this neralization was textiles.[4] In the 1850s, American industry began adapt steam and water power to production. This process picked up omentum after the Civil War, and the size of industrial enterprises owly began to grow. Between 1850 and 1870 the proportion of value ded in artisan shops, defined as having under seven employees and steam or water power, fell in 18 out of 24 of the most important dustries. By 1870 more than half of the value added in meat cking, flour milling, distilled and malt liquors, textiles, sawmills, rniture, printing, tanning, pig iron, and steam engineering was oduced in factories employing over 25 employees and an inanimate urce of power. Nevertheless, even in these dynamic sectors, firm ze remained small. In the leading 24 industries, the minimum ficient scale of firms in terms of value added was $128,000 in cotton xtiles followed by $64,000 in pig iron and millinery.[5] Even such ants of industry as McCormick in farm machinery had value added production of only $407,000 in 1870.

The fixed and working capital requirements of these establishments ere consequently small. The most important external finance need r these firms was for short-term working capital. Before the Civil ar this was largely supplied by trade acceptances. When buying raw aterials, a manufacturer could issue a trade acceptance to the sellers ho could, in turn, endorse the notes and discount them at a local nk or sell them to note brokers. The use of this instrument declined after the Civil War and was gradually replaced by the unsecure promissory note. These notes could be discounted at a bank or sold b a broker on the open market, making them commercial paper.[6] I addition to discounts, credit in the form of a loan could also b obtained from a bank by pledging some collateral, often warehous receipts, bills of lading, or documents for other commodities.

These loans and discounts tended to be of short duration. Before th Civil War the average discount period for New York banks was 4 days. Afterwards the most common maturities were 30, 60 and 9 days. It was relatively uncommon for banks to offer loans with mor than six months' maturity.[7] Although banks were the preeminen lending institutions in this period, savings banks, trust companie insurance companies, individuals and other mercantile and manufac turing firms also supplied industrial concerns with credit. In Lanc Davis' study of Massachusetts' textile firms, commercial banks wer their most important source of credit. They supplied most of the loan but the loans for under 30 days and over one year were obtained fror other sources.[8] Another feature of this market was the modest size loans and discounts. In Davis's study the largest loan was $50,000 an the smallest $68. Financial intermediaries thus had no difficulty i supplying credit to industry on this scale.

Table 6.1 provides a simple comparison of the relative size c manufacturing firms and banks. Between 1850 and 1870, the averag size of each increased, but their relative sizes changed little. If $50,00 was the largest loan demanded, the average bank, whose capital wa well over $250,000, could have accommodated such a request, eve though it would have risked one-fifth of its capital. Of course, mos loans were considerably smaller. In 1879, the average size of a loa for national banks in New York was $3,962, $2,244 in Chicago, an $1,936 in New Orleans.[9] The larger banks of the Northeast, wher most industry was located, could thus easily accommodate an industrial loan.

In the decades immediately preceding and following the Civil War there was nothing distinctive about the financing of industry in th United States. The credit needs of industry were relatively modes and could be met by short-term borrowing from banks, other financia intermediaries, or the open market using the same financial instru ments. The Civil War did bring about one important change; i brought the federal government back into the regulation of com mercial banking. The establishment of the National Banking Systen in 1864 did not immediately alter the pattern of financing industry The banks that accepted national charters did not radically chang their operations. What the associated legislation did do was to impos

Table 6.1 The relative size of manufacturing, banking and life insurance firms.

	Manufactures		Banking			Life insurance		
	Number of firms	Value added per firm (Dollars)	Number of banks	Assets per bank (Dollars)	Capital per bank (Dollars)	Number of companies	Assets per company (Dollars)	Capital per company (Dollars)
1850	123,025	3,772	824	645,631	263,350	48	237,500	
1860	140,433	6,081	1,562	640,205	270,166	43	560,465	162,791
1870	252,148	5,532	1,937	919,463	334,538	129	2,089,147	375,969
1880	253,852	7,768	3,355	1,013,115	246,200	59	7,086,441	1,213,559
1890	355,405	11,592	8,201	775,271	189,977	60	12,850,000	1,533,333
1900A	512,276	10,686	13,053	872,443	158,967	84	20,738,095	2,964,286
1900	204,754	22,696						
1909	264,810	30,815	23,734	905,410	158,001	254	14,346,457	1,862,205
1919	270,231	88,225	29,767	1,599,187	181,711	314	21,627,389	1,853,503
1929	206,663	148,024	25,568	2,828,340	381,336	438	39,913,242	3,020,548
1939	173,802	140,890	15,210	4,812,163	541,486	446	65,567,265	3,881,166
1947	240,807	308,504	14,715	11,303,840	796,398	539	95,998,145	6,374,768
1958	303,303	466,662	14,095	18,862,079	1,523,448	1,365	78,813,187	6,452,015
1967	311,140	842,010	14,267	33,615,336	2,688,091	1,723	109,481,138	9,139,872

Sources: *Abstract of the Twelfth Census, 1900* (Washington, DC, 1902), pp. 300–1.
Census of Manufactures, 1977 (Washington, DC, 1977), Table 1.
Historical Statistics of the United States (Washington, DC, 1975), Vol. 2, pp. 1019–20, 1056–61.
Note: In 1900, the Census first removed the figures for hand and neighborhood manufacturing operations, but provided figures (1900A) for comparison with previous years.

regulations on banks that, when industrial firms were transform
into large corporate enterprises, rendered them incapable of servi
all their customers' needs.

The constraints that hampered and then reduced the role of bar
in financing industrial enterprise were the general prohibition
branch banking and the limitations on the size of loans and discour
given to any single customer. The National Banking Act did r
specifically forbid branching to national banks. It only required tha
national bank's usual business be transacted in the place specified
its organization certificate. The Comptroller of the Currency int
preted this, however, as prohibiting branching.[10] This ruling was
reflection of the general hostility to banks moving beyond c
community. States could have permitted the commercial banks th
chartered to branch, but only a few states granted even limit
branching rights. The result was that in 1900, while there we
thousands of banks, only 87 of these operated a total of 1
branches.[11] The population density and economic activity where
bank located, thus, largely determined its size.

The capacity of a bank to lend to an individual firm was constrain
by the limits set by regulation on the maximum loan size. T
National Banking Act of 1864 prohibited any loan to one lender
excess of 10 per cent of a bank's capital. This ceiling was raised
1906 to 10 per cent of capital and surplus; the states also impos
constraints on the size of loans, but they were more liberal, with or
New Hampshire and North Carolina being as restrictive as t
National Banking Act. State limits commonly ranged up to 30 p
cent of capital and surplus; there were no restrictions of this kind
ten states.[12] However, this did not necessarily allow state banks
offer larger loans than national banks, because they were typica
smaller. In 1900, while the average national bank had over $1m.
assets, the average state bank had less than $300,000. This differe
tial in size was a consequence of the fact that most states banks we
established after most national banks, and their creation was pro
oted by lower state minimum capital requirements, designed to ensu
the presence of banks in small towns and rural areas.

The branching and loan size restrictions were probably not seriou
binding constraints on the commercial banks' ability to serve indust
in the first and even the second decade following the Civil W
Businesses were still of a modest size, with the obvious exception
the railroads, and commercial banks and other financial int
mediaries were able to serve their borrowing needs. The appearar
of the modern industrial enterprise devoted to mass production at t

of the nineteenth century began to change this relationship.
portant technological developments, coupled with earlier innova-
1s in transportation, communication and organization, transformed
character of American industry in a few decades.[13] These changes
;an to pick up momentum in the 1880s, as continuous process
hnologies were introduced to the production of cigarettes, matches,
1r milling, oil refining, and metals. To obtain all the benefits from
ovations in transportation, communications, and their own indus-
's technological advances, firms combined horizontally and inte-
ted vertically.

n the early stages of the formation of the large industrial
erprise, banks continued to be an important source of finance.
ny of the creators of the modern corporations went to extraordin-
lengths to cultivate bankers, to ensure that their firms had access
sufficient funds. John D. Rockefeller built up personal contacts with
veland bankers, overcoming their resistance to substantial invest-
nt in the risky business of oil refining. As Standard Oil was formed
1 expanded, Rockefeller obtained the assistance of the New York
y banks, reflecting the company's increasing needs for more
erating funds.[14] However, bank finance had its limitations, and it
yed a limited role in the consolidation movement.

n many industries, the first efforts at combination and consolida-
n were accomplished by the formation of a trust, whereby owners of
large number of firms could exchange their securities for trust
tificates. Beginning with Rockefeller's Standard Oil trust in 1882,
trust movement spread to cotton oil refining (1884), linseed oil
ining (1885), whiskey distilling (1887), sugar refining (1887) and
d smelting and refining (1887). These trust certificates remained
sely held, and a small proportion were traded on the exchanges.
ny of these trusts eventually found that conversion into a corpora-
n could increase the value of the firm, by splitting the trust
tificate into a relatively safe instrument, preferred stock, and a
atively risky one, common stock. The sugar trust converted its
tificates into half preferreds and half common stock, realizing an
preciation of 43 per cent in three months.[15]
ndustries that had not gone through the trust phase combined and
rganized via merger using stock. The wave of mergers from 1897
1902 created even more giant enterprises. The structure of
nerican industry was transformed by the creation of such firms as
ited States Steel, International Harvester, American Can, United
uit, Du Pont, and Anaconda Copper.[16] The investment banks took
lead in originating, underwriting and distributing the new

securities. Commercial banks lost their preeminent position in fin:
ing industry, as very few had any experience in investment bank
and they were prohibited from buying stock for their portfolios.

The stocks and bonds of the new corporations were placed v
wealthy individuals and other financial intermediaries, notably in:
ance companies and trust companies. Unlike banks, life insura
companies were not constrained in size. As Table 6.1 shows, banks
average, did not grow in size up to 1900. In some decades, the aver
bank, measured by assets or capital, declined, as thousands of sr
banks were chartered. By contrast, insurance companies were
geographically limited and they grew rapidly, in part, as a resul
their participation in corporate finance.[17] In addition to life insura
companies, trust companies, incorporated under liberal state chart
began to supplant commercial banks. The trust companies develc
rapidly by combining investment and commercial banking with t
trust activitieṣ. These innovative intermediaries participated in
underwriting and distribution of securities, and bought many for t
own portfolios. By 1914, the total assets of trust companies in N
York State was fast approaching the total assets of national bank:

The investment bankers who served to advise and manage the :
of the new corporations' stock also counseled them to increase t
working capital. They recommended the issuance of bonds to rem
the new giant concerns' apparent shortage of working capital. '
cotton oil trust had been forced to retain all of its profits and d
heavily on short-term loans to meet its heavy seasonal purchas
needs. Once incorporated, it sold $4m. in bonds to raise perman
working capital. The issue of stock was often accompanied by
issue of bonds as mergers typically acquired only the physical ass
and no liquid funds. Although substantially smaller than their iss
of stock, the first corporations had bond issues that ranged from $:
to $4m.[19]

The growing issue of corporate bonds reflected the inability of n
banks to meet even the short-term credit needs of their indust
customers. Any bank with pretensions of obtaining or retaining
accounts of the new industrial enterprises was faced with a seri
problem. On a microeconomic level, three individual bank histo
show how banks struggled, with varying degrees of success, to ret
their share of intermediation.

The Philadelphia National Bank aggressively courted the r
giants of industry at the turn of the century, including Swift, I
Goodrich, Westinghouse and Sears Roebuck. The bank was, howe'
frustrated by the size of loans that it could offer to its clients.[20]
1903 it became engaged in a battle with the Comptroller of

urrency, who contended that the $150,000 loans it made exceeded he legal limit of 10 per cent of capital. The bank argued that capital hould be interpreted to include capital and surplus. Before this onflict was resolved, Congress responded to general pressure from anks and specified the limit to be 10 per cent of capital and surplus, o long as no loan exceeded 30 per cent of a bank's capital. The hiladelphia National Bank tried other tactics to circumvent the legal estrictions. To give a larger loan to the Pennsylvania Railroad, it rranged for a repurchase agreement, whereby the bank would urchase securities from the railroad on the understanding that they vould be sold back to the firm at a certain time at a stipulated price.[21]

Outside of the largest cities, the inability to keep pace with the rowth of business was even more acute. Although it was a very uccessful bank, the National Bank of Commerce in Houston found tself unable to adequately serve local businesses that had become ational enterprises. In the early years of the century, the National 3ank of Commerce and other Houston banks had little to do with the najor growth industry of Texas, oil. The independents were felt to be oo risky, and companies like Texaco and Gulf Oil too big. When Gulf's redecessor company was incorporated in 1901 with $15m., its credit eeds were far larger than what any individual local bank could rovide. Thus, in 1906 and 1907, when Texaco and Gulf built nultimillion-dollar pipelines, they drew on New York and Pittsburgh or financing. Houston banks were limited to the smaller needs of andling payrolls, clearing checks and making personal loans to local xecutives.[22]

While such major city banks, as Philadelphia National, and regional anks, like the National Bank of Commerce, struggled to retain their raditional role of financing business, only a select few were flexible nough to master the changing financial environment. National City 3ank succeeded where others struggled because it moved quickly into he business of investment banking. While National City Bank could ot purchase the new industrial stocks, it did prosper by shifting its ocus from commercial to investment banking. It began this change by oining forces with Kuhn, Loeb, an investment bank that was skilled n the origination and placement of securities but lacked the banking esources and additional ability at placement that National City could ffer. Together they competed with the biggest investment banks and nderwrote the largest issues.[23] Through its close association with the ailroads, oil and other industries, the bank received very large orporate deposits. By 1905, the National City had $308m. in assets, naking it the largest bank in the nation. Its equity by 1907 was lmost $50m., which would have permitted it to make the large

short-term loans required by industry. However the bank's portfol
was instead dominated by call loans and bonds, a reflection of i
devotion to investment banking.[24] Unlike virtually all commerci
banks in the United States, National City Bank had made th
transition from being a financial intermediary of small tradition;
firms in commerce and manufacturing, to being a financial inte
mediary for the new corporate giants.

Between the Civil War and the First World War, the United Stat
acquired a distinctive form of corporate finance. The modern verticall
integrated industrial concern could not obtain the necessary fundin
from the banking sector. Federal and state regulation inhibited th
ability of banks to grow in size with industry and continue provision
short-term loans and to fund long-term investment by buying stock
Consequently, investment banks helped corporations issue bonds an
stocks that were sold primarily to the public and other financi;
intermediaries. Table 6.2 shows the distribution of nonfinanci;
business corporations securities among financial intermediaries an
the public. By 1900 commercial banks in aggregate held only a tin
fraction, 6.5 per cent, of all corporate securities. This rose only slightl
in 1910, reflecting increased purchases of corporate bonds.[25] Compe
ing financial intermediaries held almost another 20 per cent, but th
lion's share of corporate securities, well over 70 per cent, was in th
hands of the public. Regulation had divorced the business from
natural partner in corporate finance, the banking industry. Th
commercial banks were replaced as intermediaries between th

Table 6.2 Medium- and long-term debt of non-financial corporations held b
creditors.

Year	Total ($bn.)	Commercial banks	Insurance companies	Other financial intermediaries	Public
			Percentage held by		
1900	6.5	6.5	10.0	7.5	76.0
1910	14.0	9.9	11.1	6.5	72.4
1920	19.0	8.4	10.9	3.4	77.2
1930	30.0	9.5	17.2	4.2	69.1
1940	32.7	13.1	30.9	6.0	50.0

Source: Jacoby and Saulnier (1947): p. 102.
Note: Debt includes term loans.

ving public and industry by a more direct relationship between the ublic and industry, brokered by investment bankers.

anking and Corporate Finance, 1914–29

he system of corporate finance established before the First World ar was not substantially altered during the war or in the 1920s. stead, a rapidly growing economy accelerated the existing trends. ew dynamic sectors – including automobiles, radio and public ilities – were brought to the fore by technological innovation. Their nancing needs and a new merger boom increased demands for ng-term finance and investment banking services. Commercial anks, which had tentatively begun to assist with the origination, nderwriting and distribution of bonds before 1913, eagerly set up curity affiliates to act as fully-fledged investment banks and broker- es. As the demand for traditional commercial banking services agnated, this shift to investment banking proved a successful rategic move for those banks that were able to shift resources and rsonnel.

Statistics first became available in the early twentieth century, nd the reduced importance of commercial banking in the financing of nterprise is immediately apparent.[26] As seen in Table 6.3, the bulk of onfinancial corporations' external funds, 77.1 per cent, were obtained om the sales of securities in the period 1901–12. Of the remaining 2.9 per cent that were borrowed, banks provided only slightly more an half the credit. Other financial intermediaries' were encroaching n the banks' turf. In the two years before the First World War shown Table 6.4, 1900 and 1912, the banks' share of all financial termediaries assets was over 65 per cent, and the commercial banks' are was over 55 per cent. However, while banks and commercial anks offered well over 80 per cent of the loans to unincorporated usinesses in these years, their share of corporate business was far maller, approximately 55 and 46 per cent respectively. The borrow- g needs of the government during the First World War drastically educed the ability of corporations to fund their operations by the sue of new securities, as private issues were controlled by a Capital ssues Committee. During the years 1913–22 the sale of securities ccounted for only one half of the external funds raised by corpora- ons. The increased demand for borrowed funds by corporations did

Table 6.3 Sources of funds of nonfinancial corporations.

Period	Total external funds ($bn.)	Percentage of external funds from				
		Borrowing		Sale of securities		
		Total	Bank loans	Total	Stocks	Bond
1901–12	17.9	22.9	12.3	77.1	31.3	45.8
1913–22	30.1	50.5	14.6	49.8	28.2	21.6
1923–9	39.0	25.9	1.5	74.1	42.8	31.3
1930–3	−4.8	−183.3	−91.7	83.3	58.3	25.0
1934–9	0.7	−42.9	−42.9	157.1	371.4	−214.
1940–5	14.9	102.0	18.1	−2.0	23.5	−25.5
1946–9	39.3	48.3	6.1	51.4	20.6	30.8
1950–5	107.4	71.9	13.0	28.1	10.1	18.0
1956–9	71.8	61.6	17.7	38.4	12.5	25.9
1960–5	162.0	80.4	18.8	19.6	3.6	16.0
1966–70	256.4	67.2	18.5	32.8	5.4	27.4

Sources: Raymond W. Goldsmith, *Financial Intermediaries in the American Economy Since 1*(Princeton: NBER, 1958): Table 53, pp. 222–3.
Department of Commerce, *Historical Statistics of the United States* (Washington, DC: Government Printing Office, 1976), Vol 2: p. 981.
Note: Before 1950, all figures are for nonfinancial corporation. Afterwards, amounts are for business.

not, however, benefit the banks. Although total loans increas substantially, their share did not rise significantly.

In the 1920s, corporate finance reverted to the established prew pattern, beginning with a drastic reduction of the short-term de that firms had acquired during the war. For the period 1923–9 Table 6.3, all nonfinancial corporations returned to roughly t prewar pattern of external funding, with nearly three-fourths of funds being obtained through the sale of securities. The new develo ments of this period were the reversed importance of stocks a bonds, the shrinkage of commercial paper, and the virtual disappea ance of bank loans.

Table 6.3 shows that for all nonfinancial corporations, stocks to over the former prominence of bonds, accounting for almost 43 p cent of external finance. This trend was even more pronounced for t giant corporations. A National Bureau of Economic Research study 84 of the largest manufacturing firms found that stocks were t

Table 6.4 The declining importance of banks.

Year	Percentage of total assets to assets of all financial intermediaries		Percentage of total loans to corporations by financial intermediaries		Percentage of total loans to unincorporated business by financial intermediaries	
	All banks	Commercial banks	All banks	Commercial banks	All banks	Commercial banks
1900	68.1	55.5	56.6	45.3	88.0	80.0
1912	65.7	55.3	55.2	46.9	90.9	86.4
1922	57.8	44.8	54.0	45.0	92.5	88.8
1929	50.1	39.5	40.9	33.4	87.0	80.6
1933	43.8	25.3	36.2	23.6	80.4	60.7
1939	40.1	23.1	24.7	19.4	77.6	67.3
1945	45.0	28.7	23.8	20.4	88.8	86.3
1949	40.8	25.1	24.5	20.9	87.4	83.8
1952	39.4	24.9	25.4	22.1	87.7	84.6

Source: Raymond Goldsmith, *Financial Intermediaries in the American Economy* (Princeton: NBER, 1958); appendix.

preferred instrument of finance.[27] During the years 1921–7, thes firms raised $889.6m. from the sale of stocks and $318m. fro bonds. During the stock market boom of 1928–9 these firms began t substitute stock for bonds, issuing $1,064m. of stock and conducting net retirement of $400.4m. of bonds. These last few years of th decade may not, however, represent a new trend, but may instea reflect the appearance of a bubble in the stock market.[28]

In the boom times of the 'twenties, business found it easy to issu securities in the markets that were not yet regulated by the feder government. Many borrowers abandoned the commercial paper ma ket and replaced their borrowed funds with securities. This created new problem for commercial banks, because the commercial pape market had served to provide small-sized investments in industry The 10 per cent loan rule prevented many banks from directly lendin to big business, but dealers sold commercial paper from these sam firms in relatively small denominations of $2,500 to $10,000, t banks.[29] Commercial banks were thus able to hold a diversifie portfolio investment in commerce and industry. The commercial pape market, however, began to shrink after the First World War. Th number of issuing companies dropped from 4,395 in 1920 to 1,653 i 1929, producing a drop in the volume of commercial paper outstand ing from $957m. to $420m. As these firms left the market to issu securities, the commercial paper market became dominated by financ companies. The General Motors Acceptance Corporation, the Com mercial Investment Trust and the Commercial Credit Corporation an other finance companies now placed their paper directly wit corporate lenders, largely bypassing dealers and banks.[30]

On many fronts, banks' traditional commercial banking activitie were on the decline. Table 6.4 reveals that by 1929 all banks' share o financial intermediaries' assets had fallen to 50 per cent, and th commercial banks' share to under 40 per cent. Banks' loans t unincorporated business remained at prewar levels, but their percen tage of loans to corporations continued to decline, falling to 41 pe cent for all banks and 33 per cent for commercial banks in 1929. Th drastic change in corporate finance is captured even more dramatical ly by the fall in bank loans to 1.5 per cent of all external busines finance. Banks only survived as intermediaries because they held o to loans to unincorporated business and they substituted loans t corporations with real estate and call loans, and made increase purchases of securities.[31] Augmented holdings of corporate bonds kep their share of the securities in Table 6.2 relatively stable.

The problems of banks attempting to serve corporate clients becam more acute. The average bank in the 1920s was growing in size, but i

as only keeping pace with the average manufacturing firm. As seen
1 Table 6.1, the mean manufacturing firm grew from $88,000 in
alue added in 1919, to $148,000 in 1929. In terms of assets, banks
oughly kept pace, growing from $1.6m. to $2.8m. This increase in
ize was produced partly by the closure of several thousand small
anks and a merger wave in the banking industry. The average bank
vas thus able to serve only small unincorporated businesses.

Mergers in banking were largely driven by the efforts of urban
anks to increase the size of loans they could offer their customers.
'he merger wave was initiated by the Act of November 7, 1918 which
stablished a relatively simple procedure for the consolidation of
ational banks. Before the act, if two banks wished to merge one had
o be liquidated; after it, they could consolidate under either bank's
harter, subject to the Comptroller of the Currency's approval. In
919, mergers began to increase, and 172 banks with $650m. assets
nerged. These accounted for less than 2 per cent of all bank assets. At
he bank merger wave's peak, in 1929, 529 banks were merged with
5,614m. of assets, or 9.6 per cent of all banks' assets.[32] Although
ommercial loans continued to decline in importance for large corpora-
ions, the success of this consolidation movement is impressive, if only
ecause of the obstacles. Before the McFadden Act of 1927, mergers
vere limited because national banks could not have full-scale bran-
hes. This forced merged banks into one office building. Even after
927, branching was only permitted in the home-office city if state law
llowed state-chartered banks branching privileges.

A few banks did grow enough by merger to maintain large
orporations as their customers. Before the First World War, Phila-
elphia National Bank had merged with one smaller bank; after the
var it proceeded on a strategy of mergers to increase its ability to
nd. In 1918, it absorbed the Farmers' and Mechanics' Bank,
oubling its capital and enabling it to increase the maximum line of
redit from $450,000 to $900,000. It also continually added to its
urplus, so that by 1922 it was able to provide loans of $1.4m. to Ford
nd Du Pont, and $1.5m. to Bethlehem Steel and Sears Roebuck. In
926 it merged with Girard National and in 1928 with the Franklin-
'ourth National Bank, increasing its net worth to $53m.[33]

Outside of the major urban areas where banks were more geo-
raphically dispersed, it was more difficult to grow by merger. By
929, the capital and surplus of the National Bank of Commerce, one
f the largest banks in Texas, amounted to only $3m., setting the
naximum loan at $300,000. In spite of the oil boom, its principal
usiness was still the financing of the cotton trade, but even in this
eld it was becoming increasingly difficult to accommodate some

customers. The construction boom in Houston in the 1920s wa:
largely financed by insurance companies, trust companies and bank
of the Northeast. The low lending limit kept the Houston banks out o
commercial construction, and instead they financed homes and sma
ler buildings.[34]

In spite of the merger movement, commercial banks found thei
ability to accommodate corporate customers with traditional product:
declining. National banks' commercial loans as a percentage of thei
earning assets declined from 58 per cent in 1920 to 37 per cent i
1929.[35] The response of many banks was to follow the path tha
National City Bank had taken before the First World War, int
investment banking.

Before the First World War, many banks had carried out invest
ment banking activities buying bonds for their own account an
trading them for their customers. However, national banks wer
prohibited from acquiring equities for their portfolios and tradin;
them. Even before the war, banks circumvented this legal restrictior
by setting up separate security affiliates to take over their investmen
banking operations. The first of these, the First Security Company
was founded in 1908 by the First National Bank of New York
National City Bank established the second, the National City Com
pany, in 1911.[36] As the new industries grew and the demand fo
securities boomed, security affiliates increased rapidly in number
from ten in 1922 to 114 in 1931.[37] These affiliates permitted banks t
break out of their legal geographic confines. By 1930 National City
Company had 60 branches and Chase Securities Corporation 26.[38]
Although the absence of statistics makes it difficult to measure thei
success, they seem to have captured approximately half of th
originations and participations.[39]

Commercial banks were thus able to regain some of their forme
prominence by using their security affiliates as investment banks anc
brokerage houses. The trust companies' advantages over commercia
banks were also weakened, as the Federal Reserve Act of 191:
permitted national banks to handle trusts. This invasion of invest
ment banking by commercial banks was, nevertheless, a limitec
victory; and only a relatively few banks opened securities affiliates
The federal and state legislation prohibiting branching, placing
restrictions on the size of loans, and barring banks from acquiring
securities continued to prevent banks from directly participating ir
the financing of modern American corporate enterprise.

The substituion of bank finance for finance with securities before
1929 was thus, in large part, the consequence of federal and state
regulation of the banking industry. One new factor did appear on the

of the First World War, the income tax. In 1913, the Sixteenth
.endment to the Constitution was ratified, reversing the Supreme
.rt Decision of 1895 that had held that an income tax was
:onstitutional.[40] Beginning with the Revenue Act of 1913, Congress
)osed income taxes on individuals and corporations, initiating the
.ble taxation of dividends and deductibility of interest payments.
: rates were initially set very low, but they rose rapidly during the
r. By 1918, tax rates ranged from 6 per cent on incomes over
000, to 77 per cent on incomes over $1m.[41]
\fter the First World War, taxes were cut dramatically. By 1925,
. top bracket for personal income tax was reduced to 25 per cent,
. excess profits tax was removed, and the corporate income tax rate
s set at 12.5 per cent. This arrangement lowered the cost of equity
)ital compared to borrowed capital. With the tax rate set at 12.5 per
.t, a corporation needed to earn $1.136 to pay $1 of dividends, while
.eeded to earn only $1 to pay $1 of interest on debt. This gave debt
ance only a small advantage over equity finance. Studies measur-
: the joint effects of personal and corporate income tax find that up
the 1920s there was little incentive for corporate leverage.[42]
rthermore, the tax cuts of the early 1920s may have fostered some
)ectations of further reductions as the economy boomed. Any future
in the corporate tax rate would have eliminated the tax incentive
issue debt. With taxes playing a nearly neutral role, the issue of
.v equity boomed. Whereas, in the period 1901–12, $5.6bn. of stock
i $8.2bn. of bonds and notes were issued, stock gained greater
)minence in the period 1923–9, with $16.7bn. of stock and $12.2bn.
bonds issued.[43]

rporate Finance from the Great Depression to the Postwar riod

.ile the First World War temporarily altered the pattern of business
ance, the changes in regulation and taxes prompted by the New
.al and the Second World War set corporate finance on a new
.rse. Equities became less attractive, debt finance increased, and
hough banks were not restored to their early nineteenth century
)minence, their role in financing business grew somewhat.
The Great Depression, which brought about a collapse of the
iking system and widespread business failures, reduced the total
:ernal funds available to nonfinancial corporations. In the period

1930–3, as shown by Table 6.3, external funding fell by $4.8b
During the monetary contraction and banking panics, banks a
other financial intermediaries slashed their loan portfolios, and to
borrowing by nonfinancial corporations fell by $8.8bn. Bank loa
accounted for $4.4bn. of this decrease. The drop in borrowing w
partly offset by $4bn. in sales of new securities, of which $2.8bn. we
stocks and $1.2bn. were bonds. For the rest of the decade, 1934–
there was virtually no increase in total external funds to busine
Total borrowing dropped another $300m., as did bank loans. T
additional funds came from the stock market, which provided $2.6b
while the bond market contracted another $1.5bn.

It is notable that the stock market continued to provide some fun
to business during the 1930s, as the collapse of stock prices in 19
certainly made potential stock buyers more wary. The securiti
industry was hit with new regulations that increased the cost
issuing new stocks or bonds. The Glass-Steagall Act of 1933 separat
commercial and investment banking, forcing commercial banks
liquidate their security affiliates. Commercial banks were the natu
competitors of investment banks. Forcing them out of the indust
reduced competition and may have raised the cost of issuing n
securities. Congress passed two other bills governing the securiti
business, The Securities Act of 1933 and the Securities Exchange A
of 1934. The former imposed new disclosure rules for corpora
securities. This was not opposed by the investment bankers, a
probably imposed small costs.[44] On the other hand, the investme
bankers generally believed that the 1934 Act would be extreme
costly, as reflected by the sharp drop in the price of seats on the N
York Stock Exchange.[45] The magnitude of the costs imposed on n
issuers is difficult to measure, but they clearly made borrowed fun
more attractive.

Perhaps more important for external business finance was t
change in corporate taxation. Beginning in 1932, the corporate incoi
tax rate began to climb, with an increase from 12 to 13.75 per ce
By 1939 the rate had reached 19 per cent. It continued to rise duri
and after the war, until it reached its peak level of 52 per cent
1952.[46] A corporate tax rate of 52 per cent meant that to pay $1 wor
of dividends a company had to earn $2.08, while it still had only
earn $1 to pay $1 of interest on debt. When the joint effects
personal and corporate income tax are considered, a considerable bi
was now created in favor of increased corporate leverage.[47]

This dramatic increase in the cost of paying dividends had
inevitable effect on the funding of American business. As Table 6

veals, new external funding of corporations with equities fell amatically. The share of stocks dropped from 43 per cent in the 20s to just above 10 per cent in the 1950s, and well below this level the 1960s. The result of these flows was that the ratio of debt to tal capital of manufacturing firms rose from 15.2 per cent in the late 20s, to 25.1 per cent by 1964–7.[48]

Corporate finance in the postwar era heavily employed bonds, ort-term debt and loans from banks and other financial inter- ediaries. While the tax law discriminated against equities, new bond sues did not wholly replace them. This may partly be explained by e higher costs imposed by the Securities Acts of 1933 and 1934, that plied to bonds as well as stocks. The issue of bonds recovered from e low levels of the Great Depression and the Second World War, but Table 6.3 shows, they did not return to the levels of earlier in the ntury, and ranged between 15 and 30 per cent of total external nding. Thus, the principal source of external funding for corpora- ns following the Second World War was borrowed funds, which rose well over 60 per cent of all external funds in the 1950s and 1960s. ιe source of funds was the commercial paper market, which versed its decline of the 1920s. The decreased desirability of issuing curities after the passage of the Securities Acts helped to revive it. ιe volume outstanding consequently rose from $228m. in 1939 to 84m. in 1951, and then $5,946m. in 1964.[49]

The federal regulation and tax rates also made bank loans attrac- e as a source of corporate funding once again. This change can be en in Table 6.3, where bank loans as a fraction of external funding se towards 18 per cent, exceeding the levels of the beginning of the ntury. This evidence is buttressed by the figures in Table 6.4 that veal that by the 1950s banks had halted their declining relative portance as financial intermediaries. While retaining their hold on ans to unincorporated business, all banks' share of loans to corpora- ns stabilized at about 25 per cent.

The primary instrument of banks' increased lending to business was e term loan. Throughout the first four decades of the twentieth ntury any examination of bank portfolios would have shown that ost discounts and loans were still for a duration of six months or ss. This did not stop banks from making effectively longer-term ans by offering easy renewals upon· expiration. In fact, some servers claimed that a substantial fraction of bank lending was mposed of disguised long-term loans.[50] The willingness to make ficial long-term loan commitments was, however, impeded by the deral Reserve's refusal to lend to any bank except on short-term paper. Only with the Banking Act of 1935 was this policy chang permitting the Federal Reserve banks to lend to member banks any sound assets, including corporate notes with more than one ye maturity.

Term loans had several advantages over bonds. These long-te loans could be quickly arranged and tailored to the needs of t borrower and the lender. Borrowers saved on underwriting costs a other fees, and there was no wait as required by the Securities a Exchange Commission's registration rules. Issuing bonds or equit required public disclosure, but term loans kept business informat confidential. Term loans increased fairly rapidly during the late 193 In Table 6.2, they account for most of the rise in business debt held commercial banks between 1930 and 1940. By 1940 commercial bar had made $2.2bn. in term loans, while there was little increase other loans.

The term loan provided many large banks with a vital new financ instrument in the postwar period. The biggest banks that catered corporations were shorn of their security affiliates by the Gla Steagall Act. Even though many banks had initially regarded te loans with suspicion, they turned to these loans as an alternat means of supplying credit to their corporate customers.[51] Term loa did, however, have one important limitation. Like any other loan, t maximum size loan a bank could offer any customer was restricted 10 per cent of capital. To increase their lending capacity, banks acr the country merged and acquired other banks. The effects of t growth are seen in Table 6.1, where the average bank was able keep pace with the average manufacturing firm between 1939 a 1967.

In New York City the wholesale banks, including Chemical Ba Bankers Trust, and Central Hanover Trust, acquired retail bar with branching networks to augment their deposit base and capita The imperative for growth was even greater for the regional ban The banks of Houston rapidly decreased in number by merger in t 1950s, but it was not enough to allow them to offer the size of loa desired by potential corporate customers. This problem was par solved by the syndication of loans that allowed small banks originate large loans from local business and sell participations and take participations from loans originated by other banks.[53]

Interstate branching via mergers was a certain route to incre banks to a size where they could accommodate any corpor customer. While there was some reduction in the intrastate barri to branching, change was exceedingly slow; and there was virtua no discussion of eliminating the interstate branching prohibitions. For mergers within the limits of the law, the climate worsened in the 1960s. When the National City Bank applied in 1961 to the Comptroller of the Currency to acquire a suburban Westchester bank, it was turned down on the grounds that it would lessen competition. Arguments that further mergers would increase banks' market power was accepted by the Supreme Court in 1963, which blocked the merger of the Philadelphia Bank with the Girard Trust and Corn Exchange Bank. The creation of a national or even large regional branching networks was thus frustrated, and the banks' ability to take a larger share of funding business was thwarted.

By the mid-1960s banks had made a bid to increase their share of corporate finance, but they had only a marginal degree of success. American business had largely abandoned any new finance with the use of equities, and shifted to issuing bonds and borrowing from a variety of financial markets and institutions. One feature that did not change greatly was that most of the new debt was not held by banks.

The 1980s in the Mirror of History

The trends in corporate finance set in motion by high tax rates and federal regulation of securities markets in the mid-twentieth century have continued unabated. Financial innovation, from the creation of the negotiable certificate of deposit in 1961 to the present, has altered but not substantially changed these trends. Even the lowering of barriers to branching and merging for banks and the slight easing of the Glass-Steagall Act has not radically increased the role of commercial banks.

The rising level of leverage has produced a nostalgia for the old style of corporate finance with more equity owned by the general public. This earlier type of corporate finance was, however, not the result of the free operation of market forces so much as the federal and state regulations that limited the role of banks. If the regulations governing banking and securities markets were eliminated and dividends taxed only once, it is not clear what form of corporate finance would emerge. A historical perspective suggests that such a radical reform might lead to the formation of giant financial intermediaries that would become the principal owners and creditors of corporations.

Notes

[1] Kopcke (1989): p. 25.
[2] Bernanke and Campbell (1988): pp. 83–125.
[3] Although there is no clear consensus about the causes of these developments, most the blame has been levied on taxes and various agency costs. See Taggart (1985): p 13–80.
[4] Chandler (1977): pp. 51–64. In the 1832 *McLane Report*, which surveyed ten norther states, only 106 manufacturing firms had assets of $100,000 or more. Of this numbe 88 were textiles companies.
[5] Atack (1985): pp. 29–52.
[6] James (1978): pp. 54–5.
[7] James (1978): pp. 60–2. These short-term loans might be rolled over, but custome were expected to clear their accounts at least once a year.
[8] Davis (1960): pp. 5–7.
[9] James (1978): p. 70.
[10] White (1983): pp. 14–15.
[11] White (1983): pp. 13 and 159.
[12] James (1978): p. 37.
[13] Chandler (1977): pp. 240–4.
[14] Davis (1966): p. 265.
[15] Navin and Sears (1955): pp. 109–20.
[16] Nelson (1959): p. 5.
[17] Beginning in New York in 1906 with the passage of new state regulations, li insurance companies were forced to sever their close ties with investment ban (Carosso, 1970: pp. 120–6).
[18] Neal (1971): pp. 39–43.
[19] Navin and Sears (1955): pp. 120–32.
[20] Wainwright (1953): pp. 160–1.
[21] Wainwright (1953): pp. 162–5.
[22] Buenger and Pratt (1986): pp. 118–19.
[23] Cleveland and Huertas (1985): pp. 35–8.
[24] Cleveland and Huertas (1985): p. 49.
[25] Hollander (1913): pp. 793–814.
[26] The principal source on financing enterprise before 1950 is Goldsmith (1958).
[27] Koch (1943): pp. 106–7.
[28] White (1990): pp. 67–83.
[29] Baxter (1966): pp. 4–14.
[30] Baxter (1966): pp. 15–18.
[31] Jacoby and Saulnier (1947): p. 11.
[32] White (1985): pp. 286–7.
[33] Wainwright (1953): pp. 191–7.
[34] Buenger and Pratt (1986): pp. 70–9.
[35] Currie (1931).
[36] Peach (1941): pp. 61–4.
[37] Peach (1941): p. 83, Table 1. These figures are only for national banks, but it wa relatively rare for state banks to have affiliates.
[38] Preston and Findlay (1930): pp. 1153–4 and 1191–2.
[39] White (1986): p. 37.
[40] The Supreme Court decision was *Pollock v. Farmers' Loan and Trust Company.*
[41] Blakey and Gladys (1919): p. 218.
[42] Taggart (1985): pp. 45–7.
[43] Kuznets (1961): p. 278.
[44] Jarrell (1981): p. 621.
[45] Schwert (1977): pp. 136–8.

Pechman (1987): pp. 385–6. The corporate tax rate remained at 52 per cent until)62; however, it declined only very slowly. By 1983, it was still 46 per cent.

Taggart (1985): pp. 45–7.

Pechman (1987): p. 147. By 1981–3, this ratio had risen to 36.5 per cent.

The character of the market also shifted with finance companies, led by General otors Acceptance Corporation, Commercial Investment Trust and Commercial Credit >rporation, issuing about 70 per cent of all paper (Baxter, 1966: pp. 23–7).

Moulton (1918): pp. 705–31.

Cleveland and Huertas (1985): pp. 230–1.

Cleveland and Huertas (1985): pp. 239–41.

Buenger and Pratt (1986): pp. 127–30 and 186–7.

CHAPTER 7

Japan's Financial System and Industrial Innovation

KEN-ICHI IMAI

This chapter analyzes the evolution of Japan's financial system (in relation to its industrial organization) in a historical perspective, and highlights the role of the main banking system with respect to its contribution to Japanese innovations.

In the first section, Japan's corporate finance system, characterized as a credit-based system, and its relation to the "market and hierarchy framework" (Williamson, 1975) will be discussed.

The next section, after presenting our basic hypothesis of the interpenetration of organization and market by which to analyze the Japanese economy, the evolution of Japan's industrial and financial system will be studied as a developmental process, from the *zaibatsu* to business groups (after the Second World War), and further to recent network systems.

In the third section, the main banking system in Japan is discussed in our framework of interpenetration of market and organization, and its role will be described as an institutional form devised to cope with informational market failures.

In the fourth section, the relation between finance and innovation will be investigated, and the essential role of finance in sequential learning processes for innovation and in fostering dynamic key industries will be brought out.

Finally, our discussion will be summarized.

Characteristics of Japan's Financial System

A credit-based system

A well-established view characterizing Japan's financial system in comparison with those of the United States, Britain, West Germany

France is that it has four distinctive features: overlending,
rborrowing, the imbalance of liquidity between city banks and
ıl banks, and the predominance of indirect financing (Suzuki,
ı0).

'hese four characteristics are all interrelated, but usually predomi-
ıce of indirect financing has been emphasized as a special trait of
ıan's financial system. Indirect finance is a common characteristic
all mature financial markets, however, in so far as ultimate
rowers increasingly depend on financial intermedaries as financial
ısactions become complex. The ratio of financing through financial
ırmediaries to the total borrowing of non-financial sectors in 1980
; 89.9 per cent for Japan, whereas it was 81.4 per cent for the
ited States, 81.6 per cent for Britain, and 75.2 per cent for West
·many. Japan's ratio is high, but the difference is a matter of
·ree.

'rom our standpoint of discussing Japan's financial system in
ıtion to its industrial organization or innovation, we would like to
ophasize the predominance of long-term loans in corporate finance
:ombination with high debt–equity ratios in Japanese companies.
·s corresponds to the characterization by John Zysman (1983) of
ıan's financial system as a "credit-based system." He classifies
·ee distinct types of financial system: systems based on capital
·kets, with resources allocated by prices established in competitive
·kets (US and Britain); credit-based systems, with critical prices
ıinistered by the government (France and Japan); and credit-
·ed systems dominated by financial institutions (West Germany).
·ysman presents a hypothesis concerning the adjustment in these
ıncial systems as described in Table 7.1.

ancial allocation in the credit-based system

·rucially important role of financial systems is to transform savings
> investment, and to allocate funds among competing users. In a
·em based on capital markets this resource allocation is performed
·ely by the market principle, whereas in a credit-based system it is
·e in accordance with principles other than the market principle –
·example, by government administration, or by political bargaining
·ng institutions. These allocation principles can be classified as the
ıanizational principle in a broad sense. Therefore, Zysman's
·sification boils down to the dichotomy between market and
ıanization (or hierarchy), in the framework of Williamson's transac-
·ı cost economics.

Table 7.1 Financial systems and the adjustment process according Zysman.

Country	Financial system	Predicted adjustment	Actual adjustment
France ⎱ Japan ⎰	credit-based, price-administered	state-led	state-led
West Germany	credit-based, institution-dominated	tripartite-negotiated	tripartite-negotiated
Great Britain ⎱ United States ⎰	capital market-based	company-led	unclear (Britain) company-led (US)

Source: Zysman (1983): p. 94.

Japan's financial system is a credit-based system, and it is true th the resource allocation of funds is not performed at arm's length transactions in the market. It is done within an organizatio framework in which long-run relationships and intense informati exchange between banks and companies play a key role, and in wh government guidance sometimes has an influence. However, it d⊄ not mean that Japan's credit-based system is severed from the mar⊩ mechanism, let alone that it is "state-led," as Zysman insists. Inste⥂ it implies that Japanese financial allocations are performed in organized *market* by a combination of the market principle and t organization principle. We accept Zysman's definition of the "crec based system," but we cannot agree with his observation that Japa credit-based system is "state-led." It is true that Japan has adopted "artificially" low interest rate, which is administered by the Bank Japan and the Ministry of Finance, and that Japan's financial syst⊄ has been strongly regulated by the Ministry of Finance. Howev⊄ Japan's financial system is embedded in the even larger framework the market mechanism, and if we investigate its actual working detail we discover that Japanese financial allocations are m⥂ basically under the pressure of the market mechanism. For examp even in the case of interest rates, which are usually recognized governmentally administered, the actual movements of the inter rates structure are responsive to market conditions in so far as ⬩ call rate and yields on floated bonds have substantially fluctuated compensate the rigidity of administered official rates and bank dep⊂ rates, as shown in Fig. 7.1 (Kosai and Ogino, 1980).

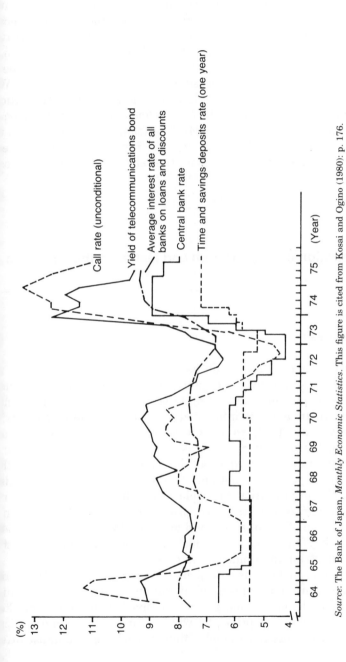

Source: The Bank of Japan, *Monthly Economic Statistics*. This figure is cited from Kosai and Ogino (1980): p. 176.

Figure 7.1 Fluctuations of various interest rates.

Particularly in the case of corporate finance, it is more appropria
to maintain that, in spite of credit rationing, Japanese credit alloc
tion has been under the pressure of market forces and the competiti
mechanism, which will be explained in detail in the following section

The essence of the Japanese economic system in general is be
analyzed by means of the dual focuses of market and organization. W
presented the analytical framework of this view as "interpenetratic
of organization and market" in the *International Journal of Industri
Organization* (Imai and Itami, 1984). The following is an attempt
analyze Japan's financial system in the framework of this inte
penetration, with special emphasis on the relationship with Japane
innovations.

Interpenetration of Organization and Market in the Japanese System

Basic hypothesis

As referred to above, the credit-based system in Japan, which
theory is administered by the organizational principle, usually ten
to work like a quasi-market. Also, as is well-known, organization
elements have in general infiltrated into the Japanese market
various ways. In short, to obtain resource allocation within a
organization, the market principle is used to a certain extent alor
with the organization principle; at the same time, allocation in tl
market arena is performed not only by the market principle but al
largely by the organization principle. Thus, both in a market ar
within an organization, the two principles coexist. We call th
"interpenetration of organization and market" (Imai and Itami, 1984
This is our key hypothesis on which we base our analysis of tl
Japanese industrial and financial systems.

The basic reason for this interpenetration is to remedy the "fai
ures" of the pure mechanism of allocation in each arena. Thu
organizational elements emerge in the market to offset mark
failures, and market-like principles will be employed within organiz
tions to remedy organizational failures such as administrati
rigidity.

he contents and degrees of market failure and of organizational
ure differ according to the stage of evolution of each market and
anization. When these failures are too great, the transaction
cerned will change its arena: i.e., the arena can change from
rket to organization, or vice versa. When the failures are in the
lium range, interpenetration occurs. Our implicit hypothesis is
t medium-range failures are so common in recent economic
tems that interpenetration usually becomes widespread.

he evolution of the Japanese economic system can be seen as a
cess of changes in the pattern of interpenetration of organizations
l markets (Imai, 1987–88). There have been three turning points in
process of Japan's industrialization. The first was the beginning of
lernization triggered by the Meiji Restoration, during which time
zaibatsu were the bastion of the entrepreneurial spirit. The second
; the period of post-war reconstruction, in which the main factor
; the dissolution of the big *zaibatsu*, with business groups engineer-
the process of rapid economic growth. The third turning point was
oil crisis, which saw the introduction and wide diffusion of
nnical innovations centered on electronics, motivated by the twin
uirements of saving energy and labor. This development trans-
ned the interfirm linkages and relations between corporations and
ks, and created the structure that is described as a network
ustrial system.

¿ *zaibatsu* as a financially controlled hierarchy

:ording to the theories commonly held in the past, the *zaibatsu*
e regarded as organizations of a limited number of big business
erprises, controlled by family ties, which directed vast economic
pires. It is a fact that from the late 1920s onwards, the *zaibatsu*
ntually turned out to conform to the common theory. However, the
ception that the *zaibatsu* were organized with the original aim of
nopolistic control alone is too one-sided. I would like to emphasize
viewpoint that the *zaibatsu* served as a source of genuine
repreneurial activity with the advent of capitalism in Japan. Such
iew holds that these organizations were necessary for starting the
ine of capitalism in the underdeveloped socioeconomic environ-
nt of the time.

n the economy of developing nations such production factors as
ital and technological manpower are extremely scarce, while the
rket itself is immature. Furthermore, the information necessary

for handling market capital or making decisions on investments
severely limited, and available only to a small number of people. It
therefore necessary to create some channels to compensate for tk
market failure, to permit capital and information to reach the mark
as and when required.

The means employed by business enterprises to cope with unce
tainty and risk in order to make decisions on large-scale investmer
are also of fundamental importance. However, in a developi
economy, institutions to facilitate dealing with uncertainty and risk
the market are not yet established. Consequently, business ent
prises have found the need to substitute intraorganizational systen
and have adopted such means as vertically integrated producti
systems, in which inputs and outputs are mutually compensated f
within the group, or by the various businesses connected to the gro
through controlling companies, thus dividing the risk among t
businesses within the group. Such measures are required becau
neither the financial market nor the stock market have matur
enough to absorb uncertainty and apportion the risk properly.

Thus, the *zaibatsu* as a powerful group of enterprises represents a
institutionalization of a mechanism formed within groups to co
pensate for the market failures in developing economies. In additio
their role can be interpreted as providing organizational innovatio
for the purpose of internally retaining the profit made from mutual
dependent activities in an immature market.[1]

An important point to be made is that the *zaibatsu* had a du
aspect. On the one hand, they functioned as a control networ
exerting direct control over their industries through holding co
panies, and indirect control through related companies. The holding
stock, the dispatching of directors to subsidiary companies, a
centralized purchases and sales were the means of this control. This
well known. However, on the other hand, the *zaibatsu* were a
market-like organizations. Within *zaibatsu* groups, each compai
behaved competitively, even though under the general direction of o
control house.[2]

This point relates to the way in which the *zaibatsu* exercis
authority. It is certain that strong authority to control constitue
companies existed in the central house. However, usually it w
exercised as a catalyst to promote mutual industrial development a
to finance strategic industrial projects in a coherent way. Th
coordination mechanism may be the origin of the Japanese way
business, utilizing organization and market in a mixed way,
expressed in our basic hypothesis.

,usiness groups" as intermediate organizations

ιe dissolution of the *zaibatsu* after the Second World War created a
ηpetitive market system in Japan, though it cannot be said that
pan began from scratch in its managerial development. The ties of
e *zaibatsu* organizations remained in a weaker form among the
ιated firms, and, in addition, such organizational principles as the
·mation of networks among people, rooted in the cultural tradition
Japan, remained substantially intact.
The interaction of these forces produced what are known as the
stwar business groups which, in the case of former *zaibatsu* groups,
ιk the following forms:

▶ There was a "presidents' club" at the core of the group, where
   periodic exchanges of information and, occasionally, decision-
   making among the member firms, were carried out.
▶ Among the member firms there was a considerable level of
   mutual long-term holding of stock for the purpose of preventing
   hostile takeover bids from outsiders.
   A large city bank operated at the center of the group, providing
   short- and long-term loans for member firms under slightly
   advantageous conditions, and in many cases was involved in the
   selection of directors.
▶ There was a general trading company at the core of the group
   which engaged in information exchange between both buyers
   and sellers.

The decisive difference between these business groups and the
ibatsu was the extent of control. As previously mentioned, the
ibatsu, through the strong connections resulting from intercom-
ny stockholding and the selection of directors, had almost total
ntrol over the decision-making of their subsidiaries. On the other
ιnd, although both the holding of stock and selection of directors
ntinued in the business groups, the connections were much weaker
d were of an entirely different nature, and therefore did not
nstitute background forces capable of substantially influencing the
cision-making process. Even were the "presidents' club" to request a
rtain change, there was no official prerogative of the association.
Organizations with such weak connections require a solid flow of
formation exchange between the member firms in order to function.
ιccessful leadership requires good decision-making, based on high-
ιality information, and changes are made on the basis of spon-
neous coordination. Otherwise, in the case of conflicting interests

among the member firms, the organizational structure binding t
is weakened and the groups disband.

Financing within the business group is perhaps a very g
example of the interpenetration of organization and market in
credit-based finance system. The member firms of a group get t
major share of financing from the main bank of the same busir
group (the definition of main bank will be given in the next secti
Clearly, this financial transaction is not a pure arm's-length mai
transaction; nor is it an internal financing either, but it is embed
in the financial market.

Within a business group, information flows more intensively
accumulates more over time between the bank and the firms. Tl
"risky" lending may be made less risky, given these informal
sources. From the firm's viewpoint, it can expect its main bank
come to its rescue at a time of financial adversity. High debt/eqi
ratios do not automatically mean a high risk of bankruptcy. Tl
banks can lend more and firms can borrow more in Japan. '
business group was a prototype of the current Japanese industrial
financial system, which will be explained in the following sections.

Interfirm relationships as informational networks

With the oil crisis as a catalyst, Japanese industries entered a i
phase – a new technological paradigm and an era of new interf
relationships.

Regarding the relationships among companies, the focus has mo
from such formal systems as mutual stockholding between compar
or the assignment of directors, to informal relationships in which
exchange of information is of primary importance. Of course, mut
stockholdings to prevent hostile takeovers are still important
many companies. However, in general, for business strategy, hun
linkages involving mutual trust are becoming more important tl
mutual stockholdings.

In this process, the handling of information has undergone a dra
change. In the case of the *zaibatsu*, crucial information such as i
technology information was exogenous and imported. In the case
business groups, it is endogenous in nature, in that the inter
transmission and processing of information is important; but as it l
been typical in the conventional activities of general trading fir
arbitraging based on information has been the main activity i
there has not been a high degree of information-creation its
However, in recent interfirm relationships (or in networks), n

formation is created through interaction (between user and produc-
·, and among production, marketing and R & D), and such creation
information becomes the driving force of business activity.

We have advanced the proposition that interpenetration of
·ganization and market occurs in order to cope with market failures
ıd organizational failures. In Japan, the cause of these failures has
ıanged from immaturity, to problems associated with information.
he main bank relationship, which will be discussed in the next
·ction, is a Japanese method used to cope with market failures
ssociated with information exchange and information creation.

he Main Bank System in Japan

ıformational market failures

ıvestment decisions are surrounded by uncertainty. Especially in a
·riod of technological innovation, decision-makers have to cope with
·nuine uncertainty, in the sense that investment risk is not only
ıcalculable but is also influenced by variables that are unknown.
·sually, technological innovation triggers a series of chain reactions
· an economic system, accompanied with unexpected repercussive
fects. We live in an age of continuous innovation and change
·iggered by information technologies.

Reducing uncertainty implies production of new information. Mar-
·t failures associated with information production are well known;
ıey include public goods property, informational asymmetry (the
.emon problem"), indivisibility, and others. In spite of these failures,
·rtain kinds of information are transacted in the market, and it is
ɔt impossible to devise several institutional designs in the market to
·oduce the information required for investment decisions. In the
nited States a number of rating companies produce information
·ncerning the creditworthiness of borrowers, for sale to financial
ıstitutions (Horiuchi, 1989).

·This may be a typical market solution, and the American financial
/stem is formulated along these lines. However, it is undeniable that
ıe market solution has severe limitations in terms of coping with
ıformational problems associated with investment and finance when
ıere are heavy market failures. Especially, as technological and
.arket information becomes more complex, the difficulty of
·mmunicating between different institutional actors increases

substantially. Usually important information in this type of situat
can be found by placing oneself in the actual situation un
observation. At the same time, accuracy and appropriateness
information can be evaluated only on a continuous basis.

In these circumstances, it is quite natural and necessary to introd
some kinds of organizational element in the market. Of course, it
possible for financial fund allocations to shift completely from t
market mode to the organizational mode; for example, to resort
internal financing within a corporation, or to government administ
tions which finance investment. However, maintaining market pr
sures which correct managerial direction is crucially important
capitalist countries, and the advantages of the market mechani
should be retained as much as possible. Therefore, an appropri
solution has to be formulated that lies between market and organi
tion. The main bank system in Japan is one possible solution
coping with the informational problems associated with investm
and finance.

The main bank relationship

In Japan a company's main bank is defined as a bank (or sometin
banks) which lends the largest share of that company's total loans
three or more consecutive years. The main bank relationship is
quasi-organizational mode of financial transactions, based on lo
term relationships between borrowers and lenders (Horiuchi, 19
and 1989). These relationships are often tightened by the ban
stockholding of borrower's equity. (The maximum amount is c
trolled by the Anti-Monopoly Law, which allows up to a 5 per ce
holding.)

These relationships were spontaneously developed during the evo
tionary process of Japan's corporate networks described above. In t
case of the *zaibatsu*, the relationships between a bank and meml
firms were quasi-internal transactions within a tightly control
combine. After the dissolution of the *zaibatsu*s, such transactions w
suddenly thrown upon the market. However, economic circumstan
after the Second World War were surrounded with genuine uncerta
ty, as mentioned above. The postwar entrepreneurs and manag
aggressively engaged in information exchange. Such exchange v
indispensable in compensating for the lack of experience of those v
had suddenly assumed responsibility owing to the purge of directors
major companies. At the same time it was necessary to decre
uncertainty and disperse the risk by obtaining information on otl

ms, thus making mutual adjustment possible. Information ex-
ange between banks and firms played a key role in this situation. It
•t only filled informational gaps between lenders and borrowers, but
so helped coordinate investment plans of related companies and
.thin groups.

The main bank relationship which was most effectively formulated
.thin business groups naturally spread to other big firms outside
ese business groups, and thence to medium- and small-sized firms.
ius, almost all companies in Japan have come to have a main bank,
id this situation has become a financial phenomenon unique to
.pan. The importance of the main bank is shown in Table 7.2
(oriuchi, 1989) as a ratio of a major company's dependence on
rrowing from the main bank to its total borrowing.

It is misleading, however, to argue that the main bank relationship
Japan is so fixed and stable that financial transactions are beyond
e scope of market forces. As Horiuchi (1989) points out: "The
.panese main bank seems to have been more changeable than

ble 7.2 The importance of the main bank in Japan*.

Unit: %

ıme of bank	1962	1967	1972	1977	1982	1986
ıi-ichi Kangyo	–	–	12.4	12.3	12.9	14.4
ıtsui	16.0	13.6	10.9	9.4	8.3	8.4
ıtsubishi	21.2	14.7	12.9	12.4	11.9	12.1
ınwa	23.4	15.8	13.6	13.7	12.8	13.5
ımitomo	21.6	17.2	13.7	11.9	11.6	12.7
ıji	21.7	17.9	15.1	12.7	11.6	13.0
kai	30.5	19.1	16.9	16.3	13.6	13.6
ıiwa	38.1	40.3	20.6	18.3	16.7	16.8
ıowa	26.0	31.9	55.8	31.6	25.6	27.6
iyo-Kobe	–	–	28.8	26.1	26.0	26.5
itama	–	–	24.8	25.4	30.1	27.0
ıkkaido Dev. Bank	21.7	34.8	16.4	10.9	16.8	14.4
kyo	47.5	35.3	27.4	20.6	18.2	19.5
J	16.1	17.1	14.0	16.0	15.0	14.8
CB	21.5	24.8	24.3	36.6	39.1	39.1
hon Saiken	n.a.	25.9	55.8	36.3	–	31.5

gures refer to the ratio of a major (i.e., listed in the first section of the Tokyo Stock Exchange)
•pany's dependence on main bank borrowing over total borrowing.
•rces: Economic Research Association, *Analysis of Major Financial Institutions' Investment and
ınce*, various issues. This table is cited from Horiuchi, 1989: p. 262.

generally believed." He found by statistical analysis that, during th
rapid growth period from the 1960s to the beginning of the 1970s, th
relationship was fairly fluid. However, he also confirmed that afte
that time the relationship became increasingly stable. The main ban
relationship is embedded in the market mechanism, and contestabili
is retained to a moderate extent; at the same time, however, it is
more intimate and long-run relationship than the bank–client rela
tionship in the financial markets of other developed countries.

Long-run behaviors

What, then, is the economic role of the main bank relationship, whic
is more than simple information exchange?

One answer is the so-called "risk-sharing hypothesis," on whic
some Japanese economists insist (for example, Nakatani, 1984). Th
hypothesis assumes that risk sharing is achieved through the "impl
cit contract" between the borrower and its main bank. However,
was difficult for me to discover direct evidence supporting th
hypothesis. As far as I know, looking at recent events, interest rat
offered in main bank relationships correspond exactly to prevailir
market rates, and there is no sign of risk sharing.

Another explanation is the hypothesis of the "delegated monitor
which suggests that the role of the main bank is to monitor borrower
corporate performance and transfer this information to other lender
taking on the responsibility of the situation. This hypothesis is qui
plausible, and there is no objection as far as its direct implications a
concerned.

However, a real problem concerns the kinds of impact created I
this role of the main bank. What kind of differences will occur in th
behavior of banks if the role of delegated monitor is borne or no
What kind of repercussions will accrue when important information
signaled by the main bank to other lenders?

My hypothesis again relates to the interpenetration of organizatic
and market. The main bank relationship is an intermediate moc
between organization and market, and therefore it can move either
the direction of market or in the direction of organization (see Figu
7.2). The movement towards market implies that the main bank do
not take an active role – instead it takes the role of delegated monito
On the other hand, the move towards organization implies that th
main bank commits itself to some company and takes strategic actic
to create mutual advantages between them. Because just by followir
the short-run market conditions it cannot create more than a

ure 7.2 The main bank relationship in the framework of organization and rket.

:rage advantage, such an active strategic move has to imply that ₊ main bank will take actions in the long-term perspective, which ʹrent market signals alone do not indicate.

The long-run strategic behavior of the main bank in the above ₁se will take the form of a strong commitment to some company. It turally induces continuous information exchange at all levels of ₋anization between the bank and the company. Information trans-tted to other lenders implies that the main bank has committed ₊lf to the future development of the company and hopes that other ʹders will follow, but when the company falls into trouble the main ₁k itself will assume the responsibility of solving the crisis.

n my view, the advantage of the main bank system lies in this ₊sibility of the bank taking an active long-term strategic role, in the ₊ve sense. But this depends on the entrepreneurship of each bank.

fact, some Japanese banks are active and some are passive, and ₊se differences have created substantial disparities among banks' ʹformances and have brought about a change of ranking among ₊jor banks.

n the next section, we draw attention to this strategic role in key ₁ustries, in order to approach the main theme of this chapter, i.e. ₊ relationship between the financial system and industrial innova-₁s in Japan.

e Role of Finance in Strategic Industries

e case of radical innovation

₊m the perspective of "innovation and finance," a crucial problem is ₊ financing of discontinuous or radical innovation. The main bank ₁tionship and information exchange between the bank and firms have contributed considerably to the promotion of financing incremental innovations. This can readily be seen from the inforn tional advantage of the main bank system described above. But wl about the case of radical innovation, or of a substantial increase investment?

An important point to be noted here is that modern technologi innovations do not arise from a vacuum. They are produced on t basis of an accumulation of technology and knowledge, and throu interactions between entrepreneurship, organizational design, co petition among rivals, and related factors. This equally applies to bc incremental innovation and radical innovation, to varying degrees. a radical innovation originates from a single entrepreneurial activi or the genius of an individual scientist, the main bank relationsl has nothing to do with its financing. However, if a discontinuous ju of technology arises out of a wide foundation of accumulated inforn tion and knowledge, continuous information exchange between investor and a lender is crucial. Without a deep understanding of t historical background of the company concerned, evaluation of innovative project is practically impossible.

Almost all of the Japanese innovations so far have been inc mental. However, there have been occasional epoch-making disc tinuous jumps of investment, which opened up new technologi frontiers. For example, aggressive investment by the Kawasaki st company in the development of the blast furnace and continuo casting during the 1950s, which was criticized as abnormal at tl time, was a big step forward in the sense that it created a strateg basis for successive technological developments. Also, the disc tinuous jump of fixed investments in computer capacities by NEC the 1970s, which will be investigated in more detail later, set t stage for a breakthrough for Japanese industries into the age microelectronics. Technologically these were not radical, but ec omically as well as organizationally they were radical, in the ser that they created new industrial paradigms and brought about "creative destruction," in the Schumpeterian sense.

"Dynamic key industries"

According to Professor Lachman (1940), we can define "dynamic k industries" as industries which are particularly sensitive to ent preneurial efforts towards change and innovation. In the case of Jap the steel industry in the 1950s and the electronic industry in t 1970s clearly belonged to the dynamic key industries. Table 7.3 sho

ɔle 7.3 The structure of Japanese industries (in terms of value added).

	1970	1975	1980	1985
	49.2	51.8	52.0	52.3
	18.4	18.2	17.7	16.0
Former K)	19.5	15.1	13.6	12.5
New K)	12.9	14.9	16.7	19.2
al	100.0	100.0	100.0	100.0

ation: C; consumer goods industries. E; Equipment goods industries (mainly machinery
istries). R; Raw materials industries (Energy, mining, chemicals, steel, ceramics, etc.). K;
iamic key industries (Computer and information services, research and education, other
rmation-related industries, telecommunication and infrastructures).
rce: Calculated from the input–output table of each year (basic tables are published by the
istics Bureau, Management and Coordination Agency, Japan).

Japanese industrial structure based on Lachman's classification. C
nds for consumer goods industries, E for equipment goods indus-
ɔs, R for raw materials industries, and K for the dynamic key
iustries defined above.
R industries, represented by the steel industry, were the former K
iustries, but their share gradually declined in the period from 1970
1985 (from 19.5 per cent in 1970, to 12.9 per cent in 1985). These
re dynamic key industries in the 1950s and 1960s. By contrast, the
w K industries, represented by the information industries in a
ɔad category, have sharply increased their share in the more recent
riod: this clearly indicates that they are becoming a strategic
iustry.
A crucial agenda for financial institutions in the age of technological
iovation is how to finance and support the development of K
iustries. The difficulty lies in the fact that demand for K products
ɔends on "expectations regarding a distant, unknown and uncertain
ure" (Lachman, 1940: p. 185). In order to finance these industries,
long-run relationship between borrowers and lenders, and con-
uous information exchange between them, are indispensable, be-
ise they require not only long-run perspectives on both sides but
·o the continuous adaptation of expectations to changing economic
cumstances during the process. The information to support invest-
·nt decisions is created through continuous interaction between the
rties and is finally condensed in terms of long-run real profit rates
d nominal interest rates. An important point related to this is that
mand for K products is also created interactively with other
iustries and firms in the process of interrelated growth of several
iustries. Future prediction of demand is difficult, but some kinds of

ex ante information would be obtainable by the intermediary activit
of a bank in this process. Also, even some forms of *ex ante* investm∢
coordination between related firms is possible, through the strate∢
action of the main bank mentioned above.

Thus the role of the main bank in fostering strategic industries is
provide information which is valid for long periods of time, wide
industrial coverage of the industries concerned and deep in ∢
perspective of technologies and market opportunities.

Another problem in K industries is that they require not o∢
financial funds for investment, but also human resources to cope w∢
new technologies and associated marketing and organizatio∢
innovations. To deprive human resources from the other C, E and
industries would not be a good strategy for the K industries, becaι
demand for K products is created by the growth of the otl
industries. Therefore, it is a better strategy to make use of on-the-∢
training as practiced in Japanese industries. However, educati∢
needs a gestation period, and until the results are fully reflected in t
form of company performance, education costs become a kind of su∢
cost.

How to recover this sunk cost is a problem which has not be∢
discussed so far, but it shapes the direction of sequential learni∢
processes (see Amendola and Gaffard, 1988). Without liquidity, fir∢
cannot allocate their resources to the education and training
workers who do not directly contribute to current production acti∢
ties. Therefore, liquid money is required to make up for this. But
the period of technological transition, firms require R & D funds,
well as funds for fixed investments embodying new technologies, a∢
they are forced to make a decision choice between human resources
& D, and new fixed investments. The latter two are fixed costs, ∤
there is a way to secure outside finance by borrowing on t
guarantee of equipment, housing and land. However, securing outs∢
finance for the creation of human resources is virtually impossib∢
and firms have to rely solely on their own liquidity.

What made it possible for Japanese firms to provide this continuο
liquidity was the sales proceeds from their current operations. M∢
Japanese firms tried to expand their sales, even if the resultant pr∢
rate was very low. Usually this is interpreted as an expansiο
oriented bias of Japanese firms sacrificing their profits. However,
our context described above, such a view may be superficial.
maintain continuous sales proceeds even when profit rates were l∢
was a good strategy by which firms could create the liquidity requir
for the creation of human resources through a learning proce∢
Japanese human resources in K industries have been gradua∢

eated through learning-by-doing and learning-by-interaction, pro-
ded by the sales proceeds produced by those learning processes
mai, 1989b).

Therefore, in order for a comprehensive strategy for K industries to
? designed and implemented, not only long-run investment funds but
so short-run liquidity are quite important. In order to secure these
nds in a comprehensive and integrated way, intensive and con-
nuous information exchange between the main bank and the
orrower firm is required. This has been the role of the main bank,
hich has contributed much towards the promotion of Japanese
novations. Illustrative evidence of this role will be given using the
xample of the semiconductor industry.

he case of semiconductors

he semiconductor industry is a representative K industry: not only
» its production and related sectors constitute a core industrial block
. the "national system of innovation" (Freeman, 1987), but also it is
idely diffused throughout all the sectors of the economy, affecting
rery sphere of social life, thus forming a key sector in the new
chnological paradigm.

Only 30 years ago the Japanese semiconductor and advanced
ectronics industry was almost nonexistent – nearly all the com-
iters were imported, and the Japanese industry was far smaller and
ore fragmented than the US and European electronics giants. The
anges that have occurred in the intervening years, which have
ought Japan to the cutting edge of advanced electronics, have been
ite spectacular. What potentials in Japan created them?

I have discussed the problem in detail in other papers; daring to
immarize them in a simplified expression, the cutting edge of
ipanese electronics has been created through a sequential learning
ocess (Imai, 1989a and 1989b).

The sequential learning process implies sequential development
om simple learning-by-doing to learning-by-interactions with other
sers and machine producers, and further to human resource creation
ocesses.

Human resource creation was crucial, and the Japanese semicon-
ictor industry actively trained its own labor within its own internal
bor market. As discussed above, in order for this in-house education
be possible, liquid money is required to recover the sunk cost of this
lucation, and in the case of Japan it was supplied by sales proceeds.
lis became possible for the Japanese semiconductor industry

through the production of standardized low-margin products, such
MOS memories, on a mass scale. From a simple perspective of pro
maximization, such a production strategy seems to be off the mar
but from our perspective it was an appropriate strategy in order
obtain liquid money continuously for the purpose of creating hum.
resources. What should be underlined is that the range of technolog
al choices available to the Japanese firms was substantially widen
during the process, and their flexible capability of adapting
turbulent economic environments increased to a large extent.

The initial stage of the learning-by-doing process began as a meth
of reducing costs and energy consumption. But its sequential develo
ment, interacting with learning by using and learning-by-interactio
changed its major role to a method of dynamic product differentiatio
Also, the pattern of innovation progressed towards an increasing
systemic type of innovation, transcending the simple product–proce
dichotomy of innovation. Japanese industrial groups and networ
type organizations were well suited to this type of systemic innov
tion.

Looking back at this sequential process, we realize how important
was that an initial start was made on a large scale. As Gunner Myrd
(1957) argued, an initial kick which goes over the threshold of t
cumulative development process is crucially important for sequenti
interrelated industrial growth. In other words, "the rate of start" is
key variable in Hicks' terminology (Hicks, 1973). The rate of sta
governs the level of resources which can be used for learning, a
ultimately determines the potentials of the human resources.

What gave this initial kick was the pioneering aggressive fix
investments by NEC in the middle of the 1970s (see Table 7.4). T
decision to undertake these investments was primarily due to t
entrepreneurial work of the then president, Koji Kobayashi (current
chairman), who had foreseen the technological and market potenti
of the merging of computers and communications ("C&C strategy,"
his terminology). However, we should not overlook the fact th
substantial support was given by the Sumitomo Bank, the main bar
of NEC,[3] for his bold investment. Indeed, NEC relied on extern
finance to the degree of as much as 85 per cent in the 197C
substantial amounts of this finance were credited from the Sumiton
Bank (see Table 7.5).

These loans represented a bold decision on the part of the Sumiton
Bank. What made it possible for the bank to take such a decision w
its degree of information and knowledge on NEC's behavior and w
of thinking, which had been accumulated through the long-run ma
bank relationship. Information-gathering at all levels of organizatio

able 7.4 Pioneering investments by NEC and other companies in semicon-
ιctor plants.

Unit: 10^8 yen

ompany	Year						1975–80 Accumulated total
	1975	1976	1977	1978	1979	1980	
EC	49	116	100	155	270	320	1,010
itachi	15	70	60	100	150	230	625
ujitsu	9	15	60	80	160	270	594
ɔshiba	30	140	50	60	100	130	510
Iatsushita	10	35	40	40	100	200	425
Iitsubishi	40	55	60	60	80	100	395
ki	11	32	42	32	55	134	306

urces: 1975–8 Nikko Research Center, April 1980.
1979–80 Nikkei Sangyo Shimbun, November 26, 1980.

able 7.5 Largest lenders to NEC, March 1980.

ender	Per cent of total loans
umitomo Bank	16.7
umitomo Trust and Bank	11.4
apan Export and Import Bank	6.7
okohama Bank	4.9
umitomo Life Insurance	4.6
ıdustrial Bank of Japan	4.3
ong-term Credit Bank of Japan	4.3
Iitsubishi Bank	4.0
yowa Bank	3.9
apan Bank and Credit Bank	2.3
otal	63.1%

urce: NEC Annual Reports.

ιcluding information concerning how human resources were being
reated as mentioned above, finally supported the decision.

This point deserves emphasis, because economic conditions at that
me surrounding the Japanese economy were quite turbulent and
ιture prospects were so uncertain that it was rather optimistic to

foresee that Japan would overcome even the oil crisis, let alone t
sharp yen appreciation. Also for NEC itself, the process of formulati
and incorporating the C&C (computer and communication) strate
was not an easy process. In an interview (Imai *et al.*, 1983), K
Kobayashi revealed that the development of the computer division
one of the main pillars of NEC was a rough process. In view of the fa
that only a very few mainframe computer manufacturers have be
able to survive in any country, it was not surprising to learn of
period when pessimism prevailed, regarding the future of NEC
computer division.

If we look at the end result, it was the bold investment decisions
Kobayashi's entrepreneurship that can be seen to have put t
company on a developmental path supported by the two pillars
C&C. But we can readily discern the importance of informati
exchange, between NEC and its main bank at all levels of t
organization and its signal effects to other lenders, and also t
significance of wider information exchange including MITI and oth
business groups behind such decisions. MITI's strong policy stance
foster Japanese information industries created increasingly optimist
expectations in related sectors, and indirectly induced the prospects
reciprocal demand creation among other business groups or industri
networks.

The Japanese system is coordinated through multilayer network
including interfirm, interindustry, bank–corporation, and gover
ment–business networks, which have their own information loops as
linkage and coordination method. The financial institutions, especial
the main banks, have acted as intermediaries of key information
these networks, and have contributed much to the promotion
Japanese industrial innovations.

Summary and Conclusion

The main points of this chapter can be summarized as follows:

(a) Japan's financial system in relation to its industrial organizatio
especially its corporate finance system, has a special trait: th
predominance of long-term loans in combination with hig
debt–equity ratios in Japanese companies. This system has bee
characterized as a "credit-based system," as compared with
"market-based system" such as in the US and Britain (in Joh
Zysman's terminology).

b) Financial allocation in Japan is performed within an organizational framework in which long-run relationships and intense information exchange between banks and companies play a key role, and in which government guidance sometimes has an influence. However, this does not mean that this system is divorced from the market mechanism; rather, it implies that Japanese financial allocations are performed in an organized market by a combination of the market principle and the organization principle.

c) The essence of the Japanese economic system is best analyzed within the framework of "interpenetration of organization and market." This interpenetration implies that to obtain resource allocation within an organization, the market principle is used to a certain extent along with the organization principle, while at the same time, allocation in the market arena is performed not only by the market principle but also by the organization principle. This is the basic hypothesis by which we have analyzed Japan's industrial and financial systems.

d) The basic reason why interpenetration occurs is to remedy market failure and organizational failure. The contents and degrees of these failures differ according to the stage of evolution of markets and organizations. The evolution of Japan's industrial and financial system can be seen as a process of changes in the pattern of interpenetration of organizations and markets to cope with both types of failure.

e) Japanese industrial and financial systems have evolved from the *zaibatsu* as financially controlled hierarchies into "business groups" as intermediate organizations, and further into informational networks based on interfirm relationships. In this evolutionary process the handling of information has undergone a drastic change. In the case of the *zaibatsu*, information was exogenous. In the case of business groups it became endogenous. However, in recent interfirm relationships (or in networks), information is created through interaction, and the creation of information becomes the driving force of business activity.

f) The main bank system in Japan is a method by which to cope with market failure associated with information exchange and information creation. The main bank relationship is a quasi-organizational mode of financial transactions that is based on long-term relationships between borrowers and lenders. The main bank assumes a role of "delegated monitor," in the sense that it monitors borrowers' corporate performance and transfers this information to other lenders taking on the responsibility of

the situation. The advantage of the main bank system lies in th
scope for banks to take an active strategic role in the long-ru
perspective, with the aim of creating mutual benefits ar
assisting in the coordination of networks.

(g) A crucial issue for financial institutions in the age of technologi
     al innovation is how to finance and support the development
     dynamic key industries. The difficulty arises because the futur
     of such industries depends on expectations which are distan
     unknown and uncertain. In order to finance these industries,
     long-run relationship between borrowers and lenders and
     continuous information exchange are indispensable. Also,
     requires the continuous adaptation of expectations to changin
     market conditions. Japanese main banks have contributed to th
     fostering of innovative firms in key industries by performing suc
     roles. The case of Japan's semiconductor industry may be seen a
     a typical example of this.

Finally, I would like to underline again the fact that the rela
tionship between Japan's financial system and its industrial syste
has been spontaneously created in an evolutionary way. It has been
changing process aimed at coping with changing market failures an
organizational failures. Rather than the stability of the relationshi
the evolutionary change necessary to meet the different challenges
the times should be emphasized. Looking at the future from th
perspective, we are able to predict that the main bank relationship i
Japan will naturally change from now on, to cope with the marke
and organizational failures of the future. The main bank relationshi
was an appropriate method to deal with the informational marke
failures which were discussed above in detail. However, the conten
of the information, and therefore the character of the market failur
associated with them, will change. Perhaps more interactive creatio
of information with heterogeneous economic agents will be require
and this will gradually alter the main bank relationship in Japa
Deregulation of Japan's financial system will promote this trend.

Notes

[1] At the same time, the formation of a group is an effective means of utilizi
entrepreneurial ability, which is of limited supply in developing nations. While th
quality of individual entrepreneurs is an important aspect of the entrepreneuri
function, the writings on entrepreneurs up to now have tended to deal with personali

an excessive extent. Entrepreneurs, like anyone else, obtain information in a social
ntext, and make judgments from their interactions with others. If some kind of
trepreneurial group is established, there is the possibility of executing the entre-
eneurial function without excessive reliance upon personal qualities. Such being the
se, considering entrepreneurs within the context of a network has a positive
gnificance. Furthermore, the success of one *zaibatsu* will propagate the success of
hers, and this will then play a pivotal role in actuating the engine of capitalism for the
tire economy.

There is much evidence that controlled companies within a *zaibatsu* behaved
dependently and competitively. Mitsubishi Economic Research Institute (1955)
mmarized this as follows: "Controlled companies could and did operate independently
coordination with the *honsha* [central house]" (p. 11). G.C. Allen (1940) wrote "A
nto [manager] who had been placed in charge of a firm where he enjoyed considerable
eedom from control would be expected in an emergency to come to the aid of the
rent concern. . . . Among the *banto* themselves there are groups in rivalry one with
other." They were controlled during times of crisis, but otherwise remained
tonomous in regard to decision-making.

The main banks of the major companies in the Japanese semiconductor industry are
follows:

ompany	Main bank
NEC	Sumitomo
Toshiba	Mitsui
Hitachi	Fuji, Daiichi Kangyo, Sanwa
Fujitsu	Daiichi Kangyo
Matsushita	Sumitomo
Mitsubishi Electric	Mitsubishi
Sanyo	Sumitomo

urrent trends

CHAPTER 8

Alternative Financial Systems in Industrial Economies, 1970–1985[1]

GIUSEPPE CONTI

Financial Typologies and Paradoxes in National Experiences

During the 1970s and 1980s the financial systems of the major industrialized countries (the United States, Japan, West Germany, France, Britain, and Italy) retained their own particular structural characteristics, especially as regards the way in which funds were applied to nonfinancial enterprises. During the 1970s there was a growing distinction between credit-oriented and market-oriented systems (Rybczynski, 1974). As is well known, this distinction is based on comparative analysis of the volume and composition of the flows of funds involved in the financing of enterprises.[2] By referring to the origins of external financial resources, a distinction can be made between market-oriented (the US and the UK) and bank-oriented countries (Japan, West Germany, France and Italy).

In the former systems, the financing of enterprises has the following characteristics: the level of self-financing is relatively high, especially with regard to external sources; rates of indebtedness in terms of flows and stocks are relatively low; an important and often predominant part of external resources derives from the issue of transferable securities in an organized secondary market; the proportion of credit obtained from financial intermediaries is not significant; as regards to loans taken out with intermediaries, short-term loans for the financing of circulating capital are the predominant form.

On the other hand, systems in which the financing of enterprises is based on credit display the following characteristics: the level of internal funding is relatively low; the level of indebtedness is higher; concerning the latter's source, it is made up predominantly of credit advanced by the banking system; the issue of fixed-interest securities

or the mobilization of risk capital furnish a modest supply of fun
the credit system in general compensates for the lack of long-te
direct finance sufficient to meet the need to invest in plant a
equipment.

During the period from 1970 to 1985 certain shifts within the t
systems occurred. The most significant of these concerned the mark
based economies where, as compared to the 1960s, enterprise finai
favored the taking-out of loans with financial institutions, tl
reducing the extent of capital-market funding. In addition, in Ang
Saxon enterprises, the contribution of funds realized through the iss
of securities became secondary. This did not, however, alter t
significance of the self-financing of such enterprises or the low lev
of their indebtedness as basic aspects orienting financial choices w
respect to the alternative model.

Certain changes concerned bank-based countries such as Ita
France, and to a lesser extent, Japan. In these countries th
emerged, especially at the end of the 1970s, the phenomenon
securitization which, though it affected the financing of the ent
economy, characterized industrial financing only marginally. A c
similarity therefore emerged between the model of financing of t
economy and the model of financing of enterprises: the structu
of financing of the economy shifted towards "direct" securiti
whereas the structure of enterprise finance continued to be based
"indirect" credit.[3] Such dualism is to be found in the Anglo-Sax
market-oriented economies themselves, due to a growth in the exte
of banks' financing of enterprises, as we have already mentioned.

The aim of this chapter is to examine these typologies in the light
the events of recent years, in order to establish whether there k
been a convergence of financial systems towards a single mod
namely, one which is market-based.

Generally the view which takes the predominance of the market
be the outcome of a greater "modernization" of the system is r
confirmed by the experience of the 1970s and 1980s. On the contra
at the level of enterprise finance, the trajectory which has be
followed has gone in the opposite direction. In all the industrializ
economies, there has been a clear predominance of bank credit a
indirect finance in the composition of the external finance
enterprises.[4] This situation did not change even at the end of t
1970s or at the beginning of the subsequent decade when prima
securities markets developed in these economies and there was
notable growth of transactions in secondary markets.

With regard to the latter aspect, an international comparis
shows the presence of phenomena which might appear paradoxic

he peculiar aspect consists in the fact that in countries having ıpital markets which are large and competitive, the financial flows btained by enterprises through new issues of shares and securities ıre more modest than in countries where capital markets are narrow ınd thin.[5] This gives rise to a relative functional and allocative fficiency of the primary market (as manifested by the mobilization of ınds for deficit sectors) which coexists with the inefficiency of the ·ansaction function relative to the secondary market, due to the mall number of operators and the low volume of transactions. Where ıe secondary market is instead relatively large and guarantees that ıe securities held in the portfolios of the various operators have a ɜrtain liquidity – thus also reducing the risk of large losses on capital ccount – the primary market does not constitute as efficient a ḥannel for the gathering and distribution of risk capital for enter- ·ises, in particular for industrial enterprises.

Before confronting these issues in the next section, in order to btain useful theoretical models, we shall first focus on certain facts; ıen, in order to obtain empirical consistency, we shall focus on ɜrtain theories. In particular, we shall concentrate on how various uthors have sought to explain the prevalence of indirect credit in the nancing of enterprises in all industrialized countries. We shall go on) deal with the role of the capital market and especially of the stock ıarket. Financial orientations in the various countries are then iscussed in relation to the central role played by financial institutions ntermediaries and market) in the structure of enterprise ownership nd control. The final section summarizes the principal conclusions ·hich emerge from our international comparison.

iversity and Paths of Development in Industrial Finance: ʾacts and Models

ʾifferences and stability of debt-ratios

ccording to Goldsmith (1969), there have been no significant ifferences at the same stage of development regarding financial rowth in industrialized and developing countries. Similarly, Gurley nd Shaw have argued that in comparison to GNP, there has been ɒng-run stability in the net indebtedness of (internal) nonfinancial ectors. This growth of debt-financing has depended on economic evelopment and on the growth of internal sources of finance (Gurley

and Shaw, 1956; Gurley, 1957). The system has reflected a basic no
of "sound finance:" without overborrowing on the part of defi
sectors or overlending on the part of agents in surplus. Consequent
at "mature" economic stages financial systems become more sophis
cated and efficient, as shown by a larger volume and higher quality
financial assets.

Generally, the aggregate financial model seems to show only o
evolutionary financial path, with secondary variants in national cas
But, at the disaggregated level, the financing of nonfinancial ent
prises shows various national patterns.[6]

The principal difference has been the relative degree of indebte
ness of nonfinancial enterprises, something which has varied a gr
deal from one country to another. During the period from 1970
1985, the relationship between debts and total assets (what is term
leverage, or more precisely the debt ratio[7]) (see Table 8.1) reach
about 85 per cent in Japan as against 37 per cent in the Unit
States. The enterprises of the other countries were to be found with
this range: in the higher part there was Germany at 77 per cent, a
Italy and France at about 68 per cent; the indebtedness of Brit
enterprises, on the other hand, was relatively low at 54 per cent.
each country, average levels of indebtedness remained relative
stable during the period. Thus, aside from intersectoral shifts a
short-term fluctuations, this seems to lead to the conclusion that t
aggregate of American or Japanese "enterprises" is coherent with
domestic norm of financial behavior related to the model of finan
predominant in the country.

The various financial trajectories are strictly related to differenc
in economic and industrial structures. It is sufficient to recall t
characteristics of the industrial systems of the various countries, t
sectoral differences in organization and size, the different degrees
uncertainty concerning expected profits in the various industr
sectors, and the specific funding requirements which together c
affect existing diversities in leverage (Bradley, Jarrell and Kim, 198
p. 876; Auerbach, 1985). National financial differences therefo
appear to reflect the average of sectoral models of enterprise finan
an average which is weighted by their respective financial nee
Inquiries of this kind would therefore require accurate in-dep
studies in the field of economic history.

National models of enterprise finance and the relative indebtedne
also depend, in part, on differences in firms' accounting systems[8] a
on different fiscal regimes.[9] But, fundamentally, historical develo
ments have oriented the way the financial function has been org
nized both within firms and externally in relation to the over

Table 8.1 Debt ratio in nonfinancial enterprises, 1970–85 (Ratio of debts to total assets, as a percentage).

	France	Italy	Germany	Japan	UK	US
1970	65.6	74.0	74.0	85.3	54.0	41.5
1971	66.0	78.1	74.5	85.4	52.9	41.1
1972	66.8	71.1	75.5	85.6	52.7	41.2
1973	67.9	69.9	76.1	86.4	54.7	41.7
1974	69.2	70.0	76.1	86.5	55.1	36.5
1975	70.3	68.4	76.0	86.5	53.5	34.7
1976	69.2	71.2	76.7	85.1	53.6	34.3
1977	69.3	69.3	76.9	84.6	53.5	34.6
1978	66.9	68.1	77.4	84.6	53.9	34.8
1979	66.8	66.7	78.0	84.6	53.5	35.2
1980	67.3	64.9	79.1	83.8	53.4	34.6
1981	69.2	65.8	79.7	83.4	54.4	34.6
1982	70.5	67.7	79.8	83.4	55.0	35.0
1983	70.7	67.9	80.0	82.9	54.0	35.5
1984	69.9	—	80.0	82.7	53.7	38.2
1985	—	—	79.9	—	—	40.5
mean	68.4	69.5	77.5	84.7	53.9	37.1
std. dev.	1.6	3.3	2.0	1.2	0.7	2.9
s/m %	2.4	4.7	2.6	1.5	1.2	7.8

Source: Ratios calculated from OECD, 1987b: tab. E.1.

financial system. Only recently, some literature has begun to analyz
the institutional channels and forms which manage the financia
resources of enterprises and their allocation, considering the shareho
ders' role, together with the functions of the stock exchange and *
various types of lenders and financiers. These relations determine th
financial structure of enterprises, the levels of indebtedness and the
long-term stability (White B., 1984; Vittas, 1986; pp. 4–7).

Enterprise finance between a single model and a plurality of models

In theoretical terms, the various approaches to industrial financ
might be divided into two categories, according to whether they adop
one or more models, and in respect to the nature of the mai
determining factors (the preferences of savers for types of financia
assets or institutional factors). The first distinction reflects th
hypothesis of a single theoretical model of finance in which th
plurality of country patterns is seen to exist only at differer
evolutionary stages, or in conditions of "financial repression" (McKin
non, 1973; Shaw, 1973). The latter distinction is based on th
alternative hypothesis that financial systems are oriented by th
demand for financial assets (with financial institutions having a
adaptative role), or that financial systems are governed by th
relationships of financial institutions (such as the stock exchang
banks and others) with borrowers and investors.

The studies follow these two main approaches. On the one han
Rybczynski's paradigm is to be placed in the category of models whic
assume the existence of one "'ideal' world financial systen
(Rybczynski, 1986: pp. 12–13 and 29), where the (strongly) marke
oriented, Anglo-Saxon economies are to be found. Their prevale
financial relations are established through large markets, in anony
mous forms, with transferable contracts. The market price mechanis
dominates investment and saving decisions. Bank-oriented systen
are seen as a deviation from the paradigm, and a sign of relativ
financial backwardness, even in countries of the same degree
economic "maturity" (Rybczynski, 1984: pp. 276–80; and Rybczynsk
1986: pp. 2–8 and 21–23).

On the other hand, the family of Modigliani-Miller models pos
ulates a financial neutrality and, consequently, a plurality of ente
prise-finance configurations which are entirely fortuitous; empiricall
some models are possible only by abandoning certain (unrealisti
hypotheses and introducing a *trait-d'union* between financial stru

e and the allocation of resources (non-neutrality). Hence the onomies of enterprise finance or models that have been empirically ertained can be attributed to the variety of fiscal regimes, to rket imperfections or to transaction costs that, in a world domin-d by uncertainty, can prevent any accurate estimate of the yields be expected from financial activity, as well as from the underlying al" activity.

Iowever, the two approaches have certain elements in common. estments which are not financed through profits (self-financing) or bugh the stock markets have been explained in terms of the ctional or structural "incompleteness" of the financial system. In er words, bank-based enterprise finance is considered to depend on tain hindrances to the full development of markets. On this point jor heuristic limits have quickly emerged. During the 1960s, the barity between the capital markets of continental Europe and the erican stock market attracted international attention.[10] The ses of the conflicting financial patterns were attributed to savers' ferences, particularly those of families, that in the European case duced narrow domestic financial markets. Moreover the con-ental European enterprise's greater resort to external funding rces (compared with investment) was attributed to another ictural difference: the weak growth in Europe of large managerial porations. The divorce between ownership and control, very rked in American corporations, increased self-financing as the ans towards further economic and financial concentration (Lintner, 9; Taggart, 1985). On the other hand, that process fostered the nation of large capital markets for larger firms.

'he thesis that Europe was doubly backward (because of narrow ck exchange markets and familial-dynastic enterprises[11]) has been ppraised. For Lamfalussy the high level of bank funding was not a sequence of institutional shortcomings, but the effect of a higher umulation ratio of European enterprises in comparison with the erican ones from 1958 to 1964. Furthermore, the tightness and itility of European financial markets was independent of savers' ferences. The direct financial investments of Europeans in secur-s were relatively higher than those of Americans. The different ction of capital markets in the US and the UK depended on the stence of large and specialized institutional investors (such as sion and life-insurance funds).[12]

ecent studies have challenged the empirical foundations of man-rialism, showing that, even in the US and UK, financial institu-s control the formation of directorates and influence the decisions nterprises.[13] This places the focus on interlocking directorates, on

group relations and on those between enterprises and capital marke
on the one hand, and between enterprises and financial institutio
on the other. It means investigating through which information s
(screening) and monitoring channels the shareholders and lenders c
influence managerial decisions, and with what kind of econom
consequences (Greenwald and Stiglitz, 1987; Dosi, 1988; Nardoz
1986b).[14]

For the 1970s and 1980s the enterprise finance problem must
redefined in order to account for the predominance of intermediari
in enterprise funding in the various countries, and the weak contrib
tion of equity finance by the stock market, especially in thc
countries where capital markets are extensive and exchanges num
ous. The emergence of credit intermediation and of allocation failu
on the part of financial markets can be understood, outside optim
market models and neutrality models, through three principal cc
tributions: the saving-investment technology of Gurley and Sha
(1967), the Hicksian distinction between an auto-economy and
overdraft economy, and the principle of increasing risk. The fi
approach analyses the greater capacity of financial intermediaries
establish themselves as compared to markets. The second shows th
fixed-price systems peculiar to intermediaries are relatively bet
adapted to the requirements of industrial financing. Finally, incre
ing risk subordinates the size of self-finance and the resort to capi
markets to bank credit and to the expansion of enterprises.

The saving-investment technology is a technology of financ
transfer from savers to investors. Any transfer of financial resour
which is not negotiated and "surreptitious" (as with administrati
transfers, or changes in relative prices) is a rudimentary a
uncompetitive technology of internal finance. The other ones, t
technologies of external finance, are more appropriate to matu
industrialized economies. Among the latter, savers prefer to h
indirect financial assets rather than acquire primary (direct) asse
owing to the former's characteristics of a steady price and yield, or
divisibility (Gurley and Shaw, 1956). From this derive lower rates
growth of direct stock, as compared to the rate of economic grow
which is sustained principally by an increase in indirect assets (Gur
and Shaw, 1957; Gurley, 1967).

A further step toward the acknowledgement of the emergence
credit-based rather than market-based systems lies in an analysis
the features and performance of the two systems. Hicks (1974:
51–4) defines two alternative typologies of the economic system: t
auto-economy and the overdraft economy. In the former, operat
principally use internal means for making investments. They co

ir negative financial balances through the issue of stocks on the
ancial market, or through the sales of financial assets on the
netary or capital markets in order to meet cash needs. The
ncipal channel of access to savings is through the financial market
ose characteristics are ones of flex price, inasmuch as the variation
interest rates depends on agents' choices of assets and on the
bitrage which they effect between the various kinds of assets.

n an overdraft economy, operators are structurally in debt,
ecially in relation to intermediaries. The latter too, if they need
uidity, must resort to credit negotiation. The principal consequence
that prices are fixed precisely in the sense that the availability of
uidity does not depend on the value of assets owned, but primarily
customer relationships which in the industrialized societies aim at
ancing productive investment projects.

The primary implications of the overdraft–auto-economy distinction
acern the role of the credit institutions. These are capable of
ercising a significant and direct influence on investment, by means
the effects of interest-rate variation (Dosi, 1988). This explains why
 consolidation of financial intermediaries is closely dependent on
 needs of the industrial structure. In particular, the banker, unlike
 auction markets, is able to take risks inasmuch as he is
oretically in a position to know "his own clients and the context in
ich they operate".[15]

There thus emerges an evaluation of the financial structure
iented to the market" (of the American and British economies) not
 a paradigm of financial development for latecomers, but as a
cific historical case.[16]

Kalecki's principle of increasing risk (Kalecki, 1971) introduces
ne evolutionary aspects. It is based on a simple proposition: a firm
ving the greater proportion of its investment financed from exter-
l sources will suffer greater losses if the investment is not
ccessful. The expansion of a firm nevertheless depends on the
dit-capital available for the financing of its activities. Creditors
sess the reliability of a firm in relation to its net worth. Therefore,
dit has a limit in enterprise capital (or risk capital) whose size
pends on the contribution of the owners, the entry of new partners
d the retention of profits. The limit can be superseded using the
recapitalist" techniques of internal finance *à la* Gurley and Shaw
volving an increase in sale prices) or by resorting to recapitaliza-
n. There is increasing risk, however, both for the shareholders and
 the controlling group, which will tend to engage in policies of
rersification in order to avoid concentrating their capital in a single
siness. From all this, it emerges that the possibility of share issues

is closely dependent on circumstances of control and on the distrib
tion of dividends and share valorization.

The instruments of internal finance and those of external finan
oriented to the market thus tend to diminish. The differences a
long-run changes in the degree of leverage are closely tied to t
techniques of external finance, that is, to the role and weight
financial intermediaries in the industrial economy. On the one ha
there is the refinement of financial techniques; on the other hand, t
organizational aspects inherent in them that devise institution
forms in order to reduce the risks associated with funding and rai
the limit of the debt ratio. Systems based on credit tend to instit
tionalize collusive relations between industry and financial inte
mediaries (according to the principle that "we're all in the same boat
– relations which the market, instead, tends to keep conflictu
("every man for himself"). It is necessary to bear in mind the
relations between industry and the banking system, in order
understand the differences between financial systems in recent year

The Capital Market and Enterprise Financing

It is now time to confront two issues. First, in what sense can o
continue to speak of economies oriented to markets, when in both t
US and the UK the greater proportion of the external finance
enterprises comes from financial intermediaries? And second, how c
we define the role of financial markets in relation to enterpri
finance, and in particular, what role is assigned to the stock market
the two models of finance?

The different degrees of leverage, the relative weight of extern
finance and the contradictory state of the stock market – which
relatively weak in terms of the contribution of funds, but extended
terms of the number of transactions, securities, and firms quoted (
vice versa) – all delineate financial systems which have differe
organizational and institutional structures – not only in quantitati
terms (such as the structure of liabilities, the flow-of-funds transfe
but also in functional terms (or in terms of economic performance).

A financial system is characterized by two factors: it takes shape
order to finance other sectors in deficit (such as the government)
other borrowers (such as households, the foreign sector and t
financial institutions themselves) and not only in order to finan

ustry (or nonfinancial firms); the structure of liabilities and the
les of enterprise finance depend on the legal status of the
erprise in question, and on the nature of relations between
ership and control, among firms, and between industry and the
ncial institutions.

Ve have already mentioned the contrast existing in certain coun-
s between the preponderance of financial intermediaries in the
ply of funds to enterprises, and the significant contribution made
ll sectors by direct assets, negotiable on a secondary market. This
gests a conflicting rule: financing the economy versus financing
erprises. In the countries in which financial instruments typical of
capital markets have constituted a large part of the net financial
vs of the entire economy, issues undertaken directly by nonfinan-
enterprises have not reached significant proportions of the overall
me of issues.

n the US, for example, the flows of direct and indirect liabilities
t of repayments) in relation to GNP were approximately equivalent
ing the period 1970 to 1984 (see Table 8.2). In 1981 there was an
rease in issues of securities, which became more important than
dit. Further growth took place in 1984, when securities rose to 17
cent of GNP, as against the 10.5 per cent of the instrument of
irect finance. In the UK the share of credit as a whole remained
atively stable, at around 13 per cent of GNP.[17] After the first half
he 1970s, total securities issues stood at around levels of 10 to 11
cent, with a comparatively small difference as compared to
irect liabilities.

n the other countries, the relative share of securities was much
er than that of credit in the whole economy: in Germany, from one
three times on average, in France slightly less, and in Japan in a
portion of one to two (see Table 8.2). In Italy, the relative
erence in question varied greatly over the same period, in spite of
fact that the flow of total funds in relation to GNP remained at
und 30 per cent. For example, in 1970, direct bonds reached 13 per
t, and indirect bonds 17 per cent; in 1984 they reached 16 per cent
against 10 per cent. Of the bank-based countries, Italy together
h France registered one of the most substantial increases in
ancing through the market. In Italy, the economy's relatively
ater dependence on the market derived mainly from the growth in
government deficit from the mid-1970s. Starting from the begin-
g of the 1980s, Italian together with French enterprises obtained a
wing proportion of capital from securities issues – something which
not happen in other countries (see Tables 8.3 to 8.8).

apan too, to some extent, experienced a similar phenomenon of an

Table 8.2 Net flow of funds of all sectors: direct finance and indirect finance.
(Total net funds raised by sectors, as a percentage of GNP)

	France			Italy			Germany			Japan			UK			US		
	Dir.	Ind.	Tot.	Dir.	Ind.	Tot.	Dir.	Ind.	Tot.	Dir.	Ind.	Tot.	Dir.	Ind.	Tot.	Dir.	Ind.	Tot.
1970	4.5	10.2	14.7	12.8	16.7	29.4	3.3	13.3	16.5	6.8	20.7	27.5	10.2	12.4	22.5	8.2	7.3	15.5
1971	4.0	20.2	24.1	11.5	30.3	41.8	4.2	15.5	19.7	9.7	27.9	37.5	5.7	30.9	36.8	6.2	10.7	16.8
1972	3.9	18.3	22.1	15.6	27.5	43.0	3.7	13.1	16.8	6.7	26.5	33.2	5.7	36.8	42.4	5.8	12.7	18.5
1973	3.0	17.2	20.1	10.1	11.4	21.5	3.6	11.1	14.7	6.7	18.1	24.8	3.6	26.0	29.6	7.3	9.3	16.5
1974	7.3	9.0	16.3	14.9	22.0	36.8	5.9	13.7	19.6	9.9	18.3	28.1	8.8	17.1	25.9	10.2	3.9	14.0
1975	5.3	15.0	20.2	11.9	18.6	30.4	4.9	13.2	18.0	10.3	18.4	28.7	6.5	13.9	20.4	9.1	7.7	16.7
1976	4.6	17.1	21.7	15.0	16.2	31.1	5.0	11.3	16.3	11.1	14.4	25.4	10.7	13.1	23.8	8.4	11.3	19.7
1977	5.9	14.9	20.8	15.3	12.9	28.2	4.9	13.9	18.7	13.5	14.1	27.5	6.1	13.5	19.6	7.7	13.5	21.2
1978	4.9	16.9	21.7	9.6	17.4	27.0	3.5	15.3	18.7	9.7	14.4	24.1	11.8	15.3	27.0	7.4	12.3	19.7
1979	6.5	17.0	23.4	10.4	22.3	32.7	4.0	14.1	18.0	9.8	14.8	24.6	10.5	15.3	25.7	8.6	8.3	16.9
1980	8.3	15.3	23.6	14.2	23.7	37.8	5.8	14.0	19.8	10.8	14.4	25.1	14.4	13.5	27.9	8.2	8.3	16.5
1981	10.4	19.9	30.2	14.7	15.3	29.9	6.3	10.1	16.4	9.2	16.5	25.7	11.2	15.1	26.2	11.4	5.5	16.8
1982	10.8	13.7	24.5	19.4	13.0	32.4	6.5	11.3	17.7	11.0	16.9	27.8	10.1	13.0	23.1	13.1	8.6	21.6
1983	10.1	15.1	25.2	14.3	16.1	30.3	5.2	11.1	16.3	9.8	14.1	23.8	9.9	11.4	21.3	11.3	12.1	23.4
1984	12.9	12.8	25.7	16.4	10.5	26.8	6.7	10.5	17.1	8.1	16.8	24.9	12.4	11.3	23.7	17.0	10.5	27.5
mean	6.8	15.5	22.3	13.7	18.3	31.9	4.9	12.8	17.6	9.5	17.8	27.2	9.2	17.3	26.4	9.3	9.5	18.8
std. dev.	2.9	3.0	3.7	2.6	5.6	5.6	1.1	1.7	1.5	1.8	4.2	3.6	2.9	7.4	5.9	2.8	2.7	3.4
s/m %	42.7	19.6	16.3	18.8	30.9	17.4	22.8	13.2	8.20	18.8	23.6	13.2	31.8	43.0	22.3	30.2	28.1	17.9

Source: Ratios calculated from OECD, 1987a; tab. 21F.7.
Note: Net flow of funds raised by domestic nonfinancial sectors (general government, nonfinancial enterprises and households), and by rest of the world and

ble 8.3   The financial structure of nonfinancial enterprises in France.
(Flow of funds as a percentage of total financial flows)

| | | | | External funds raised by | | | | |
| | | | | | Securities | | | |
	Self-finance	External finance	Bank credits	Total	shares	bonds	other	Trade credit
70	48.3	51.7	37.9	10.0	6.6	3.0	0.5	3.7
71	51.3	48.7	32.2	12.7	6.5	5.6	0.7	3.9
72	47.3	52.7	36.0	12.1	7.2	4.2	0.7	4.5
73	45.6	54.4	35.7	12.2	7.4	3.5	1.3	6.5
74	33.6	66.4	45.4	9.0	6.2	1.9	1.0	12.0
75	45.0	55.0	42.3	16.7	8.4	7.9	0.4	−4.0
76	41.5	58.5	32.9	14.7	8.3	5.2	1.2	10.9
77	40.9	59.1	42.9	12.9	6.8	4.4	1.7	3.3
78	48.8	51.2	34.1	13.4	9.1	3.6	0.7	3.7
79	47.5	52.5	35.4	12.2	7.4	3.9	0.9	4.9
80	41.0	59.0	36.6	15.7	11.7	3.6	0.5	6.6
81	36.6	63.4	43.3	15.9	12.5	2.4	1.0	4.2
82	34.8	65.2	47.0	16.1	8.5	6.5	1.2	2.1
83	37.7	62.3	38.7	19.6	12.8	5.7	1.0	4.0
84	42.6	57.4	33.1	20.1	14.8	4.7	0.5	4.2
85	48.5	51.5	31.7	19.8	14.4	5.7	−0.4	0.0
›an	43.2	56.8	37.8	14.6	9.3	4.5	0.8	4.4
‹. dev.	5.3	5.3	4.8	3.3	2.9	1.5	0.5	3.6
›n %	12.2	9.3	12.6	22.3	30.8	34.0	58.1	81.8

rce: Ratios calculated from OECD, 1987a: tab. 33.F.

:rease in bond issues – but only in the second half of the 1970s, due
a substantial growth of the public deficit, and in the 1980s due to
. increase in issues by financial institutions.[18]
If one considers the bond market (Table 8.9), net issues of
terprises as a proportion of total issues of bonds reached an average
23 per cent only in the US and in France. In the US, however, from
e first half of the 1970s, the market reduced the proportion of funds
annelled towards industry – from 36–40 per cent in 1970–1, to 18
r cent in 1983–4 (Table 8.9). This was due only in part to growth in
e issues of government bonds and in the issues of financial
stitutions, since, from the mid-1970s, enterprises themselves in-
:ased the amount of credit taken out with financial intermediaries

Table 8.4   The financial structure of nonfinancial enterprises in Italy.
(Flow of funds as a percentage of total financial flows)

				External funds raised by				
	Self-finance	*External finance*	*Bank credits*	*Securities*				*Oth*
				Total	*shares*	*bonds*	*other*	
1970	49.1	50.9	41.0	9.8	9.4	0.4	0.0	0.
1971	40.8	59.2	44.3	14.8	10.9	3.8	0.0	0.
1972	41.3	58.7	43.0	15.5	10.9	4.7	0.0	0.
1973	25.6	74.4	57.5	15.8	11.9	3.9	0.0	1.
1974	35.2	64.8	56.4	7.9	7.1	0.8	0.0	0.
1975	29.8	70.2	52.8	15.2	9.7	5.6	0.0	2.
1976	43.7	56.3	44.3	11.3	8.5	2.9	0.0	0.
1977	47.9	52.1	40.2	12.0	8.4	3.5	0.0	0.
1978	50.5	49.5	33.0	16.6	14.0	2.6	0.0	−0.
1979	53.2	46.8	38.0	8.7	7.6	1.1	0.0	0.
1980	50.4	49.6	38.7	10.4	8.6	0.3	1.5	0.
1981	42.4	57.6	42.1	14.7	13.2	0.8	0.7	0.
1982	48.0	52.0	29.9	19.2	14.4	5.3	−0.5	2.
1983	40.0	60.0	32.1	24.4	22.2	2.6	−0.3	3.
1984	34.8	65.2	41.6	16.6	15.4	1.7	−0.5	7.
1985	38.6	61.4	36.8	17.2	15.8	1.6	−0.1	7.
mean	42.0	58.0	42.0	14.4	11.7	2.6	0.1	1.
std. dev.	7.6	7.6	7.7	4.1	3.8	1.7	0.5	2.
s/m %	18.1	13.1	18.4	28.7	32.6	65.0	848.1	138.

Source: Ratios calculated from OECD, 1987a: tab. 33.F. Bank credits include trade credits.

and reduced their direct finance (see Table 8.8). In France – as
that matter in the other countries – the total value of bonds issued
enterprises went down towards the end of the 1970s. In the Brit
case, 1974 marked a break with previous years when firms' b‹
issues had been relatively high. After 1974 there were more years
which withdrawals of bonds outstripped new issues, than years
which the opposite was the case.

As far as the primary stock market is concerned, the peculiarit
are even greater. The predominantly market-based countries – t
is, those where flows of funds deriving from securities issues w‹
approximately equal to credits, as in the US and UK (Table 8.2
were countries in which the proportions of share issues by n‹

ible 8.5 The financial structure of nonfinancial enterprises in West
Germany
(Flow of funds as a percentage of total financial flows)

	Self-finance	External finance	Bank credits	Securities				Trade credit	Others
				Total	shares	bonds	other		
)70	53.2	46.8	25.4	3.2	2.2	1.2	−0.2	2.6	15.6
)71	50.6	49.4	29.8	5.6	3.2	2.8	−0.4	3.0	11.0
)72	51.5	48.5	36.6	4.6	1.7	2.4	0.4	1.7	5.6
)73	56.2	43.8	22.4	1.7	1.7	0.9	−0.9	3.3	16.4
)74	54.2	45.8	24.0	3.5	1.7	1.4	0.5	2.6	15.7
)75	63.0	37.0	13.6	2.8	3.3	−0.7	0.1	5.1	15.4
)76	60.5	39.5	20.9	2.7	2.6	0.2	−0.1	3.0	12.8
)77	63.3	36.7	19.2	1.7	1.8	0.5	−0.6	1.6	14.1
)78	70.5	29.5	19.6	1.9	2.0	−0.3	0.2	1.1	6.9
)79	63.7	36.3	26.3	0.9	1.8	−1.3	0.3	3.7	5.4
)80	55.9	44.1	24.0	3.3	2.5	0.4	0.4	1.8	15.1
)81	51.3	48.7	21.5	2.1	1.7	0.3	0.0	4.0	21.2
)82	59.4	40.6	18.7	4.2	2.3	1.6	0.3	1.4	16.2
)83	65.6	34.4	22.1	2.7	2.5	0.0	0.2	0.9	8.7
)84	63.7	36.3	19.0	2.3	1.9	0.7	−0.3	1.5	13.5
)85	65.1	34.9	18.6	4.8	2.7	2.2	0.0	0.3	11.2
ιean	59.2	40.8	22.6	3.0	2.2	0.8	0.0	2.4	12.8
d. dev.	5.9	5.9	5.1	1.3	0.5	1.1	0.4	1.2	4.2
m %	9.9	14.4	22.8	41.8	23.3	141.0	4517.3	52.7	33.2

urce: Ratios calculated from OECD, 1987a: tab. 33.F.

ιancial enterprises were significantly lower than those in bank-
ιsed countries. Columns 1 and 2 of Table 8.10 compare, as a
·oportion of GNP, net issues of all sectors of the economy taken
·gether (including the foreign sector, but mainly composed of
ιancial and nonfinancial institutions) and industrial issues alone
ιcluding capital increases not giving rise to new market issues).
·om the comparison there emerges a significant difference between
.e first and second column in countries such as the US and UK. In
ιaly and France, issues by nonfinancial corporations have been
.latively higher as a proportion of the total.[19]

Table 8.6 The financial structure of nonfinancial enterprises in Japan. (Flow of funds as a percentage of total financial flows)

	Self-finance	External finance	Bank credits	Securities			Trade credit	Oth
				Total	shares	bonds		
1970	29.7	70.3	36.0	5.1	3.7	1.4	27.5	1.
1971	29.8	70.2	53.5	5.9	3.4	2.6	6.1	4.
1972	26.7	73.3	46.3	4.4	3.5	0.9	21.3	1.
1973	25.9	74.1	31.2	4.0	2.5	1.5	39.0	−0.
1974	33.3	66.7	38.3	4.1	2.4	1.7	20.0	4.
1975	36.1	63.9	50.5	9.5	4.0	5.5	6.2	−2.
1976	31.3	68.7	37.0	4.7	2.3	2.4	26.0	0.
1977	48.0	52.0	42.9	6.7	3.9	2.9	4.2	−1.
1978	44.7	55.3	28.1	5.7	3.2	2.5	19.2	2.
1979	40.1	59.9	20.6	5.3	2.7	2.6	32.6	1.
1980	46.7	53.3	33.2	4.8	3.1	1.7	13.5	1.
1981	42.2	57.8	36.8	6.8	4.1	2.6	16.5	−2.
1982	42.9	57.1	43.8	8.0	4.6	3.4	5.3	0.
1983	45.1	54.9	39.2	6.0	2.8	3.2	9.6	0.
1984	42.7	57.3	35.4	7.0	3.1	3.9	15.5	−0.
1985	n.a.	100.0	77.9	15.1	5.2	9.9	4.6	2.
mean	35.3	64.7	40.7	6.5	3.4	3.0	16.7	0.
std. dev.	11.6	11.6	12.5	2.7	0.8	2.1	10.3	2.
s/m %	32.8	17.9	30.6	41.1	23.0	68.2	61.9	240.

Source: Ratios calculated from OECD, 1987a: tab. 33.F.

From a brief comparison with stock-market issues of ordina
shares, it is possible yet again to show that markets were a ve
restricted channel for the mobilization of risk capital or credit capi
towards enterprises, and especially nonfinancial enterprises.

The problem therefore arises of the actual function of the sto
markets in these economies, and especially in those where su
markets are very extensive. In the US and the UK, the total stock
shares amounted in 1984 to more than 50 per cent of GNP. In 1964
the US, the value of share capital was equal to that of GNP (Ta
8.11). In 1984 even the capitalization of share prices on the Tok
stock exchange had reached levels of over 50 per cent of GNP.[20]

ble 8.7 The financial structure of nonfinancial enterprises in UK. (Flow of funds as a percentage of total financial flows)

| | Self-finance | External finance | Bank credits | External funds raised by | | | | Trade credit | Others |
| | | | | Securities | | | | | |
				Total	shares	bonds	other		
70	58.4	41.6	32.1	6.8	0.8	2.6	3.4	2.7	-0.1
71	62.8	37.2	26.3	7.9	2.2	3.9	1.8	2.1	1.0
72	58.1	41.9	30.0	8.2	3.4	3.3	1.6	4.0	-0.4
73	53.7	46.3	34.7	3.4	0.8	1.0	1.6	4.4	3.7
74	53.8	46.2	34.7	2.8	0.7	-0.3	2.4	6.0	2.7
75	63.5	36.5	25.1	5.1	6.7	0.3	-1.9	2.6	3.7
76	61.1	38.9	27.5	4.8	1.5	2.0	1.3	5.8	0.9
77	73.9	26.1	18.2	3.9	3.0	-0.2	1.1	3.2	0.8
78	74.0	26.0	16.3	2.5	2.8	-0.4	0.0	4.7	2.6
79	65.6	34.4	18.6	3.4	2.0	0.0	1.4	6.2	6.3
80	64.4	35.6	26.3	5.8	3.8	0.2	1.9	1.9	1.5
81	67.4	32.6	6.8	10.8	6.8	-0.2	4.2	7.5	7.5
82	73.8	26.2	18.8	10.9	3.4	0.2	7.3	0.4	-4.0
83	76.6	23.4	13.1	4.5	6.8	-1.0	-1.3	3.9	2.0
84	81.6	18.4	9.2	7.2	4.3	-0.5	3.4	0.8	1.2
85	76.5	23.5	10.3	11.3	12.0	-1.7	1.0	1.2	0.7
an	66.6	33.4	21.8	6.2	3.8	0.6	1.8	3.6	1.9
. dev.	8.3	8.3	8.8	2.9	2.9	1.5	2.1	2.0	2.6
1 %	12.5	24.9	40.5	46.0	75.8	267.6	114.4	56.4	137.7

rce: Ratios calculated from OECD, 1987a: tab. 33.F.

s took place while on the same major stock exchanges (those of
w York, Tokyo, Osaka and London) the relationship between
nual issues of ordinary shares and end-year capitalization did not
ceed the levels of the German stock exchange and remained much
low the proportion of capital mobilized on the stock exchanges of
lan and Paris.[21]
One can suggest several explanations for these peculiarities: in the
70s and 1980s, especially in the market-oriented countries, the
nsequences of a long-term downward trend in the proportion of
ares held privately and of a long-term upward trend in the
oportion held by institutional investors became apparent. This led to

Table 8.8   The financial structure of nonfinancial enterprises in US. (Flow of funds as a percentage of total financial flows)

	Self-finance	External finance	Bank credits	Securities				Trade credit	Othe
				Total	shares	bonds	other		
1970	61.5	38.5	17.5	20.7	4.2	14.6	1.9	6.0	−5.8
1971	57.9	42.1	18.8	17.8	6.8	11.3	−0.2	6.3	−0.8
1972	54.3	45.7	25.9	11.9	5.3	6.2	0.4	11.2	−3.3
1973	47.6	52.4	29.3	8.4	3.1	4.3	1.0	15.4	−0.
1974	50.2	49.8	27.7	13.3	1.7	8.9	2.7	12.5	−3.
1975	79.0	21.0	5.8	18.1	4.8	14.6	−1.3	3.9	−6.
1976	68.5	31.5	15.9	15.0	4.0	9.5	1.5	5.0	−4.
1977	64.9	35.1	24.7	10.9	0.8	9.1	0.9	7.5	−7.
1978	57.9	42.1	24.9	8.4	0.0	7.1	1.3	13.3	−4.
1979	59.7	40.3	27.1	7.5	−1.8	6.3	3.0	12.6	−7.
1980	64.9	35.1	20.0	14.2	3.1	9.3	1.7	9.6	−8.
1981	65.4	34.6	21.7	8.8	−2.4	7.3	3.9	6.3	−2.
1982	79.5	20.5	21.7	9.3	2.8	8.2	−1.7	0.7	−11.
1983	73.2	26.8	21.3	11.7	5.5	5.0	1.2	8.0	−14.
1984	66.8	33.2	31.9	2.3	−12.3	10.7	3.9	5.8	−6.
1985	74.2	25.8	21.0	4.5	−13.5	16.0	2.1	5.8	−5.
mean	64.1	35.9	22.2	11.4	0.8	9.3	1.4	8.1	−5.
std. dev.	9.1	9.1	6.0	4.8	5.7	3.3	1.6	3.8	3.
s/m %	14.3	25.5	27.0	42.2	755.5	36.0	111.3	47.2	−59.

Source: Ratios calculated from OECD, 1987a: tab. 33.F.

a structural transformation of the stock market, in the sense that t
portfolio preferences of institutional and surplus agents dominat
those of the deficit agents. Institutional investors preferred securiti
that could be easily sold on a secondary market, and were less willi
to take on obligations and risks deriving from new share issues. T
financial institutions, especially in the US, increasingly turned to t
formation of more flexible and diversified balance sheets (Lewis, 198
Friedman, 1980; pp: 18–20, 36). The capital markets therefo
apparently reduced their contribution to capital formation and i

le 8.9 Bonds issued by nonfinancial enterprises as a percentage of total bond issues.

	France	Italy	Germany	Japan	UK	US
70	36.8	1.5	9.6	12.6	248.1	40.6
71	37.4	10.1	19.5	14.3	7.9	35.9
72	28.7	12.1	11.3	5.0	66.8	26.6
73	19.7	7.4	5.0	11.0	9.2	23.1
74	27.8	4.0	7.2	7.5	−11.1	33.1
75	40.2	10.7	−1.7	13.5	0.8	26.2
76	28.9	11.6	0.7	6.0	7.7	19.8
77	27.3	6.1	1.5	4.6	−0.6	22.6
78	20.2	4.5	−1.1	4.3	−1.8	22.2
79	23.1	4.6	−5.9	6.5	0.0	20.1
30	14.3	5.7	1.6	3.8	0.5	26.3
31	10.6	4.5	0.9	5.8	−0.9	21.8
32	16.4	12.4	3.7	6.5	0.7	13.9
33	13.9	3.0	0.1	5.2	−3.0	8.6
34	11.4	2.7	1.8	8.4	−1.3	18.3
35	12.3	1.8	5.2	12.4	−4.3	18.4
an	23.1	6.4	3.7	8.0	19.9	23.6
. dev.	9.5	3.7	5.8	3.5	61.3	7.7
%	41.0	57.2	157.8	43.6	307.4	32.8

ce: Ratios calculated from OECD, 1987a; tab. 21.F (2.c and 7.c).

•ved their efficiency in terms of the volume of transactions and of •italization on the secondary market.[22]

The existence of stable and extensive capital markets reinforces, vever, the orientations of enterprise finance, even if, in quantita-e terms, the contribution of funds goes down, as happened from the 50s onwards in the UK and the US. The stock market especially tinues to be an instrument of diversification and financial ;anization of firms. The importance of this function, which links ns to the financial system, can conflict – as actually happened in rious countries – with the stock market's other function as an trument for the mobilization of risk capital (Mayer, 1986a; Nardoz-1986b: p. 501).

Table 8.10   Share issues (as a percentage of GNP)

	France			Italy			West Germany		
	All sectors (1)	Non-financial enterprises (2)	Common stock (3)	All sectors (1)	Non-financial enterprises (2)	Common stock (3)	All sectors (1)	Non-financial enterprises (2)	Com st
1970	23.9	11.0	–	24.4	18.0	–	9.3	4.1	
1971	21.9	9.8	–	29.5	21.1	–	10.1	5.6	
1972	25.8	11.7	–	29.5	23.6	–	8.5	2.9	
1973	25.9	11.5	–	29.8	23.5	–	6.1	2.5	
1974	18.6	10.6	–	12.8	10.9	–	6.3	2.3	
1975	19.8	10.6	–	19.2	16.5	–	9.2	4.0	
1976	21.0	11.9	–	19.3	16.5	–	7.1	3.9	
1977	17.7	10.1	–	16.9	14.1	–	6.6	2.4	
1978	21.3	12.3	–	27.6	25.0	–	7.4	2.8	
1979	20.8	10.6	–	19.6	15.0	–	6.6	2.8	
1980	29.4	17.4	–	23.3	17.1	–	7.1	3.5	
1981	33.7	16.8	10.1	33.5	24.1	15.4	6.7	2.3	
1982	24.3	11.6	7.5	28.1	22.1	11.0	5.3	2.8	
1983	38.9	17.4	10.4	40.8	32.4	5.7	9.5	3.4	
1984	25.4	21.1	10.5	30.4	23.4	7.4	6.5	2.5	
1985	56.2	19.2	16.9	30.4	23.3	4.8	9.6	3.6	
mean	26.5	13.3	11.1	26.0	20.4	8.9	7.6	3.2	
std.dev.	9.4	3.6	3.1	6.9	5.2	3.9	1.5	0.9	
s/m %	35.3	26.7	27.9	26.5	25.3	43.7	19.1	26.9	5!

	Japan			UK			US		
	All sectors (1)	Non-financial enterprises (2)	Common stock (3)	All sectors (1)	Non-financial enterprises (2)	Common stock (3)	All sectors (1)	Non-financial enterprises (2)	Com s
1970	15.0	13.4	–	10.2	1.1	–	10.4	5.9	
1971	11.8	10.4	–	10.5	3.2	–	13.6	10.6	
1972	15.5	13.1	–	24.5	6.1	–	11.6	9.2	
1973	12.8	10.5	–	10.8	1.9	–	7.9	5.9	
1974	6.9	6.2	–	2.6	1.6	–	3.8	2.8	
1975	9.0	7.9	–	20.7	10.7	–	6.9	6.3	
1976	6.6	5.6	–	9.0	2.9	–	6.3	5.9	
1977	7.3	5.8	–	9.9	5.5	–	3.4	1.4	
1978	6.3	5.6	–	15.4	4.9	–	0.8	0.0	
1979	6.5	6.2	–	14.6	4.2	–	-1.6	-3.2	
1980	5.4	6.0	–	26.3	5.8	–	7.9	4.9	
1981	9.3	8.2	0.6	34.2	9.7	9.8	-1.1	-3.8	
1982	8.0	7.6	0.6	23.6	4.3	6.5	10.8	3.7	
1983	5.3	4.9	1.7	29.9	9.4	8.6	20.0	8.4	1.
1984	6.7	6.2	2.8	23.3	6.0	22.6	-8.4	-20.7	
1985	5.8	5.0	1.6	73.1	16.8	13.6	9.5	-20.7	
mean	8.7	7.7	1.4	21.2	5.9	12.2	6.3	1.0	
std.dev.	3.2	2.7	0.8	15.9	3.9	5.7	6.6	9.1	
s/m %	36.6	34.8	56.0	75.0	67.2	46.7	104.2	892.2	6

Sources and notes: In column (1) share issued (net) by domestic sectors (OECD, 1987a: tab. 21F. 7)
Column (2) share issued by nonfinancial enterprises (OECD 1987a: tab. 33F. 26). Column (3)
common stocks issued by financial and nonfinancial companies quoted at the stock exchange (FIBV
1982–6).

)le 8.11 Value of shares outstanding at the end of year and sectoral shareholders.
(Total shares as a percentage of GNP and shares held by sectors as a percentage of total holdings)

	France		Italy			West Germany		
	1981	1984	1964	1981	1984	1971	1981	1984
ares/GNP	7.5	9.9	22.4	17.2	20.4	7.8	5.9	5.8
ancial inst.			1.8	4.2	4.0			
terprises			43.5	72.8	96.0			
useholds			37.7	14.1	–			
st of the world			0.1	–	–			

	Japan			UK			US		
	1964	1981	1984	1973	1981	1984	1964	1981	1984
ares/GNP	24.4	12.7	14.5	54.8	39.1	64.0	99.6	50.9	55.2
anc. inst.	42.0	55.5	61.6	37.2	58.4	63.9	13.2	22.5	29.5
terprises	22.2	22.8	19.8	13.6	9.4	11.7	–	–	–
useholds	44.7	20.4	17.3	39.6	23.9	17.6	84.6	73.2	65.8
st of the world	–	–	–	7.1	5.0	3.8	–	–	–

rce: Ratios calculated from OECD, Financial Statistics, II, Paris, OECD, 1983 and 1985: tab. 3. The totals do not always equal 100, because of allocative discrepancies and missing sectors.

ructures of Ownership, Forms of Control and Orientation of nterprise Finance

e dynamics of financial systems have suggested evolu-nary-systemic models, in which market and bank-based financing ocedures constitute alternative forms of organization and manage-nt of the allocation of financial resources in industrialized econ-ies. Modes of allocation and processes of adjustment depend on the evalence or otherwise of a system of competitive prices (such as a ck market) as an alternative to negotiating relationships of a ateral kind, adopted by the credit institutions. We end up having stems with different mechanisms of economic regulation, including

state intervention which can exercise an adaptive or integrat
function (Cant, 1972; Zysman, 1983; Hu, 1984; Cox, 1986).

Of these regulatory mechanisms, management of ownership re
tions and of the control functions in nonfinancial enterprises occup
a central place. In modern industrial economies, the eighteen
century and preindustrial model of the owner-entrepreneur, wh
ownership and control was fused in a single individual or fam
group, has been dissolved or at least radically transformed.

In the six countries examined, different typologies of property a
control of large-scale enterprise have been dominant. Of th
typologies, some are compatible – for reasons that we shall see – w
market-based economies, others with credit-based economies. Scl
matically, it is possible to identify four types of property organizat
and relationships between industry and the financial system: int
firm share networks, or constellations of interests, in the UK and U
industrial holdings, in France and Italy; a system of combines a
reciprocal share networks, in the Japanese case; and finally,
universal banking of the German system. Such structures of ow
ership and control establish forms of relative autonomy or dependei
of the formation of capital on the financial system as a whole, w
their respective models of financial behavior of enterprises.

Polyarchies and markets in the US

Systems of share networks of a polyarchic kind established the
selves around hegemonic financial institutions, such as the fi
principal banks of New York or the British clearing banks. T
concentration of industrial shareholding in the hands of cert
financial institutions has, however, led not to models of financ
capitalism, but to the formation of interest groups which do not s
themselves up as alternatives to the financial markets which, howe
er, are charged with the function of monitoring industrial activiti
and especially quoted firms. The weak cohesion of the groups induc
firms to pursue a relative financial autonomy (involving low levels
leverage and a high degree of self-financing) and to reduce sha
issues in order not to alter "fragile" ownership equilibria.

Recent studies have, in addition, drawn attention to minori
controls – thus touching on "bank minority control" (Zeitlin, 19
Kotz, 1978) and "constrained management control" – owing to t
influence of the banks over managerial decisions (Herman, 1981). F
Soref and Zeitlin (1987) the multiproduct, multidivisional firm run
professional managers did not arise from the downfall of the capita

ass. The relative dispersal of shareholders, principally of an institu-
onal type, led to the emergence of coalitions of interests through the
echanism of logrolling or vote trading. In 1980 only a few of the 252
rgest American enterprises had majority groupings. In general,
out twenty shareholders are necessary to form a minority block, or
coalition of interests with the power to influence managerial
cision-making (Scott, 1986: pp. 137–41). In contrast to what
appened in the UK, in the US, institutional control has not emerged,
ue to the regional structure and low level of concentration of the
anking system, not to mention the rigid control of credit activities.[23]
 the US too, the household sector has further reduced its sharehold-
gs, which have become concentrated in pension funds and insurance
rms (Table 8.11). These institutional investors are controlled by the
anks' trust departments. From the immediate postwar period on-
ards, in fact, the development of the bank holding companies has
lowed the banks to incorporate the affiliated trust companies and to
xercise more direct control over such affiliates.[24] Apart from the
xisting fragmentation, a series of share networks and more solid
oss-participations have been organized around the principal finan-
al intermediaries of New York, and also around other well-estab-
shed banking groups.[25]
However, these communities of interest organized around the
nancial institutions[26] are relatively loose owing to the lack of solid
ements of cohesion and centralization. Share packages held do not
 beyond minority proportions (22 and 29 per cent of existing shares
ere held by financial intermediaries in 1981 and 1984 respectively –
e Table 8.11) and the reciprocal presence of industrialists and
ankers on the boards of directors of various companies does not
volve close and regular consultation between the banking and
dustrial boards on strategic questions going beyond specific and
nited objectives.[27] Share participations themselves are often man-
ed with portfolio-related aims in mind, and even in cases of
sagreement with the firm's management, the bank will follow the
Vall Street rule," preferring, that is, to sell, rather than exercise its
ting rights. This situation has been influenced by the same banking
les that were established at the beginning of the 1930s. With the
paration of banks and industry, large-scale American enterprises
creasingly developed their own channels of funding and sought
ternatives to domestic channels, as happened in the case of the
ultinational enterprises on the international capital markets (Pas-
é, 1979).
The paradigm of external finance of the American enterprise was
us formed and developed by sticking to a very low level of

indebtedness as compared to other countries. The flows of exterr finance have geared with intermediaries and to a lesser exte: commercial credit between firms and the securities issues, especia: bonds. Bank credit, though it grew slowly from the end of the 197(showed a variable trend during the period studied (Table 8.8). T' relative importance of trade credit probably depended on the netwo: of interfirm relations in which the degree of confidence necessary sustain commercial credit was nothing other than the reflection interfirm shareholdings – direct knowledge of the enterprise in de: which was greater in the case of shareholding chains than in that simple commercial relations.

The contribution of funds from the capital market was not massive as the extent and evolution of the American financ: markets would have led one to presume. The relatively restrict: nature of the primary stock market can be understood through t: dominant firm structure and the looseness of share networks. T: tendency of institutional shareholdings to grow since the 1960s h: helped to discourage new issues by enterprises, because a lar: proportion of institutional shareholders, having no interest in mai taining any control over the issuing enterprise, do not guarantee contribution of risk capital sufficient to support the controlling grou: In addition, enterprises have been influenced by a leverage effe: which, in market-based systems, operates in a way which is t: opposite to that in bank-based systems. In fact, in order to encoura: the take-up of new issues, even by institutional investors, firms ha: apparently had to adopt favorable dividend policies, thus restricti: their self-financing capacity.[28] Therefore the policy followed has r: been one of recapitalizing enterprises by resorting to the market, much as one of reducing relative indebtedness during the 1970s a: increasing the capacity for internal finance, as we have already see:

Institutional investors have instead sustained the bond mark: including the market for the issue of industrial bonds. Overall, t: total stock of bonds represented 58 per cent of GNP in 1964 and 198: and it rose to 71 per cent in 1984. Its composition varied between 19: and 1984: the share of the private and foreign sectors fell from 31 25 per cent, while that of the public sector rose from 69 to 75 p: cent.[29] Of private issues, over 70 per cent were absorbed by t: pension funds and insurance companies, while the banks preferr: state securities. The American bond market, too, is predominant: composed of state bonds; however, it helps to finance a relative: important part of the annual requirements of firms, and in co: parative terms it is without equals (Table 8.8).[30] The reallocation capital effected by the primary bonds market towards other secto:

·obably contributed to the growth in bank credits to firms in the last
·rt of the period.

·e City's insularity, and self-financing in British enterprises

· the UK the structure of relations between the banking system and
·ms has characteristics very similar to the American structure. The
·mily firm and the influence of prominent families among the
·areholders of British firms remained important until the 1960s.[31]
·nce then, institutional share-ownership has clearly emerged as a
·rm of defense both of the property interests of the longstanding
·dividual shareholders, and of diversification and concentration of
·ms within groups of industrialists whose weak cohesion ensured
·at the groups of the most influential families would not lose control
·mpletely (Scott, 1987: p. 219).

The dispersal of shareholders among British firms has been greater
·an among American firms. However, the shares of nonfinancial
·rporations are held by a relatively restricted number of pension
·nds. These in their turn are owned by the principal clearing and
·erchant banks, by insurance companies and investment groups. The
·nancial institutions constitute the centre of a complex polyarchy.
·round the banking core of the polyarchy, the principal shareholding
·etworks and interlocking directorates spread out. In 1976, share
·etworks formed hierarchical structures headed by hegemonic groups
·nd associated enterprises, with subordinate firms below.[32]

Since control over the banks and other financial institutions is
·xercised by constellations of interests according to a system of
·greements among syndicates of shareholders, ample room for man-
·gerial autonomy is left to affiliated companies, the pension funds and
·e various intermediaries. Institutional control of large corporations
·as grown with internally managed pension funds, so that large firms
·ave become "units of 'finance capital,' to engage in a spread of
·ctivities which cannot easily be divided into industrial, commercial
·nd banking categories" (Scott, 1986: p. 102). The system of constella-
·ons of interests means that, collectively, the latter exercise consider-
·ble power of control. This, however, prevents individual members
·om influencing the enterprise strategy. The result is that the
·arious powers cancel each other out, so that "the major shareholders
·ill tend to act as a constraint on the strategy, rather than actively
·etermining it" (Scott, 1986: p. 122).

Structures of ownership and control influence the role and function
· the financial markets. The volume of share stock is quite consider-

able and this influences the size of the secondary markets: in 1973 t
share stock rose to 55 per cent of GNP; in 1981 it was 39 per cent a
in 1984, 64 per cent – above the equivalent proportion for the U
(Table 8.11). The market is principally composed of the shares
financial institutions. In particular, between 1978 and 1985 the val
of the stock of shares of the nonbank private sector reached 47.9 p
cent of the total, the share capital of the "monetary sector" was ju
4.2 per cent of the total, while other financial institutions account
for 6.7 per cent.[33] The proportion accounted for by the capital
commercial and industrial enterprises continued, however, to
considerable, at 41.2 per cent. The principal holders were the nonbar
intermediaries themselves, with 46.9 per cent of the shares, whi
other financial institutions held 25.2 per cent. The shareholdings
nonfinancial firms amounted to only 5.8 per cent. The years followir
1978 also confirmed the long-term downward trend in the proportic
of shares held privately – which went from 18.5 per cent in 1978
12.5 per cent in 1985 – and the long-term growth in the proportic
held by other financial institutions – which went from 22.8 per cent
28.1 per cent.

The concentration of share stock in the hands of financial inte
mediaries contrasts with the significant dispersal of share package
The large banks and insurance companies, which manage about ha
the investments of the pension funds, control not less than 67 per ce
of the shares held by the latter. In addition, pension funds and ur
trusts delegate the management of a proportion of their shar
portfolios to the merchant banks, which succeed in controlling abor
18 per cent of quoted shares although they hold just 1.1 per cent.
emerges, however, that there is a clear distinction between th
holding of shares and the exercise of the rights associated with them
since the criteria by which portfolios are managed essentially serv
the aims of obtaining a source of income and realizing capital gair
(see Minns, 1988: pp. 144–5). Offsetting powers of control, th
separation between banks and industry, the City's insularity, cor
centration, and the banking cartels constitute the principal features
the British financial structure (Moran, 1984: pp. 13–16). By traditio
the clearing banks maintain client relations with industrial enter
prises, and only through them can they exercise a monitorin
function. The more active merchant banks act as financial advisors t
firms. The function of evaluating firms itself is left to stockbrokin
analysts or to external credit-rating agencies, whose judgment
influence the management of the pension funds' portfolios.[34] Wha
emerged during the 1970s was, however, an erosion of the institu
tional separation within the financial sector and a tendency toward

ιe formation of financial conglomerates, whose principal effects have
een reflected back on the financial markets themselves, thus increas-
ιg transactions and improving the auction procedures of the stock
xchange (Llewellyn, 1985: pp. 26 and 30).

The effects on enterprise finance have been a relative increase,
nce the beginning of the 1980s, in the issue of securities, especially
ιares, and a trend towards the reduction in bank credit. From a
ιoyant stock market firms have, however, obtained a relatively
mited quantity of funds as compared to all sectors taken together. In
985, which was a decidedly more favorable year, firms' issues
ιached 17 per cent of GNP, as against 73 per cent for the net issues
f other sectors (Table 8.10, columns 1 and 2). However, in relative
ιrms, not even in 1985 did the equity financing of UK firms reach the
ιvels of countries such as Italy and France (Table 8.10). British
ιterprises have maintained and increased their relative financial
utonomy: leverage has remained stable (Table 8.1), while the
roportion of internal finance has increased substantially (Table 8.7).
ι terms of enterprise finance, therefore, this is a model of separation
ιtween industry and the banking system. The model is typical of
ιarket-based systems in which the increase in firms' own funds,
ιriving from profits or risk capital provided by the market, is not
ιch as to affect firms' capitalization or their levels of indebtedness.
ιs in the case of the US, this is due to the erosion of the capacity for
ιlf-financing as a result of the distribution of dividends, and the
rosion of the increase in net worth due to the effects of the
ιpreciation. In the UK "the maintenance of a sound gearing ratio
ιquity to debt ratio) as a safety cushion, in particular, tends to play
ι important part in both financiers' and industrialists' thinking."[35]
'his creates a vicious circle, constituted by the fact that equity finance
ι generally inefficient in supplying a large volume of capital to firms
ιrough the market or profits, and therefore inadequate to increase
ιe capacity to gain access to credit. Quoted firms which, numbering
,288 in 1985 as compared to 3,316 in 1974, were more numerous
ιan the firms quoted on the American stock exchanges, cannot
ιmpensate for the rationing to which they are subject in the credit
ιarket, by an increase in share issues. These, if they were permitted
y the delicate ownership structures, would be realizable in conditions
f high or growing expected profits and generous dividend policies.[36]
ι the model of British industrial funding, net investment – and, as a
ιnsequence, an improvement in competitiveness and profitability –
ιn only be realized if adequate profits are achieved and the market is
ιnfident that firms will continue to enjoy a favorable trend in
ιturns. With a vast number of shareholdings dispersed among a

series of institutional investors, the market-oriented system can lea
to allocation distortions as well as distortions in the supervisor
function of the market, as a result of a short time-horizon whic
orients the choices of financial operators and, as a consequence, th
choices of firms, too.[37] The volatility of the primary share and bor
markets in the market-oriented countries would seem to confirm th
prevalence of such criteria.[38] A financial system with extensiv
secondary markets which guarantee the conditions of liquidity of th
financial institutions gives rise to actions aimed at the realization
windfall gains (De Cecco, 1986b and 1988).

Firms too come to enjoy some of the advantages of a flexib
management of liquidity and of the prospects of external growth
deriving from the relative dispersal of shareholdings and the volum
of shares traded on the stock exchange. Alternatively, in credit-base
systems, firms enjoy greater internal growth potential, due to th
classic effects of leverage. Among other things, credit – unlike equit
financing – makes funds for investment immediately available, an
unlike dividend payments, makes capital costs tax-deductible.

Holdings and financial orientations in Italy and France

In bank-based systems such as Italy and France, share issues an
levels of indebtedness are mutually interacting. When firms ar
unable to obtain funds in the credit market, or are able to obtain the
only on unfavorable terms, they turn to share issues in order to obtai
capital and reestablish a sound company base lost as a result of
negative trend in profits, or growing indebtedness.[40] We have alread
seen that in Italy and France, firms' indebtedness has been relativel
variable, and the acquisition of share capital relatively high.

Company readjustment of asset structures relies on the framewor
of industrial holdings. The latter comprise a number of legall
independent companies held together by a pyramid structure
formal and informal ownership and control, at the apex of which is
holding company which coordinates the activities of the entire grou
In a group structure, each single enterprise can reestablish it
creditworthiness through an increase in its registered capital, withou
this leading to a loss of control on the part of the majority shareho
ders. These retain firm control over the operating companies of th
group because, first, the pyramid system of shareholdings means tha
the possession of even a relatively limited proportion of capital i
sufficient to allow control, and second, the direct and indirec
shareholdings of the companies of the group allow a proportion

ewly issued capital to be contributed by minority shareholders or ıareholders outside the group.[41]

In the case of Italian groups where ultimate control is of a family or ıblic kind, the group has a pyramid structure with a low number of ıterlocking shareholdings and a variety of intergroup ties. This has ıcouraged collusive strategies, but has above all made the industrial ıoups less dependent on the banking system.[42] It is sufficient to point ıt that of a total share stock of around 22 per cent of GNP in 1964, ıd 17 per cent in 1981 (20 per cent in 1984), the shares held by ınfinancial firms were 43.5 per cent of the total in 1964 and 72.8 per ınt in 1981 (Table 8.11). Between 1964 and 1972 the proportion held ıivately fell from 37.7 to 14.1 per cent, while the proportion held by ıe state fell from 16.9 to 8.9 per cent. The proportion held by ıancial intermediaries, though it increased, remained slight.

Since the mid 1970s, Italian companies have reduced their indebted- ıss, something which had begun to damage their profitability and ıpacity for self-financing. The period of "debt-acquittal," accentuated ı the emergence of positive real interest rates – which led firms to ıtionalize the management of their inventories and liquidity[43] – has ıen characterized by the substitution of sources of external finance. ısues of shares have increased, especially since the beginning of the ı80s, and levels of credit have been reduced (Table 8.4).

The holding structure emerged in countries where entrepreneurship ıd managerial skills were not widely diffused, and where internal ıarkets were not very extensive. In certain historical periods these ıructural conditions led, or could have led, to industrial failures ıhich collusive company structures would have prevented, or at least ıtenuated.

In France, too, the system of holdings has been the form of ıganization of property relationships most adapted to the formation ı large, diversified companies, without compromising the persistence ı personal and family control.[44] Unlike the Italian situation, in ıance the system of groups appears to be much more diversified, ıth groups controlled by families, banks, and "loose constellations of ıterests."[45] Among groups, linked shareholdings in the large enter- ıises and share networks are frequent. The multiplicity of group ıstems has allowed the formation of various types of relations of ıllaboration and financial coordination between companies and the ınking system, from those of the Anglo-Saxon type to the collusive ıes typical of Japan and Germany. For this reason, the French ıstem seems to be intermediate between the American and Japanese ıstems, especially if one also considers the role of coordination of ıonomic activity carried out by the state.[46]

Overall, a model of enterprise finance oriented to the banks ha
been dominant: a model in which, as in the Italian case, leverage gre
until the financial stability of firms was compromised by the worser
ing economic situation, as happened in 1974.[47] In France, securitie
issues and equity finance have been channels opened up as a
alternative to the rationing of credit operating in the banking an
credit markets.[48]

Forms of collusion between banks and industry in Japan and Germany

Japan and Germany provide examples, within a credit-based eco
omy, of financial systems and relationships between industry an
banking which are different again. The high levels of enterpris
indebtedness are maintained within a system which is solidly collusiv
and cooperative, and hierarchically governed by industrial and finar
cial combines or by the universal bank. Such systems have allowe
the successful prosecution of determinate macroeconomic objective
such as the rate of growth, international competitiveness, an
domestic price stability.

In Japan, interfirm relations are structured around tight inte
locking and close shareholdings. Between 1978 and 1984, 87 per cen
of total share capital was represented by the shares of nonfinanci
enterprises, the remainder – about 13 per cent – by the shares c
private financial institutions. The latter held a proportion of share
holdings which grew from 51 per cent in 1978 to 62 per cent in 198
Firms and households hold average proportions of 22 and 20 per cen
respectively, although these are tending to decline.[49]

Even though shareholdings are centralized in the financial institu
tions, a form of nonfinancial, managerial control has emerged. Th
structure of oligarchic groups (*keiretsu*), without a holding grou
leader, took shape during the reconstruction period after the dissolu
tion of the *zaibatsu* and the family control associated with them, wit
the aim of reinforcing the large firms and preventing excessive an
damaging competition between them, while preserving the processe
of competition between firms belonging to different groups.[50]

At the end of 1978, in the 100 companies with the highest volume c
assets – among which 61 were nonfinancial firms – 75 per cent of th
equity was divided among roughly ten large financial institutions. I
a further 17 companies, the shareholdings of financial institution
represented between 50 and 75 per cent of the equity capital.[51] I

ery group the controlling shareholdings in the nonfinancial enter-
ises are centralized in the city bank and in the life insurance
mpanies of the group itself. The compactness of the leading
areholders of the group is to some extent guaranteed by the fact
at, except in a few cases, Japanese insurance companies are not
nstituted in the form of a joint-stock company. On the other hand
e banks – whose capitalization is limited – are generally partly
ned by the insurance companies themselves and by nonfinancial
ms of the group to which they belong.[52] In terms of share packages,
e centre of gravity of the group is constituted by the insurance
mpanies, but these do not constitute the core of effective control
en over the banks. The structure of shareholdings does not
nstitute the cement of intergroup relations.

The enterprises of a group are held together by reciprocal share-
ldings, but above all by credit relationships, commercial interests,
e managerial personnel, and informal committees of the chairmen of
e larger corporations.[53] Credits granted by the large banks are
ainly assigned to firms within the group, and there are special terms
cases of deferred repayments or renewals.[54]

The interfirm networks are reflected in the structure of enterprise
ancing. Firms apply for bank loans and, as an alternative, for
mmercial credits (Table 8.6). Especially during the years of reces-
n and restrictive monetary policies, bank lending was substantially
duced and commercial lending – sustained by intragroup relations
 external subcontracting – took its place. Notwithstanding the
istence of a stock market constituted – as we have seen – almost
clusively by industrial shares, Japanese enterprises have not
gaged in recapitalization practices. After 1974, with the end of the
ng period of sustained economic and industrial growth, the rate of
debtedness diminished considerably and with it also share issues
emselves (Tables 8.1 and 8.2). The close and intense relations
tween the banks and the enterprises within the group have made
licies of this kind, designed to win back the confidence of creditors,
s effective – unlike the position in Italy and France. In fact it has
en stable coalitions of managerial oligarchies which – even in
ation to the banking system as a whole – have reduced the risks
volved with credit.[55]

The network of relationships and of information between enter-
ises and banks has been further consolidated by monetary policies
ned at sustaining economic growth and indirect finance (Miyazaki,
80: pp. 60–1). Until around the end of the 1970s, a policy of
tificially low interest rates stimulated intermediation and the

banks' policies of overborrowing, becoming a decisive factor
Japanese economic and industrial development (Sakakibara a
Feldman, 1983; Suzuki, 1980 and 1986).[56]

After the second half of the 1970s, the enormous issues
government bonds helped to establish an extensive market[57] whi
has altered the environmental conditions of discretionary moneta
policy. Since the beginning of the 1980s these processes have be
accompanied by measures to gradually liberalize the capital marke
This has not, however, changed the structure of enterprise finan
(Kirby, 1980; Suzuki, 1986; Shimamura, 1989). For the moment t
greatest effects have been on financial intermediaries and markets.

Like the Japanese system, the German financial system is based
a network of relations between the banking system and indust
What is involved is a network of formal relations structured
shareholdings, the presence of bank directors on the managing a
controlling boards of companies, and informal influences exercised
the granting of loans, financial advice, and syndicates for t
placement of securities on the market. The element of cohesion
such ties is provided by the universal bank which operates in t
money and loans markets, as well as in the securities market, both
its own behalf and on behalf of third parties – not to mention
exercise of control functions over the activities of the stock exchang
subjecting it to a prudent regime of financial ratios.[58] The syste
allows the gathering, transfer and utilization of information co
cerning the firms and the problems that they may be encounterin
Relationships of negotiation and cooperation are more important th
market mechanisms in the determination of economic choices, inve
ment projects and in the procedures governing industrial activity.

The selection of industrial investment projects and firms' strategi
are influenced not only by internal hierarchies, but also by extern
and financial hierarchies. The "external" hierarchies are regulated
the *Hausbank*, on the basis of its own commercial interest, and colle
information, which they make available to the firms, about secto
and markets. Collaboration with the banks has resulted in
centralization and distribution of information, which is particular
efficient for the purposes of the international competitiveness
German firms and products.[59] This kind of system has reinforced t
hierarchical mechanisms of the selection of choices – as compared
the polyarchical mechanisms of the market. This explains, at least
part, the growth in the average performance of enterprises and t
reduction in the variance of such performance ("static efficiency"
thus encouraging the simultaneous laying down of innovative proce
ses ("evolutionary viability").[60] The formal and informal organiz

)nal structures both within and outside the firm have thus re-
forced the effects of financial leverage on enterprise growth.
In a system of internal and external hierarchies, control procedures
 not operate according to the processes of Darwinian selection of
mpetitive markets, nor through takeovers of enterprises which are
low standard in terms of efficiency and returns. The large banks
tervene in order to rescue and reorganize the firms and to avoid
llapse, and they facilitate compromise solutions among creditors
emselves (Dyson, 1986: pp. 136–8). External growth is normally
hibited by close group relations, by the coordinating function of the
.nk, and by markets which are generally restricted in terms of the
.antity of negotiable securities (Table 8.11).
The role of the universal bank and external finance in the growth
.d performance of firms depends on these relationships of ownership
.d control. In 1978, industrial shares (at market price) represented
'.4 per cent of the total; in 1985, 76.3 per cent. The shares of foreign
mpanies during the period 1978–85 represented 12.8 per cent, as
d the shares of financial enterprises.[61] During the same period the
rgest proportion – at 45.1 per cent – was held within the enterprise
ctor, while private shareholders held 17.9 per cent, the financial
stitutions 15.3 per cent, the foreign sector 12.1 per cent, and the
ate 9.7 per cent. Through their direct shareholdings and the system
 delegating votes (*Depotstimmerecht*) the three large banks (Deut-
he, Commerz and Dresdner) manage to occupy important posts on
e boards of directors and supervisory boards of many firms.[62] The
.nks' supervisory role is further facilitated by the high concentration
 firms having the form of a joint-stock company. For example, in the
id 1970s, only about 100 large firms had a turnover approaching
ree-quarters that of the total turnover of the nonfinancial
.terprises.[63] At the end of 1983, of a total of about two million
.terprises, 2,100 were joint-stock companies, and of these only 450
ere quoted on the stock exchange. By contrast, in the UK in the
me year there were 5,300 joint-stock companies, of which 2,400
ere quoted on the stock exchange (Friedmann, Ingram and Miles,
)84: p. 370). In Germany even more than in Japan, the practice of
.uity financing through the capital market has been obstructed by a
ructurally limited stock market.
The primary markets for industrial bonds in total provided less
.an 10 per cent of external funds. Firms had a high and slightly
creasing level of indebtedness over the whole period between 1970
.d 1985 (Table 8.1). However, self-financing has not only outstripped
.e proportion of external finance (Table 8.5), but in relative terms
.s exceeded the self-financing of enterprise in the other countries;

German firms have also enjoyed greater stability during the period
has been argued that, besides supplying a significant proportion of
means of external finance, the banks have carried out with so
efficiency the operation of guiding firms towards profitable objecti
and productive efficiency.[64] Collusive activities between industry a
the banks have probably contributed to the search for alternat
channels of financing for firms during periods of credit restriction
domestic markets, as is demonstrated by the trend in bank lendi
and foreign loans (other loans) in the financing of German enterpri
(Table 8.5).

Concluding Remarks

Summarizing, it seems possible to suggest, first, that the bar
oriented countries tend to favor a logic of accumulation and
economic performance of a long-run kind. Market-oriented syste
on the other hand, display market efficiency in terms of transactio
information, and liquidity. These systems are consistent with ec
omies in which the various financial institutions, firms, the state a
foreign operators compete among themselves for the acquisition a
allocation of financial resources, or in order to change their own as
structure in response to market signals.

Second, the stock markets do not generally serve well the purpo
of industrial financing. Even in the countries where they are partic
larly active as primary markets, or, where the instruments of dir
finance are numerous, two situations are found: either direct finar
represents a secondary form of financing – as in the case of equ
finance in France and Italy – or else the markets finance enterpri
to a much lesser extent than they do other sectors of the economy,
in the case of the bond market in the US.

Third, in both systems debt financing and indirect finance a
factors essential to firms' growth. Bank credit constitutes the basis
the structure of firms' external financing, and is a decisive element
investment choices and in financial management in periods of falli
profits. In market-based systems, resort to financial intermediaries
to some extent offset by issues of securities and by trade credit. T
joint leadership role of the banks in industrial financing, and t
weight of internal finance, has led to a relatively low level
indebtedness, which has allowed only exceptional and seconda
access to the direct forms of finance typical of flex-price markets. T

*olution of leverage, especially in the American case, has suffered *e consequences of the deterioration in the state of credits of the *ancial markets. In fact, in the presence of the economic problems *hich emerged during the 1970s (the reduction in profits, the rise in *terest rates, greater instability, etc.), the leverage of American firms *s been further reduced – in contrast with the stability or inverse *end recorded for firms in the other countries. In the United *ingdom, however, firms have increasingly turned to bank lending.

Fourth, the size of the stock market – corresponding to the *minance of the joint-stock company and the relative dispersal of *dustrial ownership – if accompanied by loose forms of control and *bject to the threat of takeovers or the overthrow of existing *liances, has led to a structural weakness in the stock market as a *annel for risk capital by enterprises. This is what happened in the *K and the US. By contrast, in the bank-oriented countries where *e control of firms has taken the form of industrial or industrial-*ancial holdings, equity finance has been particularly active. The *ntribution of equity financing to stock capital has had the function *'reestablishing the accessibility of credit, and has helped to maintain *gh levels of bank lending.

Bank-oriented finance and high ratios of indebtedness have turned *t to be compatible with a wider range of structures of ownership *nd control of enterprises. In the bank-based systems, with a greater *spersal of shareholdings, various kinds of interfirm agreement for *e formation of majorities, and collusive relations between industry *nd the banking system, the stock markets have contributed relative- limited proportions of capital to enterprises – as, for that matter, *as happened in the market-based countries (apart, perhaps, from the *se of the US, due to the peculiar importance of the bond market).

The last point concerns the trends which emerged between 1970 *nd 1985. During this period, the tendency of financial systems was *wards despecialization – towards a breakdown of the institutional *undaries separating the various financial and nonfinancial oper-*tors. The global increase in competitiveness also lowered the bound-*ies between domestic and international financial markets. These *nportant changes do not, at least so far, seem to have altered *nterprise finance, nor to have affected those equilibria of ownership *nd control which regulate its basic orientations.

In global terms, economic systems have strengthened financial *struments, negotiations, and the typical relationships of markets. *owever, especially in the bank-based systems, this has not "disorien-*ted" enterprise finance. In the market-based systems, enterprise *nance has run counter to the trend, further developing institutional relations of a hierarchical kind with the banking system. This is way of reducing instabilities in auction markets and of managi funds, liquidity and risks in more "closed" markets governed discretionary policies.

Apart from this, the bank-oriented systems could encounter diffic ties in, for example, the maintenance of current levels of enterpr debt, should the claims of other sectors on internal financial resour intervene (as seems to be the case in Italy and France). Mc solidly-based industrial systems having very close industry–banki relations have, as in the Japanese case, minimized the effects of t strong pressure of public debt on enterprise finance. The globalizati of the financial markets could, for some of these systems, increase t efficiency of financial intermediaries and bring advantages to the operating on an international scale, thus allowing access to consid able flows of capital at lower cost, without, however, uprooting t financial and banking system from the accumulation process.

Notes

[1] I would like to acknowledge helpful suggestions and comments by Marcello de Cec and the many discussions about the historical perspectives with Tommaso Fanfani a Renato Giannetti. I would like to thank also Francesco Cesarini and Joseph Stiglitz w read and commented on an earlier draft of this chapter. Usual disclaimers apply.

[2] The basic accounting scheme takes into account the formation of the net financ saving or deficit, distinguishes between internal and external enterprise finance, and reference to the latter considers the origins and modes of transfers of resour from surplus agents to deficit agents. The annual accounting identity is sho schematically as follows: sources $(S + P)$ = uses $(I + A)$, where S is gross saving, P is increase in liabilities, I is gross physical investment, and A is net acquisition of financ assets. The credit or debit balance (net financial saving) is defined as $S - I$, equal $A - P$. Capital transfers have not been included in the analysis.

The terms "enterprises" or "industry" simply indicate the "nonfinancial enterprise sector, which includes industrial and nonindustrial enterprises.

[3] "Direct" or "primary" securities refer to all the financial assets issued directly sectors in deficit and acquired by sectors in surplus. "Indirect" or "secondary" financ assets, on the other hand, are represented by the liabilities of financial intermediar whose function is to gather funds from agents in surplus and lend them to agents deficit, or in other words, to substitute primary for secondary assets.

[4] Cf. De Cecco, 1989. See also De Cecco, 1986: p. 171.

[5] This is especially true if we compare the US and the UK, on the one hand, with Ita and France on the other.

[6] Even in the case of the United States, however, the relative stability of debt-financi indicators from the early postwar years to the 1980s came about as a result of heightened variation in the proportions of nonfinancial enterprises, of households and government. Cf. Friedman, 1980; Pollin, 1985; Taggart, 1985.

[7] In spite of the variety of definitions of leverage (or gearing), for simplicity we ha used the terms "rate of indebtedness" and "leverage" interchangeably.

[8] Cf. Sarathy and Chatterjiee, 1984; and Suzuki and Wright, 1985: p. 99.

n the consistency of this hypothesis see Taggart, 1985 and Mayer, 1987.
Between the late 1950s and the early 1960s, European enterprises, unlike American
s, had been able to maintain a rate of accumulation above their profitability and
-financing capacity. Enterprise expansion had depended not on profits, but predomi-
atly on external sources. This situation gave rise to a high level of demand for funds,
ich spilled over on to the American financial markets, where capital could also be
ained on more favorable terms. The American monetary authorities, however, were
rried about the balance of payments deficit that developed in the wake of European
ance of payments surpluses. So, the major responsibility for the basic disequilibria in
international payments system tended to be attributed to the backwardness of the
ropean financial markets. One of the most influential supporters of this thesis is
adleberger, 1966. The EEC Segré report (*Development of European Capital Market*,
36) and that of the OECD commission on invisible transactions (*Capital Markets
dy: General Report*, Paris 1967), expressed themselves in analogous terms. A
erent interpretation and an historical reassessment is to be found in De Cecco, 1976:
393–4.
Cf. in particular Chandler and Daems, 1974: pp. 9–11; and Chandler and Daems,
30.
See Lindsay and Sametz, 1967: pp. 386 and 475.
Cf. Zeitlin, 1974: pp. 1099–1106; Kotz, 1978; Herman, 1981; Pitelis and Sugden,
36; Scott, 1986; Cosh and Hughes, 1987. For a historical-evolutionary focus on group
uctures see Chandler's comparative analysis, 1986: pp. 50–62; and Sapelli (1987: pp.
7–9, 353).
n this sense the market-oriented finance of enterprises is not simply an indicator of
antitative funding from stock exchange markets, but a concept which can characte-
e international differences in leverage ratios. The granting of more substantial
dits might have limited managerial control by the oversight of the banks.
atrolling or minority interests, even if confined to the exchange of information rather
n being directive and strategic, would have led the banks to play a role "normally"
igned to the market and shareholders, with all the drawbacks involved in the free
cretion of a "visible hand" potentially able to interfere at various levels, from the
rket price to management (Stiglitz, 1985).
n the bank-oriented system, the low level of managerial autonomy did not restore to
market the role of enterprise-monitoring which remained in the hands of the
ncipal shareholder or of the banking system. At the level of the financial
figuration, institutional control over management turned out to be less exacting in
ms of the risk of failure expressed by the firm's leverage. A majority shareholder
ld thus aim at expansion of the enterprise, by making use of external capital offered
the banking system.
De Cecco, 1986a: p. 174. See also De Cecco, 1989: pp. 201–3.
This overturns the conventional view, held in an extreme form, by Rybczynski, 1986.
This is true if one excludes the years 1971 to 1974, when indirect instruments grew
ably. This happened for a variety of reasons, among which was the adoption of
npetition and credit control, followed by a wave of speculation that also affected the
don stock exchange without, however, significantly affecting the increase in new
1es, particularly the share issues of nonfinancial enterprises. See Bonaiuti, 1988: p.
5. During these years, securities issues of nonfinancial enterprises fell. Share issues
reased as a percentage of GNP only in 1972 (see Table 8.10).
or example, from 1974 to 1976, issues of public bonds increased from Y4,564bn. to
1,657bn. In 1980 the bonds issued by financial institutions were of a value of
,700bn. and in 1983, Y9,541bn. This was slightly less than half the issues of public
ds in the same year reaching a total of about Y30,000bn. of bonds issued (cf. OECD,
37a: tab. 21.F/21). Cf. also Suzuki, 1986; Dotsey, 1982.
t is necessary to point out that these data overestimate the contribution to firms of
ital deriving from the stock exchange, inasmuch as they also include increases in
al capital due to direct contributions by partners, and such accounting operations as
nges in the firm's legal status, mergers and acquisitions.
Cf. FIBV, 1985. For the other countries the OECD data do not diverge very much

from those of the FIBV, even if they include the value of shares not quoted on the sto
exchange.
[21] For example, in 1985, the ratio between issues and capitalization in New Yc
reached 1.3 per cent, which was the same as in 1981. In Japan, the relationship was (
per cent in 1981 and 0.3 per cent in 1985. The ratio was higher in London at 2.5 an(
per cent during the same years. In Germany the ratio was 2.3 and 2.4 per cent, while
Italy it was 2 and 4 per cent. In France it was 14.4 and 13 per cent. Calculated fro
FIBV, *Rapport*, various years.
[22] Mayer (1986b: p. 11) has reached analogous conclusions. See also Tobin, 1984.
[23] See in particular Coulbeck, 1984: pp. 170–3.
[24] See Scott, 1986: pp. 136, 146; Maycock, 1986.
[25] Cf. Kotz, 1978: pp. 70–1, 84–9, 97 and 110–13; Scott, 1986: pp. 149–50, 153. *
example of group structure is the case of Citicorp, analyzed by Coulbeck, 1984:
198–211.
[26] With the other studies quoted, see also Mizruchi, 1982; and Mintz and Schwar
1985.
[27] Cf. Scott, 1987: p. 222. See also Vittas, 1986: pp. 5, 8–9; and also Vittas, 1978:
13–14, 19–21.
[28] Every year, from 1970 to 1985, the American enterprises have increased their r
distribution of dividends: see OECD, 1987b: tab. E.2.
[29] Calculated from OECD, 1987a: tab. 22.B. According to certain estimates, from 19
to 1985 public bonds represented 45 per cent of GNP, corporate securities 17 per ce
and securities issued by financial institutions 9 per cent. Calculated from US Bureau
the Census, various years.
[30] The trend, however, shows a relative reduction in the proportion of industrial issu
In fact while the proportion of new issues by financial firms has grown at a rate simi
to that of state issues and has continued to represent about 29 per cent of total issu
the proportion of industrial issues fell from 40–36 per cent in 1970–1 to 18 per cent
1984–5.
[31] The historical reasons for this have been explained by Hannah: 1983, pp. 58–65.
[32] See Scott, 1986: pp. 87, 91–2, 94, 99, 101, 117, 119.
[33] Calculated from CSO, 1987 (tab. S7 D–F e H–K).
[34] Cf. Vittas, 1986: pp. 5, 11. By contrast, for Lisle-Williams (1986: p. 248) "t
merchant banks unavoidably act as clearing houses for intelligence, and as the Cit
impersonal network is dense, extensive and efficient in conveying information, th
judgements of corporate strength and weakness help to determine the terms on whi
companies obtain finance." Recently Scott (1987: p. 221) has asserted that the histori(
separation between City and industry "has gradually been abolished." The thesis o'
British financial capitalism has, however, been rejected by Ingham, 1984: pp. 50-
205–20.
[35] Hu, 1975: p. 50. Cf. also White B., 1984: pp. 14, 24.
[36] The gearing ratio has been considered as a sort of financial counterpart of t
stagnation of British industry. See Carrington and Edwards, 1979: pp. 31, 36–8 a
218–21.
[37] Cf. Nardozzi, 1986b: pp. 512–19, 524. The arguments developed by Dosi (198
concerning the conflict between static and dynamic efficiency in bank and mark(
oriented systems are also particularly interesting.
[38] See, for the various countries, the standard deviation of issues in the period 1970–
(Tables 8.9, 8.10, and 8.3–8.8). The phenomenon is discussed with reference to t
1960s by Hu, 1975: pp. 30–3.
[39] It has, for example, been argued that a large part of the growth of enterprise debt
the US during the 1980s can be attributed to the volume of shares withdrawn
through operations of leveraged buyout – following the wave of mergers a
acquisitions: see Wilson *et al.*, 1986: p. 514. For the British case, an important debate
the causes of industrial concentration in the 1960s and 1970s has led some to mainte
that the internal growth of enterprises has been the principal factor, and acts of merg
secondary (see Prais, 1976; Hart and Clarke, 1980), while more convincingly – giv

detailed historical evidence reported – other authors have shown the decisive
»rtance of the merger waves in the growth of manufacturing enterprises (see
nah and Kay, 1977).
theoretical model of this process has been developed by Greenwald and Stiglitz,
*: p. 12.
*. Brioschi, 1988: p. 223. More generally see also Mosconi and Rullani, 1978; and
chiati, 1989.
»e Brioschi, 1988: pp. 225 and 231.
n these aspects cf. Macchiati, 1985; Onado, 1986: pp. 19–21.
*. Caron, 1974, pp. 129–30; Lévy-Leboyer, 1979: pp. 146–7, 153–4, 157, 172–3; and
Lévy-Leboyer, 1980: pp. 121–2, 138, 142 and 154–5.
*. Scott, 1987: p. 228.
*. Zysman, 1983; Vittas, 1986.
his turns out to be confirmed, even though fixed tangible assets – and thus net
:h – accounted at their historical cost, were revalued. Doing this would not change
interest payments of enterprises either; cf. the revaluations computed by Carrera de
el, 1987.
his has depended on the economic and monetary policies adopted, cf. Nardozzi, 1983:
55–85; Feroldi, 1985; Barzaghi, 1988a.
alculated from Statistics Bureau, various years (tab. 12–5, A). OECD data (1987a;
22.B) show that in 1964, 44.7 per cent of existing shares were still privately held,
gainst 8.2 per cent held by the banks, 7.4 per cent by the insurance companies and
per cent by the nonbank credit institutions. By 1981 the private share had fallen to
per cent, while the shares of banks and insurance companies had risen to 23.7 and
per cent respectively. The proportion held by nonbank intermediaries had fallen to
per cent.
Cf. in particular Miyazaki, 1980. Imai (1980: pp. 76, 81–2) has emphasized the
sive role of the MITI in the organization of Japanese enterprises, through antireces-
cartels and "investment adjustment," with the aim of improving the international
petitiveness of Japanese enterprises. On group organization see also Alhadeff, 1975;
namura, 1978.
f. Nishiyama, 1984: pp. 125, 137–40.
ee Nishiyama, 1984: pp. 129–31 and 163.
f. Kojima and Ozawa, 1984; Scott, 1986: pp. 167–8 and Vittas, 1986: pp. 4, 7, 10.
ee Scott, 1986: p. 186; and Shimamura: 1989, p. 48.
ott has defined the Japanese structure as an oligarchy of combines. In particular,
rfirm relations are very close in traditional groups such as Mitsubishi, Mitsui and
iitomo, whose industrial interests predominantly concern the extractive, chemical,
l and mechanical engineering industries. More recently formed groups on the other
d – such as Sanwa, DKB and Fuyo – being tied to industrial sectors of more recent
vth, have more "fragile" interfirm structures, much more similar to those of the
lo-Saxon countries; cf. Coulbeck, 1984: pp. 230–3; and also Scott, 1986: pp. 191–2,

ee also Bank of Japan, 1973; Royama, 1983–4; Toniolo, 1985; and Ikeo, 1987. Imai
i0) and Boltho (1985) have emphasized the effects on economic growth of the
inistrative guidance of the MITI.
ı 1964 the total value of debentures barely reached 25.3 per cent of GNP. In 1981 it
hed 69.3 per cent and in 1984, 86 per cent. The heavy issues by the state dragged
issues of the financial institutions along behind them, but not industrial issues; cf.
ƆD, 1987a: tab. 22.B (our calculations).
f. Locatelli, 1987; and Barzaghi, 1988b: pp. 73–5 and 78.
mong others see Coulbeck, 1984, p. 336; Dyson: 1986: pp. 124–6.
ccording to Dosi (1988), a trade-off between static and dynamic efficiency would
* be posed where there was cumulative technical progress, that is, where the
»vative project is not subject to failure. On the empirical side, such hypotheses are
irmed by Prais, 1981 (chapter 5).
alculated on the basis of data drawn from the Deutsche Bundesbank, various years.

[62] The concentration of shareholdings among the credit institutions is high: it
sufficient to point out that in terms of nominal capital, five banks held more than 50
cent of the shares held by the credit institutions in 1974. In the same ye
representatives of the banks sat on the board of directors of 59 of the 66 enterpri
quoted on the stock exchange. In only eight cases was only one representative involv
cf. Eckstein, 1980: p. 467.

[63] At the end of 1972, this limited group was among the 2,300 joint-stock compan
(controlled by the *Aktiengeseltz* of 1965) as against the more than one-hund
thousand limited liability companies (*Gesellschaft mit beschrankter Haftung*).
Beeny, 1975, pp. 8–9.

[64] See Cable, 1985a and 1985b.

ational Specificities and Current endencies in Financial Systems[1]

GIANGIACOMO NARDOZZI

analyzing the relationship between the peculiarities of individual economic systems and their more general trends requires a just proportioning between theory and history that is often difficult to achieve. In the case of financial systems, the task is made even more arduous by the absence of a predominant theory. There is no shortage of accurate studies concerning the history of the major financial systems; what is lacking, however, is a solid theory to explain the dynamics of financial systems.

Monetary economics is based solely on the role of money in determining general equilibrium. In the main monetary theories, financial institutions either do not matter (monetarism) or are considered exogenous and are molded to a specific context – the Anglo-Saxon one (neo-Keynesian, or the neoclassical synthesis of Keynes) (Tonveronachi, 1989). Growth theory, an area very neglected nowadays, does not adequately integrate the real and financial aspects (Vicarelli, 1979; Ciocca, 1982). A confirmation of this comes from the fact that in the most refined theory of structural dynamics and growth, that developed by Pasinetti (1981), money and financial transactions do not play important roles (Nardozzi, 1983a). The economics of information applied to financial intermediation (for a recent survey, see Gertler, 1988) has made important contributions to determining sufficient conditions for the existence of institutions different from the centralized markets. But if one wants to use this theory in analyzing financial system dynamics, it presents the same limitations outlined by Schumpeter in his *Theory of Economic Development* when he defended the incompatibility between the Walrasian model and the understanding of development. In order to understand the way in which information problems are solved, it is necessary to use a static approach, which is inadequate for studying the system's dynamics and trends.

However, a relationship between financial institutions and grow
is present in Goldsmith's (1969) financial accounting and relat
statistics. But this monumental research has not been updated, an
thus, does not include the revolution which financial systems ha
experienced in the course of the last fifteen years (for a critic
appraisal see Della Torre, 1985 and 1987).

This being the state of the most consolidated theories, I will try
deal with the connections between national peculiarities and mo
general trends in the financial systems, gathering ideas and analys
from a diverse array of literature which includes contributions
Marx, Schumpeter, Wicksell, Keynes, and subsequent elaborations
post-Keynesians and "circuit" theorists (very recent works whi
attempt to systematize the latter schools are Graziani and Mess
(1988) and Rogers (1989)).

By combining various ideas from the above-mentioned "classic
with the reformulations and developments of the two other schools,
seems to me that we can obtain a set of consistent propositions th
are coherent and compatible with the "economics of informatio
results, open to considering national specificities of financial systen
yet general enough to grasp common trends. This set of propositio
will be presented in the first section of this chapter, underlining the
implications for the analysis of financial systems. In the subseque
section I will show how this analytical framework is empirical
verified, by observing different financial systems. In the third sectior
will use this framework to interpret current tendencies, criticizing t
idea that they are expressions of a "natural" and progressi
evolution in the structure of financial systems. I will show, on tl
contrary, that they do not constitute an irreversible moveme
towards a general model of the financial system that is altogeth
"better" than the previous ones.

The Analytical Framework

Four basic propositions

Stripped to the bone, the foundations of monetary theory on which tl
analysis of financial systems rests are formed by four propositior
which I shall confine myself to stating with reference to the ma
literature.

THE MONETARY AND FINANCIAL INSTITUTIONS ARE IMPORTANT, SINCE
Y ARE EXPRESSIONS OF AN ECONOMIC ORGANIZATION — CAPITALISM —
H CANNOT BE OTHER THAN A MONETARY ECONOMY

s means that the main characteristics of the financial system are
ved from the working mechanism (production and reproduction) of
talism, and not from the services which "financial firms" offer to
onal and maximizing individuals according to the general econ-
c equilibrium model (macro approach versus micro approach).
his proposition expresses the common conviction of Marx,
umpeter and Keynes that the links between finance and the
tioning of the economic system have to be found in the organiza-
of production (monetary theory of production). Schumpeter, as is
known, derives the need for credit and banks from the creation of
chasing power by innovative entrepreneurs, which is the genuine
ression of capitalism. Keynes, in the earlier draft of the second
pter of his *General Theory*, cites Marx as the forerunner of his
inction between the "entrepreneur economy" and the "cooperative
omy" (on this distinction, see Nardozzi (1983b), Kregel (1984),
ers (1989)). With this distinction, Keynes introduces money as an
ntial element in capitalistic production, as it is necessary to pay
es in legal tender (entrepreneur or "money wage" economy) and
in goods, as in the "cooperative economy." The "monetary theory
roduction" also forms the foundation for the "circuit" theories
mitt, 1988).

WITH REFERENCE TO THE PRODUCTION MECHANISM, MONEY SHOULD BE
SIDERED AS CREDIT WHICH IS NECESSARY TO OBTAIN THE PRODUCT, AND
AS A STOCK FOR FACILITATING EXCHANGES OF AN ALREADY PREDETER-
ED PRODUCT

s point, already clear in the critique of Marx to Fullarton, was
en up by Hilferding (in *Das Finanzkapital*) with the distinction
ween circulation credit and capital credit. In the same tone,
umpeter differentiated between normal credit and abnormal credit
ch governs the definition of the bank as creator, and not just
rmediary, of purchasing power. Keynes deals with this question
cially in the debate with Ohlin and Robertson on the "finance
ive," which was then resumed by the post-Keynesians (for a
vey of the recent "debate on the debate," see Graziani (1984)).
ey as credit determined by production is the manifesto of the
cuit" theorists.

(C) CREDIT CANNOT BE CONSIDERED AS A GOOD WHOSE PRICE (
INTEREST RATE) IS DETERMINED BY SUPPLY AND DEMAND

This proposition, which clearly results in Wicksell's case of a "p
credit economy" (*Interest and Prices*), was recently taken up
Stiglitz and Weiss (1988). In this respect, the imperfections of
information approach converge with the Keynesian and post-Keyn
ian thesis of "credit rationing."

(D) THE RATE OF INTEREST IS A MONETARY PHENOMENON DETERMIN
INDEPENDENTLY OF THE PROCESS WHICH GENERATES PROFITS IN THE R
SECTORS (Rogers, 1989 p. 169)

There are no "natural forces" which determine the interest r
Instead, it is a conventional phenomenon (Keynes, 1936; for simil
ities with Marx, see Panico, 1983). Its value varies more w
fluctuations in liquidity preference than with changes in the mor
supply (Kregel, 1984). Liquidity preference is the expression of
"degree of confidence" which determines the amount of the premi
to be offered to induce people not to hoard. The degree of confidenc
affected by the amount of certainty/uncertainty determined by
overall economic policy (and not only by monetary policy).

These four propositions are very general, and convey more of a vis
than a theory. But from these fundamentals we derive more spec
implications for the analysis of the financial systems, which I
develop in the following paragraphs.

Credit and financial intermediation

Credit is not provided by the market, but rather by the banks wh
administer the payments system acting as "social accountants."[2] Th
it is necessary to distinguish between credit and what can be cal
"financial intermediation." The former generates purchasing pov
through the creation of deposits that constitute means of payme
the latter transfers already existent purchasing power from lenders
borrowers through both deposits collected and invested that do
constitute means of payment and through services returned in
markets in which funds are transferred by the purchase of securiti

In financing productive activity, credit can completely substit
financial intermediation. This substitution occurs in Wicksell's p
credit economy, or in the overdraft economy of Hicks (1974) (her

French school that has some contacts with the "circuit" theorists
I the post-Keynesian theorists; see Lavoie (1985) and Maricic
88)). However, reverse substitution, i.e. credit being substituted by
ancial intermediation, encounters some limitations. Schumpeter's
ory and Keynes' "finance motive" deduce that firms' need for
iidity can be satisfied by the market, and not by bank credit, only
diverting from other uses the purchasing power accumulated in the
m of stocks through an increase in the velocity of money and in the
erest rate. On the other hand, if we want to resort to "external"
ney, created by external accounts or treasury financing, its use in
ancing economic activity is contingent upon the government deficit,
ernal accounts, and central bank policies and meets with limita-
is stemming from information imperfections. Consequently,
hough there is competition between credit and financial inter-
diation, the relation between the two is asymmetric, since it is
onceivable that financial intermediation should completely substi-
e credit, which implies that it is not possible to suppose a complete
istitution of banks by markets.

n this perspective, banking disintermediation, which constitutes an
portant phenomenon of the recent structural transformations in
financial systems, is not an indication of market superiority over
iks. Rather, its origin must be sought in generally accidental
torical factors.

stomer vs. market relationship

edit is provided on the basis of customer relations that utilize
vate information deriving from the administration of the payments
tem. This information determines not only the understanding of
lenders' businesses, but also the Keynesian degree of confidence
ich serves as a shield against the uncertainty dominating the
imates of future yields to firms (Nardozzi, 1986a).

redit tends to prefer uses at predetermined values, and thus
erates, through rationing, generally in a fix-price system (Goodhart,
36; De Cecco, 1986). Financial intermediation, however, employs
:tion markets using public information (even if often integrated
:h the confidence stemming from the names of the banks involved).
us, financial intermediation operates in a flex-price system.

'or the part carried out with credit and the part carried out with
ancial intermediation by banks, the allocation of financial resources
urs outside the market. It takes place through "voice" selection
:chanisms, rather than "entry-exit" mechanisms (as Zysman

asserts, adopting Hirschman's framework, quoted in Dosi (198
Here we see the importance of the relations between banks and fi
and of their institutional connotations in analyzing financial syste

Definition of "financial structure"

The financial structure of an economy can be defined by the rela
weight of credit and financial intermediation. This definition se
more suitable than that which contrasts direct circuits (markets)
indirect circuits (intermediaries). Actually, the traditional distinc
between market-oriented financial systems (the Anglo-Saxon o
and intermediary-oriented ones (those of Continental Europe) is
supported by the intermediation ratio (the ratio between finar
assets of intermediaries and liabilities of nonfinancial sectors), wl
is high in all systems. This distinction is, however, verified in
degree of bank intermediation (the ratio between financial asset
banks and financial liabilities of nonfinancial sectors) which
stitutes an approximate index of the weight of credit assets
financial flows (Nardozzi, 1983b and 1988a).

On the impossibility of defining an "optimal" financial structure .

There is no theoretical basis on which to define an optimal finan
structure which can serve as a model for financial systems. It is t
that a financial structure can be evaluated in terms of its efficie
and stability; however, the concept of efficiency can take differ
meanings and efficiency in one sense may not imply another typ
efficiency (for an appraisal of the efficiency–performance relationsl
see Tonveronachi (1989), Ch. 3). In financial markets it is necessar
distinguish what Tobin (1984) calls "information-arbitrage efficien
from "fundamental valuation efficiency." The first, which chara
rizes the large markets of the major financial centers, does not im
the second. Thus, we see a confirmation of Keynes' thesis (1936,
12) according to which it is precisely stock market liquidity t
demands a "convention," ignoring the value of securities based
estimates of firms' future earnings.

   For the financial system as a whole, however, it is necessary to r
to Tobin's "functional efficiency" rather than to the "allocat
efficiency" (in a static sense), which loses its significance if taken
of the Walrasian context. But "functional efficiency" has many fac

nder the quantitative profile of financing capital accumulation, the ıancial structures in which market-orientation prevails over credit em less efficient than those in which credit prevails (for past history e Gerschenkron's argument; for present comparisons see Conti 987), Mayer (1989)). And less developed and liquid stock markets fer greater financing flows to firms than those that are more :veloped (Nardozzi, 1986a; IRS, 1988). In a qualitative light, based ı the rate of innovation and ensuing performances of industrial ructures, Dosi (1988c) has recently argued that "credit-based" 'stems are less capable than "market-based" systems of promoting ıe exploration of new technological paradigms when "the innovative »portunities are high and the innovative competences are quite ffused throughout the economy." Finally, in considering the function ' capital control in financial systems, Stiglitz (1985) has argued that ıniversal banking" is more efficient than a "marked-based" system.

If all these results, which already leave a lot of room for uncertainty . evaluating the merits and shortcomings of different financial ructures, are combined with considerations concerning stability, the ıestion is unlikely to be solved once and for all. We do not need to ·call the vast amount of literature on the subject to assert that as a ıysiological characteristic of financial systems, instability is an ıtegral part of the analytical framework considered earlier. Instabil- y takes on different forms according to the financial structure, the ructure of the productive system, the relationship between banks ıd industry, and the goals and instruments of monetary policy (in ıe FI.SI.MO. Group this has been dealt with by Bonaiuti (1987)). hus, not even stability lends itself to measurements which are .dependent of place and time.

These analytical points referring to the performance of financial ructures agree with the results of historical research, at least in the ay they are synthesized by Cameron (1967, 1972) (see also Ciocca 982)). They suggest comparisons between different financial struc- ıres, based not on reference to some optimal (or "natural") system, ıt on the evaluation of comparative advantages and disadvantages eighed with the characteristics (and economic policies) of different :onomies.

. . and of thinking in terms of irreversible progressive structural ∙ndencies of financial systems

rom the preceding points we can conclude that theory does not ıentify any irreversible tendency towards the emergence of one

particular financial structure that is more advanced than the othe
It follows that:

(a)   We are not allowed to consider the recent evolution of financ
      systems as progress towards better patterns. This is not to de
      the progress that has been made in the micro aspects
      intermediaries and markets thanks to technological, organiz
      tional, and institutional innovations. However, it does 1
      imply that this progress necessarily corresponds to better agg
      gate performance in the efficiency and stability of financ
      structures (the "second best" theorem applies to this argume
      see Tonveronachi (1989)).

(b)   Neither are we allowed to think of deregulation and regulati
      processes, which have accompanied recent transformations,
      the outcome of a natural evolution (for an evaluation of the
      processes stressing national peculiarities, see Nardozzi (1988b)

National Specificities (Models of Financial Systems)

Defining a financial system model

In the 1970s, the financial systems of the major economies s1
showed greatly differing structural characteristics. Sharp differenc
in regulation accompanied these structural differences.[3]

If we define a financial system *model* as the whole financ
structure and the regulation applied to it, we may say that in t
group of G7 nations, different models of financial systems exist whi
represent individual national specificities. This is not just a simp
tautology, because the concept of model allows regulation to
considered as an integral part of the financial system, and not jus1
set of restrictions imposed from the outside on a system that, if l
alone, could work freely (Nardozzi, 1988a).

These different models have not directly controlled performance
the respective economies so as to constitute an unequivocal "stru
ture–performance" relationship that can be ordered according
preference. The analytical framework outlined earlier in this chapt
was confirmed by empirical evidence.

vo opposing models: the United States and Germany

is not within the scope of this chapter to describe the various models
financial systems. However, in order to clarify my argument, it is
cessary to keep in mind the essential features of two models: those
the United States and of Germany. In the 1970s, these were at the
posite ends of a scale along which we could situate the other
stems, and transformations in banking and finance in recent years
n be seen as a process of synthesizing the two systems, as we shall
e.[4]

Looked at from the perspective of our analytical framework, the
nerican model before deregulation was the most meticulous applica-
n of the distinction between credit and financial intermediation,
ile the German model was the opposite.

In the American model, credit activity was carried out by com-
ercial banks which operated the payments system. Financial inter-
ediation was performed both by organizations that collected deposits
t used as means of payment (thrift institutions) and by financial
ndepository institutions.

The ban on commercial banks operating in the securities market
cked the possibility of taking advantage of the strong position
termined by the credit activity that combines the privileges of the
eation of money with those of managing payments. This ban
oided subjecting the growth of the capital market to banking
tivities beyond mixing together financial and monetary roles, which
a potential generator of financial instability. This model entrusted
imarily the market with allocating financial resources, and legisla-
rs were clearly concerned that the market's growth should not be
peded by competition with the banks. The prohibition against
rning interest on checking accounts and the regulation of maximum
tes returned on savings accounts (Regulation Q) were measures
ken with this goal in mind (Evans, 1984).

A necessary complement to legislation so narrowly prescribing the
le of banks is the regulation of capital markets. Introduced by the
w establishing the SEC, the regulation of capital markets ensures
at prices are correct indicators of the values they represent
andatory disclosure) and that the behavior of the intermediaries
es not undermine trust in the markets (professional honesty rules,
ntrol of insider trading, etc.).

If the American model exalts the contractual relations typical of the
pital market, the German model highlights the importance of
lations typical of the credit activity. The "universal bank" combines

in one body all the functions that in the American case are carried o
separately by banks and specialized intermediaries. For the Germe
bank, financial intermediation is the natural extension of its cred
activity. The two activities mutually support each other, in th
information deriving from the management of payments is direct
(and internally) used for financial intermediation, while the acco
panying shareholding of firms reveals an ample flow of information
the creditworthiness of the borrower companies (through ban
participating in administrative boards). Consequently, the capit
market is dominated by banks. The capital market acts as a tool f
maintaining the relationship between banks and industry that
characteristic of universal banking, and not, as in the American cas
as an alternative source of funding. Contractual relations that a
established in the market are actually the outcome of custom
relations characteristic of banking. Thus, the allocation of financi
resources is based not on information revealed to specialized inte
mediaries and the market by transparency, but rather on the bank
knowledge of firms, and their control capability. This distinctic
makes the American philosophy of regulating the capital mark
completely alien to the German model.

Current Tendencies

Some well-known stylized facts . . .

A recent phenomenon since the 1970s has been the closing of the ga
between financial system models, and the overcoming of nation
specificities deep-rooted in the history of individual countries. Th
"institutional despecialization" has accompanied the widespread ph
nomenon of credit despecialization" which has considerably blurre
the distinctions between intermediaries and between market se
ments.

The current tendency to surmount national specificities has take
place through four well-known structural changes which ha
affected, to different extents, the major financial systems:

(a)   a wave of financial innovations (for a taxonomy, see BIS (1986)
(b)   a "securitization" (in the broad sense of development in financi
      intermediation through markets, to the detriment of ban
      credit). This development was brought about by competitic

against banks, but has also taken the form of substituting credit relations with market relations on the part of banks (securitization in the strict sense) (for a survey of facts and theories, see Gardener (1987));
internationalization of financial systems and globalization of markets;
an extended process of reregulation, designed to overcome the segmentation of financial systems and to develop the markets and make them more efficient (Nardozzi, 1988b).

and their interpretation as the outcome of a "natural evolution"

these facts seem to strengthen the vision of a progressive and -way evolution of financial systems that sees the surpassing of the vidual peculiarities of the models through the affirmation of the ·ket as the regulator of financial flows, delayed until now by iating historical contingencies and/or regulations. It is the asser- ., then, of a more advanced single "market-oriented" model like the ʒlo-Saxon one. This thesis is very clearly stated in the "stages of ιncial development" theory by Rybczinski (1984, 1985) which ɛs up the deterministic vein present in the historical studies by schenkron and in the statistical studies by Goldsmith.
.t the heart of Rybczinski's theory is the assumption that market tions are superior to the customer relations of bank credit. He ɛrts the existence of a "natural evolution" of the financial system, ɕh moves through the progressive stages of "bank oriented," ɪrket oriented," and finally "strongly market oriented" structures . where financial institutions increasingly dispose of and trade in ɪr assets – the process described as securitization – and where .ncial risk hedging markets play a predominant role" (Rybczinski, 5: p. 39)). This "natural evolution" creates a "virtuous cycle of ɑnce," since ". . . by improving the risk-assuming and risk-bearing ɑcity of an economy the evolution of the financial system helps to ·ease capital formation, savings and economic growth; this in turn sts the further transformation of the financial system, raising in risk-bearing ability, investment and saving – and so on in a uous circle of advance" (ibid.).
ccording to Rybczinski, current tendencies confirm this natural ɪution towards more advanced financial structures, because they w the shift of systems that were already at the "market-oriented" ʒe (United States, United Kingdom) towards the more advanced or ongly market-oriented" stage; they also show "bank-oriented"

systems (France, Italy, Germany) moving towards the "mark oriented" stage.

It would be superfluous to underline how greatly this interpretat of recent tendencies contrasts with the analytical framework outlin earlier in this chapter. On the other hand, it is also unnecessary note that overcoming national specificities, and developing and perf ting the markets, seem to be occurrences contrary to that analy al framework, which, instead, implies the persistence of differe models of financial systems. Moreover, there are several factu methodological and theoretical points that cast doubt over t possibility of providing a deterministic interpretation such as that Rybczinski.

The following sections will be devoted to these points.

A different interpretation

I shall begin with a fact that I believe is widely known but perha not made explicit enough in the literature which deals with the rece changes in the financial systems: the importance of the history of t American financial system in promoting the four changes list above. The invention and development of new financial instr ments and related markets, securitization, and deregulation a all events originating in the United States and/or in internation activities developed first and primarily by the major American ban

The importance of the American financial system in generating n trends and passing them on to the rest of the world is not surprisin given the country's size and its leadership role. And it is a histori constant which De Cecco (1976, 1984, 1985) has called to a attention for some time.

This fact questions the method used in analyzing the dynamics financial systems. If the world financial system is composed unequal partners (according to the approach of J.H. Williams follow by De Cecco (1976)), should we not analyze the dynamics of t dominant system before defining the general tendencies?

But how should we analyze it? From the approach which I outlin earlier, a suggestion arises: that of evaluating the *coherence* of t model. As we have seen, the configuration and regulation of financial system allows for several solutions, and it is not possible identify an "optimal" one. Thus, the forces which determine t dynamics cannot be sought after in the area of a "natural" "optimal" configuration. Rather, they must be found in the logic th holds together the model (internal coherence) or in the relationsh tween the model and the environment in which it operates (external 1erence).

According to this dialectic approach (for the distinction with Kane's)81) "regulatory dialectics," see Nardozzi (1988a)) a model tends to ange when it contains constituent elements that lead to its being 2rcome (internal incoherence factors), or when it becomes incom- tible with the surrounding environment (external incoherence tors). Applying this approach to the two models of the United 1tes and Germany, examined earlier, it seems possible to deduce it while the German model is incoherent with the development of ancial intermediation based on the markets, the American model is t. In the German case, such development undermines the basis of 3tomer relations typical in universal banking – providing firms, on : one hand, with the alternative of resorting to the market for .g-term financing, and, on the other hand, making less justified the ns' submissions to banks through detention of their permanent ldings (Steinherr and Huveneers (1989)).

The American model, as it operated in the 1970s, was certainly 1erent with the existence of a large market in which financial ermediation could take place. However, this does not mean that :h a model was also coherent with developments in financial ermediation which question the primary role of banks. More :cifically, the "pure" specialization principle is actually an exalta- n of the specificity and importance of banks. Thus, it cannot reach : point of contradicting its own premises. In the words of the 3sident of the Federal Reserve Bank of New York, E. Gerald rrigan:

While one can readily picture a financial system in which the role of the ecurities markets is very limited, one is hard pressed to visualize a ontemporary financial system in which credit intermediaries are not a najor feature of the financial and economic landscape. To put it directly, he credit intermediaries provide certain functions which cannot be as eadily performed by the securities markets, at least as we know them.
(Corrigan, 1987: p. 31)

hus, a massive substitution of credit by the financial intermedia- 1 relationship based on market instruments poses internal coher- 'e problems not only to the German model, but also to the 1erican model. The difference between the two is that, as far as 1ctural dynamics is concerned, while the first model inhibits ovations which could shake its foundations, the second model ourages them. In fact, in the German case, universal banking ninates financial intermediation by heightening credit activity l curbing the development of the alternative financial market instruments. In the American case, banking was blocked, in the pi competition within the financial system, by the rigid regulation due the full realization of the specialization principle. This encouraged competition to introduce new financial instruments that tended develop markets and financial intermediation to the point of exc sively constraining banks. Thus, in the American model there was *internal* incoherence factor stemming from the fact that the comp tion between credit and financial intermediation can encourage development of market instruments and markets that eventua became contradictory to the specialization principle.

On the basis of these considerations, we can see the stylized fa that I mentioned earlier triggered by the incoherence of the Ameri model. It is a question of internal incoherence in which exter incoherence factors were implanted, such as the explosion of inflat and rising interest rates brought about by Volcker's monetary poli

An exact verification of this thesis requires a reconstruction of recent history of the American financial system considerably lar than I have been able to do. I shall limit myself here to mentionin few essential points.

The reactiohs of the major American banks to the segmentatior the American financial system after the banking reforms of the 19 were diverse, and have been brilliantly described by De Cecco (19 1984, 1985). Several innovations preceded those of the 1970s, such CDs (Citicorp, 1961), short-term promissory notes (FNB of Bost 1964) and the Eurodollar market as a fund-collecting source (si 1966). These innovations (new instruments and new financial n kets) were the outcome of internal incoherence in the Ameri model. They answered the need to defend the positions of the ma commercial banks, which were constrained in their expansion Regulation Q (Eisenbeis, 1982). On the other hand, they ended promoting market financial intermediation that competes with cre which is the very distinctive feature of banks.

In this system, already shaky due to internal incoherence, w implanted the turbulent effects of the external climate: rising inflat and rising interest rates. These external factors weigh heavily credit activity, acting on both liabilities and assets of banks. Rega ing the first, even for the most liquid deposits, depositors try to obt interest rates that compensate for inflation. This requirement upheld by nonbanking financial intermediaries (money mar mutual funds) or directly by nonfinancial institutions (trading c panies) that offer financial products to which payment services connected.

The advantages of deposits over securities (absence of price risk

w transaction costs) have been reduced because of lowering transac-
n costs and innovations in techniques and instruments for covering
k that, for securities, offer good risk–return combinations. This is
e reason for the extraordinary growth in institutional investment,
rough which these advantages can be achieved (Cumming, 1987).
Concerning assets, banks themselves have limited the supply of
aditional credit openings (as they had become too risky, thus
quiring their own capital, and costly, due to rate fluctuations) in
vor of financing carried out by market instruments (securitization).
The extension of financial intermediation based on market instru-
ents, which is detrimental to the traditional banking relationships
aracteristic of credit activity, is the reaction by the American
ancial system to the rigidity of the model conceived in the 1930s.
is response has undermined the foundation of that model: the
gmentation of the financial system deriving from a meticulous
plication of the specialization principle. Deregulation is the final
tcome of incoherence in the American model. The DIDMCA of 1980
d the Garn-St Germain Act of 1982 constitute an initial overcoming
segmentation in the financial system. Deregulation is now going on
th the resettlement of the whole financial system, as outlined by
rrigan (1987), which is the ultimate overcoming of the specializa-
n model in favor of the junction, even if within bank holding
mpanies, of credit and market financial intermediation.

. and its implications on the evaluation of current tendencies

cording to the interpretation I have sketched above, recent tenden-
s are not the outcome of a "natural evolution" that unavoidably
ds to the market as regulator of financial flows. It is not a question
"natural" evolution, since it is largely the outcome of a crisis in a
tional model, that of the United States. This evolution does not
en signify the triumph of the market, since it stems from overcom-
g the model that most exalted the market's role in the financial
termediation reigning in banks. In the 1970s and 1980s, it was the
nerican model that entered into a crisis, and not the opposing
rman model which exalts the role of banks over the market.
Of course, in the mean time, financial intermediation which passes
rough the market has developed greatly. But this development,
ng with the internationalization of financial relations, has re-
firmed the importance of banks, which was slipping in the American
del of rigid specialization. As De Cecco (1986a) points out, it is only
means and not an end.

The financial revolution which we have witnessed has led to convergence in the models of various financial systems, which ca briefly be described by saying that there is more banking in tl once "market-oriented" models and more market in the once "ban oriented" models. Today we are moving towards a "transnation model" in which the major German universal banks are confrontii the major banking and financial holdings, which originated in cou: tries with specialization models but are now also spreading in Fran (*archipels bancaires*) and in Italy (*gruppi polifunzionali*). It is a mod which unites two previously separate features: the importance of tl bank as typified by the old continental European models, and tl importance of the market, as typified by the old Anglo-Saxon mod Thus, the dialectic that once made these models opposite is no reaching a synthesis.

Might we suggest that this "transnational model" is better than i precedents? The approach followed here denies the possibility answering this question, suggesting, rather, that internal and exte nal coherence be evaluated in order to identify the tendencies.

In this light, I shall offer a few conclusive remarks, taking up tl last of the four basic propositions stated earlier, which concerns tl interest rate. If the behavior of the interest rate (its level ar variability) can be traced back to the certainty (in the Keynesi: sense) which economic policy is capable of offering investors, we ca outline two alternative scenarios for the future.

The first scenario foresees a general uncertainty stemming fro agreement difficulties among three very different leaders (the Unit States, Japan, Germany). This uncertainty keeps interest rates ar volatility high (due to frequent changes in short-term expectation: which are transmitted to the financial assets markets.

This outlook favors finance growth (as has been seen in rece years), but at the same time contains instability risks underevaluat by financial intermediaries (because of the increasing availability individual hedging instruments). The October 1987 crash did n cause a financial crisis, and we can be optimistic about the solidity the financial system (though such optimism should be cautious, : Kindleberger (1988) suggests). But even leaving aside the risk of financial crisis, could the markets and the securities industry endu another show of volatility of those proportions? Wouldn't the marke end up being drastically rearranged?

The second scenario foresees a world economic policy that co siderably lowers uncertainty, thereby lowering interest rates ar their volatility. This outlook, so favorable for the economies, would n

so for the financial assets markets, which would become less
ıportant.

I think the stability pattern that the financial systems of the G7
ıtions are leaning towards must be evaluated keeping in mind these
·ssible alternatives, which cast serious doubts on the theory of the
atural evolution" of financial systems. I am also aware that the
·proach I have followed here is more fragmentary and less precise in
·oviding results than the "progressive" vision of development stages
the financial systems. But, if nothing else, this may avoid forcing
story down unalterable paths, and will open up a fruitful inter-
ange of ideas between historians and economists.

otes

ʌany of the ideas offered here are the result of participating in the research group on
inance Systems: Theory and Comparative Issues," which was formed in 1983 by the
ıiversities of Florence, Siena and Modena (FI.SI.MO Group), and enjoyed the
ıancial support of the Italian Ministry of Education. I am grateful to all the
·rticipants who took part in the stimulating discussions, and to Gianni Bonaiuti
ʒarding the preparation of this chapter.
Ihis role of banks has been especially highlighted by Schumpeter in his posthumous
ok *Das Wesen des Geldes*, the Italian version of which (G. Nardozzi ed., *L'essenza
lla moneta*) has been published thanks to Cassa di Risparmio di Torino, 1991. This
ıme role of banks has also recently been observed by Stiglitz and Weiss (1988).
Ihe terms "regulation" and "deregulation" have been used to describe the American
ıse, where government intervention is carried out by means of a net of precise rules.
ıis, however, is just one of the many ways for regulating a financial system. Other
ıys, especially the European ones, consist in the attribution of vast, and discretional,
·wers to the controlling bodies (Italy, France) or in "gentlemen's agreements" (UK).
ıese latter ways may make the relative financial systems scarcely appear to be
ʒulated, while they are actually very well controlled. In this chapter I will give the
·m "regulation" a wider meaning than that used in the United States.
Ihis summary description of the models draws extensively from Nardozzi (1988a) and
based on specific research work by Bonaiuti (United States) and Barzaghi (Germany),
ntained in Nardozzi (1988b).

References

Abramovitz, M. (1986), "Catching Up, Forging Ahead, and Falling Behind" *Journal of Economic History*, 46: pp. 385–406.

Aghion, P. and Bolton, P. (1988), *An Incomplete Contract Approach* **t** *Bankruptcy and the Financial Structure of the Firm*, MIT, Department **o** Economics Working Paper 484.

Akerlof, G. (1970), "The Market for 'Lemons': Quality Uncertainty and th Market Mechanism," *Quarterly Journal of Economics*, 90: pp. 488–500.

Akerlof, G. and Stiglitz, J. (1969), "Capital, Wages and Structural Unemploy ment," *Economic Journal*, Vol. LXXIX, June: pp. 269–81.

Alchian, A. and Demsetz, H. (1972), "Production, Information Costs an Economic Organization," *American Economic Review*, 62: pp. 777–95.

Aldcroft, D.H. (1964), "The entrepreneur and the British economy 1870 1914," *Economic History Review*, 17, August: pp. 113–34.

Alhadeff, D.A. (1975), "Bank-Business Conglomerates – the Japanese Exper ence," *Banca Nazionale del Lavoro Quarterly Review*: n. 114, pp. 232–67.

Allen, C.C. (1940), "Japanese Industry: Its Organization and Development **t** 1937," in Boody, Schumpeter, E. ed., *The Industrialization of Japan an Manchukuo, 1930–1940: Population, Raw Materials and Industry*, Macmi lan, New York.

Amendola, M. and Gaffard, J.L. (1988), *The Innovative Choice. An Econom Analisis of the Dynamics of Technology*, Basil Blackwell, Oxford and Ne York.

Andrade, E.N. da C. (1946), *Industrial Research: 1946*, Bodley Head, Londor

Andrews, P.W.S. and Brunner, E. (1951), *Capital Development in Iron an Steel*, Blackwell, Oxford.

Aoki, M. (1986), "Horizontal versus Vertical Information Structure of th Firm," *American Economic Review*, 76 (5), Dec: pp. 193–224.

Aoki, M. (1988), *Information, Incentives and Bargaining in the Japanes Economy*, Cambridge University Press, Cambridge.

Aoki, M. (1990a), "The Participatory Generation of Information Rents and th Theory of the Firm," in Aoki, M., Gustafsson, B. and Williamson, O.E. (eds pp. 26–51.

Aoki, M. (1990b), "Towards an Economic Model of the Japanese Firm *Journal of Economic Literature*, XXVIII, March: pp. 1–27.

Aoki, M., Gustafsson, B. and Williamson, O.E. (1990), *The Firm as a Nexus Treaties*, Sage Publications, London.

Aoki, M. and Rosenberg, N. (1989), "The Japanese Firm as an Innovatin Institution," in Shiraishi, T. and Tsuru, S. (eds), *Economic Institutions in Dynamic Society*, Macmillan, London: pp. 137–54.

Arthur, W.B. (1988), "Competing Technologies: An Overview," in Dosi, G., Friedman C., Nelson, R., Silverberg, G. and Soete, L. (eds), *Technical Change and Economic Theory*, Frances Pinter, London.

Asquith, P. and Mullins, D. (forthcoming), "Returns and Default Rates on High Yield Bonds," *Journal of Finance*.

Atack, Jeremy (1985), "Industrial Structure and the Emergence of the Modern Industrial Corporation," *Explorations in Economic History*, 22, January: pp. 29–55.

Auerbach, A.J. (1985), "Real Determinants of Corporate Leverage," in B.M. Friedman (ed.), *Corporate Capital Structure in the United States*, University of Chicago Press, Chicago and London: pp. 301–22.

Baker, W.J. (1970), *A History of the Marconi Company*, Methuen, London.

Bank of Japan (1973), *Money and Banking in Japan*, Macmillan, London.

Barnett, C. (1986), *The Audit of War: The Illusion and Reality of Britain as a Great Nation*, Macmillan, London.

Barzaghi, A. (1988), "La Francia," in Nardozzi, G. ed., *Sistemi creditizi a confronto*: pp. 113–55.

Barzaghi, A. (1988) "La Repubblica Federale Tedesca," ibid., pp. 71–111.

Baskin, J. (1988), "The Development of Corporate Financial Markets in Britain and the United States, 1600–1900," *Business History Review*, 62.

Baxter, N.D. (1966), *The Commercial Paper Market*, Bankers Publishing Company, Boston.

Beeny, J.H. (1975), *European Financial Reporting* 1. *West Germany*, The Institute of Chartered Accountants in England and Wales, London.

Beer, J.J. (1958), "Coal-Tar Dye Manufacture and the Origins of the Modern Industrial Research Laboratory," *Isis*, 49: pp. 123–31.

Berglof, E. (1990), "Capital Structure as a Mechanism of Control: a Comparison of Financial Systems," in Aoki, M., Gustafsson, B. and Williamson, O.E. (eds), *The Firm as a Nexus of Treaties*, Sage Publications, London: pp. 26–51.

Bernanke, B.S. (1983), "Nonmonetary effects of the Financial Crisis in the Propagation of the Great Depression," *American Economic Review*, 73, June: pp. 257–76.

Bernanke, B.S. and Campbell, J.Y. (1988), "Is There a Corporate Debt Crisis?," *Brookings Papers on Economic Activity*: n.1: pp. 83–125.

Best, M.H. and Humphries, J., "The City and Industrial Decline," in Elbaum, B. and Lazonick, W. (eds).

Binmore, K., Rubinstein, A. and Wolinsky, A. (1986), "The Nash Bargaining Solution in Economic Modelling," *Rand Journal of Economics*, 17 (2), Summer: pp. 176–88.

BIS (Bank for International Settlements) (1986), *Recent Innovations in International Banking*, BIS, Basel.

Blakey, R.G. and Gladys, C.B. (1919), "The Revenue Act of 1918," *The American Economic Review*, 9, June: pp. 213–43.

Boltho, A. (1985), "Was Japan's Industrial Policy Successful?," *Cambridge Journal of Economics*: pp. 187–201.

Bonaiuti, G. (1987), "Una nota su instabilità, struttura e regolamentazione degli intermediari," *Note Economiche*.

Bonaiuti, G. (1988), "Il Regno Unito," in Nardozzi, G. (ed.), *Sistemi creditizi a confronto*: pp. 157–211.

Bordo, M.D. (1987), "Explorations in Monetary History: A Survey of the Literature," *Explorations in Economic History*, 23.

Bordo, M.D. and Schwartz, A.J. (eds) (1984), *A Retrospective on the Gol Standard, 1821–1931*, University of Chicago Press, Chicago.

Born, K.E. (1977), *Geld und Banken im 19. und 20. Jahrhundert*, Alfre Kroner, Stuttgart.

Borrus, M.G. (1988), *Competing for Control*, Ballinger, Cambridge, MA.

Bradley, M., Jarrell, G.A. and Kim, E.H. (1984), "On the Existence of a Optimal Capital Structure: Theory and Evidence," *Journal of Financ* XXXIX: n. 3, pp. 857–78.

Brainard, W.C., Shoven, J.B. and Weiss, L. (eds) (1980), "The Financia Valuation of the Return to Capital," *Brookings Papers on Econom. Activity*, 2: pp. 453–511.

Brioschi, F. (1988), "Struttura proprietaria e comportamento concorrenzial del sistema industriale italiano," in Bianchi P. ed., *Antitrust e grupi industriali*, Bologna, Il Mulino: pp. 221–33.

Buenger, W.L. and Pratt, J.A. (1986), *But Also Good Business, Texa ,Commerce Banks and the Financing of Houston and Texas, 1886–198* A&M University Press, College Station, Texas.

Bunting, D. (1971), "The Truth about 'The Truth About the Trusts,'" *Journa of Economic History*, 31.

Bunting, D. (1974), *Statistical View of the Trusts*, Greenwood Press, Wes port.

Business Week (1989), "Is the US Selling Its High-Tech Soul to Japan?, 6/26/89: pp. 117–18.

Business Week (1988), "Special Report: Learning to Live with Leverage. 11/7/88: pp. 138–56.

Buxton, N.K. and Aldcroft, D.H. (eds) (1979), *British Industry Between th Wars*, Scolar Press, London.

Byatt, I.C.R. (1979), *The British Electrical Industry 1875–1914*, Oxfor University Press, Oxford.

Cable, J.R. (1985a), "Capital Market Information and Industrial Performanc. the Role of West Germany Banks," *The Economic Journal*, 95: pp. 118–32

Cable, J.R. (1985b), "The Bank–Industry Relationship in West Germany Performance on Policy Aspects," in Schwalbach J. ed., *Industry Structur and Performance*, Edition Sigma, Berlin: pp. 17–40.

Cameron, R. (1961), *France and the Economic Development of Europ* Princeton University Press, Princeton.

Cameron, R. (ed.) (1967), *Banking in the Early Stages of Industrializatior* Oxford University Press, New York and London.

Cameron, R. (ed.) (1972), *Banking and Economic Development*, Oxfor University Press, New York.

Campbell, R.H. (1985), *Scotland 1707: the Rise of an Industrial Societ* (Second edn), John Donald, Edinburgh.

Cant, B.R. (1972), *Britain's Economic Problems in International Historica Perspective*, Manchester Business School, Manchester.

Caron, F. (1974), "Investment Strategy in France," in Daems, H. and Van de Wee, H. (eds): pp. 96–144.

Caron, F. (1979), *An Economic History of Modern France*, Columbia Universi ty Press, New York.

Carosso, V.P. (1970), *Investment Banking in America*, Harvard Universit Press, Cambridge, MA.

Carosso, V.P. (1987), *The Morgans. Private International Bankers, 1854*

1913, Harvard University Press, Cambridge, MA.

arrera de Morel, B. (1987), "Les entreprises françaises sont-elles trop endettées?," *Banque*: n. 473: pp. 541–6.

arrington, J.C. and Edwards, G.T. (1979), *Financing Industrial Investment*, The Macmillan Press, London and Basingstoke.

hampernowne, D.C. (1953), "A Model of Income Distributions," *Economic Journal*, LXIII: pp. 318–51.

handler, A.D. (1974), "Structure and Investment Decisions in the United States," in Daems, H. and Van der Wee, H. (eds).

handler, A.D. (1976), "The Development of Modern Management Structure in the US and UK," in Hannah, L. ed., *Management Strategy and Business Development*, Macmillan, London.

handler, A.D. (1977), *The Visible Hand: The Managerial Revolution in American Business*, Harvard University Press, Cambridge, MA.

handler, A.D. (1978), "The United States: Evolution of Enterprise," in *The Cambridge Economic History of Europe*, in Mathias, P. and Postan, M.M. (eds).

handler, A.D. (1980a), "The United States: Seedbed of Managerial Capitalism," in Chandler, A.D. and Daems, H. (eds).

handler, A.D. (1980b), "The Growth of the Transnational Industrial Firm in the United States and the United Kingdom: A Comparative Analysis," *Economic History Review*, 2d ser., 33.

handler, A.D. (1986), "Managers, Families, and Financiers," in Robayashi, R. and Morikawa, H. (eds), *Development of Managerial Enterprise*, University of Tokyo Press, Tokyo: pp. 35–63.

handler, A.D. (1990), *Scale and Scope*, Harvard University Press, Cambridge, MA.

handler, A.D. and Daems, H. (1974), "The Rise of Managerial Capitalism and its Impact on Investment Strategy in the Western World and Japan," in Daems, H. and Van der Wee, H. (eds): pp. 1–34.

handler, A.D. and Daems, H. (eds) (1980), *Managerial Hierarchies. Comparative Perspectives on the Rise of the Modern Industrial Enterprise*, Harvard University Press, Cambridge, MA, and London.

handler, A.D. and Salsbury, S. (1971), *Pierre, S. Du Pont and the Making of the Modern Corporation*, Harper & Row, New York.

iocca, P. (1982), *Interesse e profitto*, Il Mulino, Bologna.

iocca, P. and Toniolo, G. (1984), "Industry and Finance in Italy, 1918–1940," *Journal of European Economic History*, 13.

lapham, J.H. (1926), *An Economic History of Modern Britain, Vol. 1: The Early Railway Age 1820–1950*, Cambridge University Press, Cambridge.

leveland, H.B. van and Huertas, T.F. (1985), *Citibank. 1812–1970*, Harvard University Press, Cambridge, MA.

oase, R. (1988), *The Firm, the Market and the Law*, Chicago University Press, Chicago.

ohen, J. (1977), *Finance and Industrialization in Italy, 1844–1904*, Arno Press, New York.

ohen, W.M. and Mowery, D.C. (1989), *The Influence of the Correlates of Firm Size on Product-Line R&D Investment*, unpublished MS.

ommittee on Commercial and Industrial Policy after the War (1918), *Final Report*, HMSO, London.

onti, G. (1987), "Sistemi di finanza di impresa: un confronto internazionale," in FI.SI.MO, *Tendenze dei sistemi finanziari: fatti e problemi interpretativi* Siena.

Corrigan, E.G. (1987), "Financial Innovations in International Financia Markets," in *United States in the World Economy*, Chicago Universit Press, Chicago: pp. 257–64.

Cosh, A.D. and Hughes, A. (1987), "The Anatomy of Corporate Contro Directors, Shareholders and Executive Remuneration in Giant US and UI Corporations," *Cambridge Journal of Economics*, XI: n. 4, pp. 285–313.

Cottrell, P.L. (1980), *Industrial Finance, 1830–1914: The Finance an Organisation of English Manufacturing Industry*, Methuen, London.

Cottrell, P. (1990), "Britain," in Cameron R. and Bovykin V. (eds), *Interna tional Banking and International Finance*, Oxford University Press, Ne York.

Coulbeck, N. (1984), *The Multinational Banking Industry*, Croom Helm London and Sydney.

Cox, A. (ed.) (1986) *State, Finance and Industry. A Comparative Analysis c Post-War Trends in Six Advanced Industrial Economies*, Wheatshea Books, Brighton.

Creamer, D., Dobrovolsky and Borenstein, I. (1960), *Capital in Manufactur ing and Mining. Its Formation and Financing*, Princeton.

Cremer, J. (1990), "Common Knowledge and the Coordination of Economi Activities," in Aoki, M., Gustafsson, B. and Williamson, O.E. (eds): pp 53–76.

CSO (1987) (Central Statistical Office), *Financial Statistics*, HMSO, London September.

Cumming, C. (1987), "The Economics of Securitization," *Federal Reserve Ban. of New York Quarterly Review*.

Currie, L. (1931), "The Decline of the Commercial Loan," *Quarterly Journal c Economics*, 45, August: pp. 698–709.

Daems, H. (1975), *The Holding Company. Essays on Financial Inter mediatives, Concentration and Capital Market Imperfections in th Belgian Economy*, Katholieke Universiteit, Department Economie, Leuver n. 16.

Daems, H. and Van der Wee, H. (eds) (1974), *The Rise of Manageria Capitalism*, Leuven University Press/M. Nijhoff, Louvain and The Hague.

David, P.A. (1975), *Technical Choice, Innovation, and Economic Growth* Cambridge University Press, New York.

Davis, L.E. (1960), "The New England Textile Mills and the Capital Markets A Study of Industrial Borrowing, 1840–1860," *Journal of Economic History* 20, March: pp. 1–43.

Davis, L.E. (1966), "The Capital Markets and Industrial Concentration: Th US and UK, A Comparative Study," *Economic History Review*, XIX:, pp 255–72.

Davis, L.E. (1967), "The Capital Markets and their Concentration: the U. and UK. A comparative Study," reprinted in *Purdue Faculty Papers i Economic History, 1956–66*, Purdue University Press, Purdue.

Davis, L.E. and Gallman, R. (1978), "Capital Formation in the United State during the Nineteenth Century," in Mathias, P. and Postan, M.M. (eds).

Davis, L.E. and North, D.C. (1971), *Institutional Change and America Economic Growth*, Cambridge University Press, New York.

Cecco, M. (1976), "International Financial Markets and US Domestic
olicy since 1945," *International Affairs*: pp. 381–99.
Cecco, M. (1984), *International and Transnational Financial Relations*,
luropean University Institute Working Paper n.84/121, Florence.
Cecco, M. (1985), "Modes of Financial Development in American Banking:
)ynamics and World Financial Crises," in *Development, Democracy and the*
rt of Trespassing. Essays in Honour of Albert Hirschman, ed. by Foxley,
\., McPherson, M.S., O'Donnell, G., University of Notre Dame Press, Notre
)ame, Ind.
Cecco, M. (1986), "Innovazione finanziaria e teoria monetaria," *Note*
'conomiche.
Cecco, M. (1988), "Le imprese tra banca e finanza," *L'Industria*, n.s., IX: n.
, pp. 5–13.
Cecco, M. (1989), "Alternative Modes of Financial Organization," in
\essides C., King T., Nuti, M. and Sokil, C. (eds), *Financial Reform in*
'ocialist Economies, Washington – Florence, Economic Development Insti-
ute of the World Bank – European University Institute: pp. 196–204.
lla Torre, G. (1985), "Book review of R. Goldsmith, The Financial
)evelopment of India Japan and United States," *Moneta e Credito*.
lla Torre, G. (1987), "Le tendenze dei sistemi finanziari nell'approccio
,uantitativo di R. Goldsmith," *Quaderni dell'Istituto di Economia dell'Uni-*
•ersità di Siena.
rtouzos, M., Lester R. and Solow, R. (eds) (1989), *Made in America*, MIT
'ress, Cambridge, MA.
utsche Bundesbank (various years), *Monthly Report*, May.
:kson, P.G.M. (1967), *The Financial Revolution in England. A Study in the*
)evelopment of Public Credit, 1688–1756, St. Martin's, London.
si, G. (1984), *Technical Change and Industrial Transformation*, Macmillan,
.ondon and St. Martin's Press, New York.
si, G. (1988a), *Institutions and Markets in a Dynamic World*, The
Manchester School.
si, G. (1988b), "Sources, Procedures, and Microeconomic Effects of Innova-
ion," *Journal of Economic Literature*, 26: pp. 1120–71.
si, G. (1988c), Finance, Innovation and Industrial Change, paper presented
it the Conference on "The Markets for Innovation, Ownership and
'ontrol," Stockholm, 12–15 June.
si, G. (1990), "Finance, Innovation and Industrial Change," *Journal of*
'conomic Behavior and Organization.
si, G. and Orsenigo, L. (1988), "Coordination and Transformation: an
)verview of Structures, Behavior and Change in Evolutionary Environ-
nents," in Dosi G., Freeman C., Nelson, R., Silverberg, G. and Soete, L.
eds), *Technical Change and Economic Theory*, Francis Pinter, London, and
'olumbia University Press, New York.
si, G., Teece, D.J. and Winter, W. (1991), "Toward a Theory of Corporate
'oherence: Preliminary Remarks," in Dosi, G., Toninelli, P.A. and Giannet-
i, R., *Technology and Enterprise in a Historical Perspective*, Oxford
Jniversity Press, Oxford.
si, G., Tyson, L. and Zysman, J. (1988), "Trade, Technologies and
Development," in Johnson C., Tyson, L. and Zysman, J. (eds), *Politics and*
°roductivity, Ballinger, Cambridge, MA.

Dotsey, M. (1982), "Japanese Monetary Policy, a Comparative Analysi *Bank of Japan – Monetary and Economic Studies*, IV: n. 2, pp. 105–27.

Dubois, A.B. (1938), *The English Business company after the Bubble A 1720–1800*, The Commonwealth Fund, New York.

Dyson, R. (1986), "The State, Banks and Industry: The West German Cas in Cox, A. (ed.), pp. 118–41.

Eagly, R. and Smith, V.V. (1976), "Domestic and International Integration the London Money Market, 1731–1789," *Journal of Economic History*, 3(

Eaton, J. (1986), "Lending with Costly Enforcement of Repayment a Potential Fraud," *Journal of Banking and Finance*, 10: pp. 281–93.

Eaton, J., Gersovitz, M. and Stiglitz, J. (1986), "Pure Theory of Country Ris] *European Economic Review*, 30, No. 3, June: pp. 481–513; also NB] Working Paper No. 1894, April 1986 and NBER Reprint #793.

Eaton, J. and Gersovitz, M. (1981), "Debt with Potential Repudiatic Theoretical and Empirical Analysis," *Review of Economic Studies*, Vol. 4 pp. 289–309.

Eckstein, W. (1980), "The Role of the Banks in Corporate Concentration West Germany," *Zeitschrift für gesamte Staatswissenschaft*, 136: pp. 46(82.

Edelstein, M. (1982), *Overseas Investment in the Age of High Imperialis, The United Kingdom, 1850–1914*, Methuen, London.

Edwards, J.R. (1981), *Company Legislation and Changing Patterns Disclosure in British Company Accounts, 1900–40*, The Institute of Cha tered Accountants, London.

Edwards, R.C. (1975), "Stages in Corporate Stability and Risks of Corpora Failure," *Journal of Economic History*, 35: pp. 418–57.

Eisenbeis, R. (1982), "Regulation and Deregulation of Banking," *The Banke Magazine*.

Elbaum, B. and Lazonick, W. (eds) (1986), *The Decline of the Briti Economy*, Clarendon Press, Oxford.

Evans, G. (1984), "The Evolution of Financial Institutions and the Ineffectiv ness of Monetary Policy," *Journal of Economic Issues*.

Fama, E.F. (1970), "Efficient Capital Markets: a Review of Theory a] Empirical Work," *The Journal of Finance*, 25, May: 383–417.

Fama, E.F. (1976), *Foundations of Finance*, Basic Books, New York.

Fazzari, S.M. and others (eds) (1988), "Financing Constraints and Corpora Investment," *Brookings Papers on Economic Activity*, 1: pp. 141–95.

Ferguson, C.H. (1983), "The Microelectronics Industry in Distress," *Technol gy Review*.

Ferguson, C.H. (1988), "From the People Who Brought You Voodoo Eco omics," *Harvard Business Review*.

Feroldi, M. (1985), "Monetary Mechanisms and Exchange Rates in Franc(in De Ménil G. and Westphal, U. (eds), *Stabilization Policy in France a] the Federal Republic of Germany*, Elsevier Science Publishers, Amsterda] New York, Oxford: pp. 227–62.

FIBV (Fédération Internationale des Bourses de Valeurs) (1985), *Rappo Paris.

Flaherty, T.M. and Hiroyuki, I. (1984), "Finance" in Okimoto, D. *et al.* (ed] *Competitive Edge, The Semiconductor Industry in the US and Japo* Stanford University Press, Stanford.

Florida, R.L. and Kenney, M. (1988), "Venture Capital-Financed Innovati(and Technological Change in the USA," *Research Policy*, 17: pp. 119–37.

ey, D. and Sidrauski, H. (1970), "Portfolio Choice, Investment and
irowth," *American Economic Review*, Vol. 60: pp. 44–63.

eman, C. (1962), "Research and Development: A Comparison between
ritish and American Industry," *National Institute Economic Review*, 20.

eman, C. (1982), *The Economics of Industrial Innovation*, Francis Pinter,
ondon.

eman, C. (1987), *Technology Policy and Economic Performance, Lessons
rom Japan*, Pinter Publishers, London and New York.

edman, B.M. (1980), "Postwar Changes in the American Financial Mar-
ets," in Feldstein, M. (ed.), *The American Economy in Transition*, The
Jniversity of Chicago Press, Chicago and London: pp. 9–78.

edmann, W., Ingram, D.H.A. and Miles, D.R. (1984), "Business Finance in
he United Kingdom and Germany," *Bank of England Quarterly Bulletin*,
XIV, September: n. 3, pp. 368–75.

ambos, L. (1966), *Competition and Cooperation*, Johns Hopkins University
ress, Baltimore, Md.

e, D. and Hellwig, M. (1985), "Incentive-Compatible Debt Contracts I: The
ne-Period Problem," *Review of Economic Studies*, October: 52, pp. 647–64.

e, D. and Stiglitz, J. (1989), *A Simple Proof that Futures Markets are
lmost Always Informationally Inefficient*, NBER Working Paper #3209.

rdener, E. (1987), "Securitisation and the Banking Firm," *Revue de la
anque*.

rschenkron, A. (1962), "Economic Backwardness in Historical Perspective,"
dem., *Economic Backwardness in Historical Perspective*, Harvard Universi-
y Press, Cambridge, MA.

rtler, M. (1988), "Financial Structure and Aggregate Economic Activity:
n Overview," *Journal of Money, Credit and Banking*.

dsmith, R.W. (1958), *Financial Intermediaries in the American Economy
ince 1900*, NBER and Princeton University Press, Princeton.

dsmith, R.W. (1969), *Financial Structure and Development*, Yale Universi-
y Press, New Haven and London.

dsmith, R.W. (1985), *Comparative National Balance Sheets*, University of
hicago Press, Chicago.

od, F. (1973), "Backwardness and the Role of Banking in XIX Century
uropean Industrialization," *Journal of Economic History*, 33.

odhart, C.A. (1969), *The New York Money Market and the Finance of
rade, 1900–1913*, Harvard University Press, Cambridge, MA.

odhart, C.A. (1986), "Why Do Banks Need a Central Bank," *Oxford
conomic Papers*.

rte, J.F. (1989), *Testimony before the Subcommittee on Science, Research,
nd Technology, Committee on Science, Space, and Technology*, US House
f Representatives, July 13.

aham, M.B.W. (1988), "R&D and Competition in England and the United
tates: The Case of the Aluminum Dirigible," *Business History Review*, 62:
p. 261–85.

aziani, A. (1984), "The Debate on Keynes' Finance Motive," *Economic
Notes*.

aziani, A. and Messori, M. (eds) (1988), *Moneta e Produzione*, Einaudi,
urin.

eenwald, B. and Stiglitz, J. (1987), "Money, Imperfect Information, and
conomic Fluctuations," *National Bureau of Economic Research – Working
aper*, March: n. 2188.

Greenwald, B. and Stiglitz, J. (1988), "Money, Imperfect Information ₁
Economic Fluctuations," in *Finance Constraints. Expectations* ₄
Macroeconomics, Kohn, M. and Tsiang, S.C. (eds), Oxford University Pr
Oxford: pp. 141–65.

Greenwald, B. and Stiglitz, J. (1990), "Financial Market Imperfections ₄
Productivity Growth," *Journal of Economic Behavior and Organization.*

Greenwald, B., Stiglitz, J., and Weiss, A. (1983), "Informational Imperfecti
in the Capital markets and Macro-economic Fluctuations," *Ameri*
Economic Review, Vol. 74, No. 1, May 1984: pp. 194–9 (paper presente₄
the American Economic Association, December).

Grossman, S. and Hart, O.D. (1980), "Takeover Bids, the Free Ride Probl
and the Theory of the Corporation," *Bell Journal of Economics*, 11: n.2,
42–64.

Grossman, S. and Stiglitz, J. (1977), "On Value Maximization and Alterna₄
Objectives of the Firm," *Journal of Finance*, XXXII, No. 2, May:
389–402.

Grossman, S. and Stiglitz, J. (1980), "Stockholder Unanimity in the Makin₄
Production and Financial Decisions," *Quarterly Journal of Economics*,
No. 3, May: ˜pp. 543–66.

Gurley, J.G. and Shaw, E.S. (1956), "Financial Intermediaries and
Saving-Investment Process," *Journal of Finance*, XI.

Gurley, J.G. and Shaw, E.S. (1957), "The Growth of Debt and Money in
United States, 1800–1950: A Suggested Interpretation," *The Review*
Economics and Statistics, XXXIX: n. 3, pp. 250–62.

Gurley, J.G. and Shaw, E.S. (1967), "Financial Structure and Econoₘ
Development," *Economic Development and Cultural Change*, IV: n. 3,
257–68.

Hall, B.H. (1988), "The Effect of Takeover Activity on Corporate Resea
and Development," in Auerbach, A. (ed.), *Corporate Takeovers: Causes* ₄
Consequences, University of Chicago Press, Chicago.

Hall, R. and Jorgenson D. (1967), "Tax Policy and Investment Behavi₄
American Economic Review, Vol. 57: pp. 391–414.

Hannah, L. (1974a), "Managerial Innovation and the Rise of the Large-S₄
Company in Great Britain," *Economic History Review*, 2d ser., 28.

Hannah, L. (1974b), "Mergers in British Manufacturing Industry, 18₄
1919," *Oxford Economic Papers*, new ser., 26.

Hannah, L. (ed.) (1976), *Management Strategy and Business Developm₄*
Macmillan, London.

Hannah, L. (1980), "Visible and Invisible Hands in Great Britain,"
Chandler A.D. and Daems H. (eds).

Hannah, L. (1983), *The Rise of the Corporate Economy* (Second ed
Methuen, London and New York.

Hannah, L. and Kay, J.A. (1977), *Concentration in Modern Industry. The₄*
Measurement and the U.R. Experience, Macmillan Press Ltd, London.

Hannaway, J. (1989), *Managers Managing: The Workings of an Administ₄*
tive System, Oxford University Press, Oxford.

Hart, O.D. (1975), "On the Optimality of Equilibrium When the Mar₄
Structure is Incomplete," *Journal of Economic Theory*, 11: pp. 418–43.

Hart, P.E. and Clarke, R. (1980), *Concentration in British Indus₄*
1935–75. A Study of the Growth, Causes and Effects of Concentration
British Manufacturing Industries, Cambridge University Pr₄
Cambridge.

awtrey, R. (1919), *Currency and Credit*, Longmans, Green and Co., New York.

ein, C. and Mirowski, P. (1987), "Interest Rates and Crowding Out during Britain's Industrial Revolution," *Journal of Economic History*, 47.

erman, E.S. (1981), *Corporate Control, Corporate Power*, Cambridge University Press, Cambridge.

icks, J. (1973), *Capital and Time*, Clarendon Press, Oxford.

icks, J. (1974), *The Crisis in Keynesian Economics*, Oxford University Press, Oxford.

ilferding, R. (1909), *Das Finanzkapital*, Berlin.

irschleifer, J. (1966), "Investment Decisions under Uncertainty: Applications of the State-Preference Approach," *Quarterly Journal of Economics*, 80: pp. 252–77.

odder, J.E. (1988), "Corporate Capital Structure in the United States and Japan: Financial Intermediation and Implications of Financial Deregulation," in Shoven, J.B. (ed.), *Government Policy Towards Industry in the United States and Japan*, New York, Cambridge University Press, Cambridge.

ollander, J.H. (1913), "Security Holdings of National Banks," *American Economic Review*, 3, December: pp. 793–814.

olmes, A.R. and Green, E. (1986), *Midland: 150 Years of Banking Business*, Batsford, London.

oriuchi, A. (1989), "Informational Properties of the Japanese Financial System," *Japan and the World Economy*, 1, n. 3, July: pp. 255–78.

oriuchi, A. *et al.* (1988), "What Role Has the 'Main Bank' Played in Japan," *Journal of the Japanese and International Economies*, 2, n. 2, June: pp. 159–80.

u, Y.S. (1975), *National Attitudes and the Financing of Industry*, Political and Economic Planning, London.

u, Y.S. (1984), *Industrial Banking and Special Credit Institutions. A Comparative Study*, Policy Studies Institute, London.

eo, K. (1985), *Nihon no Kinyu Shijo to Soshiki* (Japan's Financial Market and Organization), Toyo Keizai Shimpo-sha, Tokyo.

eo, K. (1987), "Japan's Financial System: A Micro Approach," *Japanese Economic Studies*, XVI, Fall, n. 1: pp. 60–77.

nai, K. (1980), "Japan Industrial Organizations" in Sato K. (ed.), *Industry and Business in Japan*, M.E. Sharpe, Inc. and Croom Helm, New York and London: pp. 74–135.

nai, K. (1986), "Japan's Industrial Policy for High Technology Industry," in Hugh P. (ed.), *Japan's High Technology Industries*, University of Washington Press, Seattle.

nai, K. (1987–88), "The Corporate Network in Japan," *Japanese Economic Studies*, vol. 56, n. 2, Winter: pp. 3–37.

nai, K. (1989a), "Japanese Pattern of Innovation and Its Commercialization Process," Paper presented at the Conference "Economic Growth and the Commercialization of New Technologies," Stanford University, September 11–12.

nai, K. (1989b), "Latecomer Strategies in Advanced Electronics – Lesson from the Japanese Experience, Paper presented at the OECD Development Center's Conference on "Technological Change, and the Electronic Sector: Perspectives and Policy Options for Newly Industrializing Countries," June: Paris.

Imai, K. *et al.* (1983), "Interview with Mr Koji Kobayashi (Chairman NEC)," *Business Review* (in Japanese), Institute of Business Resear Hitotsubashi University, vol. 31, n. 1, August, published by Chikura-sho

Imai, K. and Itami, H. (1984), "Interpenetration of Organization and Marke Japan's Firm and Market in Comparison with the U.S.," *Internatior Journal of Industrial Organization*, n. 2: pp. 285–310.

Ingham, G. (1984), *Capitalism Divided? The City and Industry in Brita Social Development*, Macmillan, London.

IRS (Istituto per la Ricerca Sociale) (1988), *Rapporto sul mercato azionar* Edizioni Il Sole 24 Ore, Milan.

Itoh, I. (1987), "Information Processing Capacities of the Firm," *Journal Japanese and International Economics*, Sept. (3): pp. 299–326.

Jacoby, N.H. and Saulnier, R.J. (1947), *Business Finance and Banki* National Bureau of Economic Research, New York.

James, J.A. (1978), *Money and Capital Markets in Postbellum Ameri* Princeton University Press, Princeton.

Jarrell, G.A. (1981), "The Economic Effects of Federal Regulation of t Market for New Security Issues," *Journal of Law and Economics,* December.

Jeffreys, J.B. (1938), "Trends in Business Organization in Great Britain sin 1856," University of London, unpublished Ph.D. dissertation.

Jeidels, O. (1905), *Das Verhältnis der deutschen Grossbanken zur Industr mit bes. Berücksichtigung der Eisenindustrie*, Leipzig.

Jensen, M. and Meckling, W. (1976), "Theory of the Firm: Manager Behavior, Agency Costs and Ownership Structure," *Journal of Financ Economics*, 3: pp. 305–60.

Jensen, M. and Meckling W. (1986), "Theory of the Firm, Manageri Behavior, Agency Costs and Capital Structure," *Journal of Financ Economics*, 3 (4), Oct.: pp. 305–60.

Jones, R. and Marriott, O. (1975), *Anatomy of a Merger: A History of GEC A and English Electric*, Jonathan Cape, London.

Kaldor, N. (1956), "Alternative Theories of Distribution," *Review of Econom Studies*, 23: pp. 83–100.

Kalecki, M. (1939), *Essays in the Theory of Economic Fluctuations*, Allen Unwin, London.

Kalecki, M. (1971), "Entrepreneurial Capital and Investment," in Kalecki, N *Selected Essays on the Dynamics of the Capitalist Economy 1933–197* Cambridge University Press, Cambridge: pp. 105–9.

Kane, R. (1981), "Accelerating Inflation, Technological Innovation and tl Decreasing Effectiveness of Banking Regulation," *The Journal of Financ*

Kaplan, A.D.H. (1964), *Big Business in a Competitive System*, Brookin Institution, Washington, D.C.

Kennedy, W. P. (1976), "Institutional Response to Economic Growth: Capit Markets in Britain to 1914," in Hannah, L. (ed.), *Management Strategy ar Business Development*, Macmillan, London.

Kennedy, W.P. (1987), *Industrial Structure, Capital Markets, and t Origins of British Economic Decline*, Cambridge University Pres Cambridge.

Kennedy, W.P. and Britton, R., "Portfolioverhalten und wirtschafliche Er wicklung im spaten 19. Jahrhundert. Ein Vergleich zwischen Grossbrita nien und Deutschland. Hypothesen und Spekulationen," in Tilly, R. (ed.): p 45–89.

ynes, J.M. (1936), *The General Theory of Employment Interest and Money*, Macmillan, London.

ynes, J.M. (1979), *Collected Writings* (D. Moggridge, ed.), Macmillan, London, Vol. XXIX.

ndleberger, C.P. (1966), "Balance of Payments Deficits and the International Market for Liquidity," in Kindleberger, C.P., *Europe and the Dollar*, MIT Press, Cambridge, MA: pp. 1–26.

ndleberger, C.P. (1987), "Banking and Industry between the Two World Wars: An International Comparison," *Journal of Economic History*: pp. 7–27.

ndleberger, C.P. (1988), "Il 'lunedì nero' del 1987: considerazioni in prospettiva storica," *Rivista di Storia Economica*.

rby, J.E.W. (1980), "The Japanese and Their Changing Economic Environment," in Norbury, P. and Bownas, G. (eds), *Business in Japan. A Guide to Japanese Business Practice and Procedure*, Macmillan, London and Basingstoke: pp. 85–94.

ch, A.R. (1943), *The Financing of Large Corporations, 1920–39*, National Bureau of Economic Research, New York.

cka, J. (1978), "Entrepreneurs and Managers in German Industrialization," in Mathias P. and Postan, M.M. (eds).

cka, J. (1980), "The Rise of the Modern Industrial Enterprise in Germany," in Chandler, A.D. and Daems, H. (eds).

ike, K. (1984), "Skill Formative Systems in the US and Japan: a Comparative Study," in Aoki M. (ed.), *The Economic Analysis of the Japanese Firm*, North-Holland, Amsterdam: pp. 47–75.

ike, K. (1988), *Understanding Industrial Relations in Modern Japan*, Macmillan, London.

jima, K. and Ozawa, T. (1984), *Japan's General Trading Companies Merchants of Economic Development*, Development Centre of OECD, Paris.

pcke, R.W. (1989), "The Roles of Debt and Equity in Financing Corporate Investments," *New England Economic Review*, July/August: pp. 25–48.

rnai, J. (1980), *The Economics of Shortage*, North-Holland, Amsterdam.

sai, Y. and Ogino, U. (1980), *Nihon Keizai Tenbo* (A Survey of the Japanese Economy), Nihon Hyoron-sha, Tokyo.

tz, D.M. (1978), *Bank Control of Large Corporations in the United States*, University of California Press, Los Angeles.

egel, J.A. (1984), "Monetary Production Economics and Monetary Policy," *Economie et Societé*, Serie Monnaie et Production n.1.

ah, E. and Meyer, J.R. (1959), *The Investment Decision*, Harvard University Press, Cambridge, MA.

uznets, S. (1961), *Capital in the American Economy, Its Formation and Financing*, NBER and Princeton University Press, Princeton.

chman, L.M. (1940), "A Reconsideration of the Austrian Theory of Industrial Fluctuations," *Economica*, 7, n. 26, May: pp. 179–96.

mfalussy, A. (1968), *Les marchés financiers en Europe*, P.U.F., Paris.

mmert, W.B. (1989a), "The Bubble Act and the Mysterious Retreat of the Eighteenth Century Stock Market: An Answer to Mirowski," unpublished MS, London School of Economics.

mmert, W.B. (1989b), "Political Constraints and Economic Performance: Banking in England and Scotland, 1700–1850," unpublished MS, London School of Economics.

moreaux, N. (1985), The *Great Merger Movement in American Business, 1895–1904*, Cambridge University Press, New York.

Landes, D. (1969), *The Unbound Prometheus*, Cambridge University Pres
Cambridge.

Lavington, G.E. (1921), *The English Capital Market*, Methuen, London.

Lavoie, M. (1985), "Credit and Money: the Dynamic Circuit, Overdra
Economics and Post-Keynesian Economics," in *Money and Macro Policy*
M. Jarsulic (ed.), Kluwer-Nijhoff.

Lazonick, W.A. (1981), "Factor Costs and the Diffusion of Ring Spinning
Britain prior to World War I," *Quarterly Journal of Economics*, 96: p
89–109.

Lazonick, W.A. (1983), "Industrial Organization and Technological Chang
The Decline of the British Cotton Industry," *Business History Review*, 57: p
195–236.

Levin, R., Klevorick, A., Nelson, R. and Winter, S. (1987), "Appropriating t
Returns from Industrial R&D," *Brookings Papers on Economic Activity*: p
783–820.

Lévy-Leboyer, M. (1964), *Les Banques Europeennes et l'industrialisatio
internationale dans la première moitié du XIX siècle*, Presses Universitair
de France, Paris.

Lévy-Leboyer, M. (1978) "Capital Investment and Economic Growth
France, 1820–1930," in Mathias, P. and Postan, M.M. (eds).

Lévy-Leboyer, M. (1979), "Le patronat français, 1912–1973," in M. Lév
Leboyer, (ed.), *Le patronat de la seconde industrialisation*, Les Editio
Ouvrières, Paris: pp. 137–88.

Lévy-Leboyer, M. (1980), "The Large Corporation in Modern France,"
Chandler, A.D. and Daems, H., pp. 117–60.

Lewchuk, W. (1985), "The Return to Capital in the British Motor Vehic
Industry, 1896–1939," *Business History*, 27, March: pp. 3–25.

Lewis, M. (1987), "Personal Financial Services in the United States:
Transatlantic Perspective," in Goodhart, C., Currie, D. and Llewellyn, D.
(eds), *The Operation and Regulation of Financial Markets*, Macmilla
London: pp. 54–77.

Lichtenberg, F.R. and Siegel, D. (1989), "The Effects of Leveraged Buyouts o
Productivity and Related Aspects of Firm Behavior," unpublished MS.

Lindsay, J.R. and Sametz, A.W. (1967), *Financial Management. An Analytic
Approach*, R.D. Irwin Inc., Homewood, Ill.

Lintner, J. (1959), "The Financing of Corporations," in Mason, E.S. (ed.), *T
Corporation in Modern Society*, Harvard University Press, Cambridge, M
pp. 166–201.

Lisle-Williams, M., "The State, Finance and Industry in Britain," in Cox, A
pp. 231–61.

Llewellyn, D.T. (1985), "The Changing Structure of the UK Financial System
The Three Banks Review, March: n. 145, pp. 19–34.

Locatelli, R. (1987), "Il ruolo delle banche nell'intermediazione in titoli societa
e nell'acquisto di partecipazioni industriali: un'indagine comparativa," in
Cesarini (ed.), *Banche, intermediari finanziari e mercato azionario. Espe
ienze a confronto*, Angeli, Milan: pp. 35–43.

Lockwood, W.W. (1968), *The Economic Development of Japan* (Second edn
Princeton University Press, Princeton.

Lucas, A.F. (1937), *Industrial Reconstruction and the Control of Competitio
Longman, London.

Macchiati, A. (1985), *Il finanziamento delle imprese industriali in Italia*,
Mulino, Bologna.

chiati, A. (1989), "La holding come intermediario finanziario. Contributo
r un'analisi," *Finanza imprese e mercati*, I: n. 1, pp. 27–47.

Leod, B. and Malcomson, J. (1986), "Reputation and Hierarchy in Dynamic
odels of Employment," mimeo, University of Southampton.

rosty, H.W. (1907), *The Trust Movement in British Industry*, Longmans,
reen, London.

ath, G. and Postlewaite, A. (1990), "Workers versus Firms: Bargaining
er a Firm's Value," *Review of Economic Studies*, 57: pp. 369–80.

icic, A. (1988), "Apporti e limiti della nozione di economia di inde-
tamento in una prospettiva keynesiana," in Graziani and Messori (eds).

tin, A. (1976), *James, J. Hill and the Opening of the Northwest*, Oxford
niversity Press, New York.

z, E. (1968), *Österreichische Industrie- und Bankpolitik in der Zeit Franz
sephs I*, Europa Press, Vienna, Frankfurt and Zurich.

hias, P. and Postan, M.M. (eds) (1978), *The Industrial Economies: Capital,
abour and Enterprise*, vol. 7 of *The Cambridge Economic History of Europe*,
ambridge University Press, Cambridge.

cock, J. (1986), *Financial Conglomerates: the New Phenomenon*, Gower,
ldershot.

er, C. (1986a), "Financial Innovation: Curse or Blessing?," *Oxford Review
Economic Policy*, II: n. 4, pp. x–xiii.

er, C. (1986b), "New Issues in Corporate Finance," Centre for Economic
olicy Research, Discussion Paper n. 181.

er, C. (1987a), "Financial Systems and Corporate Investment," *Oxford
eview of Economic Policy*, III: n. 4, pp. i–xvi.

er, C. (1987b), "The Assessment: Financial Systems and Corporate
vestment," *Oxford Review of Economic Policy*, 3, Winter: pp. i–xvi.

er, C. (1989), "The Influence of the Financial System on the British
orporate Finance," paper prepared for the Conference "The Separation of
dustry and Financial Intermediaries," Centre for Monetary and Financial
conomics, Università Bocconi, Milan.

loskey, D.N. (ed.) (1971), *Essays on a Mature Economy: Britain after 1840*,
ethuen, London.

ouldrick, P. (1984), "Operations of the German Central Bank and the
ules of the Game, 1879–1913," in Bordo, M.D. and Schwartz, A.J. (eds).

innon, R.I. (1973), *Money and Capital in Economic Development*, The
rookings Institution, Washington, DC.

er-Thurow, G. (1982), "The Industrialization of Invention: A Case Study
om the German Chemical Industry," *Isis*, 73: pp. 363–81.

ie, R. (1986), "The London and New York Stock Exchanges, 1850–1914,"
urnal of Economic History, 46.

ns, R. (1988), "The Management of Shareholdings in Large Manufacturing
ompanies," in Harris L., Coakley, J., Croasdale, M., Evans, T. (eds), *New
erspectives on the Financial System*, London – New York – Sydney, Croom
elm: pp. 143–69.

tz, B. and Schwartz, M. (1985), *The Power Structure of American Business*,
ae University of Chicago Press, Chicago and London.

on, J. (1986), "Financial Panics: the Seasonality of the Nominal Interest
ate and the Founding of the Fed," *American Economic Review*, 76.

wski, P. (1981), "The Rise (and Retreat) of a Market: English Joint Stock
ares in the Eighteenth Century," *Journal of Economic History*, 41,
ptember: pp. 559–77.

Mitsubishi Economic Research Institute (1955), *Mitsui-Mitsubishi-Sumito*
Mitsubishi Economic Research Institute, Tokyo.

Miyazaki, Y. (1980), "Excessive Competition and the Formation of Keirets
in Sato, R. (ed.), *Industry and Business in Japan*, M.E. Sharpe, Inc. *è*
Croom Helm, New York and London: pp. 53–73.

Mizruchi, M.S. (1982), *The American Corporate Network 1904–1974*, S*è*
Publications, Beverly Hills and London.

Mizruchi, M.S. and Schwartz, M. (eds) (1987), *Intercorporate Relations. 1*
Structural Analysis of Business, Cambridge University Press, Cambrid

Modigliani, F. and Miller, M. (1958), "The Cost of Capital, Corporation Fina*è*
and the Theory of Investment," *American Economic Review*, 48, June:
261–7.

Mokyr, J. (1985), *The Economics of the Industrial Revolution*, Rowman *è*
Allanheld, Totowa, NJ.

Moran, M. (1984), *The Politics of Banking. The Strange Case of Competit*
and Credit Control, Macmillan, London.

Morgan, E. V. and Thomas, W.A. (1962), *The Stock Exchange: its History o*
Functions, Elek, London.

Mosconi, A. and Rullani, E. (1978), *Il gruppo nello sviluppo dell'impr*
industriale. Con un'analisi del caso FIAT, ISEDI, Milan.

Moulton, H. G. (1918), "Commercial Banking and Capital Formation," *Jour*
of Political Economy, 26, July: pp. 705–31.

Mowery, D.C. (1981), "The Emergence and Growth of Industrial Research
American Manufacturing, 1899–1946," Ph.D. diss., Stanford Universit

Mowery, D.C. (1983), "Industrial Research, Firm Size, Growth, and Surviv
1921–1946," *Journal of Economic History*.

Mowery, D.C. (1984), "Firm Structure, Government Policy, and the Organi
tion of Industrial Research: Great Britain and the United States, 19(
1950," *Business History Review*.

Mowery, D.C. and Rosenberg, N. (1989), *Technology and the Pursuit*
Economic Growth, Cambridge University Press, New York.

Mowery, D.C. and Rosenberg, N. (1990), *The Growth of US. Industr*
Research, CEPR Discussion Paper #182, Center for Economic Pol
Research, Stanford.

Myers, S. and Majluf, N. (1984), "Corporate Financing and Investm*è*
Decisions When Firms Have Information that Investors Do Not," *Journa*
Financial Economics, 11: pp. 187–221.

Myrdal, G. (1957), *Economic Theory and Under-developed Regions*, Ger
Duckworth, London.

Nakagawa, K. (1974), "The Structure and Motives of Investment by Priv*è*
Enterprises in Japan before the Second World War," in Daems, H. and V
der Wee, H. (eds).

Nakatani, I. (1984), "The Economic Role of Financial Corporate Grouping,'
Aoki M. (ed.), *The Economic Analysis of the Japanese Firm*, Elsevi
Amsterdam: pp. 227–48.

Nardozzi, G. (1983a), *Tre sistemi creditizi. Banche ed economia in Franc*
Germania e Italia, Il Mulino, Bologna.

Nardozzi, G. (1983b), *Structural Trends of Financial Systems and Cap*
Accumulation: France, Germany, Italy, Commission of the European Co
munities, Directorate General for Economic and Financial Affairs, Econo
Papers n. 14.

dozzi, G. (1983c), "Schumpeter e l'economia monetaria," in *Società viluppo Impresa*, by Filippini, C. and Porta, P. (eds), IPSOA, Milan.

dozzi, G. (1986a), "Credito e banca in un sistema finanziario innovativo," *anca Toscana Studi e Informazioni*.

dozzi, G. (1986b), "Il mercato azionario: quale modello per l'economia aliana?," in *Oltre la crisi* (by Ente per gli studi monetari, bancari e nanziari L. Einaudi (ed.)), Il Mulino, Bologna.

dozzi, G. (1988a), "Sulla dinamica strutturale dei sistemi finanziari," paper resented to the Società Italiana degli Economisti, Rome.

dozzi, G. (ed.) (1988b), *Sistemi creditizi a confronto*, Servizio Studi della amera dei Deputati, Roma.

ional Research Council (1933, 1940, and 1946), *Industrial Research aboratories of the United States*, Bulletins 91, 104, and 113, Washington, C.

in, T.R. and Sears, M.V. (1955), "The Rise of a Market for Industrial ecurities, 1887–1902," *Business History Review*, June: pp. 109–20.

l, L.D. (1971), "Trust Companies and Financial Innovation, 1897–1914," *usiness History Review*, 45, Spring: pp. 35–51.

l, L.D. (1987), "The Integration and Efficiency of the London and msterdam Stock Markets in the Eighteenth Century," *Journal of Economic History*, 47.

son, R.L. (1959), *Merger Movements in American Industry 1895–1956*, rinceton University Press, Princeton.

son, R.L. and Winter, S. (1982), *An Evolutionary Theory of Economic hange*, The Belknap Press of Harvard University Press, Cambridge, MA.

hiyama, T. (1984), "The Structure of Managerial Control: Who Owns and ontrols Japanese Business," in Sato, K. and Hoshino, Y. (eds), *The natomy of Japanese Business*, M.E. Sharpe, Inc. and Croom Helm, New ork, London and Sydney: pp. 123–63.

rth, D.C. (1986), "The New Institutional Economics," in *Journal of nstitutional and Theoretical Economics (Zeitschrift fur die gesamte Staaswissenschaft)*, 142.

CD (1987a), *Financial Statistics*, II, OECD, Paris.

CD (1987b), *Financial Statistics*, III, OECD, Paris.

nstead, A.L. and Goldberg, V.P. (1975), "Institutional Change and American Economic Growth: A Critique of Davis and North," *Explorations in conomic History*, 12: pp. 193–210.

ado, M. (1986), "Il finanziamento delle imprese. Un tentativo di sintesi," in *dem* (ed.), *Sistema finanziario e industria*, Il Mulino, Bologna: pp. 7–27.

senigo, L. (1989), The *Emergence of Biotechnology*, Frances Pinter, London.

nico, C. (1983), "Analysis of the Relationship between the Rate of Interest nd the Rate of Profit," in *Keynes' Economics and the Theory of Value and istribution*, Eatwell, J. and Milgate, R. (eds), Duckworth, London.

ppi, F.U., Kappelhoff, P. and Melbeck, C. (1987), "Die Struktur der Jnternehmensverflechtung in der Bundesrepublik," *Kölner Zeitschrift fur oziologie und Sozialpsychologie*, 39: pp. 693–717.

sinetti, L. (1962), "Rate of Profit and Income Distribution in Relation to the ate of Economic Growth," *Review of Economic Studies*, 29: pp. 267–79.

sinetti, L. (1981), *Structural Change and Economic Growth. A Theoretical ssay on the Dynamics of the Wealth of Nations*, Cambridge University ress, Cambridge.

Pastré, O. (1979), *La stratégie internationale des groupes financiers ame cains*, Economica, Paris.

Patrick, K. (1967), "Japan, 1868–1914," in Cameron, R. (ed.), *Banking in Early States of Industrialization*.

Pavitt, K. (1984), "Sectoral Patterns of Innovation. Toward a taxonomy an theory," *Research Policy*.

Pavitt, K. (1991), "Some Foundations for a Theory of the Large Innovat Firm," in Dosi G., Toninelli, P.A. and Giannetti, R., *Technology a Enterprise in a Historical Perspective*, Oxford University Press, Oxford.

Payne, F.L. (1967), "The Emergence of the Large-Scale in Great Brita 1870–1914," *Economic History Review*, 2d ser., 20.

Payne, F.L. (1978), "Industrial Entrepreneurship and Management in Gr Britain," in Mathias, P. and Postan, M.M. (eds).

Peach, W.N. (1941), *The Security Affiliates of National Banks*, The Jof Hopkins University Press, Baltimore.

Pechman, J.A. (1987), *Federal Tax Policy*, Brookings Institution, Washingt DC.

Penrose, E.P. (1959), *The Theory of the Growth of the Firm*, Blackw Oxford.

Pitelis, C.N. and Sugden, R. (1986), "The Separation of Ownership a Control in the Theory of the Firm. A Reappraisal," *International Journal Industrial Organization*, IV: pp. 69–86.

Platt, D.C. (1986), *Britain's Investment Overseas on the Eve of the First Wo War*, Oxford University Press, London.

Pohl, M. (1982), *Konzentration im deutschen Bankwesen. 1848–1980*, Knaf Frankfurt.

Pollard, S. (1965), *The Genesis of Modern Management*, Edward Arno London.

Pollard, S. (1989), *Britain's Prime and Britain's Decline: The British Econo 1870–1914*, Edward Arnold, London.

Pollin, R. (1985), "Stability and Instability in the Debt-Income Relationshij *American Economic Review*, 75, 1985: n. 2, pp. 344–50.

Porter, P.G. (1974), "Typologies of Investment Strategies in the Unit States," in Daems, H. and Van der Wee, H. (eds).

Prais, S.J. (1976), *The Evolution of Giant Firms in Britain. A Study of t Growth of Concentration in Manufacturing Industry in Britain 1909–? Cambridge University Press, Cambridge.

Prais, S.J. (1981), *Productivity and Industrial Structure. A Statistical Stu of Manufacturing Industry in Britain, Germany and United States*, Ca bridge University Press, Cambridge.

Pressnell, L.S. (1956), *Country Banking in the Industrial Revolutic* Clarendon Press, Oxford.

Preston, H.H. and Findlay, A.R. (1930), "Era Favors Investment Affiliate *American Bankers Association Journal*, 24: pp. 1153–4 and 1191–2.

Ravenscraft, D.J. and Scherer, F.M. (1987), *Mergers, Sell-Offs, and Econon Efficiency*, Brookings Institution, Washington, DC.

Reader, W.J. (1975), *Imperial Chemical Industries: A History*, Oxford U versity Press, Oxford, vol. 2.

Reader, W.J. (1976), *Metal Box: A History*, Heinemann, London.

Reader, W.J. (1979), "The Chemicals Industry," in Buxton, N.K. and Aldcro D.H. (eds), *British Industry between the Wars*, Scolar Press, London.

ch, F. (1951), *The Molding of American Banking*, 2 Vols., New York.

, R.B. and Mankin, E. (1986), "Joint Ventures with Japan Give Away
r Future," *Harvard Business Review*.

er, R. (1987), *Geldtheorie*, Springer Verlag, Berlin, Heidelberg and New
rk.

er, R. (1988), "The New Institutional Economics applied to Monetary
nomics," *Journal of Institutional and Theoretical Economics*, 144:
208–24.

er, J. (1910), *Die deutschen Grossbanken und ihre Konzentration*,
cher, Jena.

er, J. (1911), *The German Great Banks and their Concentration*,
pared for the National Monetary Commission, US Government Printing
fice, Washington, DC.

an, M. (1990), "What is Vertical Integration?," in Aoki M., Gustafsson B.
d Williamson, O.E. (eds), pp. 53–76.

nson, J. (1956), *The Accumulation of Capital*, Macmillan, London.

rs, C. (1989), *Money, Interest and Capital*, Cambridge University Press,
ambridge.

R. (1984), "Orange Juice and Weather," *American Economic Review*, 74,
cember: pp. 861–80.

nberg, N. (1974), *Perspectives on Technology*, Cambridge University
ess, Cambridge.

nberg, N. (1982), *Inside the Black Box*, Cambridge University Press,
mbridge.

nberg, N. and Steinmueller, W.E. (1988), "Why Can't Americans Learn
be Better Imitators?," *American Economic Review*.

vsky, H. (1961), *Capital Formation in Japan*, Free Press, Glencoe, Ill.

, S. (1973), "The Economic Theory of Agency: The Principal's Problem,"
nerican Economic Review*, May: pp. 134–9.

ow, W.W. (1960), *The Stages of Economic Growth*, Cambridge University
ess, New York.

ama, S. (1983–4), "The Japanese Financial System: Past, Present, and
ature," *Japanese Economic Studies*, XIII, Winter: n. 2, pp. 3–32.

elt, R.P. (1988), "Theory, Strategy, and Entrepreneurship," in Teece, D.J.
d.), *The Competitive Challenge*, Ballinger, Cambridge.

czynski, T.M. (1974), "Business Finance in the EEC, USA and Japan,"
he Three Banks Review*: n. 103, pp. 58–72.

czynski, T.M. (1984), "Industrial Finance System in Europe, U.S. and
pan," *Journal of Economic Behaviour and Organization*: V, pp. 276–80.

czinski, T.M. (1985), "Financial Systems, Risk and Public Policy," *The
oyal Bank of Scotland Review*: n. 148, pp. 35–45.

czinski, T.M. (1986), *The Internationalization of the Financial System and
e Developing Countries. The Evolving Relationship*, Washington, The
orld Bank, World Bank Staff Working Papers: n. 788.

man, W. (1989), *Venture Capital Industry in the United States*, Harvard
usiness School Working Paper.

akibara, E. and Feldman, R.A. (1983), "The Japanese Financial System in
omparative Perspective," *Journal of Comparative Economics*, VII: n. 1, pp.
-24.

er, M.S. and Weinhold, W.A. (1980), *Merger Trends and Prospects*, report
r the Office of Policy, US Department of Commerce, Washington, DC.

Sanderson, M. (1972), "Research and the Firm in British Industry," *Sci* *Studies*, 2: pp. 107–51.

Sapelli, G. (1987), "Gruppi d'impresa e trasformazione della sovranità p lare," *Stato e mercato*: n. 21.

Sarathy, R. and Chatterjiee, S. (1984), "The Divergence of Japanese and Corporate Financial Structure," *Journal of International Business Stu* XV, n. 3, pp. 75–89.

Saul, S.B. (1979), "The Engineering Industry," in Buxton N.K. and Ald D.H. (eds).

Saville, J. (1955), "Sleeping Partnership and Limited Liability, 1850–1ε *Economic History Review* 8.

Schiller, R.J. (1981), "Do Stock Prices Move Too Much to be Justifie Subsequent Changes in Dividends?," *American Economic Review*, 71, J pp. 421–36.

Schmitt, B. (1988), "Circuito economico e moneta bancaria," in Grazian and Messori M. (eds).

Schumpeter, J. (1971), *Teoria dello sviluppo economico*, Sansoni, Florence

Schwert, G.W. (1977), "Public Regulation of National Security: A Test of Capture Hypothesis," *Bell Journal of Economics*, 8, Spring.

Scott, J. (1986), *Capitalist Property and Financial Power. A Compara Study of Britain, the United States and Japan*, Wheatsheaf Bo Brighton.

Scott, J. (1987), "Intercorporate Structures in Western Europe: a Comp tive Historical Analysis," in Mizruchi, M.S. and Schwartz, M. (eds).

Scott, W.R. (1912), *The Constitution and Finance of English, Scottish Irish Joint Stock Companies to 1720*, Cambridge University Press, C bridge, vol. 1–vol. 3.

Shaw, E.S. (1973), *Financial Deepening in Economic Development*, Ox University Press, New York.

Shimamura, T. (1989), "Japan's Financial System: Creation and Chang *Japanese Economic Studies*, 17, n. 3: pp. 43–88.

Shleifer, A. and Vishny, R. (1988), "Managerial Entrenchment," pε presented to a conference at Princeton University.

Snowden, K. (1987), "American Stock Market Development and Performai 1871–1929," *Explorations in Economic History*, 24.

Solow, R. (1956), "A Contribution to the Theory of Economic Grov *Quarterly Journal of Economics*, LXX, February: pp. 65–94.

Soref, M. and Zeitlin, M. (1987), "Finance Capital and the Internal Struct of the Capitalist Class in the United States," in Mizruchi M.S. and Schwε M. (eds), pp. 56–84.

Statistics Bureau – Management and Coordination Agency (various yea *Japan Statistical Yearbook*, Printing Bureau of the Ministry of Fina Tokyo.

Steinherr, A. and Huveneers, C. (1989), "Universal Banking: A View Inspi by German Experience," paper prepared for the Conference "The Sepa tion of Industry and Financial Intermediaries," Milan.

Stigler, G.J. (1968), "Monopoly and Oligopoly by Merger," in Stigler G.J. (ε *The Organization of Industry*, Irwin, Homewood, Ill.

Stiglitz, J. (1969), "A Re-Examination of the Modigliani-Miller Theore *American Economic Review*, 59, No. 5, December: pp. 784–93 (presente the 1961 meetings of the Econometric Society, Washington, DC).

itz, J. (1972a), "Some Aspects of the Pure Theory of Corporate Finance: nkruptcies and Take-Overs," *Bell Journal of Economics*, 3, No. 2, itumn: pp. 458–82.

itz, J. (1972b), "On the Optimality of the Stock Market Allocation of vestment," *Quarterly Journal of Economics*, February, 86, No. 1: pp. –60.

itz, J. (1974a), "Incentives and Risk Sharing in Sharecropping," *Review of onomic Studies*, 41, April: pp. 219–55.

itz, J. (1974b), "On the Irrelevance of Corporate Financial Policy," nerican *Economic Review*, 64, December: pp. 851–66 (presented at a nference in Hakone, Japan, 1970).

itz, J. (1982), "Ownership, Control and Efficient Markets," in *Financial onomics: Essays in Honor of Paul Cootner*, by Sharpe W.F. and Cootner (eds.), Prentice Hall, Englewood Cliffs, NJ: pp. 118–58.

litz, J. (1985), "Credit Markets and the Control of Capital," *Journal of oney, Credit and Banking*, 17, No. 1, May: pp. 133–52.

litz, J. (1986), "Towards a More General Theory of Monopolistic Competi-)n," in *Prices, Competition and Equilibrium*, Pestor M. and Quandt R.E. ds), Barnes and Noble Books, Totowa, NJ: pp. 22–69.

litz, J. (1988a), "Why Financial Structure Matters," *Journal of Economic :rspectives*, 2, Fall, n.4: pp. 121–6.

litz, J. (1988b), "Money, Credit and Business Fluctuations," *The Economic ecord*, December: pp. 307–22.

litz, J. (1989), "Using Tax Policy to Curb Speculative Short-Term rading," Conference on Regulatory Reform of Stock and Futures Markets, olumbia University, May.

litz, J. and Weiss, A. (1981), "Credit Rationing in Markets with Imperfect iformation," *American Economic Review*, 71, No. 3, June: pp. 393–410.

litz, J. and Weiss A. (1983), "Incentive Effects of Termination: Applica- ons to the Credit and Labor Markets," *American Economic Review*, ecember, 72: pp. 912–27.

:litz, J. and Weiss, A. (1986), "Credit Rationing and Collateral," in *Recent evelopments in Corporate Finance*, Jeremy Edwards, Julian Franks, Colin layer and Stephen Schaefer (eds), Cambridge University Press, New York: p. 101–135.

:litz, J. and Weiss, A. (1987), "Credit Rationing with Many Borrowers," in merican *Economic Review*, March, pp: 228–31.

:litz, J. and Weiss, A. (1988), "Banks as Social Accountants and Screening evices for the Allocation of Credit," in *The Monetary Economics of John 'icks*, Courakis A. and Goodhart, C. (eds), Macmillan.

ımers, L. and Summers, V. (1989), "When Financial Markets Work Too Vell: A Cautious Case for a Securities Transaction Tax," paper presented) the Annenberg Conference on Technology and Financial Markets, Vashington, DC, February.

)ple, B., "Aspects of Private Investment Strategy in Great Britain," in)aems, H. and Van der Wee, H. (eds).

:uki, S. and Wright, R.W. (1985), "Financial Structure and Bankruptcy Lisk in Japanese Companies," *Journal of International Business Studies*, (VI, n. 2: pp. 97–110.

uki, Y. (1980), *Money and Banking in Contemporary Japan*, Yale Jniversity Press, New Haven.

Suzuki, Y. (1986a), *Money, Finance, and Macroeconomic Performan*
  Japan, Yale University Press, New Haven and London.
Suzuki, Y. (1986b), "A Comparative Study of Financial Innovation, Dere
  tion and Reform in Japan and the United States," *Bank of Jap*
  Monetary and Economic Studies, IV, October, n. 2: pp. 147–59.
Sylla, R. (1972), "The United States, 1863–1913," in Cameron R.
  Banking and Economic Development.
Taggart, R.A. Jr. (1985), "Secular Patterns in the Financing of US Cor
  tions," in Friedman B.M., *Corporate Capital Structures in the United S*
  University of Chicago Press, Chicago.
Teece, D. (1988), "Technological Change and the Nature of the Firm," in
  G., Freeman, C., Nelson, R., Silverberg, G. and Soete, L. (eds), *Tech*
  Change and Economic Theory, Francis Pinter, London, and Colu
  University Press, New York.
Thorelli, H.B. (1954), *Federal Antitrust Policy*, Johns Hopkins Unive
  Press, Baltimore, Md.
Tilly, R. (1966), *Financial Institutions and Industrialization of the Rhine*
  1815–1870, University of Wisconsin Press, Madison.
Tilly, R. (1974), "The Growth of Large-Scale Enterprise in Germany sinc
  middle of the Nineteenth Century," in Daems, H. and Van der We
  (eds).
Tilly, R. (1982), "Mergers, External Growth and Finance in the Develop
  of Large-Scale Enterprise in Germany," *Journal of Economic History*
  pp. 629–58.
Tilly, R. (ed.) (1985), *Beitrage zur Quantitativen Vergleichenden U*
  nehmensgeschichte, Klett-Cotta, Stuttgart.
Tilly, R. (1986), "German Banking, 1850–1914: Development Assistan
  the Strong," *Journal of European Economic History*, 15: pp. 113–52.
Tilly, R. (1989a), "Banking Institutions in Historical and Compar
  Perspective: Germany Great Britain and the United States in
  Nineteenth and Early Twentieth Century," *Journal of Institutional*
  Theoretical Economics (Zeitscrift fur die gesamte Staatswissenschaft),
  n.1.
Tilly, R. (1989b), "Some Comments on German Foreign Portfolio Investm
  1870–1914," unpublished Conference Paper.
Tobin, J. (1984), "On the Efficiency of the Financial System," *Lloyds B*
  Review, n. 153: pp. 1–15.
Tolliday, S. (1979), "Industry, Finance and the State: An Analysis of
  British Steel Industry during the Inter-War Years," D. Phil. th
  University of Cambridge.
Tolliday, S. (1986), "Steel and Rationalization Policies, 1918–1950,'
  Elbaum B. and Lazonick W. (eds).
Toniolo, G. (1985), "Intermediazione finanziaria e sviluppo economic
  Giappone: nota sul periodo 1952–1972," *Politica Economica*, I, n. 2:
  259–77.
Tonveronachi, M. (1989), *Struttura ed evoluzione dei sistemi finanziari*, Ba
  Popolare dell'Etruria e del Lazio.
Townsend, R. (1979), "Optimal Contracts and Competitive Markets
  Costly State Verification," *Journal of Economic Theory*, October, 21:
  265–93.
Tyson, R.E. (1968), "The Cotton Industry" in Aldcroft, D.H. (ed.),
  Development of British Industry and Foreign Competition, Universit

ilasgow Press, Glasgow.
Bureau of the Census (various years), *Statistical Abstract of the United States*, Washington, DC.
arelli, F. (ed.) (1979), *Capitale industriale e capitale finanziario: il caso italiano*, Il Mulino, Bologna (Introduction).
tas, D. (ed.) (1978), *Banking Systems Abroad. The Role of Large Deposit Banks in the Financial Systems of Germany, France, Italy, the Netherlands, Switzerland, Sweden, Japan and the United States*, Inter-Bank Research Organization, London.
tas, D. (1986), "Banks' Relations with Industry: An International Survey," *National Westminster Bank Quarterly Review*, February: pp. 2–14.
inwright, N.B. (1953), *The History of the Philadelphia National Bank*, Villiam Fell Co., Philadelphia.
ite, B. (1984), "International Differences in Gearing: How Important are They?," *National Westminster Bank Quarterly Review*, Nov: pp. 14–25.
ite, E.N. (1983), *The Regulation and Reform of the American Banking System. 1900–1929*, Princeton University Press, Princeton.
ite, E.N. (1985), "The Merger Movement in Banking, 1919–1933," *Journal of Economic History*, 45, June: pp. 285–91.
ite, E.N. (1986), "Before the Glass-Steagall Act: An Analysis of the nvestment Banking Activities of National Banks," *Explorations in Economic History*, 23: pp. 33–55.
ite, E.N. (1990), "The Stock Market Boom and Crash of 1929 Revisited," *Journal of Economic Perspectives, 4*, Spring: pp. 67–83.
ite House Science Council (1988), *High-Temperature Superconductivity: Perseverance and Cooperation on the Road to Commercialization*, Office of Science and Technology Policy, Washington, DC.
cksell, K. (1936), *Interest and Prices*, Macmillan, London.
iener, M.J. (1981), *English Culture and the Decline of the Industrial Spirit, 1850–1980*, Cambridge University Press, Cambridge.
ilkins, M. (1989), "The Free-Standing Company: an Important Type of British Foreign Direct Investment," *Economic History Review*, 41.
illiamson, J.G. (1984), "Why was British Growth So Slow During the Industrial Revolution?," *Journal of Economic History*, 44.
illiamson, O.E. (1975), *Markets and Hierarchies: Analysis and Antitrust Implications*, The Free Press, New York.
illiamson, O.E. (1985), *The Economic Institutions of Capitalism*, The Free Press, New York.
ilson, C.M. (1954), *The History of Unilever*, Cassell, London, vol. 1.
ilson, J.F., Fogler, E.M., Freund, J.L. and Van der Yen, G.E. (1986), "Major Borrowing and Lending Trends in the US Economy, 1981–85," *Federal Reserve Bulletin*, August: pp. 511–24.
amamura, K. (1972), "Japan, 1868–1930: A Revised View," in Cameron R. (ed.), *Banking and Economic Development*.
amamura, K. (1978), *Entrepreneurship, Ownership, and Management in Japan*, in Mathias, P. and Postan, M.M. (eds).
eitlin, M. (1974), "Corporate Ownership and Control: The Large Corporation and the Capitalist Class," *American Journal of Sociology*, 79, n. 5: pp. 1073–119.
ysman, J. (1983), *Governments, Markets, and Growth. Financial Systems and the Politics of Industrial Change*, Martin Robertson, Oxford.

Author Index

Note: Numbers preceded by the letter n refer to the number of the note which appears on the page indicated: for example, 245n50 refers to note 50 which can be found on page 245.

ubject Index